MW01258361

Social Media
in
Sport

Theory and Practice

EMERGING ISSUES AND TRENDS IN SPORT BUSINESS

Series Editor: Norman O'Reilly *(University of Guelph, Canada)*

Emerging Issues and Trends in Sport Business - Vol. 2

Social Media
in
Sport
Theory and Practice

Editors

Gashaw Abeza
Towson University, USA

Norm O'Reilly
University of Maine, USA

Jimmy Sanderson
Texas Tech University, USA

Evan Frederick
University of Louisville, USA

 **World Scientific**

NEW JERSEY · LONDON · SINGAPORE · BEIJING · SHANGHAI · HONG KONG · TAIPEI · CHENNAI · TOKYO

Published by

World Scientific Publishing Co. Pte. Ltd.

5 Toh Tuck Link, Singapore 596224

USA office: 27 Warren Street, Suite 401-402, Hackensack, NJ 07601

UK office: 57 Shelton Street, Covent Garden, London WC2H 9HE

British Library Cataloguing-in-Publication Data
A catalogue record for this book is available from the British Library.

Emerging Issues and Trends in Sport Business — Vol. 2
SOCIAL MEDIA IN SPORT
Theory and Practice

ISBN 978-981-123-765-2 (hardcover)
ISBN 978-981-123-766-9 (ebook for institutions)
ISBN 978-981-123-767-6 (ebook for individuals)

For any available supplementary material, please visit
https://www.worldscientific.com/worldscibooks/10.1142/12299#t=suppl

Desk Editor: Sandhya Venkatesh

Typeset by Stallion Press
Email: enquiries@stallionpress.com

Editors

Gashaw Abeza (Ph.D.) is recognized as one of the leading scholars in the field of social media in sport. He is currently an Assistant Professor at Towson University. Dr. Abeza has a long-standing and ongoing research program studying the impact of social media on the sport industry and its implications for society at large. He has written extensively on the topic of social media in sport, publishing over 45 journal articles and book chapters in outlets such as *Communication and Sport, International Journal of Sport Communication (IJSC), Journal of Sport Management, Journal of Strategic Marketing,* among others. He is the co-author of two previous books: one, on e-sport titled *Implications and Impacts of eSports on Business and Society* (IGI global, 2019) and a second, on sport marketing titled *Canadian Sport Marketing* (Human Kinetics, in press). Prior to returning to academia, Abeza had a successful career in sport management and marketing at a global level, and currently provides consultancy services to a range of sports organizations around the world. Abeza serves as an *ad hoc* reviewer for a number of academic journals and was a special issue guest editor for *IJSC* on the topic of "*Contemporary Issues in Social Media in Sport.*" Currently, he serves on the editorial boards of seven different academic journals: *International Journal of Sport Communication; Sport, Business, and Management; Journal of Relationship Marketing;*

International Journal of eSports Research; Journal of Global Sport Management, Sport Marketing Quarterly, and *International Journal of Sports Marketing and Sponsorship.* Before joining Towson University, Abeza taught graduate and undergraduate courses at the Southern Methodist University (Dallas, TX, USA) and the University of Ottawa (Ottawa, ON, Canada).

Norm O'Reilly (Ph.D.) is recognized as one of the leading scholars in the business of sports. He is currently the Dean of the Graduate School of Business at the University of Maine. Dr. O'Reilly has a keen interest in social media and its role in achieving the business objectives of brands who sponsor sports, sports properties, and agencies who support these brands and properties. An active scholar, with 16 books and more than 145 journal publications, scholarship in social media is a prominent element of his work. For instance, the Canadian Sponsorship Landscape Study, for which Dr. O'Reilly is the founding and lead researcher, includes a series of questions related to social media that have informed industry practice and academic research. A recipient of the Career Achievement Award by the American Marketing Association's Sport Marketing Special Interest Group and the "Five to Watch" under-40 sport industry award, Dr. O'Reilly has taught at Guelph, Ohio, Ottawa, Stanford, Syracuse, Ryerson, Athabasca, Laurentian and the Russian International Olympic universities.

Jimmy Sanderson (Ph.D.) is currently an Assistant Professor in the Department of Kinesiology and Sport Management at Texas Tech University. Dr. Sanderson maintains an active research agenda focused on social media and sport, and has published over 80 journal articles and book chapters. He is the author of two previous books on social media and sport — *It's a Whole New Ballgame: How Social Media is Changing Sport* and *Developing Successful Social Media Plans in Sport Organizations* with Dr. Chris Yandle. He regularly consults with and speaks to sports organizations on social media-related topics. Dr. Sanderson has been cited in a variety of news outlets on social media and sport, including *USA Today*, ESPN.com, *Sports Illustrated,* and *The Washington Post*. Dr. Sanderson has taught at Arizona State University and Clemson University.

 **Evan Frederick** (Ph.D.) is currently an Associate Professor of Sport Administration within the Department of Health and Sport Sciences at the University of Louisville. His primary research interest is the intersection of sport and social media. Specific areas of interest include image repair, perceptions of athlete activism, and discussions of socio-cultural and political issues via social media. Frederick's work in these areas was recently cited in the *Washington Post*. Frederick has published 40 peer-reviewed articles and book chapters in outlets such as *Communication and Sport,* the *International Journal of Sport Communication, Journal of Sports Media, Sport in Society, Mass Communication and Society,* and *Online Information Review*. Frederick currently serves on as the Chair for the *International Association for Communication and Sport* and as an editorial board review member for *Communication and Sport*. Previous to the University of Louisville, Frederick taught at the University of New Mexico and the University of Southern Indiana.

Foreword

Dr Lawrence A Wenner, Von der Ahe Professor of Communication
and Ethics, Loyola Marymount University

Founding Editor, Communication & Sport Journal

As someone who has long focused his research agenda on communication and sport, it certainly is time for a comprehensive book on sport and social media. The area has become a dominant one in the study of sports communication, both in sports management programs as well as in communication and media studies. The book, *Social Media in Sport*, is edited by an "A team" of sports communication scholars, Gashaw Abeza, Norm O'Reilly, Jimmy Sanderson, and Evan Frederick, and features a distinguished cast of leading international scholars who have contributed to diverse understandings about the nexus of sport and social media.

Social media, whether one engages with some, many, or none of its platforms, is a ubiquitous feature of contemporary life. Along with gigantic major platforms at the top of the social media heap, such as Facebook, YouTube, WeChat, and Instagram, each with over a billion active users, that have come to define the mainstream, lesser but still heavily "populated" platforms such as TikTok, Sina Weibo, Snapchat, Reddit, Pinterest, and Twitter all swing considerable weight as well, each with over 300 million active users (Statistica, 2020). However, taken in the context of the history of communication technology, it is important to recognize that social media is merely a blip on a long timeline.

Yet, for digital natives, such as those in Gen Z and some Millennials, it may seem that social media has always existed. And indeed, some (Standage, 2013) have made the case that all media is social, and that social media has been with us for thousands of years. But this is hindsight and a specious stretch. Indeed, the term "social media" really was not even voiced until the early 1990s (Bercovici, 2010). And even the term, let alone the concept, really was not much used until the late 1990s as early platforms such as those from AOL, Classmates, SixDegrees, and iVillage moved beyond the more arcane bulletin board systems (BBSs) that drew early attention by the more "nerdy" early technological adopters (cf. Bercovici, 2010, "Timeline of social media," 2020).

Today, social media is increasingly in our faces. In a way, it is the new "prime time." If one wants to socialize or connect, it is a convenient meeting place. If one wants to market products or services in a targeted way or win the hearts and minds of voters to win elections or fundraise, it is now the most potent power tool in one's kit. If one wants to disrupt truthful reports by branding them as fake news, challenge grounded reality with disinformation asserting lies as facts, or spread unfounded conspiracy theories undergirded by little or specious evidence, it is at your service. Both benign and malignant, there is little doubt that social media, with its powers to strategically target, engage, and build collective action, is a media form unlike any that we have seen before.

Given these attributes, it is not surprising that social media has been readily adopted by both sports organizations and fans. It is both a sports star and media star, a conduit for sports commerce connecting sports entities to fans and building community among fans. Still, as a (perhaps not nerdy enough) boomer who was not one of those earlier adopters, I have often been more a scholarly skeptic (cf. Wenner, 2014a, 2014b) rather than an evangelist for or enthusiastic user of social media in the context of the field of sport.

Indeed, I have been only an occasional user, more an observer looking in from the outside, satiating my curiosity about how this will all play out in the broader fields of communication and sport as more and more digital natives (such as the ones featured in this book) joined the scholarly ranks in an area where I had been an early settler making a case for its importance. As such, especially given that my "legacy" status has been grounded in understandings of "legacy" media, I may seem to some an odd choice for penning a foreword to this book.

Still, rest assured, I am no Luddite, even though not a digital native. Yet, I have seen a lot of "new" technology come, go, and become "old." Time and time again, I have seen the nimbleness of legacy media being able to adapt to and repurpose new media to advance their goals. Indeed, new technology was a focus early in my career. My first published study (Wenner, 1975) considered the promise of "new technology" and how it might be facilitated through public policy. So early on I got the allure of new communications technologies as shiny pennies calling out to scholars, full of potential as "game changers" in how humans interact. In the last 100 or so years, a parade of new communication technologies has arrived on the scene. All were thought to be threatening in their own ways, both to earlier established legacy media and for what "traditionalists" feared the new technology would do to human sensibilities and relations.

Another overarching truism about the introduction of new communication technologies is that human needs often have had little to do with their development. Here, scientists break new technological ground by inventing new forms (moving pictures, "talkies," radio, television, personal computers, mobile phones). As often as not, they have done so with only an inkling of their application or potential, rather than in clear response to some deafening urgency of human need or clear understanding of how the technology might play out in culture or commerce.

Rather, "needs" for new communication technologies evolved as they were discovered by early adopters and imagined by manufacturers and marketers. Simply put, we often did not know we had "needs" for new communication technologies until appealing corporate narratives made their case for their essential value in the hopes of igniting contagion. Thus, a backdrop for this story, and it is true as well in the specific case of sport and social media that is considered in this book, is that technological invention comes first, often preceding (and necessarily searching for yet established) needs. Of course, this may be seen as an essential chicken or the egg kind of question or one about the cart getting before the horse. But this frame is important to understanding social media more generally and more specifically how social media has come to be used (and abused) for both fun and profit in sporting contexts.

The evolution of inquiry on sport and social media may be seen as one of moving from zero to sixty. In the larger contexts of research on sports communication, it has gone from nothing to an oddity at the margins to something central and important. Certainly, it was not really to be found on the map in early inquiry on media and sport. For example, in the mid to late 1980s, when I put together *Media, Sports, and Society* (Wenner, 1989), a volume that in hindsight might be considered the first "handbook" on the scholarly study of media and sport, social media, as a term, concept, or practice had yet to arrive. At the time, concerns over "new technology" and sport largely centered around marketplace shifts to cable from over-the-air television (cf. Bellamy, 1989). Certainly, in the backdrop, precursors to the modern Internet, such as the U.S. Department of Defense funded Advanced Research Projects Agency's ARPANET and the U.S. National Science Foundation's NSFNET project aimed at advancing and connecting supercomputing, were nascent but promising developments ("History of the Internet," 2020). If there was much "socializing" going on in such domains of the visionary scientists and "nerds" who saw promise in what eventually materialized as the commercially driven Internet we know today, it was unlikely that much concerned the world of sports.

By the mid-1990s, noise about the "World Wide Web" (the dominant term at the time with acronym WWW), facilitated by the rise of commercial Internet service providers (ISPs) and others who saw promise in an emergent digital communication marketplace, was beginning to be heard throughout the halls of academia. Thus, in planning a second research "handbook" on the fusion of media and sport in the mid-1990s, *MediaSport* (Wenner, 1998), I felt compelled to include an "obligatory" chapter on what was then characterized as sport in cyberspace or, more succinctly, "cybersport." Here, there was a very basic challenge: there was not very much "there there" or obvious expert scholars. Although there were early explorations into fantasy sport online bulletin boards (Walker *et al.*, 1993), a series of "help" articles in the *Journal of Sport and Social Issues* by Malec (1995a, 1995b, 1996) touting the value of the WWW as a resource for sports scholars, and Maloni, Wolff, Greenman, and Miller's (1995) *Netsports* popular press guide to sports on the "information highway," broad social inquiry about what the Internet portended for sport and its marketplace had not yet been mounted. In this void, I recruited Steve McDaniel and Chris Sullivan (1998) to take a stab at conceptualizing what the nexus of sport and cyberspace might yield and mean.

While at that time McDaniel and Sullivan (1998) really had few tea leaves to read, their work was helpful in both situating the nascent state of affairs in the "Wide World of Cybersport" and posing approaches that could be taken to study the sport–Internet nexus by examining cybersport objects, instances, and experiences. They charted the early toehold strategies of legacy sport media organizations and established sports organizations who were feeling their way about what the WWW could do and, most particularly, what it could do for advancing branding and building loyal and engaged fan communities. Most presciently, their analysis pointed to the rise of "co-promotion" between media and sports outlets on the web that was beginning to "blur some of the social and commercial boundaries within the mediated sports production complex, as first conceptualized by Wenner (1989)" (McDaniel and Sullivan, 1998, p. 271). While they did not use the term, they predicted the inevitability of the "prosumer" by noting how "sports fans are now able to produce sports sites for themselves" (p. 271).

While McDaniel and Sullivan's (1998) work set the stage, stimulating scholarly realization of the importance that research on cybersport would come to play, little focused research on the nexus of sport and social media may be found in scholarly journals in the first five years of the 21st century. Indeed, early in the "aughts," social media had not yet mainstreamed. Three developments, a considerably more encyclopedic handbook on sports media (Raney and Bryant, 2006), the publication of the first research quarterly on sports communication in 2008, and stocktaking in a small but influential volume (Sanderson, 2011) fueled and enabled inquiry on sport and social media.

The main service of the Raney and Bryant (2006) handbook was in making a case that research on media and sport more broadly had matured. While only three of its thirty-some chapters focused exclusively on "sports online," their inclusion signaled rising importance of emergent new forms in the media space. All in all, the chapters continued to speak more to the promise of new online media than established impact. Nonetheless, that a founding figure in media and sport research, Michael Real (2006), very convincingly argued that the future cultural impacts of sport on the web promised to be paradigm-changing wielded considerable influence on scholars seated in communication and media studies. Included as well were two other future/potential-oriented chapters. Mahan and McDaniel's (2006) treatment pointed to the relevance of cybersport to the sports management and marketing scholarly community and Leonard's (2006) exploration of the "untapped potential" of virtual sports gaming portended other avenues for social inquiry about online sports communities.

If there was ever a "starting gun" to research on sport and social media, it was sounded by the 2008 launch of the *International Journal of Sport Communication* (*IJSC*) by its founding editor Paul Pedersen as the first quarterly research journal on sports communication. Importantly, Pedersen, who was one of the first to make the case for the study of strategic sports communication in sports management, perhaps more than any one scholar, saw how valuable social media could be to sports marketing, public relations, and promotional communication. Stimulated by the start of more prominent social media platforms such as My Space, Facebook, and Twitter earlier in the "aughts," *IJSC* became a magnet outlet for a second wave of mediasport scholars who were "digital natives," many if not most schooled in the myriad of sports management programs that rose during this same period, but some in select communication and media studies programs that had begun to recognize the legitimacy of the sport context as well.

Out of this latter context in communication and media studies came Jimmy Sanderson's (2011) *It's a Whole New Ballgame: How Social Media is Changing Sports*. Quite amazingly written while a graduate student, Sanderson's book served as a concise and convincing treatise about the ways in which social media was changing, and was further going to change, how culture and commerce engaged with sport. His arguments and evidence clearly showed how social media at the nexus of sport was not something at the margins, but rather had become integral to the definition of what sports media had become. Further, Sanderson's work was a landmark in considering the organizational implications of social media to both sport and media organizations, and his understandings of how this would play out in the marketplace made a good case that social media would become a dominant force in connecting athletes and fans.

That these three developments ushered in legitimacy for a focus on social media and sport was mirrored in the attention that this nexus received in handbooks that followed. Here, Pedersen's (2015) *Routledge Handbook of Sport Communication* raised the bar yet further as a comprehensive handbook for the broader area of inquiry. Featuring not only an essential framing chapter on the theoretical opportunities presented by social media by Sanderson (2015), the rising importance of the role that social media was more and more playing in the sport marketplace was reinforced by a breakout section focused on sports communication in new and emerging media, featuring some ten chapters on cybersport topics, all with "social" components that had been foreshadowed in earlier work by McDaniel and Sullivan (1998).

Providing further evidence that research on sport and new media, with social media as the glue that held together its importance, had moved from the periphery of inquiry on communication and sport to its center was the publication of Billings and Hardin's (2016) *Routledge Handbook of Sport and New Media*. Such a volume would not have been fathomable even ten years prior. The study of cybersport had come of age, and this volume, in its thirty-some chapters, provides seminal focus on research foundations, production processes, the shaping, marketing, and branding of messages, audience experiences and fanship, and identity formations in digital mediasport spaces. Clearly, the nexus of social media and sport had come of age in research on sports communication.

However, what remained was the need for a more focused book on sport and social media. To my mind that is what Gashaw Abeza, Norm O'Reilly, Jimmy Sanderson, and Evan Frederick have put together, along with their distinguished cast of contributors, in the book ahead, *Social Media in Sport.* It is hard to imagine a more systematic treatment of the topics essential to understanding the sport and social media nexus. Here, you will find thoughtful treatments that situate social media in sport, overview the research agenda, and draw out our understandings of how online communities in sport are formed and function. Considered are essential snapshots of how social media is used in both major and minor sports, how social media informs and is used in sports and media organizational decision-making, and how data analytics and management guide strategies in the marketplace. The workings of social media in marketing contexts, from relationship marketing to brand management to sponsorship shaping, are broken out in thoughtful detailed treatments. The relationship of social media to legacy sport media, the legal issues that its employ may raise, and how social media can play an essential role in managing crisis communication are all considered. Crucially, the challenges of the digital divide that can fracture access is considered in a breakout chapter on diversity and inclusion at the nexus of sport and social media. Finally, bottom line issues of revenue generation and consideration of effective ways to strategically manage social media in contemporary sporting environments are given careful treatment. In sum, the analyses that you will find in *Sport and Social Media* cover all of the essential bases for those interested in how social media has changed the face of our contemporary experiences with sport.

Lawrence A. Wenner
Port Townsend, Washington, USA

REFERENCES

Bellamy, R. V. (1989). Professional sports organizations: Media strategies. In L. A. Wenner (Ed.), *Media, Sports, and Society* (pp. 120–133). Newbury Park, CA: Sage.

Bercovici, J. (2010). Who coined 'social media'? Web pioneers compete for credit. *Forbes*. Available at https://www.forbes.com/sites/jeffbercovici/2010/12/09/who-coined-social-media-web-pioneers-compete-for-credit/?sh=6d85acb851d5.

Billings, A. C. and Hardin, M. (2016). *Routledge Handbook of Sport and New Media*. London: Routledge.

History of the Internet (2020). Wikipedia. Available at https://en.wikipedia.org/wiki/History_of_the_Internet.

Leonard, D. (2006). An untapped field: Exploring the world of virtual sports gaming. In A. A. Raney and J. Bryant (Eds.), *Handbook of Sports and Media* (pp. 426–442). Mahwah, NJ: Lawrence Erlbaum.

Mahan, J. E. and McDaniel, S. R. (2006). The new online arena: Sport, marketing, and media converge in cyberspace. In A. A. Raney and J. Bryant (Eds.), *Handbook of Sports and Media* (pp. 443–468). Mahwah, NJ: Lawrence Erlbaum.

Malec, M. A. (1995a). Sports discussion groups on the Internet. *Journal of Sport and Social Issues, 19*(1), 108–114.

Malec, M. A. (1995b). The wonderful World Wide Web of sports: Another Internet resource. *Journal of Sport and Social Issues, 19*(3), 323–326.

Malec, M. A. (1996). Usenet news groups: Another Internet resource. *Journal of Sport and Social Issues, 20*(1), 106–109.

Maloni, K., Wolff, M. Greenman, B., and Miller, K. (Eds.) (1995). *Netsports: Your Guide to Sports Mania on the Information Highway*. New York: Random House:

McDaniel, S. R. and Sullivan, C. B. (1998). Extending the sports experience: Mediations in cyberspace. In L.A. Wenner (Ed.), *MediaSport* (pp. 266–281). London: Routledge.

Pedersen, P. M. (Ed.) (2015). *Routledge Handbook of Sport Communication*. London: Routledge.

Raney, A. A. and Bryant, J. (2006), *Handbook of Sports and Media*. Mahwah, NJ: Lawrence Erlbaum.

Real, M. R. (2006). Sports online: The newest player in mediasport. In A. A. Raney and J. Bryant (Eds.), *Handbook of Sports and Media* (pp. 183–197). Mahwah, NJ: Lawrence Erlbaum.

Sanderson, J. (2011). *It's a Whole New Ballgame: How Social Media is Changing Sports.* New York: Hampton Press.

Sanderson, J. (2015). Social media and sport communication: Abundant theoretical opportunities. In P. M. Pedersen (Ed.), *Routledge Handbook of Sport Communication* (pp. 56–65). London: Routledge.

Statistica (2020). Most popular social networks worldwide as of October 2020, ranked by number of active users. Available at: https://www.statista.com/statistics/272014/global-social-networks-ranked-by-number-of-users/.

Timeline of social media (2020). Wikipedia. Available at: https://en.wikipedia.org/wiki/Timeline_of_social_media.

Standage, T. (2013). *Writing on the Wall: Social Media — the First 2,000 Years.* New York: Bloomsbury.

Walker, J. R., Rylands, C., Hiltner, J. R., and Bellamy, R. V. (1993). Talking about the game: A content analysis of a fantasy baseball bulletin board. Paper presented at the annual convention of the Speech Communication Association, Miami, FL.

Wenner, L. A. (1975). Cable TV access and public policy. *Intellect, 104*(December), 246–248.

Wenner, L. A. (Ed.) (1989). *Media, Sports, and Society.* Newbury Park, CA: Sage.

Wenner, L. A. (Ed.) (1998). *MediaSport.* London: Routledge.

Wenner, L. A. (2014a). Much ado (or not) about Twitter? Assessing an emergent communication and sport research agenda, *Communication and Sport, 2,* 103–106.

Wenner, L. A. (2014b). On the limits of the new and the lasting power of the mediasport interpellation. *Television and New Media, 15*(8), 732–740.

Lawrence A. Wenner is Von der Ahe Professor of Communication and Ethics at Loyola Marymount University in Los Angeles. He is founding editor of the bi-monthly research journal *Communication and Sport,* and former two-term editor of the *International Review for the Sociology of Sport* and the *Journal of Sport and Social Issues.* With ten books and over 140 scholarly journal articles and book chapters, his recent research focuses on sport media, gender, and commodity culture. His upcoming books include the *Oxford Handbook of Sport and Society* and *American Sport in the Shadow of a Pandemic: Communicative Insights* (with Andrew Billings and Marie Hardin).

Contents

Chapter 1

Introduction to Social Media in Sport

Kevin Hull* and Gashaw Abeza†

*University of South Carolina, United States
†Towson University, United States

CHAPTER OBJECTIVES

After reading this chapter, you will be able to do the following:

- Understand the definition of social media
- Describe the history of social media
- Recognize the defining characteristics of social media
- Identify the different types of social media platforms
- Describe the current trends in social media
- Classify the different types of social media users
- Recognize the dimensions of social media use by different stakeholders
- Identify key skills necessary to manage social media platforms

KEY TERMS

Content communities	Social media influencers
Defining characteristics	Social media platforms
Discussion sites	Social media users
Engage in conversation	Social network

1

INTRODUCTION

The rapid technological advancements in the past decade have accelerated the scope, magnitude, and penetration of social media's reach. Faster Internet broadband, easily accessible portable devices, large digital data storage possibilities, and global interconnectedness have all fast-tracked the growth and expansion of social media. The past decade has seen the emergence of a range of platforms (e.g., Facebook, Twitter, YouTube, SnapChat, Weibo, TikTok) that are used by various entities (e.g., individuals, groups, businesses, governments) for different purposes (e.g., retailing, education, politics, social movement, health, sport). During this period, the social media platforms themselves have evolved. Whether serving as simple mediums for information exchange and staying in touch with people or providing venues on which events are live streamed, these platforms provide a place for influencers to endorse products, news stories to break, sponsored ads to appear in our newsfeeds, and photo editing to take place (tasks that are no longer left to professionals). The online atmosphere has transformed how different entities create, share, and consume information.

Consider the following examples, seemingly unrelated to each other, and think about the scope, penetration, and magnitude of social media reach in the past few years. As of early 2021:

- Facebook (started in 2004) has 2.7 billion monthly active users.
- Instagram (started in 2010) has over 1 billion monthly active users.
- Twitter (started in 2006) has 330 million monthly active users.
- Pinterest (started in 2010) has 335 million monthly active users.
- Snapchat (started in 2011) has 101 million monthly active users.
- TikTok (started in 2016) has 800 million monthly active users.

In the sports world, the popularity and acceptance of social media by the industry's various stakeholders, including athletes, coaches, managers, executives, teams, leagues, fans, events, and sports governing bodies have been widespread. Some examples as of early 2021 include:

- ESPN on Twitter (@espn) has 36.1 M followers
- FC Barcelona on Facebook (@fcbarcelona) has 102.5 M followers
- Cristiano Ronaldo on Instagram (@cristiano) has 242 M followers
- WWE YouTube Channel has 69.4 M subscribers
- UFC on TikTok (@ufc) has 4.7 M followers
- Seattle Seahawks head coach @PeteCarroll on Twitter has 2.2 M followers
- Nike has representatives with more than 20 different Twitter accounts

Social media's role in sport has exhibited growing complexity and increasing omnipresence. Therefore, the purpose of this chapter is to discuss some of the basics of social media and set the foundation for it has impacted sport. Specifically, the chapter covers the definition of social media, its history and evolution, its different platforms, its user types, its dimensions of use, some of its popular sites, and its impact on the sport industry.

SOCIAL MEDIA IN SPORT: KEY CONCEPTS

WHAT IS SOCIAL MEDIA?

While the task of defining social media might seem easy, it is anything but. In fact, 100 different people striving to define it might produce 100 different answers. Social media takes many different forms, and some of the most popular examples include social networking sites such as Facebook and Twitter and content-sharing sites such as YouTube, Instagram, and Snapchat. Given the expansive nature and scope of social media, it is not surprising that various authors provide numerous definitions. The term *social media* might have no universally recognized definition, but looking at the formation of the phrase can offer some clarity. Social media is a construct from two areas of research, communication science and sociology

(Peters *et al.*, 2013). The "social" aspect of social media comes from sociology, in which users such as individuals, groups, or organizations are connected, network, and exchange content within their online community. The "media" aspect of social media comes from the world of communication and is simply identified as a mode of information delivery. Therefore, the combination of these elements leads to a basic understanding that social media refers to the way in which individuals, groups, or organizations in a network form relationships to generate and exchange information with each other, unlike the hierarchical structure of information flow that unidirectionally passes over from one entity to others. Hence, dialogue or conversation is a vital part of social media. In this chapter, **social media** is defined as comprising those *online resources open to the public (e.g., blogs, social networks, content communities, and discussion sites) that people use primarily to share content (e.g., text, photo, audio files, and video) and engage in multi-way conversation on Internet applications (e.g., Facebook, Twitter, YouTube).*

LEARNING ACTIVITY 1

Pick your favorite sports team and review their social media accounts. Pick one of these accounts and examine the last 25 posts from that account. What type of posts are these? Who is the audience for these posts? What is the team trying to accomplish by sending these messages? Any summary comments you can make on your observations?

THE EMERGENCE AND GROWTH OF SOCIAL MEDIA

The mass media and access to information has been impacted by different technologies that have emerged over the course of the past 100 years. Telephones (in the 1870s) and radio (in the 1920s) played a significant role in the development of broadcast media. The television (in the 1940s) played a substantial role in the expansion and development of the mass media and access to information. The emergence of personal computers (in the 1970s) and the

Internet and World Wide Web (in the 1990s) offered further progression with the introduction of freedom of choice and more accessible information. Cell phones (in the 1980s and 1990s) and then smartphones (in the 2000s) brought access to information even further, making it digital and shared in real time via different social media platforms (in 2000s). As Shotsberger (2000) reported, it took radio 38 years, television 13 years, and the Web four years to reach 50 million users. However, it only took two years for Facebook to reach 50 million users, thus illustrating the increasing speed at which social media is expanding. Hundreds of active social networking sites, one type of social media platform, have been introduced since the creation of Six Degrees, the first recognized social media platform, in 1997.

This growth and evolution have resulted in some social media platforms having extremely short lifespans that include dramatic falls from glory. At one point, the video-based platform Vine had 200 million users, but less than three years later, it was out of business (Newton, 2016). While there have been several platforms that have come and gone since 1997, most of the current major social media sites emerged in the years since 2002.

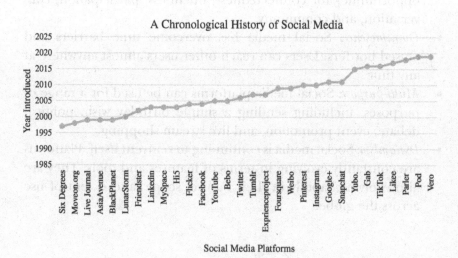

Figure 1: A Chronological History of Social Media

DEFINING CHARACTERISTICS OF SOCIAL MEDIA

As online resources that people use primarily to create and share content and to engage in conversation, social media platforms have certain **defining characteristics**. In this chapter, the authors extend the work of Hennig-Thurau *et al.* (2010) and briefly describe seven of these characteristics:

- *User-Generated Content*: Users produce the content (e.g., text, photos, videos) as opposed to the original Web in which one-way messages were largely supplied by publishers.
- *No "Gate Keeper"*: Users can create and post content without third-party permission (e.g., a newspaper editor), which has made real-time information exchange an inherent characteristic of today's society.
- *Content Availability*: Users' social media activities are visible to others and can be seen immediately after being produced and also long afterward.
- *Community Driven*: Users can create, listen, learn, contribute, and circulate interests, experiences, and comments that provide opportunities for connectedness, openness, participation, conversation, and community.
- *Omnipresence*: Social media has overcome time barriers and erased borders. Users can reach other users almost anywhere at any time.
- *Multi-purpose*: Social media platforms can be used for a range of purposes, including sending a simple birthday wish, political debate, event promotion, and live stream shopping.
- *Dynamism*: Social media is continuing to reinvent itself. Platforms are constantly evolving in terms of features and tools. They are also evolving rapidly in their nature, scope, and extent of use across the globe.

LEARNING ACTIVITY 2

Pick a sporting event that happened before social media began in the year 1997. For example, you could pick the 1986 Masters Golf Tournament where legend Jack Nicklaus won his 5th and final Masters at the age of 46. For the sporting event that you chose, assume social media was available then and create an entire social media portfolio consisting of 20 different social media messages from various platforms. How would the athletes, teams, media, and fans all discuss that event if it happened today?

SOCIAL MEDIA PLATFORMS

In the discussion of social media, most people primarily think of social networking sites such as Facebook or Twitter. However, social media also includes resources that people use to share content and engage in conversation, such as blogs and discussion sites. Based on the various types of applications and extending the work of Constantinides and Fountain (2008) and Abeza and O'Reilly (2018), we classified **social media platforms** into *four major categories: social networks, content communities, blogs, and discussion sites.* These platforms are briefly described, along with corresponding sports-related examples.

- *Social network*: A platform that allows users to initiate communication with other users who share their interests by posting information, comments, messages, and images and creating a community for participation. Common communication points with which to initiate conversations on social networks include status updates in Facebook and tweets on Twitter. Some examples include NBA Facebook (www.facebook.com/nba), ESPN's Twitter (@espn), and FC Barcelona's Facebook (@fcbarcelona).

- *Content communities*: Content communities are platforms that are predominately dependent on videos, photos, and audio files from the users themselves. Like social networking sites, users can engage in discussions with other content community members regarding video or photo content posted on a site. Some examples include Cristiano Ronaldo's Instagram (@cristiano), WWE's YouTube Channel, UFC's TikTok (@ufc), and Cristiano Ronaldo's Snapchat (@CristianoRonaldo).

- *Blogs*: Blogs are online journals or personal websites usually managed by an individual. Entry times are stamped on each posting and displayed in reverse chronological order. Readers can post a response to a specific entry, allowing the author of the initial content to read these responses and react to readers' comments, creating a virtual dialogue. Regular readers of blogs can develop relationships with one another through their own frequent comments. Since the development of social networks, blogs are now traditionally fan driven and created, including pages for the Seattle Mariners (www.ussmariner.com) and the Toronto Maple Leafs (www.mapleleafshotstove.com).

- *Discussion sites*: Discussion sites (e.g., Reddit, Quora) are platforms on which users with similar interests share ideas on different topics, activities, and concerns. On discussion sites such as forums and message boards, messages are often approved by a moderator before they are made available to the public. Once they are approved, users engage in conversations in the form of posted messages. Examples include the Calgary Flames forum (http://fans.flames.nhl.com/community/) and the New York Giants Board (https://thegiantsboard.proboards.com/).

As Wakefield and Wakefield (2016) stated, these platforms have common attributes such as (1) user profile, (2) user access to digital content, (3) a user list of relational ties, and (4) user ability to view and traverse relational ties.

POPULAR SOCIAL MEDIA SITES

An attempt to list all of the social media platforms that have existed could lead to the creation of an extremely long list, especially since many have existed only for a short while. Some social media networks either dropped dramatically in popularity (such as Myspace) or went away completely (such as Vine). Seven of the more popular social media sites are discussed as follows.

FACEBOOK

Founded in 2004 as *The Facebook*, the original goal of Facebook was to connect college students on the campus of Harvard University. However, it quickly expanded to include users around the world. The hub of the site is each individual user's news feed, on which information and stories from people or businesses with which the user has connected will show up for the user to read. These posts can comprise text, photos, or videos. Users can simply read/watch the post, and they also have the opportunity to like, comment on, or share the post with their own followers. In addition, users can post their own updates that can be seen by other users of the site. In 2016, Facebook launched Facebook Live, which allowed users to stream live video straight from their mobile device to their news feed.

INSTAGRAM

Instagram, started in 2011, is a photo and video-sharing social media site in which users create posts that have a visual element with a caption accompanying the image/video. Much like Facebook (which acquired Instagram in 2012), users decide which accounts they want to follow, and then posts from those selected accounts will show up in the users' feeds. These posts can then be liked or commented on for added engagement.

PINTEREST

Pinterest (launched in 2010) is a social media site that is often described as an online pinboard. Users share ideas for fashion, food, home design, and other creative outlets by creating "pins" that are essentially online bookmarks. Users can then collect these pins on various pinboards on their profile page. Of Pinterest's monthly users, the majority are women. In fact, 42% of American adult women said they used the platform, compared to just 15% of men (Perrin and Anderson, 2019).

SNAPCHAT

First released in 2011, the social media Snapchat was one of the fastest-growing social networks in the world by 2020. The messaging network allows users to post photos and videos (known as "snaps") that disappear from the site after a set number of seconds. Additionally, users can put their "snaps" in a sequence that viewers can watch as a "story." The service of sending disappearing messages to each other is popular among people aged 25 and younger (Clement, 2019).

TIKTOK

TikTok became available worldwide in 2018. It is a video-sharing social media platform. TikTok videos are short, with the network capping the length at 15 seconds each (Matsakis, 2019). The content is traditionally set to music, with users lip-syncing or dancing along with the song. Starting with its United States debut in 2018, TikTok has been primarily popular with a younger audience, as 69% of the users are between the ages of 13 and 24 (Sehl, 2020).

TWITTER

Twitter, which was launched in 2006, allows users to send messages, or tweets, that are a maximum length of 280 characters. Tweets can contain news, commentary, personal information, embedded photos or videos, or links to articles or videos. These tweets are then displayed immediately on users' timelines after being posted. Twitter users follow other accounts that have content that interests them and get the latest information from those accounts delivered directly to their Twitter timeline.

YOUTUBE

YouTube is a video-sharing social media that allows individuals and businesses to upload videos directly to the Internet. The network was created in 2005 and purchased by Google in 2006 (LaMonica, 2006). Viewers can rate, share, and comment on the content, while also having the option to subscribe to channels that interest them.

SOCIAL MEDIA USERS

Users join a given platform for different reasons, including the ability to connect with others, access news stories, share information, and be entertained. However, not all social media users are the same. Users' levels of participation range from passive visitor to committed contributor. For example, while some users visit a social media site multiple times a day every day, others log on much less frequently. One may use some platforms often, but never visit a different social media site. Harridge-March and Quinton (2009) proposed that there were different types of social media users based on how frequently they visit various platforms. However, as social media has evolved, so have the types of users. Therefore, using Harridge-March and Quinton's categories as a guide, we grouped social media users into *six different types*.

- "Lurkers" are users who prefer to observe before making contributions, mainly with an intention of familiarizing themselves with the site's culture.
- "Newbies" are those who have just started to contribute to discussions but do not exhibit tangible commitment or engagement.

- "Onlookers" are those who are accustomed to a site but post occasionally, share less details about themselves, and set their online information to "private." The primary purpose of their usage is to stay up-to-date within their social networks.
- "Minglers" are those discussants who post comments but with no particular regularity.
- "Devotees" are those who are committed in terms of time and energy and make frequent comments with a high degree of substance. This group of users can be referred to as evangelists/insiders/celebrities.
- "Influencers" are those who have a sizeable number of followers, who respond to the needs and interests of their digital community, and whose followers consider them both sources and guides. As such, **social media influencers** have persuasive power and likely shape their followers' attitudes.

Two observations are worth noting here: First, the classification does not apply across all platforms but indicates a user's involvement level at each individual platform. For example, someone can be a newbie on Snapchat, a mingler on Twitter, a celebrity on Facebook, and an influencer on Instagram. Hence, if someone is a mingler on one platform, it does not mean that the user is necessarily one on all other platforms as well. Second, users (particularly influencers) have the ability to accumulate cultural capital by sharing information with members of their digital communities on a regular basis and with a high degree of substance. As these users gain sizeable numbers of followers, they become social media influencers. Narratives communicated by social media influencers are often perceived as compelling, sincere, and reliable by members of their digital community (Lim *et al.*, 2017). Particularly, elements of cultural capital such as relatability, accessibility, and intimacy give rise to authority, leading consumers to value social media influencers' recommendations.

One of the remarkable aspects of social media is how it connects people who normally would never interact. In fact, these unfamiliar users can often create the most meaningful impact. Users often

follow and interact with people they know, so messages are traditionally shared among people who already have the same opinions and
beliefs. However, when those messages venture outside that circle,
users can have a greater influence because they can reach people
not in their immediate circle. The strength of weak ties theory states
that people have strong ties with those whom they know closely, such
as family or friends. However, people also have many casual acquaint-
ances, such as coworkers or friends of friends, with whom they have
weak ties of relationships. In the spreading of information, the weak
ties are often more effective in getting the message out to a new and
wider audience because those within the same friend circle often all
know each other already (Granovetter, 1973).

DIMENSIONS OF SOCIAL MEDIA USE
IN SPORT

Social media has had a tremendous impact on the world of sport.
Impacting teams, athletes, fans, and other similar stakeholders,
social media most obviously influences sport through the fact that
nearly everything and everyone involved has their own account. For
example, no matter which social media network they choose, fans of
the Boston Red Sox can follow the accounts of the Red Sox, Major
League Baseball, individual players, other Red Sox fans, and journalists who report on the team. These accounts all have a similar
focus of the Red Sox, but the goals of each differ. While the use of
social media by some of these stakeholders is briefly discussed in
what follows, Figure 2 showcases the dimensions of social media use.
Users create content that appears on social media platforms and is
received by the audience. Due to the two-way nature of social media,
audiences can engage with that content directly through the users
who created it. In the social media-based exchange of information,
sports entities (e.g., professional sports — covered in Chapter 4,
minor sports — covered in Chapter 5) use social media for different
purposes such as relationship marketing (Chapter 8), branding
(Chapter 9), sponsorship (Chapter 10), crisis communication
(Chapter 13), etc.

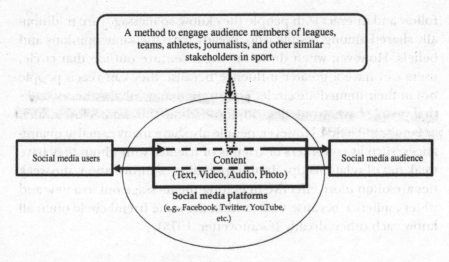

Figure 2:   Social Media Use in Sport

TEAMS AND LEAGUES

Teams and leagues have a variety of different purposes for using social media, but ultimately each one is related to generating excitement surrounding the team. In their study that involved 26 professional sports teams from the four major leagues in North America, Abeza, O'Reilly, and Seguin (2019) reported that professional teams' objectives for social media use can be categorized as one of the six types: interaction, news updates about the team (such as scores, schedule, and awards), ticket sales, sponsorship, public relations, and customer service. A study that looked exclusively at how Major League Baseball teams were using Instagram revealed that posts fell into one of four categories: business objectives (such as selling tickets or merchandise), sporting objectives (such as game action), charitable organizations (such as visits to hospitals), or non-baseball-related posts (Kim and Hull, 2017).

While they may not be overtly promoting ticket and merchandise sales, many of the posts on social media are ultimately designed to motivate fans to open their wallets. A study of Spanish-language Instagram accounts for baseball teams found that posts actively showcased more Hispanic players and cultural events. These pictures received more likes and comments than posts that did not have a Hispanic element in them (Hull *et al.*, 2018). These Spanish-language accounts were getting Hispanic fans excited about the team by showcasing Hispanic players, perhaps leading to those fans buying tickets or merchandise.

LEARNING ACTIVITY 3

Watch a sporting event on television or on stream and see how the event is discussed on the various social media outlets. How are they different? How are they the same?

ATHLETES

Athletes have some of the largest followings on social media, and they have embraced the medium in many different ways. In one of the first studies of athletes using Twitter, research demonstrated that sports stars utilized the social network to create positive exposure for themselves, engage fans, and increase their own visibility (Pegoraro, 2010). Little has changed since that early research. A study of golfers during the Masters Tournament found that many of the participants spent their time away from the course sending out tweets to their followers about everything from what they bought in the gift shop to on-course strategy (Hull, 2014).

Ultimately, many athletes use social media as a way to showcase their lives when not playing their sport. They might show pictures of their family, talk about their hobbies, and discuss their opinions on social issues. For example, basketball player LeBron James expressed his support for Hillary Clinton on social media in her quest for the presidency in 2016, while also later calling President Donald Trump a "bum" (Hastings, 2019). Some athletes have used social media to give fans a behind-the-scenes look at their lives. In 2018, Serena Williams tweeted about postpartum depression after having a baby, earning praise from many fans for her honesty (Young, 2018). However, some of these posts, while giving the athletes an opportunity to display a different side of their personalities, can also get athletes into trouble. Hours after winning the Heisman Trophy in 2018, quarterback Kyler Murray had to apologize for anti-gay tweets that he had sent years earlier (ESPN, 2018). In their study that investigated 17 of the world's highest-paid professional athletes' use of their own social media channel, Abeza *et al.* (2017) reported that all the top athletes used their platform for endorsement. For example, Cristiano Ronaldo sending Tweets that endorse Nike's soccer boots or Maria Sharapova tweeting: "My secret to natural beauty is out thanks to @AvonInsider!". Similarly, LeBron James has over 70 million followers on Instagram, and uses the platform to promote brands such as GMC Hummer, nutrition brand Ladder Sport, and Nike (Lane, 2020). These posts can be big business for the athletes, as LeBron James earns US$300,000 per sponsored Instagram post (Lane, 2020).

FANS

Fans who rely on online news outlets to get the latest information are often considered "connected" fans, and they can access most information they seek about their team online (Hull and Lewis, 2014). These connected fans are not necessarily more passionate or dedicated than those of previous generations; they are simply using new methods to acquire their sports news. However, social media has much of what connected fans are looking for (i.e., immediacy and interactivity). The ability of social media outlets to deliver news instantly allows fans to access the latest information at once. Immediately after a game concludes, fans can log onto their favorite social media network to access the final score, photos from the game, statistics, and videos of interviews afterwards. Some social networks, such as Facebook and Twitter, can also include links to stories that contain more information for fans who are looking for additional details. Social media serves as a venue where fans reunite outside of the stadium and access content to react to and bond over, which could be from the team to fans or fans to fans (Abeza *et al.*, 2017).

The interactive elements of social media are appealing to fans because they allow like-minded people from all across the world to connect over a specific topic. For example, on Twitter, users can write messages to each other using the @ symbol, creating a situation in which the tweet will show up directly in the recipient's timeline. The use of hashtags can also connect fans by allowing those who click on them to get a variety of posts all about that topic. These hashtags, such as #NBATwitter, have created what one Twitter executive called "a virtual sports bar," where fans of the game can discuss various topics together (McCarthy, 2019). While social media users can connect with other fans, possible interaction with athletes could be the most significant draw. Before social media, any face-to-face interactions were at highly scripted events such as charity events or autograph signings. Now fans can send a social media message to an athlete, and the athlete might respond. This interactivity can make the relationship feel like more than just a one-way friendship.

JOURNALISTS

The sports media uses social media to provide updates for their audience. For example, if a trade happens in basketball, instead of having to wait until the 6 o'clock news or the morning newspaper, media members can now instantaneously deliver that information directly to their audiences' social media timelines. The majority of journalists said that they not only post their breaking news on social media, but they also monitor those posts looking for updates from other journalists (Willnat and Weaver, 2014). This is discussed in much more detail in Chapter 11. Additionally, social media allows journalists to showcase a different side of their personalities by sending posts that are more about their personal lives and less about news and scores.

However, journalists might be among the most impacted entities in terms of their employment and the ability to break the news. As early works (e.g., Schultz and Sheffer, 2010) reported, the impact of social media has been significant, particularly on the newspaper business. With teams, leagues, and players all having the ability to connect with users directly, many are simply avoiding journalists when delivering news. For example, when LeBron James announced he was signing with the Los Angeles Lakers in 2018, he did not need ESPN or a traditional media outlet to make the announcement. Instead, the agent for James broke the news himself on Twitter (Joseph, 2018). Therefore, one of the primary purposes for following journalists — to get the latest news — can now be fulfilled directly through the athletes or teams themselves. Relatedly, citizen journalism is also a culture that has expanded with the growth of social media. In citizen journalism, ordinary sports fans can report and disseminate news and information about players, coaches, managers, etc. For example, posting pictures of Lionel Messi's summer vacation 2020 in Ibiza with family on Instagram.

PRACTITIONER PERSPECTIVE

Practitioner: Shannon Gross, Director of Content Strategy for the Dallas Cowboys

Education: University of Louisiana at Monroe, BA Mass Communications

Shannon Gross has been with the Dallas Cowboys for 17 years, ten of those years as Social Media Manager. He recently assumed the

(*Continued*)

position of Director of Content Strategy. In his role, he oversees the programming department, and develops and manages social media strategies for the Dallas Cowboys, Dallas Cowboys Cheerleaders, and AT&T Stadium.

Question: Can you tell us the changes that you have observed in the social media world in the past five years?

Shannon Gross: There are a few, so let us look at the six major changes for now. One is the way that social media is structured within sports. It used to be one staff intern that used to run the social media department. Now, most social media departments have three or four full-time people that are running social media platforms.

Two, a huge emphasis is now placed on fan engagement. Not only do you want to put out good quality content, but you want fans to respond. You want them to interact and engage with your posts. Teams are now trying to find out what attracts and engages fans. Is it behind-the-scenes access or is it player interviews? In sports, fans want access, autographs, selfies, and want to be on the sidelines. The question would be, how do you give access without giving away a competitive advantage? How can you bring somebody into a team meeting room without giving away the different plans for the week, and that is kind of what teams are trying to figure out. Even if the social media teams want all the access, coaches might not agree. They may say, "we are trying to win football games. You just stay out of the coaching business and behind-the-scene stuff."

Three, the ownership is being supportive now. Teams have become content creators more so than they have been in the past. For example, for the draft this year, we got more behind-the-scenes access than we ever have. The ownership is now telling us, "we understand you need this. Let us know what you need."

Four, social media departments have shifted from repurposing content to creating their own unique content that is geared

(*Continued*)

(*Continued*)

specifically toward social channels and toward all the different formats within these different channels. For example, YouTube is for long-form content, while Instagram has short-form content. Instead of taking content that was made for TV and the website and converting it to social media, departments are now producing content for specific platforms and then putting it on TV.

Five, more behind-the-scenes stories are being put out by players than teams. For example, we may not have access to players like we have always had in the past. This is going to be a game changer for us. We are, in a way, competing with our own players. Players now are coming into the league raised on social media. They have been doing social media since they were in junior high and high school. Whenever we started this, social media was new and our players were not in the same position. They may not have even be bothered with it. Now, we have college graduates that are coming in that have their own social media management teams that follow them around. They may have their own videographers and photographers. They have people that run their social accounts. So, one of the challenges is how do you get that access that sometimes they want for themselves? As athletes get more social media savvy, they realize that they can turn this into a revenue stream long after they retire. I think that is going to be a big challenge going forward.

Six, people are more interested in shorter and shorter content. That is why, partly, TikTok is such a big deal. On TikTok, you can scroll through 100 videos in about 20 minutes. So, we are trying to keep people's attention and trying to find the new thing. We know that there are platforms that come and go; you do not want to get too late of a start, but you also don't want to adopt something that's not going to be around. Along with this, some teams may have a traditional fan base. We have a lot of nostalgia around our brand. A team like the Chargers just moved to Los Angeles, and they kind of revamped their whole social strategy. They can do a lot of cutting-edge stuff that may not work for us. So, I think

(Continued)

finding what resonates with fans and then sticking with that and keeping true to that is always a challenge.

Question: Can you share with us a couple of major technological advancements that you observed recently in one or two of the popular social media platforms?

Shannon Gross: Live streaming and shorter content. I think live video in general kind of changed the game. On Facebook, Instagram, and YouTube, there is live stream which was not there a few years back. Video live streaming, one may argue, could have played a major role for the development of Snapchat that led to the development of TikTok. People are consuming content at shorter and shorter increments. With TikTok, a ten-second video seems to grab people's attention.

Another major change is that social media platforms are serving you content that you did not ask for, but that you want and that you want to see without you subscribing to it. Across all platforms, users do not even have to subscribe to somebody's channel. TikTok, Instagram, YouTube, Facebook, and others bring similar content into your feed to what you may have accessed previously. It is sort of "Here's where you spend most of your time," and then it's going to suggest those videos to you.

Question: Can you give us one or two unique features of each of the popular platforms, namely, Facebook, Twitter, YouTube, Instagram, and Snapchat?

Shannon Gross: Facebook is for a large-scale audience. It has the widest demographics: older, younger, family, friends from high school, and college. Twitter is where you go to keep up with breaking news. Uniquely, when you tune into a broadcast, one social platform you see most that's integrated into a broadcast is Twitter. Instagram, as a visual platform, started off with just photos

(Continued)

(Continued)

and now has video, tagging locations, and filters. Instagram Stories are unique. It's a lot easier for a platform to pull other people into a conversation because we can see people log in and you can click on them and have a one-on-one conversation. YouTube gives you a unique ability to create a channel, and it sorts your interests by playlists. It has its own way to serve content as the algorithms let you see content that you normally would not see. It is unique, and we do not appreciate it enough. YouTube Live is a great addition, too. Snapchat's uniqueness is its introduction of consuming video vertically. Most screens are horizontal like the TV experience. When you have an iPad, you turn it sideways. With Snapchat, you have vertical videos, and you see people now programming for vertical video. In the beginning, Snapchat didn't have any type of analytics, and it was not easy putting our content on the platform when we couldn't measure analytics and data. Now, they provide some analytics.

KEY SKILLS FOR PRACTICE

Social media is constantly evolving. As stated previously in this chapter, the technology advances quickly, so social media practitioners must stay ready to use the latest technology and develop the skills needed to run a popular account. For example, running a social media account requires more than just sending messages, as multimedia elements are now prominently featured on most accounts. Therefore, those working in social media should develop graphic design and video editing skills so that they can include those types of content with their messages.

Additionally, running a social media account might seem like a lot of fun, but it is a tremendous amount of work. Particularly, running a social media platform for a sport organization requires skills, creativity, and dedication. These and other practical guidelines are discussed in Chapter 16. For example, the social media team members for the Boston Red Sox often work more hours than players themselves. For a 7 p.m. game, the team starts work at around 9:30 a.m. and works all the way through beyond the final inning (McCaffrey, 2019). Time management becomes an important skill in social media management, as they need to balance speed, creativity, and accuracy during long days. While it would be nice if all interactions with the public were positive, a great deal of a social media manager's time is spent dealing with negative content. A person responsible for social media platforms needs to determine what is an appropriate tone for the social media account by establishing boundaries regarding specific topics, language, and ethics.

TRENDS AND CURRENT ISSUES

Social media platforms allow users to share personal photos, videos, and information with friends, family, and followers throughout the Internet. However, there are concerns that this personal information can be used for purposes that were not originally intended by the user. This leads to concerns about issues of privacy on social media. About 80% of social media users said that they were concerned about advertisers and businesses having access to their personal information (Rainie, 2018). However, keeping this information safe from unwanted viewers is a difficult task. Some social media users reported that they had difficulty managing their privacy controls due to confusing directions.

Some question how those who use social media can even expect a sense of privacy. Users readily share their physical location, family photos, and personal anecdotes with the public; perhaps they give up any rights to privacy by doing so. In 2010, Facebook founder Mark Zuckerberg said that wanting privacy was no longer an expected behavior among people. He stated, "People have really gotten comfortable not only sharing more information and different kinds, but more openly and with more people. That social norm is just something that has evolved over time" (Kirkpatrick, 2010).

Despite that opinion, millions of social media users have stated that they are concerned about protecting their individual data. Only 9% of social media users said they were "very confident" that social media companies would protect their personal data (Rainie, 2018). This has created worries in users about data security. Some popular games and applications on Facebook have shared users' information with advertising companies. For example, the company that created the game *Farmville*, in which Facebook users tend to virtual crops on their virtual farm, had access to players' gender, age, occupation, hobbies, interests, zip codes, and friend lists (Thulin, 2018).

In 2018, the United States Congress took note of these privacy and data concerns, summoning Zuckerberg to Washington D.C. to answer questions about how Facebook protects users' data. Zuckerberg told Congress that users could delete the information they had put into the website, but some writers found that very little personal information could actually be replaced (Chen, 2018). The hearings resulted in promises from the United States government to look into how to regulate what social media companies collect from users and what these companies end up doing with that data (Wichter, 2018).

CHAPTER SUMMARY

The history of social media is a short but incredibly innovative journey. Early social media sites had small followings with limited features. The first few recognized sites simply allowed users to send messages to those people who were connected to them. Now, social media sites offer users the ability to post live videos, photos, and up-to-the-second news updates that show up immediately in a user's timeline. Some of the most popular social media sites have over one billion users throughout the world. For sports fans, teams, players, and journalists, social media has changed how games are consumed by the public. Sports news updates are reported instantly on social media, athletes can interact directly with fans, and teams can generate excitement among fans about upcoming events. However, social media is much more than just posting funny images and videos. Practitioners work long hours (see Chapter 16) and often interact with negative messages, all while worrying about data security and the privacy involved with their accounts. In its short time of existence, social media has grown tremendously, and has a bright future ahead.

KEY RESOURCES

- Presentations from the 2020 International Conference on Social Media and Society, https://socialmediaandsociety.org/smsociety-presentations-2020/.
- Is traditional sports journalism still relevant in the age of social media? https://www.dw.com/en/is-traditional-sports-journalism-still-relevant-in-the-age-of-social-media/a-43687112.
- Trends: Facebook Live and Sports Publishers, https://www.facebook.com/facebookmedia/blog/trends-facebook-live-and-sports-publishers.
- TikTok: Sports' next great social media venture? https://frntofficesport.com/tiktok-in-sports/.
- Twitter craze is rapidly changing the face of sports, https://www.si.com/more-sports/2009/06/05/twitter-sports.

TEST YOUR KNOWLEDGE

1. Identify four concepts that are included in the definition of social media. Use the definition that is introduced in this chapter.
2. What are the four types of social media platforms? Briefly discuss each.
3. Six different types of social media users are identified in this chapter. Identify and describe each briefly.
4. What are the defining characteristics of social media? Briefly discuss each.
5. Pick your preferred three social media sites and identify, at least, three major differences and three similarities among each platform.
6. Identify three key skills necessary to manage social media platforms and discuss them briefly.

REFERENCES

Abeza, G. and O'Reilly, N. (2018). Social, digital, and mobile media in sport marketing. In Schwarz, E. and Hunter, J. (Eds.), *Advanced Theory and Practice in Sport Marketing* (3rd Ed.), Routledge.

Abeza, G., O'Reilly, N., and Seguin, B. (2019). Social media in relationship marketing: The perspective of professional sport managers in the MLB, NBA, NFL, and NHL. *Communication and Sport*, 7(1), 80–109.

Abeza, G., O'Reilly, N., Séguin, B., and Nzindukiyimana, O. (2017). The world's highest-paid athletes, product endorsement, and Twitter. *Sport, Business and Management*, 7(3), 332–355

Chen, B. X. (2018). I downloaded the information that Facebook has on me. Yikes. *The New York Times*. Retrieved from https://www.nytimes.com/2018/04/11/technology/personaltech/i-downloaded-the-information-that-facebook-has-on-me-yikes.html.

Clement, J. (2019). Percentage of U.S. internet users who use Snapchat as of 3rd quarter 2019, by age group. Retrieved from https://www.statista.com/statistics/814300/snapchat-users-in-the-united-states-by-age/.

Constantinides, E. and Fountain, S. J. (2008). Web 2.0: Conceptual foundations and marketing issues. *Journal of Direct, Data and Digital Marketing Practice*, 9(3), 231–244.

ESPN (2018). Heisman Trophy winner Kyler Murray apologizes for anti-gay tweets. Retrieved from https://www.espn.com/college-football/story/_/id/25490250/heisman-trophy-winner-kyler-murray-apologizes-anti-gay-tweets.

Granovetter, M. S. (1973). The strength of weak ties. *American Journal of Sociology*, 78, 1360–1380.

Harridge-March, S. and Quinton, S. (2009). Virtual snakes and ladders: Social networks and the relationship marketing loyalty ladder. *The Marketing Review*, 9(2), 171–181.

Hastings, J. (2019). Athletes and the quest for balance on social media. Retrieved from https://theundefeated.com/features/athletes-and-the-quest-for-balance-on-social-media/.

Hennig-Thurau, T., Malthouse, E. C., Friege, C., Gensler, S., Lobschat, L., Rangaswamy, A., and Skiera, B. (2010). The impact of new media on customer relationships. *Journal of Service Research*, 13(3), 311–330.

Hull, K. and Lewis, N. P. (2014). Why Twitter displaces broadcast sports media: A model. *International Journal of Sports Communication*, 7(1), 16–33.

Hull, K. (2014). A hole in one (hundred forty characters): A case study examining PGA tour golfers' Twitter use during The Masters. *International Journal of Sport Communication*, 7(2), 245–260.

Hull, K., Kim, J. K., and Stilwell, M. (2018). Fotos de Beisbol: An examination of the Spanish-language Instagram accounts of Major League Baseball teams. *Howard Journal of Communications*, *30*(3), 249–264.

Joseph, A. (2018). LeBron James announced that he would be joining the Lakers in the least dramatic way. Retrieved from https://ftw.usatoday.com/2018/07/lebron-james-lakers-klutch-announcement-nba-free-agency-los-angeles-rich-paul-reaction.

Kim, J. K and Hull, K. (2017). How fans are engaging with baseball teams demonstrating multiple objectives on Instagram. *Sport, Business and Management*, 7(2), 216–232.

Kirkpatrick, M. (2010). Facebook's Zuckerberg says the age of privacy is over. *The New York Times*. Retrieved from https://archive.nytimes.com/www.nytimes.com/external/readwriteweb/2010/01/10/10readwriteweb-facebooks-zuckerberg-says-the-age-of-privac-82963.html.

LaMonica, P. R. (2006). Google to buy YouTube for $1.65 billion. Retrieved from https://money.cnn.com/2006/10/09/technology/googleyoutube_deal/.

Lane, B. (2020). LeBron James earns $300,000 per sponsored Instagram post and is the NBA's highest paid social media influencer. Retrieved from https://bit.ly/3iwqDJd.

Lim, X. J., Radzol, A. M., Cheah, J., and Wong, M. W. (2017). The impact of social media influencers on purchase intention and the mediation effect of customer attitude. *Asian Journal of Business Research*, 7(2), 19–36.

Matsakis, L. (2019). A beginner's guide to TikTok. Retrieved from https://www.wired.com/story/how-to-use-tik-tok/.

McCaffrey, J. (2019). Life on the social media front lines: Voices of Red Sox mix snark with ceremony. *The Athletic*. Retrieved from https://theathletic.com/1235357/2019/09/24/life-on-the-social-media-front-lines-as-the-face-of-the-team-red-sox-staffers-mix-snark-with-ceremony/.

McCarthy, M. (2019). NBA and Twitter team up to bring "virtual sports bar" to life. Retrieved from https://frntofficesport.com/nba-twitter-finals/.

Newton, C. (2016). Why Vine died. Retrieved from https://www.theverge.com/2016/10/28/13456208/why-vine-died-twitter-shutdown.

Pegoraro, A. (2010). Look who's talking — Athletes on Twitter: A case study. *International Journal of Sport Communication*, 3(4), 501–514.

Perrin, A. and Anderson, M. (2019). Share of U.S. adults using social media, including Facebook, is mostly unchanged since 2018. Retrieved from https://www.pewresearch.org/fact-tank/2019/04/10/share-of-u-s-adults-using-social-media-including-facebook-is-mostly-unchanged-since-2018/.

Peters, K., Chen, Y., Kaplan, A. M., Ognibeni, B., and Pauwels, K. (2013). Social media metrics — A framework and guidelines for managing social media. *Journal of interactive marketing, 27*(4), 281–298.

Rainie, L. (2018). Americans' complicated feelings about social media in an era of privacy concerns. Retrieved from https://www.pewresearch.org/fact-tank/2018/03/27/americans-complicated-feelings-about-social-media-in-an-era-of-privacy-concerns/.

Schultz, B. and Sheffer, M. L. (2010). An exploratory study of how Twitter is affecting sports journalism. *International Journal of Sport Communication, 3*(2), 226–239.

Sehl, K. (2020). 20 important TikTok stats marketers need to know in 2020. Retrieved from https://blog.hootsuite.com/tiktok-stats/#:~:text=TikTok%20has%20a%20reputation%20for,of%20the%20app's%20user%20base.

Shotsberger, P. G. (2000). The human touch: Synchronous communication in web-based learning. *Educational Technology, 40*(1), 53–56.

Thulin, L. (2018). The roots of Cambridge Analytica scandal. Retrieved from https://slate.com/technology/2018/03/farmville-helped-sow-the-seeds-of-the-cambridge-analytica-scandal.html.

Wakefield, R. and Wakefield, K. (2016). Social media network behavior: A study of user passion and affect. *The Journal of Strategic Information Systems, 25*(2), 140–156.

Wichter, Z. (2018). 2 days, 10 hours, 600 questions: What happened when Mark Zuckerberg went to Washington. *The New York Times.* Retrieved from https://www.nytimes.com/2018/04/12/technology/mark-zuckerberg-testimony.html.

Willnat, L. and Weaver, D. (2014). The American journalist in the digital age. Retrieved from http://news.indiana.edu/releases/iu/2014/05/2013-american-journalist-key-findings.pdf

Young, A. (2018). Why Serena Williams sharing 'postpartum emotions' is so important. USA Today. Retrieved from https://www.usatoday.com/story/life/allthemoms/2018/08/07/serena-williams-postpartum-maternal-childbirth-complications/925122002/.

https://doi.org/10.1142/9789811237669_0002

Chapter 2

Research in Social Media and Sport

Edward (Ted) M. Kian* and Jimmy Sanderson†

*Oklahoma State University, United States
†Texas Tech University, United States

CHAPTER OBJECTIVES

After reading this chapter, you should be able to do the following:

- Identify some of the key theories and conceptual frameworks used to study social media in sport
- Describe topical areas that researchers are studying in use of social media in sport
- Identify how sports and social media research can be beneficial to sports organizations and their stakeholders
- Identify emerging research areas in sport and social media
- Describe future research direction in sport and social media

KEY TERMS

Agenda setting

Conceptual framework

Critical/cultural theories

Critical race theory

Framing

Maladaptive parasocial interaction

Parasocial interaction

Self-presentation

Social identity theory

Uses and gratification theory

Virtual maltreatment

INTRODUCTION

Social media has become a prominent part of the sport industry. Over the past decade, sports organizations have increasingly adopted social media platforms and integrated them into their customer service, public relations, and marketing functions, among others. Additionally, social media has revolutionized all communications, and — specific to sport — audiences now have access to a host of athletes through their social media platforms such as Instagram, Twitter, and Snapchat, and they can potentially interact and converse with athletes in these spaces as well. Athletes have utilized social media to showcase more of their personality as well as to advocate for social and political change. These outcomes are just a few of the ways that social media has influenced the sport industry. As social media has grown and become a key communication channel in the sports world, so too has research about social media and its intersection with sport. Researchers have examined topics ranging from how athletes present themselves on platforms such as Instagram (Geurin-Eagleman and Burch, 2016), benefits and challenges that athletes face with social media (Hayes *et al.*, 2019), how sports mangers utilize social media for relationship marketing (Abeza, *et al.*, 2019), and how young athletes may be vulnerable to sexual abuse through platforms such as Snapchat (Sanderson and Weathers, 2020).

Researchers studying social media and sport take a variety of approaches in their research. Some researchers seek to explain and predict behavior seen on social media (Achen *et al.*, 2018), while others examine the lived experiences of athletes (Browning and Sanderson, 2012) and other sports stakeholders (Abeza *et al.*, 2019) with social media. Still, some other researchers dissect and analyze how social media may reinforce power disparities (Thorpe *et al.*, 2017), social problems such as racism (Kilvington and Price, 2019), homophobia (Rodriguez, 2017), and misogyny (Litchfield *et al.*,

2018). Still others look at how conversations on social media related to sports issues reflect contemporary societal values (Foote *et al.*, 2017). Sports and social media researchers also study a variety of contexts including professional sports (Clavio and Kian, 2010), intercollegiate athletics (David *et al.*, 2018), international sports (Hölzen and Meier, 2019), Olympic sports (Geurin and McNary, 2020), and youth sports (Frederick and Clavio, 2015). Researchers also may focus their efforts on specific platforms such as Facebook (Vale and Fernandes, 2018); Instagram (Toffoletti *et al.*, 2019); Twitter (Naraine *et al.*, 2019); and Snapchat (Billings *et al.*, 2017). Some of the areas that sports and social media research tends to focus on include:

- Athlete experiences with social media
- Organizational management of social media
- Organizational use of social media (e.g., marketing)
- Social media and sports media
- Social media and societal issues that can be understood through sport
- Fan behavior on social media
- Legal and ethical issues associated with social media (e.g., social media policies, ambush marketing).

Research in sport and social media can help sports organizational personnel have empirical information that can assist in better managing their social media platforms, and most researchers hope that their studies will be of practical application to sports organizational personnel. The purpose of this chapter is to provide an overview of the theoretical developments and conceptual frameworks in use of social media in the field of sport, discuss emerging research topics in social media in sport, and identify future research directions in social media in sport.

> ## LEARNING ACTIVITY 1
>
> Take a few minutes and go to the Google Scholar portal and type in "Sport and Social Media." Scroll through the results. Find an article title that looks interesting to you and click on it. Then, read the article abstract. What topical area of sport and social media is this research addressing? What is the context of focus? What method did the researchers use? What were the author(s)' primary findings? What contributions do the author(s) claim to make?

RESEARCH IN SOCIAL MEDIA AND SPORT: KEY CONCEPTS

THEORETICAL DEVELOPMENTS AND CONCEPTUAL FRAMEWORKS IN SOCIAL MEDIA IN SPORT

Social media and sports researchers employ theories and conceptual frameworks to help guide their investigations. A **theory** is a system of ideas or principles that helps explain phenomena such as behavior, while a **conceptual framework** is used to make distinctions and help organize ideas. Theories have generally been tested and validated over time, whereas a conceptual framework may have limited applicability or more/less relevance to certain kinds of contexts/behaviors. Some of the more prominent theories and conceptual frameworks used in social media and sports research will now be discussed.

AGENDA SETTING

Agenda Setting is a theory that discusses how media organizations get people to think about certain topics based on the frequency and salience (e.g., information on the home page or headline) of coverage (McCombs and Shaw, 1972). The main premise of agenda setting is that by frequency, positioning, and giving some topics more coverage, media organizations can influence what audiences think is important. For example, you might visit the homepage of a news organization like CNN or Fox News. What stories/topics are featured prominently on the home page? In the sport industry, agenda setting has been observed with media coverage. For instance, researchers have found that male athletes typically receive more coverage than female athletes (Frederick *et al.*, 2015), which may lead audiences to think about and value men's sports more than women's sports.

LEARNING ACTIVITY 2

Visit the homepage of a sport media organization such as ESPN, CBS Sports, or Yahoo! Sports. Examine the content on the homepage. What sports are featured? What athletes are featured? What insights can you draw about what this particular media organization is trying to get the audience to think about?

Whereas agenda setting has largely been a function of mass media organizations (e.g., ESPN), the advent of social media has created some shifts in agenda-setting, as sports organizations, athletes, fans, and other sports stakeholders can engage in agenda-setting by how frequently and prominently they post about specific topics. Indeed, considering how quickly a social media post can go "viral," social media is a powerful way for sports organizations, athletes, and other sports stakeholders to advance ideas (Hull *et al.*, 2017). For example, Hull (2014) examined how student-athletes at the University of North Carolina-Wilmington were able to use the hashtag #Fight4UNCSwimandDive to save the swimming and diving teams from being cut by the athletic department. Hull *et al.* (2017) used agenda setting to explain how the University of Houston used the hashtag #HTownTakeover marketing and branding campaign to promote success in the football program. They found that over the course of the season, the #HTownTakeover was used in 57.3% of the tweets posted by the football program's Twitter account. Hull *et al.* (2017) observed how the University of Houston football team was able to use agenda-setting with the hashtag to keep fans reminded of how important the campaign was and to associate the campaign with a winning football culture. Agenda-setting also can occur as audiences debate sports information and news on social media. For example, Woo, Brigham, and Gulotta (2020) examined how Twitter users debated and discussed the case of former NFL player Ray Rice's striking his fiancée. The authors observed that as users conversed around this story, they deviated from dominant ways the story was being reported and challenged others regarding the way they were interpreting the story.

FRAMING

Framing is a theory that has historically been used to study mass media. According to this theory, framing occurs when news organizations emphasize or select particular phrases, images, or wording to generate specific interpretations in the audience (Entmann, 1993). With the advent of social media, framing has evolved as mass media organizations are no longer the sole producers or gatekeepers of media content. While sports media organizations and sports media members still engage in framing, athletes and sports organizations can also generate content to tell their stories and to "frame" or **counterframe** (challenging how the media is reporting an incident). For example, Sanderson (2011) discussed that one of the primary benefits that social media provided athletes was the capability to challenge and contest how they were portrayed in the mass media. In an early study, Sanderson (2010) found that supporters of Tiger Woods used Woods's Facebook page to counter and challenge how the mass media was portraying his infidelity, portraying Woods as a human being who had made a mistake, and whose private life was being unnecessarily exploited. Fans also can use social media to contest and challenge how the media is portraying their fan base and to challenge cultural stereotypes. As one example, Burch *et al.* (2015) examined how, in response to the Vancouver riots after the National Hockey League's Canucks won the Stanley Cup, fans used Twitter to dispute perceptions of Canadian hockey fans and disassociated themselves from the rioters.

In another work, Romney and Johnson (2019) studied Instagram images from four major sports networks in the United States. The study found that women were featured much less frequently than men, and when female athletes were shown, it was often in non-athletic roles and shown alongside men. In this particular case, through framing, women's sports were shown in ways that did little to challenge their position. Coche (2017) found that female athletes challenged traditional stereotypes through their written content on Twitter, but observed that their visual images tended to reinforce their femininity through posting personal rather than athletic photographs.

CRITICAL/CULTURAL THEORIES

Researchers also employ critical and cultural theories to examine sport and social media. These theories focus on cultural and social formations and structures and tend to operate from a framework that a particular group of people is oppressed because of social structures. The theoretical approaches used in this area help to highlight social inequity and raise awareness and advocate for equality, social reform, and social justice. Researchers utilize these theories to show how social media can be used to understand social conditions through issues that occur in sport, as well as to highlight how sports stakeholders (e.g., athletes) challenge social norms. Tofoletti and Thorpe (2018) discussed how female athletes use social media to present themselves in empowering and entrepreneurial ways. Grounded in feminist approaches, they discussed how social media enabled female athletes to enact new strategies for identity construction to market themselves. Litchfield *et al.* (2018) utilized this approach to examine social media comments directed at tennis player Serena Williams relating to her race, gender, and sexuality. They found that social media users engaged in verbally hostile commentary towards Williams on the basis of her gender and ethnicity and sexualized her in problematic ways. Their study illustrated the abuse that women in sport often endure and suffer and highlighted the structural norms in sport that open women up to criticism when they excel or try to enter male-dominated sports (e.g., women who are hired as assistant coaches in male sports). Other researchers using feminist approaches have examined social media as becoming more dynamic spaces for women's sports to receive coverage (Litchfield and Kavanagh, 2019), to showcase the online harassment female sports journalists face on social media (Antunovic, 2019), and how Muslim women athletes use social media to challenge stereotypes (Ahmad and Thorpe, 2020).

Researchers have utilized **critical race theory** to help understand topics such as social media users' reactions to athletes' activism efforts (Frederick *et al.*, 2017; Frederick *et al.*, 2019). Critical race theory is predicated on notions that racism is normalized in American society and is (re)produced in ways that promote power differences between Whites and Blacks. Researchers have used this theory to understand how people respond to athletes who advocate for social justice around topics such as racism (Frederick *et al.*, 2019). For instance, Frederick *et al.* (2017) analyzed Facebook comments in response to protests by University of Missouri football players regarding racism on campus. Using critical race theory, they found that responses both minimized racism and encouraged student-athletes to advocate for racial equality, while other comments suggested that student-athletes had no business engaging in activism. These comments reinforced ideas that student-athletes should accept the status quo and be grateful for their scholarships.

Frederick *et al.* (2019) analyzed Facebook comments in response to a speech at the 2016 ESPYS by NBA players LeBron James, Dwyane Wade, Chris Paul, and Carmelo Anthony advocating for racial justice around police brutality directed at African Americans. They found that comments reflected the complicated nature of race relations in the United States as while some people praised the athletes for their activism, others suggested that racism was manufactured and questioned whether law enforcement reform was needed. The authors noted that these comments also reflected deeply embedded cultural stereotypes and beliefs that are difficult to change. Additional research has utilized critical race theory to understand public reactions to incidents that occur in sport. As one example, Foote *et al.* (2017) used this approach to investigate Twitter comments related to NFL player Adrian Peterson being accused of child abuse. Their analysis of the discourse showed how cultural values around parenting and governmental overreach shaped responses to this incident. Researchers also have used critical race theory to examine how users responded to athletes engaging with President Donald Trump via Twitter (Frederick *et al.*, 2020), and to understand racism directed towards Black athletes through social media (Oshiro *et al.*, 2020).

PARASOCIAL INTERACTION

Parasocial interaction is a theory that discusses how people interact and form relationships with media figures in ways that resemble actual, social interaction, but differ because they are mediated and one-sided (Horton and Wohl, 1956). People have traditionally engaged in parasocial interaction with media figures such as celebrities, newscasters, and athletes. With the advent of social media, fans have arguably more of a direct link to athletes, and commenting/ posting to an athlete's Twitter or Instagram account appears to be the modern-day version of writing a fan letter. Early work in parasocial interactions and athletes/sports figures on social media looked at how athletes kept fans updated and engaged via Twitter (Kassing and Sanderson, 2010), and ways that athletes utilized social media to promote parasocial interaction, or more two-way interaction (Frederick *et al.*, 2014; Sanderson, 2013a). Kassing and Sanderson (2015) extended parasocial interaction to function as "circumsocial," which accounted for athletes using social media by rotating between messages that were uni-directional, while at other times, being willing to engage and converse with fans.

Whereas **parasocial interaction** is largely expressed through positive behavior (e.g., support, praise), researchers also have discovered that fans can engage in negative and destructive behaviors that are conveyed through social media. This trend has given rise to the notion of **maladaptive parasocial interaction**, or interaction that is hostile and relationally inappropriate. Sanderson and Truax (2014) utilized this approach to examine Twitter responses to

University of Alabama placekicker Cade Foster after he missed three field goals during a rivalry football game against Auburn University in 2013. They found that Twitter users responded with death threats and other vitriolic comments along with ridiculing and belittling Foster. For context, in the 24-hour-period after the game, Foster's Twitter account was mentioned over 12,000 times. Sanderson *et al.* (2020) used maladaptive parasocial interaction to examine Twitter comments directed at Chicago Bears kicker Cody Parkey after he missed a potential game-winning field goal in the 2018 NFL Playoffs. They also found that people directed death threats and other anger-laced comments at Parkey, such as requesting he leave the city and that he commit suicide.

SELF-PRESENTATION

Just as social media has opened up opportunities for athletes to counteract how they are framed in the media, it also has allowed them to take more control over their **self-presentation**. Through self-presentation, people emphasize or highlight traits that they feel are important for others to know and which likely reflect how they want others to view them. Self-presentation has been conceptualized as either being "front stage" or "back stage." Front-stage behavior is often tailored for public consumption and puts forward a very polished and manicured presentation. Conversely, back-stage presentation is closer to who the real person is and is less scripted. To help conceptualize these differences, think about how some Instagram users may portray themselves in very precise ways that may not reflect how the person actually lives. In face-to-face interaction, a person may try to highlight certain self-presentation aspects yet may be subjected to cultural and social norms that influence how people view them. Through social media, athletes and other sports figures can select and emphasize attributes that they feel are important, and which may counter as they are normally viewed or presented to the public through mass media. Geurin-Eagleman and Burch (2016) investigated Olympic athletes' self-presentation on

Instagram and found that female athletes were more likely to post photos of themselves than male athletes, and that athletes who posted the most variety of photos received the most fan engagement. They also discussed the importance of athletes posting pictures that aligned with their personal brand. Bigsby *et al.* (2019) examined high school athletes' Twitter accounts and found that athletes who engaged in more self-promotion and ingratiation were correlated with receiving new offers from potential schools.

While some athletes have the ability to counter stereotypes or challenge portrayals through social media, this may not always be the case. Li *et al.* (2017) found that male student-athletes were more likely to self-present on social media through athletic poses, while female student-athletes portrayed themselves in more stereotypical, feminine ways. Weathers *et al.* (2014) had similar findings through their study of the Twitter accounts of sports broadcasters Kirk Herbstriet and Erin Andrews. They found that Herbstriet mostly self-presented through sports knowledge and football expertise, while Andrews's self-presentation tended to focus on more gender-stereotyped traits as make-up and shopping. However, social media can also serve as a mechanism for women to generate more coverage for their sports (Litchfield and Kavanagh, 2019). Researchers also have used self-presentation theory to explore cultural differences in how athletes self-present on social media (Xu and Armstrong, 2019).

LEARNING ACTIVITY 3

Go to one of your social media profiles for which you have an active account that you check regularly. Take the time to review the last 15–30 days of your postings. Review how you are self-presenting? What kinds of traits and qualities are you emphasizing or highlighting? Anything you would change? How do you think it looks on you if you were job hunting?

Note: If you do not have a social media account, complete the activity using a social media account of one of your friends.

SOCIAL IDENTITY THEORY

Many people derive satisfaction and identity fulfillment through group membership. For instance, if you follow a sports team, television show, or Pinterest community, why do you do so? What value do you get from your membership with this group? **Social identity theory** (Tajfel and Turner, 1986) helps to understand group affiliation and how people may respond when group membership is threatened. People tend to refer to the groups they belong to as "in" groups, with groups who are different from them as "out" groups. For example, think about a sport rivalry such as between the New York Yankees and Boston Red Sox. How do you think Yankee and Red Sox fans view themselves? How do they perceive fans of the other team? Social identity theory helps us understand the value that people place on group membership and how they respond when group membership is threatened (Sanderson *et al.*, 2016). For instance, think about how fans might respond when a star player decides to leave via free agency? Or how a fan of a college football team may feel when a high school recruit who has stated they will attend the school de-commits and decides to attend another school? These decisions can impact fans as they may feel that the athlete is communicating that their "group" is not as good as another "group." This threat can prompt sports fans to communicate abusive and hostile comments on social media.

For instance, Sanderson (2013b) analyzed Facebook comments related to University of Cincinnati head football coach Brian Kelly leaving the school to become the head football coach at the University of Notre Dame. In studying a Facebook group that was entitled "Get out of our city Brian Kelly," Sanderson observed that fans managed the social identity threat associated with Kelly leaving by disparaging Kelly and suggesting that he no longer reflected group values. Some fans also engaged in threats on Kelly's life and conveyed that they hoped he died. In another study, Sanderson *et al.* (2016) used social identity theory to examine how fans of the St. Louis Rams responded to players Stedman Bailey, Tavon Austin, Jared Cook, Chris Givens, and Kenny Britt walking onto the field during player introduction with arms locked in a "hands up gesture." The players behavior was in response to the death of African American male Michael Brown in Ferguson, Missouri, and was a gesture adopted by those who were questioning police brutality targeted at African Americans. They found that fans responded to this gesture by suggesting the players be cut, burning their team apparel, and alerting team sponsors on Twitter to cancel their sponsorships. Through these actions, these individuals severed their ties with the team, as they felt by supporting the players, the Rams had deviated from shared group values predicated on supporting law enforcement.

USES AND GRATIFICATIONS

People have a variety of needs and motivations that they seek to meet when they use various media. **Uses and gratifications theory** (Katz *et al.*, 1974) helps explain why people consume the media they do and what needs they seek to fill through their consumption. Researchers have applied uses and gratifications theory to help understand why sports stakeholders such as athletes and fans use certain social media platforms. Browning and Sanderson (2012) employed this theory to understand why student-athletes use Twitter. They found three primary motivations for use: (a) keeping in touch with others; (b) communicating with followers; and (c) accessing information. Hambrick *et al.* (2010) studied professional athletes' uses of Twitter and observed that athletes used Twitter to post mostly about non-sports-related topics. They also found that the more interactive an athlete was on Twitter, the bigger his/her audience became.

Much of the research employing uses and gratifications has focused on sports consumer behavior (Clavio and Kian, 2010). Billings *et al.* (2017) invoked uses and gratifications theory to understand sports fans' motivations for using Snapchat. They found that people spent more time following sports on Snapchat than other social media platforms such as Twitter. They also found that people who reported higher levels of sports fandom were more likely to use Snapchat to follow sports. Gibbs *et al.* (2014) investigated Canadian

Football League fans' motivations for Twitter and discovered four primary motivations: (a) interaction, (b) promotion, (c) live game updates, and (d) news. Smith *et al.* (2019) found that sports fans used Twitter to supplement their sports viewing and reported higher enjoyment when using social media while watching live sporting events. Uses and gratifications have also been applied to explore cultural differences with sports consumption. Billings *et al.* (2019), found that U.S. sports fans possessed more motivations with Facebook than Twitter, while Chinese users reported that they obtained higher gratification fulfillment than American participants. Researchers have also discovered that gender and team identification can predict the use of certain social media platforms (Haugh and Watkins, 2016), and that sports fans seek to fulfill different needs through different social media channels (Lewis *et al.*, 2017).

LEARNING ACTIVITY 4

Think again about one of the social media platforms you use consistently. But choose a different one than the one you used in Learning Activity 1. Ask yourself, why do you use it? What motivates you to use it? What gratifications are you seeking to fulfill through it?

Note: If you do not use social media, complete the activity using another form of media that you do consume such as a television show, video game, or podcast, etc.

CONCEPTUAL FRAMEWORKS

Several conceptual frameworks have been used to study social media and sports topics. Witkemper *et al.* (2016) developed a typology, or classification system, to describe social media use in sport. The authors suggested that social media use in sport could be analyzed based on levels of user interactivity (e.g., high, low) and user involvement or activity (e.g., high low) through four quadrants: (1) high interactivity and high involvement; (2) high interactivity and low

Table 1. Social Media Use in Sport.

Type	Characteristics	Example
Cooperation Community	Low Interactivity, High Accomplishment	Public Relations Team Promotions Fans using Social Media to locate team information
Competition Community	High Activity, High Interactivity	Social Media for Play-by-Play Creating Interactive Competitions
Proactive Community	High Interactivity, Low Activity	Social Media Users providing product or service reviews
Passive Community	Low Activity, Low Interactivity	Posting news stories Posting blog entries

Table 2. Framework for Virtual Abuse Athletes Experience on Social Media.

Abuse Type	Example
Physical	Social media user threatening an athlete with harm or wishing death on an athlete
Sexual	Social media users threatening athlete with rape or other non-consensual sexual acts
Emotional	Social media user wishing an illness like cancer on an athlete
Discriminatory	Social media user who makes disparaging remarks about an athlete's race, gender, or sexuality

involvement; (3) low interactivity and high involvement, and (4) low interactivity and low involvement. These quadrants are summarized in Table 1.

In their work, Kavanagh, Jones, and Sheppard-Marks (2016) created a framework for virtual maltreatment, which captured the abusive behavior athletes receive on social and digital platforms. Table 2 summarizes each type of abuse with an example.

EMERGING RESEARCH TOPICS IN SOCIAL MEDIA AND SPORT

Social media is a massive topic to stay abreast of and researchers face challenges with staying current with the constantly changing landscape of social media and the accompanying effects and out-comes it creates. Whereas early research focused more on content approaches to sport and social media (e.g., by looking at what ath-letes or sports organizations were posting) research is now moving beyond this area to look more at effects and outcomes of social media. One emerging area pertains to athletes' social media con-sumption and potential effects. Hayes *et al.* (2019) looked at why athletes use social media while at competitions and found that ath-letes reported that it helped them stay connected to family and friends and minimized their stress during competitions. This find-ing contrasts with popular messaging around athletes' use of social media (e.g., being a distraction). Yet, there are ways for social media to distract athletes (Hayes *et al.*, 2020) and these barriers need to be looked at and addressed. For example, Browning and Sanderson (2012) found that student-athletes reported checking social media mentions during halftimes of games. The effects of social media use by athletes during competitions remains inconclusive and there is a need for sports and social media researchers to continue to investi-gate this topic and work with sports organizations on strategies to manage and minimize potential negative effects for athletes.

There is also a need for research that looks at athletes' social media use on platforms where they may share content that has little to do with their athletic identity. For example, many athletes play video games, and while video games are not inherently "social media", looking at how athletes such as Major League Baseball player Trevor May uses YouTube to stream games is a growing area of emphasis. Other research has found that athletes connect with their peers on other teams through video games and stay connected to family and friends (Sanderson *et al.*, 2020). Looking at athletes' interaction and engagement with audiences through video games would be an important endeavor to pursue. Additionally, athletes' growing consumption of video games also may create organizational friction, and taking organizational management approaches to this topic would be worthwhile. For instance, how should teams react when a player speaks critically of the organization which employs them during a video game stream? As one example, in July 2020,

Chicago Bulls basketball player Daniel Gafford criticized then head coach Jim Boylen on a Twitch stream (Conway, 2020). Specifically, while streaming a game of NBA2K. Gafford stated, "He [Boylan] aight. I don't like him a lot, but he's OK. Got some things he can work on, got some things he can do better as a person and as a coach" (Conway, 2020, para. 4). This comment quickly became public with multiple news outlets reporting it. The media attention focused on Gafford's comments put the Bulls in a public relations dilemma of having to respond to a player criticizing a coach on a video game stream, an incident they were likely unaware of until reported in the media.

Another emerging research trend centers on the increasing use of social media by athletes and sports organizations for activism and advocacy related to social and political issues. Previous research indicates that athletes often receive negative feedback on social media when engaging in activism (Frederick *et al.*, 2017) and some fans threaten to stop supporting a team or going to games because of the political statements made by sports organizations and athletes. However, in 2020, with the rise of social issues into prominence and many athletes taking a stand, it was quite likely that this had changed/is changing. It will be important to look at how sports organizational personnel manage these reactions and how they try and appease various stakeholder groups. Similarly, it appears that sports organizations are becoming more active in posting political and social commentary through team social media accounts. Consider the Tampa Bay Rays, who on July 24, 2020, posted, "Today is Opening Day, which means it's a great day to arrest the killers of Breonna Taylor" (Varn, 2020). While the Rays could have taken a number of approaches to promote the season resuming, they chose to focus specifically on the Taylor case, and in so doing, raised the ire of local law enforcement (Varn, 2020). Understanding the strategic approaches that teams are using to address/respond to social and political causes will be important to shape our understanding of organizational social media strategy. For example, in August 2020, after Milwaukee Bucks players elected to not play a scheduled playoff game against the Orlando Magic in response to the police shooting of Jacob Blake in Kenosha, Wisconsin, a city in close proximity to Milwaukee, it quickly became a national news story with polarizing views being expressed through social media. The Bucks organization was faced with a choice of not getting involved, or expressing support or criticism of the players. The Bucks decided to post a public message of support for the players on its Twitter account, an action that illustrates the increasing shift for sports organizations to be more vocal about supporting social justice activism.

A third emerging area to consider is the evolution of social media platforms and how different sports stakeholders utilize these channels. TikTok has quickly emerged as a popular social media platform, and many athletes and sport organizations have created TikTok accounts to meet audiences on this platform. Evaluating what kind of content sports stakeholders are posting and assessing what content is strategically suited for TikTok can help inform our knowledge of how emerging platforms are adopted and used by sports organizations, athletes, and fans. A fourth emerging area pertains to what might be termed "digital archaeology" or the public mining of old social media content that is then exposed, often at inopportune times for athletes. For example, athletes such as Kyler Murray, Josh Allen, Trea Turner, and Josh Hader have had people expose social media content posted by these athletes when they were teenagers, which created public relations issues for the athletes, the agencies that represent them, and the sports organizations that employ or had just drafted them. In response, there has been a surge of news articles centered on athletes' "scrubbing" their social media accounts. Research that examines these incidents, people's motivations for digging for old content, and the implications for athletes and sports organizations will be important to undertake.

FUTURE RESEARCH DIRECTIONS IN SOCIAL MEDIA IN SPORT

Social media is constantly changing, so in some ways, trying to predict future research directions seems impossible. However, several directions are mentioned here. First, social media platforms seem to be taking a more prominent role in sports media. For example, people now watch games through platforms such as Twitter and Facebook, and YouTube Live. Twitch is home to a huge volume of esports streaming. What role might social media play in the future of sports broadcasts and sports media? Would a company like Facebook ever bid on sports media rights? Second, the sport industry, like many others has been significantly impacted by the global COVID-19 pandemic. For a time, the sport industry was shut down, and for those sports organizations who have resumed competition, they have done so with no or limited fans present. This outcome has taken away a primary content piece for sports organizations for their social media strategy. Future research can investigate how sports organizations are compensating for the lack of games as well as limited or no fans at games to keep fans engaged.

Third, future research can look at organizational implications stemming from social media. For example, during the summer of 2020, a picture surfaced of Oklahoma State University head football coach Mike Gundy wearing an OAN (a media outlet that has been associated with alt-right views) shirt. In response, many people took to Twitter to express their displeasure with Gundy, including then-standout Oklahoma State running back Chuba Hubbard (Pickman, 2020). In response to Hubbard's post, Gundy issued an apology, held a meeting with players, and agreed to make changes to the program's culture (Taylor, 2020). In a similar incident, in June 2020, West Virginia University football player Kerry Martin tweeted about encounters with defensive coordinator Vic Koenning that Martin suggested were discriminatory (Brocato, 2020). Koenning was placed on suspension and a voluntary separation was announced (Kercheval, 2020). Future research can examine the impact of these kinds of incidents and how they might assist sports organizations in more proactively dealing with issues, rather than waiting for them to be reported on social media before change is addressed.

KEY SKILLS FOR PRACTICE

While you may or may not pursue a career as a sports and social media researcher, there are many research functions that people in the sport industry perform. Some of these are highlighted as follows:

Designing Research: Sports organizations are constantly seeking to improve, and research can help produce evidence that assists sports organizations in their effort to make informed decisions. Sports leaders have to be able to understand what areas need investigation and how research can help answer important organizational questions. For example, a marketing manager for a minor league hockey team determines that the organization needs to focus on three social media platforms. To determine which platforms provide the most value for the organization, the marketing manager designs questions about audience engagement that can be answered through analyzing engagement with the organization's social media accounts.

Data collection: Sports organizations regularly seek feedback from different stakeholder groups via surveys, interviews, focus groups, and social media campaigns. Understanding how to collect data and the best methods to select to obtain data is a routine task for many sport industry professionals in functional areas like marketing and sales. In social media, there are a number of different data mining software applications (for more, see Chapter 7). Some of these include Sisense, SQL Server Analysis Services (SSAS), Oracle Data Mining (ODM), and Rapid Minder. For example, a sport organization could use data provided by the analytic programs of Facebook, Twitter, Instagram, and YouTube to analyze what kinds of content is connecting with their respective target audiences.

Data analysis: Sports organization personnel must analyze data after they are collected and be able to report that data in meaningful ways to executives and decision-makers. For example, if a marketing professional meets with a focus group of season-ticket holders to assess their input on the in-venue experience, these data will have to be analyzed and reported. As you will read in Chapter 7, the science of analyzing and interpreting social media data has been propelled by various computational and methodological advancements including audio analytics (e.g., speech analytics), video analytics (e.g., edge-based analytics), and text analytics (e.g., sentiment analysis). Using the preceding example, the sport organization could use information from survey participants to understand the audience response to social media content, and could classify responses by things such as age, location, and frequency of participant engagement with the organization's content.

Implementation: Sports organization personnel must implement action when they assess and evaluate research. Using the preceding example, perhaps after analyzing data from social media, a sport organization learns that younger people in the local community engage more with content about the organization's efforts in the community, while media personnel engage with the organization's content when it is anchored on news and information about the team.

CHAPTER SUMMARY

Social media plays a prominent role in the sport industry. Social media researchers are actively investigating the many ways that social media can help us understand it's influence on different areas of the sport industry. Sports and social media researchers are interested in a variety of topics ranging from social media use in sports marketing, to athletes and branding through social media, to training and education around social media, and how social media and sport can be used to understand society and social issues. Social media and sports research is a valuable tool for the industry and can help industry personnel better understand benefits, problems, and implications associated with social media.

KEY RESOURCES

- *Communication & Sport* — https://journals.sagepub.com/home/com.
- *International Journal of Sport Communication* — https://journals.humankinetics.com/view/journals/ijsc/ijsc-overview.xml.
- *Journal of Sports Media* — https://muse.jhu.edu/journal/402.

TEST YOUR KNOWLEDGE

1. What is a theory? How is it different from a conceptual framework?
2. What have researchers found in their investigation of how athletes present themselves on social media?
3. Which theoretical perspective might be best suited for a researcher who wanted to study reactions on Twitter to the NBA protests in August of 2020?
4. In what ways does framing benefit athletes on social media?
5. Which theoretical perspective might be best suited to explain why athletes use TikTok?
6. What can athletes do to guard against their old social media content being publicly exposed?
7. Think of a research question that would help a sport organization better understand some aspect of social media?

REFERENCES

Abeza, G., O'Reilly, N., and Seguin, B. (2019). Social media in relationship marketing: The perspective of sport managers in the MLB, NBA, NFL, and NHL. *Communication and Sport, 7,* 80–109.

Achen, R. M., Kaczorowski, J., Horsmann, T., and Ketzler, A. (2018). Exploring off-season content and interaction on Facebook: A comparison of U.S. professional sport leagues. *International Journal of Sport Communication, 11,* 389–413.

Ahmad, N. and Thorpe, H. (2020). Muslim sportswomen as digital space invaders: Hashtag politics and everyday visibilities. *Communication and Sport, 8,* 668–691.

Antunovic, D. (2019). "We wouldn't say it to their faces:" Online harassment, women sport journalists, and feminism. *Feminist Media Studies, 3,* 428–442.

Bigsby, K. G., Ohlmann, J. W., and Zhao, K. (2019). Keeping it 100: Social media and self-presentation in college football recruiting. *Big Data, 7,* 3–20.

Billings, A. C., Qiao, F., Conlin, L., and Nie, T. (2017). Permanently desiring the temporary? Snapchat, social media, and the shifting motivations of sports fans. *Communication and Sport, 5,* 10–26.

Billings A. C., Broussard, R. M., Xu, Q., and Xu, M. (2019). Untangling international sports social media use: Contrasting U.S. and Chinese uses and gratifications across four platforms. *Communication and Sport,* 7, 630–652.

Brocato, J. (2020). Vic Koenning placed on leave after Kerry Martin's allegations of mistreatment. *MetroNews.* Retrieved from https://wvmetronews.com/2020/06/23/wvu-safety-kerry-martin-accuses-dc-vic-koenning-of-mistreatment/.

Browning, B. and Sanderson, J. (2012). The positives and negatives of Twitter: Exploring how student-athletes use Twitter and respond to critical tweets. *International Journal of Sport Communication,* 5, 503–521.

Burch, L. M., Frederick, E. L., and Pegoraro, A. (2015). Kissing in the carnage: An examination of framing on Twitter during the Vancouver riots. *Journal of Broadcasting and Electronic Media,* 59, 399–415.

Clavio, G. and Kian, E. M. (2010). Uses and gratifications of a retired female athlete's Twitter followers. *International Journal of Sport Communication,* 3, 486–500.

Coche, R. (2017). How athletes frame themselves on social media: An analysis of Twitter profiles. *Journal of Sport Media,* 12, 89–112.

Conway, T. (2020). Bulls' Daniel Gafford rips Jim Boylen on Twitch video: "I don't like him a lot." *Bleacher Report.* Retrieved from https://bleacherreport.com/articles/2901106-bulls-daniel-gafford-rips-jim-boylen-on-twitch-video-i-dont-like-him-a-lot.

David, J. L., Powless, M. D., Hyman, J. E., Purnell, D. J., Steinfeldt, J. A., and Fisher, S. (2018). College student athletes and the psychological impacts of Twitter use. *International Journal of Sport Communication,* 11, 163–186.

Entmann, R. M. (1993). Framing: Towards clarification of a fractured paradigm. *Journal of Communication,* 43, 51–58.

Foote, G., Butterworth, M., and Sanderson, J. (2017). Adrian Peterson and the "Wussification of America:" Football and myths of masculinity. *Communication Quarterly,* 65, 268–284.

Frederick, E. L. and Clavio, G. (2015). Blurred lines: An examination of high school football recruits' self-presentation on Twitter. *International Journal of Sport Communication,* 8, 330–344.

Frederick, E., Burch, L. M., and Blaszka, M. (2015). A shift in set: Examining the presence of agenda-setting on Twitter during the 2012 London Olympics. *Communication and Sport,* 3, 312–333.

Frederick, E., Sanderson, J., and Schlereth, N. (2017). Kick these kids off the team and take away their scholarships: Facebook and perceptions of athlete activism at the University of Missouri. *Journal of Issues in Intercollegiate Athletics, 10*, 17–34.

Frederick, E., Pegoraro, A., and Sanderson, J. (2019). Divided and united: Perceptions of athlete activism at the ESPYs. *Sport and Society, 22*, 1919–1936.

Frederick, E. L., Pegoraro, A., and Schmidt, S. (2020). "I'm not going to the f***ing White House": Twitter users react to Donald Trump and Megan Rapinoe. *Communication and Sport.* Advance online publication. Doi: 10.1177/2167479520950778

Frederick, E., Lim, C. H., Clavio, G., Pedersen, P. M., and Burch, L. M. (2014). Choosing between the one-way or two-way street: An exploration of relationship promotion by professional athletes on Twitter. *Communication and Sport, 2*, 80–99.

Geurin-Eagleman, A. N., and Burch, L. M. (2016). Communicating via photographs: A gendered analysis of Olympic athletes' visual self-presentation on Instagram. *Sport Management Review, 19*, 133–145.

Geurin, A. N. and McNary, E. L. (2020). Athletes as ambush marketers? An examination of Rule 40 and athletes' social media use during the 2016 Rio Olympic Games. *European Sport Management Quarterly.* Advance online publication. doi: 10.1080/16184742.2020. 1725091

Gibbs, C., O'Reilly, N., and Brunette, M. (2014). Professional team sport and Twitter: Gratifications sought and obtained by followers. *International Journal of Sport Communication, 7*, 188–213.

Hambrick, M. E., Simmons, J. M., Greenlagh, G. P., and Greenwell, T. C. (2010). Understanding professional athletes' use of Twitter: A content analysis of athlete tweets. *International Journal of Sport Communication, 3*, 454–471.

Haugh, B. R. and Watkins, B. (2016). Tag me, tweet me if you want to reach me: An investigation into how sports fans use social media. *International Journal of Sport Communication, 9*, 278–293.

Hayes, M., Filo, K., Riot, C., and Geurin, A. (2019). Athlete perception of social media benefits and challenges during major sporting events. *International Journal of Sport Communication, 12*, 449–481.

Hayes, M., Filo, K., Geurin, A., and Riot, C. (2020). An exploration of the distractions inherent to social media use among athletes. *Sport Management Review.* Advance online publication. doi: 10.1016/j.smr.2019.12.006.

Hölzen, M. and Meier, H. E. (2019). Do football consumers care about sport governance? An analysis of social media responses to the recent FIFA scandal. *Journal of Global Sport Management, 4*, 97–120.

Horton, D. and Wohl, R. R. (1956). Mass communication and parasocial interaction. *Psychiatry, 19,* 215–229.

Hull, K., Lee, J., Zapalac, R., and Stilwell, M. (2017). H-town takeover: Social media agenda setting and branding efforts at the University of Houston. *Journal of Issues in Intercollegiate Athletics, 10,* 162–181.

Kassing, J. W. and Sanderson, J. (2010). Fan-athlete interaction and Twitter, tweeting through the Giro: A case study. *International Journal of Sport Communication, 3,* 113–128.

Kassing, J. W. and Sanderson, J. (2015). Playing in the new media game or riding the virtual bench: Confirming and disconfirming membership in the community of sport. *Journal of Sport & Social Issues, 39,* 3–18.

Kavanagh, E., Jones, I., and Sheppard-Marks, L. (2016). Towards typologies of virtual maltreatment: Sport, digital cultures, and dark leisure. *Leisure Studies, 35,* 783–796.

Katz, E., Blumler, J. G., and Gurevitch, M. (1974). Utilization of mass communication by the individual. In J. G. Blumler and E. Katz (Eds.), *Uses of mass communication* (vol. III, pp. 19–32). Beverly Hills, CA: Sage.

Kercheval, B. (2020). West Virginia 'mutually agrees to separate' with defensive coordinator Vic Koenning. CBSSports.com Retrieved from https://www.cbssports.com/college-football/news/west-virginia-mutually-agrees-to-separate-with-defensive-coordinator-vic-koenning/.

Kilvington, D., and Price, J. (2019). Tackling social media abuse? Critically assessing English football's response to online racism. *Communication and Sport, 7,* 64–79.

Lewis, M., Brown, K. A., and Billings A. C. (2017). Social media becomes traditional: Sport media consumption and the blending of the modern information pathways. *Journal of Global Sport Management, 2,* 111–127.

Li, B., Stokowski, S., Dittmore, S. W., Malmo, J. R., and Rolfe, D. T. (2017). A case study of self-representation on Twitter: A gender analysis of how student-athletes portray themselves. *Global Sports Business Journal, 5,* 61–75.

Litchfield, C. and Kavanagh, E. (2019). Twitter, Team GB, and the Australian Olympic team: Representations of gender in social media spaces. *Sport in Society, 22,* 1148–1164.

Litchfield, C., Kavanagh, E., Osborne, J., and Jones, I. (2018). Social media and the politics of gender, race, and identity: The case of Serena Williams. *European Journal for Sport and Society, 15,* 154–170.

McCombs, M. E., and Shaw, D. L. (1972). The agenda-setting function of the mass media. *Public Opinion Quarterly, 36,* 176–187.

Naraine, M. L., Wear, H. T., and Whitburn, D. J. (2019). User engagement within the Twitter community of professional sport organizations. *Managing Sport and Leisure, 24,* 275–293.

Oshiro, K. F., Weems, A. J., and Singer, J. N. (2020). Cyber racism towards black athletes: A critical race analysis of http://TexAgs.com online brand community. *Communication & Sport.* Advance online publication. doi: 10.1177/2167479520911888

Rodriguez, N. S. (2017). #FIFAputos: A Twitter textual analysis over "puto" at the 2014 World Cup. *Communication and Sport, 5,* 712–731.

Romney, M. and Johnson, R. G. (2019). The ballgame is for the boys: Visual framing of female athletes on national sports networks' Instagram accounts. *Communication & Sport.* Advance online publication. doi: 10.1177/21674759519836731

Pickman, B. (2020). Oklahoma State's Chuba Hubbard says he will 'not be doing anything' with school following photograph of Mike Gundy. *SI.com.* Retrieved from https://www.si.com/college/2020/06/15/chuba-hubbard-oklahoma-state-mike-gundy-shirt.

Sanderson, J. (2010). Framing Tiger's troubles: Comparing traditional and social media. *International Journal of Sport Communication, 3,* 438–453.

Sanderson, J. (2011). *It's a whole new ball game: How social media is changing sports.* New York, NY: Hampton Press.

Sanderson, J. (2013a). Stepping into the (social media) game: Building athlete identity via Twitter. In R. Luppicini (Ed.), *Handbook of research on technoself: Identity in a technological society* (pp. 419–438). New York: IGI Global.

Sanderson, J. (2013b). From loving the hero to despising the villain: Exploring sports fans social identity management on Facebook. *Mass Communication and Society, 16,* 487–509.

Sanderson, J. and Truax, C. (2014). "I hate you man!": Exploring maladaptive parasocial interaction expressions to college athletes via Twitter. *Journal of Issues in Intercollegiate Athletics, 7,* 333–351.

Sanderson, J. and Weathers M. (2020). Snapchat and child sexual abuse in sport: Protecting child athletes in the social media age. *Sport Management Review, 23,* 81–94.

Sanderson, J., Frederick, E., and Stocz, M. (2016). When athlete activism clashes with group values: Social identity threat management via social media. *Mass Communication and Society, 19,* 301–322.

Sanderson, J., Browning, B., and DeHay, H. (2020). "It's the universal language:" Investigating student-athletes' use of and motivations for playing Fortnite. *Journal of Issues in Intercollegiate Athletics, 13,* 22–44.

Sanderson, J., Zimmerman, Stokowski, S., and Fridley, A. (2020). "You had one job!": A case study of maladaptive parasocial interaction and athlete maltreatment in virtual spaces. *International Journal of Sport Communication, 13,* 221–238.

Smith, L. R., Pegoraro, A., and Cruikshank, S. A. (2019). Tweet, retweet, favorite: The impact of Twitter use on enjoyment and sports viewing. *Journal of Broadcasting & Electronic Media, 63,* 94–110.

Taylor, J. (2020). In Twitter statement, Chuba Hubbard explains he wasn't wrong for what he said, but reiterated he was wrong for how he went about it. *NBCSports.* Retrieved from https://collegefootballtalk.nbcsports.com/2020/06/16/oklahoma-state-football-chuba-hubbard-wasnt-wrong-with-what-he-said-but-how-he-said-it/

Thorpe, H., Toffoletti, K., and Bruce, T. (2017). Sportswomen and social media: Bringing third-wave feminism, postfeminism, and neoliberal feminism into conversation. *Journal of Sport and Social Issues, 41,* 359–383.

Tofoletti, K. and Thorpe, H. (2018). Female athletes self-representation on social media: A feminist analysis of neoliberal marketing strategies in "economies of visibility." *Feminism and Psychology, 28,* 11–31.

Toffoletti, K., Pegoraro, A., and Comeau, G. (2019). Self-representations of women's sports fandom on Instagram at the 2015 FIFA Women's World Cup. *Communication and Sport.* Advance online publication. doi: 10.1177/2167479519893332.

Vale, L. and Fernandes, T. (2018). Social media and sports: Driving fan engagement with football clubs on Facebook. *Journal of Strategic Marketing, 26,* 37–55.

Varn, K. (2020). Pinella sheriff to Rays: Breonna Taylor tweet was 'just wrong' and 'reckless.' *Tampa Bay Times.* Retrieved from https://www.tampabay.com/news/pinellas/2020/07/30/pinellas-sheriff-to-rays-breonna-taylor-tweet-was-just-wrong-and-reckless/

Weathers, M., Sanderson, J., Matthey, P., Grevious, A., Tehan, M., and Warren, S. (2014). The tweet life of Erin and Kirk: A gendered analysis of sports broadcasters' self-presentation on Twitter. *Journal of Sports Media, 9,* 1–24.

Witkemper, C., Blazska, M., and Chung, J. (2016). Establishing a typology of social media uses in the sport industry: A multidimensional scaling study. *Communication and Sport, 4,* 166–186.

Woo, C. W., Brigham, M. P., and Gulotta, M. (2020). Twitter talk and Twitter sharing in times of crisis: Exploring rhetorical motive and agenda-setting in the Ray Rice scandal. *Communication Studies, 71,* 40–58.

Xu, Q. and Armstrong, C. L. (2019). #SELFIES at the 2016 Rio Olympics: Comparing self-representations of male and female athletes from the U.S. and China. *Journal of Broadcasting and Electronic Media, 63,* 322–338.

Chapter 3

Online Communities in Sport

David Wagner

Munich Business School, München, Germany

CHAPTER OBJECTIVES

After reading this chapter, you should be able to:

- Distinguish between on-domain communities and communities hosted on social media
- Categorize different types of communities in different sports business contexts
- Analyze and assess online community success in the context of sports management
- Describe and assess business impacts of sports communities
- Recognize the key tasks and skills required for community managers
- Outline future trends and directions for communities in the field of sports management

KEY TERMS

Business impacts

Community health

Community management

Community success

On-domain communities

Online communities

Sport communities

INTRODUCTION

Online communities have been part of the technological developments surrounding social media. Often, the terms social media and online communities are used interchangeably, however, there are some noteworthy distinctions, which we will explore in this chapter. **Online communities** can be defined as "virtual space(s) where people come together with others to converse, exchange information or other resources, learn, play, or just be with each other" (Kraut and Resnick, 2011, p. 1). Online communities are social in nature and usually aimed at sustaining relationship building among members. Traditionally, researchers have emphasized a commonality among community members, for example, through the existence of shared experiences, conditions, goals, or convictions (Sproull and Arriaga, 2007). More recent studies of online communities present them as new organizational forms, because they differ in the way tasks are divided and allocated, as well as in respect to the way information flows are designed and rewards distributed, (i.e., key parameters of organization design, Puranam *et al.*, 2014). Even if not all of them classify as new organizational forms, they frequently extend beyond digital marketing and have the potential to shape the digital strategies and competitive advantages of modern organizations (Bussgang and Bacon, 2020; Wagner *et al.*, 2017).

The field of sport provides a fertile ground for online community building (Lupinek, 2019; Popp and Woratschek, 2016). There are several reasons for this. First, emotional bonds between fans are a defining feature of sport; fans are often passionate about the teams they support and are actively seeking to engage in exchanges with other fans (Smith and Stewart, 2010). Second, fandom of a specific team or discipline can be viewed as creating a shared identity which binds community members together (Lock and Heere, 2017). In fact, research has shown that engagement in **sports communities** enhances identification with the organization, team, and stadium attendance (Yoshida *et al.*, 2015). As we will see later, there are different types of communities when it comes to the objectives they are designed to meet. Communities may cater to sports entities at different levels. For example, there are online communities operating at the team level (e.g., Manchester United), at the association level (e.g., English Premier League), at the sport level (e.g., soccer), or sport at large. The mini cases provided in this chapter illustrate some of these online communities.

As an introductory example, you can think of Reddit, the news site and self-proclaimed "front page of the Internet" (Reddit, 2020a), as hosting multiple sports-related communities. The biggest and most general one, Reddit Sports, has more than 17 million subscribers and ranks 26th in size compared to all communities hosted on the platform. On average, Reddit Sports receives 42 posts and 243 comments per day (Subreddit Stats, 2020). Furthermore, there are more than 70 subreddits, i.e., dedicated forums to specific topics, in the field of sport, featuring all major leagues and numerous smaller sports disciplines (Reddit, 2020b).

Based on the definition of online community introduced above, one could argue that the primary community may be identified by common emotional bonds and a shared identity. For example, take a basketball team, and its primary community would be the sum of all fans of the team. However, the primary community may be dispersed and interact across multiple physical and digital channels. Fans of a team, for instance, would meet physically at games or in sports bars, or distant fans of the team can come together and unite on digital channels, including different social media sites, with a dedicated online community being one — potentially the most important one — of them.

This chapter focuses explicitly on self-hosted communities or so-called **on-domain communities** (which are hosted on the web presence of a specific sport entity, therefore the name *on-domain*). They are treated as an independent class of communities, apart from Facebook, Instagram, Twitter, and the other prominent social media platforms. On-domain communities come with certain advantages and disadvantages, requiring online marketing and social media teams to weigh them carefully before opting for one or the other. Integrating and accounting for on-domain communities in sport will help professionals evaluate strategic options and implications when deciding where to invest scarce digital marketing budgets.

LEARNING ACTIVITY 1

In your experiences being online, have you come across any self-hosted or on-domain communities in a general business context? How about communities in a field related to sport (e.g., health, tourism)? How about specific ones in the context of sports business? What makes them communities, i.e., what is it that binds their members together? Please identify examples and briefly discuss them.

HISTORY

Some of today's online communities were started in the 1990s as forums or message boards, but, as growth continued, were later migrated to more modern technology infrastructure. The online community phenomenon is strongly related to the rise of the Internet (Kim, 2000) and, more specifically, the proliferation of Web 2.0. While the first generation of Internet-based applications, i.e., static web pages, largely carried one-way messages supplied by publishers, Web 2.0 incorporated participatory and collaborative content (e.g., text, audio files, photo, video), produced and controlled by users. The term Web 2.0 denotes the shift in the nature of these applications (O'Reilly Media, 2005), which was essential for more sophisticated community-building to take place. Scholars of sports management and sports marketing have since discovered online communities as a worthy sub-field of investigation (Lupinek, 2019; Popp and Woratschek, 2016). Lately, sports management scholars have focused on the topics of digital transformation (Ströbel *et al.*, 2021) and digital innovation (Ratten, 2016), yet online communities remain an integral part of these conversations. That is because they (still) are novel, digital channels with significant untapped potential to create value for a multitude of sports stakeholders, such as fans, players, coaches, league officials, club owners, club executives, suppliers, event organizers, publishers, sponsors, and many more.

ONLINE COMMUNITIES IN SPORTS: KEY CONCEPTS

WHAT KIND OF COMMUNITY IS RIGHT FOR ME? EXPLORING COMMUNITY TYPES

The term community, with its positive connotation and focus on shared conviction or interest, is appealing to many, especially from a marketing perspective. For this reason, the community label is commonly used in practice, whereas, in theory, this would be hard to defend. Thus, we should be careful when distinguishing between different types of communities. This chapter deliberately starts with the term online community in its general notion. The following is an overview of the different community types as they can be found in the world of sports (adapted from Wagner *et al.*, 2016).

BRAND COMMUNITIES

Brand communities are virtual spaces that specifically focus on an organization's brand or product (Muniz and O'Guinn, 2001). The Harley Owners Group by Harley Davidson is frequently cited as an example of a successful brand community. Brand communities also seem to have attracted most of the research attention in the field of sports management and marketing (Lupinek, 2019). This may not be surprising, given that consumers normally like to engage in a dialogue surrounding their hobbies, in particular, sport. Mini Case 1 presents an example of a brand community run by FC Bayern München.

MINI CASE 1 — A BRAND COMMUNITY HOSTED BY A CLUB: FC BAYERN MÜNCHEN

Community site: FCB Forum available at https://forum.fcbayern.com/.

Fußball-Club Bayern München, commonly known as FC Bayern Munich, is a professional German sports club based in Munich, Germany. It is best known for its professional soccer team, which plays in the Bundesliga, the top tier of the German soccer league, and is the most successful club in German soccer history. FC Bayern won a record 30 national titles and 20 national cups, along with numerous European honors.

FC Bayern Munich is not only the best football club on the field, it is also a German social media champion, placed at the top of the Social Media Index 2020, curated by the International Football Institute (FC Bayern Munich, 2020). FC Bayern's social media team is active on the main social media platforms — Facebook, Instagram, Twitter, and YouTube — but it also runs its own community forum, which was founded in 2006. The FCB Forum is publicly accessible and integrated into the FC Bayern Munich website. As of August 2020, the FCB Forum has 2,860 topics, 2,342,097 posts, and 9,868 members. Fans talk about the team, rumors of players' changes, practice, and much more. Through the use of gamification, community members can collect points, e.g., for starting a discussion, commenting, or liking others' contributions. Based on these points, a ranking is built, retaining a competitive element. Through the FCB Forum, supporters from around the world have the opportunity to become "more than just a fan."

THEMED OR BRANDED COMMUNITIES

In contrast to a brand community, where the focus is on a specific brand or its products, a themed community addresses a theme of general interest to many. Popp and Woratschek (2016) suggest that some organizations may find it attractive to widen the scope of an online community beyond their immediate product or service. As a consequence, they introduce the term branded communities to denote a brand's sponsorship of a themed community. A good example of a branded community in sport is fussball.de (http://www.fussball.de/), a soccer portal, which is run by the German Football Association in cooperation with Deutsche Telekom, a telecommunication provider (see Mini Case 2). Examples of other themed communities include sports technology (https://www.starters.co/latest) or communities dedicated to specific sport disciplines, such as soccer (https://www.reddit.com/r/soccer/).

MINI CASE 2 — A THEMED COMMUNITY HOSTED BY AN ASSOCIATION: FUSSBALL.DE

Community site: Fussball forum available at http://www.fussball.de/ugc/-/foren/11#!/.

Fussball.de is a platform provided by the DFB, the German Football Association, one of the biggest professional associations in the world (Deutscher Fußball-Bund, 2020). Fussball.de is the central portal for amateur soccer in Germany. The portal is developed and maintained by Deutsche Telkom (Deutscher Fußball-Bund, 2019), a German telecommunications firm, which is a sponsor of both FC Bayern Munich and the German Football Association (Deutsche Telekom, 2020). With help of the community, the DFB aims to establish a lively exchange of opinions about German amateur soccer, coaches, games, and players. The community is structured around subforums focused on men's football, women's football, and youth football, with further subdivisions in each category. Beyond a regular (fan) profile, through which members can create and share content, there is also the option to register a player profile. After verification, this extended profile allows the automatic publication of additional personal data in the user´s profile of the DFBnet database, for example, the personal club history or player statistics.

SERVICE COMMUNITIES

Service communities, as the name implies, focus specifically on the service component of a specific brand or product. They are often more problem-centered and designed to quickly answer fan/consumer questions about certain products or resolve complaints. The community-aspect comes into play when both formal customer support specialists, paid by the organization, as well as motivated community members, normally volunteers, answer the questions posted. While improving service is a concern to sports organizations and research has shown that social media is used specifically for this purpose (Abeza *et al.*, 2017), there is a lack of examples for dedicated service communities in the domain of sports management. However, plenty of examples exist in other industries, such as consumer electronics (https://www.dell.com/community), telecommunications (https://crowdsupport.telstra.com.au/, which includes a sport subsection), or travel (https://community.withairbnb.com/).

INNOVATION COMMUNITIES

Often based on the concept of open innovation, innovation communities are focused on integrating (lead) users and other external stakeholders into organizational problem-solving (Chesbrough, 2003). A prime example of such an innovation community is OpenIDEO, which serves as a platform to bring 'problem sponsors' and 'problem solvers' together, often with a focus on grand societal challenges. One of the more recent sports-related challenges carried out on OpenIDEO is the Nike Circular Innovation Challenge, seeking to create waste-free products using Nike Grind materials (https://challenges.openideo.com/challenge/nike-design-with-grind/top-ideas). Initially, more than 400 ideas were generated by contest participants, of which 12 were later selected and further developed jointly with Nike, Inc.

INTERNAL COMMUNITIES

Social intranets, or social network sites used in work settings, have become a standard instrument to connect internal stakeholders of organizations, often employees of large organizations. For example, Nike, Adidas, and other multinational sports organizations all run social intranets to connect their global workforces. Through social intranets it is possible to set up and support internal communities that share certain interests or work collaboratively on joint projects, (e.g., novel products, Wagner *et al.*, 2017). Internal communities may prove particularly valuable to membership-based organizations, such as sports clubs and sports associations, where members are often geographically dispersed and do not interact personally on a day-to-day basis. In a survey about the use of digital instruments in voluntary sports clubs across Germany and Austria, administered to club chairs, board members, and executive directors, Ehnold and colleagues (2020) found that internal and external communication is the most frequently cited category of digital instruments in use, reported by 93.7% of respondents.

(ONLINE) COMMUNITIES OF PRACTICE

Communities of Practice were popularized by Wenger (2000) and describe the exchange and learning processes among peers who work in similar functional roles. Culver and Trudel (2008) apply the concept of Communities of Practice to the field of sports management, citing multiple examples of coaching communities. While existing studies were conducted in offline settings, usually by interviewing coaches, there is an opportunity for these Communities of Practice to assemble in virtual spaces. The International Coaching Federation, for example, sponsors a number of virtual Communities of Practice (https://coachfederation.org/communities-of-practice) on the topics of, for instance, career coaching, coaching science, and ethics.

The above-mentioned community types may be viewed as generic types, and in isolation, but they may also come in mixed forms. The main point of the discussion was to make readers aware of the conceptual differences between and the application of different community types across the spectrum of sports management.

LEARNING ACTIVITY 2

Take a look at the following communities and assess whether they fit any of the categories introduced above. Do they neatly fit one category? What criteria would you use to assign them to a particular classification? Discuss your assessment with a classmate.

1. https://www.reddit.com/r/nba/
2. https://www.theamericanoutlaws.com/
3. https://innovation.ispo.com/pages/ueber
4. https://www.usaultimate.org/

WHAT KIND OF COMMUNITY IS RIGHT FOR ME? EXPLORING COMMUNITY TYPES

WHY CHOOSE AN ON-DOMAIN COMMUNITY? FACTORS TO CONSIDER FROM A BUSINESS PERSPECTIVE

As outlined earlier, the decision for or against an on-domain community is somewhat strategic and the following section outlines relevant criteria which need to be considered.

COMMUNITY AND DATA OWNERSHIP

On-domain communities can also be called proprietary communities. That is because they are owned and operated by their host organizations. This is in stark contrast with creating a specific page or profile on a social media site, where the account (and the content produced by it) belongs to the platform that runs the service, e.g., Facebook. In fact, owning the data that is generated in the community and having access to user profiles (and thus, the possibility to directly interact with fans/consumers) may be considered some of the key drivers to set up an on-domain community.

COMMUNITY GOVERNANCE

Community governance is about control and direction of the community. Contrary to social media outlets, where the big platforms decide on the rules that are being enforced, on-domain communities enable community hosts to develop and enforce their own community rules. Many of you will have seen 'netiquettes' on community sites that describe the behavioral norms guiding social interactions. These may include details about what kind of content is desirable in a community, the type of language that is deemed adequate, and how rules are being enforced. The Australian Institute of Sport, for example, has developed a guideline that can be used and adapted by all kinds of sports organizations (https://www.ais.gov.au/networks/social-media-principles). Governance also includes autonomy over strategic decisions, such as whether and how online advertising or sponsorships can be integrated into the community (i.e., its monetization).

COMMUNITY DESIGN

The big social media sites are often the benchmark and role models for community sites. Many of the core functionalities and design features observed on major social media sites will inspire the design of community sites. Nevertheless, the ultimate decision of how a community will look like and which components it will have rests with the host. While it may be desirable for many to be able to design a community platform from scratch, it can also be pricey. Having some default options to draw on may be beneficial to community hosts, especially to novices who may not have a clear idea what an optimal community design should entail.

WEBSITE AND E-COMMERCE INTEGRATION

Many organizations still focus their online marketing endeavors on their website, which means that the website is the central hub through which all other channels get connected. This model is often referred to as a hub-and-spoke model in digital marketing. One of the key advantages of on-domain communities is the fact that they are *on-domain*, meaning that they are normally part of a domain of a specific website (e.g., community.companyxyz.com). This, in turn, means that the social interactions with fans/consumers take place on home turf (i.e., the company's website) which, among other things, helps to enhance search engine rankings. The benefit may be even bigger if there is a tight integration with the company's e-commerce offerings (i.e., their web shop), as it facilitates easier access to different offerings. For example, there is a high chance for a visitor to navigate directly from a community discussion to the online shop in order to purchase an item that was featured in the discussion.

COSTS INVOLVED

On-domain communities are (initially) more expensive to set up than communities run on social media sites. Although revenue models of software providers differ somewhat, the general cost structure for on-domain communities usually consists of the following pillars:

monthly basic fees for use of the software (often dependent on the different modules used), fees tied to the number of members in a community (i.e., community size), fees tied to the visits to a community (i.e., community attention), and fees for customizations (i.e., the adjustment of the software to the individual needs of each community host). There are further costs involved for the marketing of the community, so that host organizations get potential members to visit the site and sign up. Ultimately, there is also an overhead for **community management** activities, (i.e., the manpower required to moderate and run the community). Indeed, 6-to-7-digit community budgets (on an annual basis) are not unusual for larger organizations (Ellermann *et al.*, 2016).

DOES IT WORK? ASSESSING COMMUNITY SUCCESS

Of course, managers of online communities will be interested in and evaluated on how well their communities are doing. Their main objective is to develop a thriving community. That may sound easier than it is. Researchers have found that most communities struggle to activate their members. According to Nonnecke and Preece (2000), up to 90% of community members never become active upon joining a community, with lurking behavior (i.e., passive observation) being a dominant and common problem (Kokkodis *et al.*, 2020).

According to Wagner *et al.* (2014), the extent to which an online community's vital systems are performing well is referred to as online **community health**. The authors, based on previous research, interviews with community managers, and a dataset from MOTOR-TALK, Europe's biggest Auto and Motor Community, derived seven dimensions of online community health. These seven dimensions are presented in Table 1.

It is worth mentioning that for some of the dimensions introduced above, indicators for measurement are readily available (e.g., the quantity of content measured by new threads and posts),

Table 1. Dimensions of Community Health.

Dimension	Description
Content (quantitative)	Content is normally considered the life blood of communities. It denotes the addition of new content, such as new threads and new posts.
Content (qualitative)	Value of content in the eyes of the community members (i.e., information quality or, alternatively, social satisfaction online).
Interactivity	A high level of interactivity can be characterized by long threads with many posts and many community members contributing to it. This equals more individual viewpoints being heard and/or a broader integration of expertise.
Atmosphere	The general 'touch and feel' of the community (e.g., flaming and constructiveness of exchanges). Community members need to feel comfortable in order to contribute. Highly relevant in the context of hate-speech, prevalent in many online spaces.
Members	The number of community members. Of particular interest is the retention of central or core community members over time. Monthly active users seem to be an established metric frequently reported in the media.
Responsiveness	Responsiveness denotes the tendency for community members to respond to queries by others. A response may provide answers to a question, advice, or support to someone in need as well as opinions on a discussion topic. The timeliness of the response also matters.
Trust	The ability to trust people's actions or what they say. Members who have a longer track record in the community or those with a significant amount of contributions are likely to be more trustworthy. Such details are often provided on profile pages and serve as signals to other community members. Highly relevant in the context of online mis-information.

Source: Adapted from Wagner *et al.* (2014), pp. 7–8.

while for others, measurement is much trickier and requires more sophisticated ways of working with available data, or, in their absence, simple proxies that can be used instead.

PRACTITIONER PERSPECTIVE

Practitioner: Bianca Oertel, Senior Community Manager & Team Lead at MOTOR-TALK, Europe's biggest Auto and Motor Community.

Education: Master's degree in business administration with a specialization in marketing, HTW Berlin — University of Applied Sciences.

MOTOR-TALK.de was founded in Berlin in 2001 as a special interest community through an integration of 30 automotive forums. Since then, it has evolved into Europe's largest online community focused on cars and car-related topics. Besides cars and motorcycles, motor sport is an important thematic pillar. The community, consisting of 4.5 million unique users, attracting 4.1 million unique visitors a month, has produced more than 60 million posts, which appear in roughly 700 thematic and branded forums, with distinct sub-communities dedicated to the Formula 1 and private motor sport, as examples. In 2015, the company was acquired by Mobile.de GmbH, Germany's largest vehicle trading platform, and a subsidiary of eBay.

From 2004 to 2010, Bianca Oertel studied marketing at HTW Berlin. During her studies, she started working for MOTOR-TALK in the field of community management. Today, she is a

Senior Community Manager and runs a community management team, which includes both employees and volunteers (moderators). Besides her job at MOTOR-TALK, she is a member of the German Association for Community Management (BVCM) and an examiner in the certification program for social media and community professionals, which the association runs. Since 2010, she has been organizing Berlin's Stammtisch of social media and community managers, a community of practice. "At MOTOR-TALK, the community management team is the interface between the company and our community of users. We are here to protect the interests of both parties; that is our primary mission."

Note: The original interview was published in German in Clauss *et al.* (2020). For the purpose of this chapter, it was shortened and translated into English by the author.

LEARNING ACTIVITY 3

Take a look at one of the communities that has been introduced in this chapter. Following this examination, take a more detailed look at a couple of threads (approximately 5 to 10) and try to assess the dimensions of community health introduced above, both objectively and subjectively. Would you classify the community as healthy? Why or why not? Discuss your results and support your argument.

WHAT DO WE GET OUT OF IT? BUSINESS IMPACTS OF COMMUNITIES

In a recent survey of the German Association for Community Management (BVCM), Clauss *et al.* (2019) surveyed more than 300 social media and community managers about the specific business objectives they are pursuing with their activities. The study found that the participants' primary goal was the increase of media reach, which 78% of them named as an objective. Next on the list are increasing engagement (61%), brand awareness (54%), and customer retention (34%). A considerable number (43%) of them stated that they were interested in winning new customers, and 27% of them directly attempt to increase sales. This is roughly in line with a comparable survey by The Community Roundtable (Happe and Storer, 2020), based in the United States.

In one analysis of the 'social dollars' generated by a customer community, Manchanda and colleagues (2015) take a look at customer expenditures after joining a community of a multichannel entertainment products retailer. They found that there is a significant increase in customer expenditures that is explained by the social behaviors of community members. More active members (in terms of posting) and better-connected members (in terms of friendship ties created) contribute 3% and 16%, respectively, to the additional expenditures generated by the community. They further calculate that the community broke even with about 33,000 community members. However, the community counted more than 260,000 members within the first 15 months after the community launch, thus making the community a "very profitable investment" (Manchanda *et al.*, 2015, p. 384).

The objectives above mainly relate to the class of external communities, i.e., of those facing external stakeholders, such as fans/customers. As mentioned in the section on community types, there are also internal communities, such as the social intranets that connect members of (voluntary) sports organizations or communities of practice. Here, the goals differ somewhat. Internal communities, according to Clauss *et al.* (2019), are normally aimed at connecting employees or community members (indicated by 93%), accessing expertise (indicated by 87%), and identifying experts (indicated by 47%), as well as strengthening collaboration (indicated by 80%). Interestingly, engagement, named by 60% as an explicit goal, scores equally high for both internal and external communities.

KEY SKILLS FOR PRACTICE

In previous studies of social media and community managers by the German Association for Community Management, Ellermann *et al.*

(2016) distinguished between five broad sets of skills, based on routine tasks these professionals engage in on a daily basis.

STRATEGIC SKILLS

Community managers will normally develop their own community strategy, which requires a plan for implementation, the development of performance measurement indicators and routines for continuous measurement, the drafting of reports for senior management, but also the promotion of the community both internally and externally as well as the benchmarking against competitors. Many of the inputs for these documents were discussed in the sections above. Importantly, the community strategy is rarely a stand-alone document. Very frequently, it relates and feeds directly into the broader marketing, innovation, or digital (transformation) strategies, thereby aligning with corporate strategy.

CONTENT PRODUCTION

As mentioned in a number of chapters in this book, content production and distribution are central aspects of online community work. This includes the planning, production, and scheduling of internal content and curation of externally produced content. Social media and community managers are also frequently involved in conceptualizing and running campaigns of different sorts. Importantly, given the nature of social media and the multiple content formats used in different settings, content no longer just represents texts, but images, infographics, voice-recordings, video, and more. A comparison of social media and community managers reveals that content production is the most time-consuming category of work for social media managers.

NURTURING SOCIAL INTERACTIONS

Community managers need to find creative ways to activate the community and foster social interactions. They do this by recruiting new community members, writing responses to queries and requesting contributions, connecting community members with each other, designing incentive programs for power users and recruiting (volunteer) moderators who will help with the management of sub-communities, e.g., local chapters. A comparison of social media and community managers reveals that nurturing social interactions is the most time-consuming category of work for community managers. Thus, for the community manager, the work is more about creating leverage (through community members) than producing the content alone.

LEADERSHIP SKILLS

Community managers are normally part of a community team and may thus find themselves in different leadership roles. They may, for example, recruit additional people to their team, be responsible for developing individual team members in certain areas, coordinating service providers, and leading project teams. The leadership category does not seem to be prevalent in terms of where most time is spent on a daily basis, however, it is an important category. Specifically, it is telling that social media and community managers frequently seem to be engaged in cross-functional teams and initiatives, e.g., with marketing, product development, or innovation units, thereby having to leverage soft power — or distributed leadership — instead of being formally in the position to determine the team's course of action.

TECHNICAL SKILLS

Ultimately, there are also a number of technical skills required for the work in this domain. Social media managers are used to working with a number of content-related and analytics tools, such as content management systems (e.g., Wordpress), image processors and video cutting (e.g., the Adobe Suite), social media management systems (e.g., Hootsuite), social media monitoring solutions (e.g., Brandwatch), or web analytics (e.g., Google Analytics). The work of community managers may be slightly more technical, because, specifically in the case of on-domain communities, community managers are frequently overseeing development work. This may include coordination with internal or external software developers, for example, being able to articulate (unique) technical requirements or new feature requests and, thereby, influence the future development of the underlying community software. In case of a community migration, knowledge of relational databases and data structures is important.

TRENDS AND CURRENT ISSUES

KEEPING UP WITH THE FIELD'S SPEED OF DEVELOPMENT

One of the key challenges for most social media and community management teams is the field's speed of development. New platforms are joining the social media ecosystem on a regular basis, sometimes changing the types of media used, e.g., the recent focus on voice and video, and frequently introducing new features, such as stories or moments. Think of TikTok or Snapchat as some of the latest entrants to the field. Keeping up with these developments and translating current trends into community features is a recurring challenge for community managers.

COMMUNITIES FOR MARKETING AND INNOVATION

The field of user innovation has witnessed a rise in popularity over recent years. There is much potential for including lead users in initiatives surrounding new product development or the enhancement of existing products. Currently, however, innovation communities are just a small niche in the community space. Social media and community management teams are frequently unaware of this opportunity. This does not come as a surprise, given that community teams are normally reporting to marketing departments (Clauss *et al.*, 2019). This may also explain the prominence of brand communities in sports. It is time for innovation departments to step up and get involved. Never before has it been so easy to reach out to diverse stakeholders and leverage open innovation in the field of sports management (Ratten, 2016).

THE RISE OF COMMUNITIES IN ESPORTS

Esports is a field that is particularly conducive to community building. Game publishers have a long track record for running communities. This makes a lot of sense, since players are already interacting in a digital environment and are normally sophisticated users of digital technologies (Kramer *et al.*, 2021). It seems natural to establish a virtual community where professional and personal exchanges can take place, and bonds between players of certain game titles can develop. The rise in popularity of esports over the recent years has lead to a growth in potential community members. As a result of the spread of the Corona pandemic in early 2020, severe lockdowns were implemented in many countries around the world. Esports has been a beneficiary of the pandemic, with player numbers and revenues surging during the lockdown. In conjunction, community participation (e.g., at EA Games) increased significantly.

CHAPTER SUMMARY

This chapter is about online communities in sport. While communities may be hosted on social media sites, the focus of this chapter is to shed light on proprietary or so called on-domain communities as a specific class of communities. The chapter started with a short review of the history of online communities and situating the phenomenon in the field of sports management. It then described different types of online communities in the context of sports management. Judging from a business perspective, the chapter discussed important factors to consider which distinguish on-domain communities from other social media platforms. A system for the measurement of success was put forward, followed by a discussion of **business impacts** of online communities. Key skills for community managers were then described. The chapter concluded with future trends and developments at the intersection of communities and sports management.

KEY RESOURCES

Software providers in the field of online communities:
   Providers of internal communities:

- Higher Logic: https://www.higherlogic.com/
- Jive: https://www.jivesoftware.com/
- Microsoft Sharepoint: https://www.microsoft.com/en-us/ microsoft-365/sharepoint/collaboration

   Providers of external (customer) communities:

- Brandslisten: https://www.brandslisten.com/
- Khoros: https://khoros.com/
- Vanilla: https://vanillaforums.com/en/

   Providers of innovation contests and communities:

- Hyve: https://www.hyve.net/en/
- InnoCentive: https://www.innocentive.com/
- OpenIDEO: https://www.openideo.com/

Professionalizing the discipline of community management worldwide:

- CMX Hub: https://cmxhub.com/
- The Community Roundtable: https://communityroundtable. com/
- German Association for Community Management: https://www. bvcm.org/

TEST YOUR KNOWLEDGE

1. Name few reasons why sport is a fertile ground for online community building.
2. What has Web 2.0 to do with online communities?

3. What are some of the key differences between communities hosted on social media compared to on-domain communities?
4. Name and explain the generic types of communities that were introduced in this chapter. Please give an example for each.
5. Why would you consider an on-domain community as a potential alternative to hosting a social media community? Please explain the underlying factors.
6. What is community health? How can you measure it?
7. What are some business objectives for running communities? To what extent do objectives differ for internal and external communities? Why?
8. What are some of the key skills that community managers need to possess?
9. Please name and explain three trends in sports communities.

Acknowledgment: We would like to thank Marie-Louise Braun, a graduate student from the Master in Sports Business and Communication program, for help with literature search as well as the collection and review of mini cases presented in this chapter.

REFERENCES

Abeza, G., O'Reilly, N., and Seguin, B. (2017). Social media in relationship marketing: The perspective of professional sport managers in the MLB, NBA, NFL, and NHL. *Communication and Sport*, 2167479517740343. https://doi.org/10.1177/2167479517740343.

Bussgang, J. and Bacon, J. (2020). When community becomes your competitive advantage. *Harvard Business Review*. https://hbr.org/2020/01/when-community-becomes-your-competitive-advantage.

Chesbrough, H. W. (2003). *Open innovation: The new imperative for creating and profiting from technology.* Harvard Business School Press.

Clauss, A., Collet, S., Laub, T., Lämmer, S., Schnurr, J.-M., and Wagner, D. (2019). *Social Media und Community Management 2018.* Bundesverband Community Management e. V. für digitale Kommunikation und Social Media. https://www.bvcm.org/bvcm-studie-2018/.

Clauss, A., Collet, S., Laub, T., Lämmer, S., Schnurr, J.-M., and Wagner, D. (2020). *Profilinterviews zu den BVCM-Berufsbildern.* Bundesverband

Community Management e. V. für digitale Kommunikation und Social Media. https://www.bvcm.org/wp-content/uploads/2020/04/Profilinterviews-zu-den-BVCM-Berufsbildern.pdf.

Culver, D., and Trudel, P. (2008). Clarifying the concept of communities of practice in sport. *International Journal of Sports Science and Coaching*, *3*(1), 1–10.

Deutsche Telekom. (2020). *Commitment to soccer pays off.* https://www.telekom.com/en/company/details/commitment-to-soccer-pays-off-506620.

Deutscher Fußball-Bund. (2019). *DFB-Premium-Partner Deutsche Telekom.* https://www.dfb.de/verbandsstruktur/partner-des-dfb/deutsche-telekom/.

Deutscher Fußball-Bund. (2020). *About DFB.* https://www.dfb.de/en/about-dfb/.

Ehnold, P., Faß, E., Steinbach, D., and Schlesinger, T. (2020). Digitalization in organized sport — usage of digital instruments in voluntary sports clubs depending on club's goals and organizational capacity. *Sport, Business and Management: An International Journal, ahead-of-print* (ahead-of-print). https://doi.org/10.1108/SBM-10-2019-0081.

Ellermann, B., Enke, S., Laub, T., Lämmer, S., Schnurr, J.-M., and Wagner, D. (2016). *Social-Media- und Community-Management in 2016.* Bundesverband Community Management e. V. für digitale Kommunikation und Social Media. https://www.bvcm.org/bvcm/ausschuesse/forschung/bvcm-studie-2016/.

FC Bayern Munich. (2020). *FC Bayern are also German champions on social media.* https://fcbayern.com/en/news/2020/07/fc-bayern-are-social-media-champions-of-germany.

Happe, R. and Storer, J. (2020). *The State of Community Management 2020.* The Community Roundtable. https://communityroundtable.com/what-we-do/research/the-state-of-community-management/the-state-of-community-management-2020/.

Kim, A. J. (2000). *Community Building on the Web: Secret Strategies for Successful Online Communities.* Peachpit Press.

Kokkodis, M., Lappas, T., and Ransbotham, S. (2020). From lurkers to workers: Predicting voluntary contribution and community welfare. *Information Systems Research, 31*(2), 607–626. https://doi.org/10.1287/isre.2019.0905.

Kramer, K., Wagner, D., and Scheck, B. (2021). Reaping the digital dividend? Sport marketing's move into esports: insights from Germany.

European Journal of International Management, 15(2/3), 339–366. https://doi.org/10.1504/EJIM.2021.10032384.

Kraut, R. E. and Resnick, P. (2011). *Building Successful Online Communities: Evidence-Based Social Design.* MIT Press.

Lock, D. and Heere, B. (2017). Identity crisis: A theoretical analysis of 'team identification' research. *European Sport Management Quarterly, 17*(4), 413–435.

Lupinek, J. M. (2019). Tracing the ABC's of brand community. *International Journal of Sports Marketing and Sponsorship, 20*(2), 291–306. https://doi.org/10.1108/IJSMS-09-2017-0103.

Manchanda, P., Packard, G., and Pattabhiramaiah, A. (2015). Social Dollars: The Economic Impact of Customer Participation in a Firm-Sponsored Online Customer Community. *Marketing Science, 34*(3), 367–387. https://doi.org/10.1287/mksc.2014.0890.

Muniz, A. M., and O'Guinn, T. C. (2001). Brand community. *Journal of Consumer Research, 27*(4), 412–432. https://doi.org/10.1086/319618.

Nonnecke, B. and Preece, J. (2000). Lurker demographics: Counting the silent. *Proceedings of the SIGCHI 2000 Conference on Human Factors in Computing Systems,* 73–80. https://doi.org/10.1145/332040.332409.

O'Reilly Media. (2005). *What Is Web 2.0.* http://oreilly.com/web2/archive/what-is-web-20.html.

Popp, B. and Woratschek, H. (2016). Introducing branded communities in sport for building strong brand relations in social media. *Sport Management Review, 19*(2), 183–197. https://doi.org/10.1016/j.smr.2015.06.001.

Puranam, P., Alexy, O., and Reitzig, M. (2014). What's "New" About New Forms of Organizing? *Academy of Management Review, 39*(2), 162–180. https://doi.org/10.5465/amr.2011.0436.

Ratten, V. (2016). Sport innovation management: Towards a research agenda. *Innovation, 18*(3), 238–250. https://doi.org/10.1080/14479338.2016.1244471.

Reddit. (2020a). *Reddit.* https://www.reddit.com/.

Reddit. (2020b). *Reddit Sports.* https://www.reddit.com/r/sports/wiki/related.

Smith, A. C. T. and Stewart, B. (2010). The special features of sport: A critical revisit. *Sport Management Review, 13*(1), 1–13. https://doi.org/10.1016/j.smr.2009.07.002.

Sproull, L. and Arriaga, M. (2007). Online Communities. In H. Bidgoli (Ed.), *Handbook of Computer Networks* (pp. 898–914). John Wiley & Sons,

Inc. http://onlinelibrary.wiley.com/doi/10.1002/9781118256107. ch58/summary.

Ströbel, T., Stieler, M. and Stegmann, P. (2021). Guest editorial. *Sport, Business and Management: An International Journal, 11*(1), 1–9. https:// doi.org/10.1108/SBM-03-2021-124.

Subreddit Stats. (2020). *Subreddit Stats.* https://subredditstats.com/.

Wagner, D., Richter, A., Trier, M., and Wagner, H.-T. (2014). Toward a Conceptualization of Online Community Health. *ICIS 2014 Proceedings.* http://aisel.aisnet.org/icis2014/proceedings/SocialMedia/21.

Wagner, D., Wagner, H.-T., and Ellermann, B. (2016). Online Communities als Quelle von Ideen und Innovationen. *Ideen-und Innovationsmanagement, 1*, 7–11. https://doi.org/10.37307/j.2198-3151.2016.01.04.

Wagner, D., Wenzel, M., Wagner, H.-T., and Koch, J. (2017). Sense, seize, reconfigure: Online communities as strategic assets. *Journal of Business Strategy, 38*(5), 27–34. https://doi.org/10.1108/JBS-09-2016-0088.

Wenger, E. (2000). Communities of Practice and Social Learning Systems. *Organization, 7*(2), 225–246. https://doi.org/10.1177/135050840072002.

Yoshida, M., Heere, B., and Gordon, B. (2015). Predicting behavioral loyalty through community: Why other fans are more important than our own intentions, our satisfaction, and the team itself. *Journal of Sport Management, 29*(3), 318–333. https://doi.org/10.1123/jsm.2013-0306.

https://doi.org/10.1142/9789811237669_0004

Chapter 4

Social Media Use in Major Sports

Matthew Zimmerman*, Kelsey Slater†, and Lauren Burch‡

*Mississippi State University, United States
†North Dakota State University, United States
‡Loughborough University London, United Kingdom

CHAPTER OBJECTIVES

- Identify the distinct elements of major sports from a social media perspective
- Evaluate how the different stakeholders in major sports use social media
- Describe the importance of social media use for sporting events
- Distinguish between the different objectives which teams, leagues, and national governing bodies have when using social media

KEY TERMS

Authenticity

Customer relationship
  management systems

Engagement

Major sport

National governing body

Social media strategy

INTRODUCTION

"Anybody in Norfolk play FIFA15, I will come to your house & politely embarrass you on Xbox One in front of your family & friends..."

It was a simple tweet, the type of phrasing the average enthusiastic and confident video game player of any age would send. After receiving a significant response, the gamer then wrote, "Fool think I won't pull up to his house & go straight to the refrigerator then beat him in FIFA15, he gone learn today..." The exchange led to a meetup in which the individual who sent the original tweet and the person who responded each won a match in EA Sports' FIFA15 video game on Xbox One. Afterward, there was a group photo, as the host and his friends enjoyed meeting the person behind the original tweet — former star NFL wide receiver Chad Johnson (Dubin, 2015). Johnson had already earned a reputation as one of the more engaged athletes on Twitter, regularly responding to fans and frequently displaying a personality on the medium. When he was released by the New England Patriots at the age of 34, his Twitter bio indicated that he was "UNEMPLOYED" and his new profile photo showed Johnson sitting on a suitcase, hitchhiking.

Johnson's is not the only notable sports-related Twitter feed with a sense of humor and engagement. For instance, the expansion of Las Vegas Golden Knights' quick rise in the National Hockey League continues to be accompanied by a social media presence that can best be described as eccentric (Snel, 2018), which is discussed in more detail in Chapter 6. Social media offers relationship marketing opportunities — that is, the chance to build a long-term dialogue with fans that may lead to sales and a deeper commitment — between fans and major professional sports leagues (Abeza *et al.*, 2019). As the dynamic interrelationship between social media and marketing benefits (branding, sponsorship, endorsements, sales promotion) have become clearer, most sports figures and organizations have increased their utilization of the various platforms. In addition to showing the aforementioned sense of humor and engagement, individual athletes as well as teams and governing bodies can seize the opportunity to bypass traditional media filters and take their messages directly to their fan base and other potential customers and consumers. This is notable since the opportunity for the more individualized presentation can allow individual athletes to provide a more complex image compared to the usual simplistic stereotypes and tropes (Coche, 2017). Ultimately, when athletes and organizations utilize social media as part of a messaging strategy, the "social" aspect occurs as fans have the opportunity to respond and make comments of their own (Anagnostopoulos *et al.*, 2018).

This chapter focuses on the use of social media by individuals and organizations involved in what can be defined as **major sports**. This includes American football, basketball, baseball, hockey, the world's game — soccer, and mega-events such as the World Cup and the Olympic Games. These major sports are defined by their level of popularity both in their home nations and worldwide in terms of participation, spectator attention, and media exposure including television rights (Willis, 2020). For example, North American professional team sports have four unique features that distinguish them from other sports (Gladden and Sutton, 2014). These include interdependence (teams need to compete and cooperate simultaneously — e.g., profit sharing), structure and governance (leagues, owners, board of governance, administrative unit), labor-management relations (collective bargaining, free agency, salary caps, and a player draft), and the role of electronic and new media. Professional team sports generate billions of dollars each year through media rights, gate receipts, luxury seating, sponsorships, and properties (Gladden and Sutton, 2014). This chapter also discusses social media usage by individuals and organizations associated with the major revenue-producing sports at the U.S. college level — football, and men's and women's basketball (Ordway, 2020). Research has indicated that sports seeking greater popularity might utilize social media due to its immediacy, low cost, and lack of need for traditional media coverage (Kassing and Sanderson, 2010). However, major sports and larger sports organizations also seek to utilize social media for similar reasons of message control in speed and content, lack of cost, and creating a connection with fans and other interested parties (Geurin and Burch, 2017).

In a similar fashion to the experiences of non-athlete individuals on social media, athletes using social media also have had their share of adventures. Perhaps most famously, in October 2012, then-freshman Ohio State backup quarterback Cardale Jones barely had a place on the depth chart, but soon found a place of infamy. He tweeted "Why should we have to go to class if we come here to play FOOTBALL, we ain't come to play SCHOOL, classes are POINTLESS." Within five years, Jones had led the Buckeyes to the first College Football Playoff Championship, retweeted the original tweet with a lament on how "stupid" it had been, and created an Instagram post making fun of his earlier youthful misdeed the day he graduated from Ohio State University. The name Cardale Jones remains somewhat synonymous with the original tweet, but his later deft usage of Twitter and Instagram invited a reassessment from fans and media on multiple social media platforms (Lesmerises, 2017).

Earlier in the same year that Jones committed his initial gaffe, professional sports organizations in the United States were testing the limits of social media engagement. During the NHL's Stanley Cup playoffs, the Los Angeles Kings eliminated the top-seeded Vancouver Canucks in the first round. The organization's celebratory tweet read, alluding to the Canucks' lack of mass popularity and overall negative perception by fans of other Canada-based NHL franchises, "To everyone in Canada outside of B.C., you're welcome." In this case, Kings players distanced themselves from the tweet quickly, citing respect for the Canucks (Fitz-Gerald, 2012). Such instances of candid expression on social media have helped cement social media's place in the sports conversation. As fans seek a higher level of connection with the sports entities in which they are interested, the use of social media by those entities has increased exponentially. Most sports organizations (e.g., teams, leagues, national and international governing bodies) have a presence on social media. Facebook and Twitter are the most popular text-based platforms. As discussed in Chapter 1, Instagram, YouTube, Pinterest, Snapchat, and TikTok are also the commonly used social media sites.

The next section of this chapter will examine more specifically the use of the various social media platforms by sports-related individuals and organizations in major sports.

LEARNING ACTIVITY 1

Examine the social media sites (Facebook, Instagram, and Twitter) of a single sport organization. Compare the number of followers or likes and then analyze the types of posts including how many words, links, videos, photos, and calls to action are present. Also, look for overlap in messaging between the different mediums. Compile your results and discuss your findings with your classmates.

SOCIAL MEDIA AND MAJOR SPORTS: KEY CONCEPTS

Social media is an opportunity for individuals and organizations in sport to grow and cultivate their audience. Content communicated on the various social media platforms is used to share information, promote offerings, and possibly entice a potential commitment in the form of purchases of tickets, merchandise, or services. As noted above, sports fans can be found on different platforms such as Facebook, Twitter, Instagram, Snapchat, and more recently TikTok, which has become a preferred short-video platform. The use of Snapchat and TikTok is noteworthy, as sports fans tend to utilize social media when they are looking to consume sports-related short videos (Moran, 2019). Among fans of athletes, the use of TikTok for personal videos has led to a perception of higher **authenticity** (Su *et al.*, 2020). Authenticity, or acting genuine, is important in social media use as pages that are perceived by fans as authentic are more likely to maintain a fan base (Kucharska *et al.*, 2020). Part of the continued conversation with fans can help forge and develop a deeper connection between a fan base and a sports organization, with fan groups forming while sports teams and leagues become closer to the fans as opposed to being a massive corporate entity (Abeza *et al.*, 2019).

Ultimately, fans and interested parties who utilize social media are seeking information and interaction, and it is imperative that sports-related entities understand how to provide these benefits (Gibbs *et al.*, 2014). In addition, the nature of social media as online communication with a worldwide reach casts each platform as a potential vehicle for continuing engagement. Fan attachment to a sport organization remains even as individuals might physically move from the team's locations or origin, and social media offers an easy opportunity for an organization to maintain a connection with such individuals (Collins *et al.*, 2016). For the fan, retaining a level of association with a team often can have a direct positive effect on an individual's potential purchase intention in terms of merchandise as well as tickets to an event, which an organization's official social media feeds can serve to encourage (Park and Dittmore, 2014).

Different social media platforms have different metrics of **engagement** including likes, favorites, retweets, and comments, all of which can be used to evaluate performance on social media, which is a topic discussed in detail in Chapter 15. A number of athletes in major sports, similar to Chad Johnson, use Twitter to talk about their personal lives and engage with fans. As Doyle *et al.* (2020) reported, soccer athletes have increased fan engagement on Instagram when they posted high quality photographs or pictures with teammates. Understanding the different ways to use the various social media channels is important for athletes and organizations to optimize fan engagement. (See Chapter 15 for social media management practical guidelines). For an organization, it is important to create a social media schedule, preferably built around the sports calendar, emphasizing certain events and maintaining a steady flow of information from multiple platforms. Notably, organizations must also be flexible in these schedules, as unforeseen events outside of the sporting realm may affect leagues and teams. In 2020, the COVID-19 pandemic led to a massive rescheduling of sports leagues worldwide, with some championship contests being completely canceled (ESPN, 2020). Throughout the resulting uncertainty, sports organizations were able to continue communicating important information while also reaffirming their presence in the community (Sharpe *et al.*, 2020).

In addition, identifying interested segments in the potential marketplace (e.g., students, parents, individuals categorized into demographic groups by age, gender, race, and income) is key in creating and developing a **social media strategy**. In terms of identifying and cultivating the potential audience, surveys and focus groups as well as social media polls and inquiries allow an organization to gain a higher level of knowledge regarding their target publics (Achen, 2016). The resulting databases, or **Customer Relationship Management (CRM) systems**, assist organizational representatives in determining and managing what types of messages might best reach certain segments of the potential customer base. Notably, in a survey of soccer supporters in Europe to discover motivations for their use of social media to engage with soccer clubs, Vale and Fernandes (2018) found that fans seek information, agency (e.g., the ability to make individual choices within fandom) as fans, and affection for the brand. Belonging to a group and having the ability to interact were also paramount desires, indicating that each sport organization should provide fans with knowledge and the opportunity to become part of something, including a general feeling of belonging with the fan base, or more specifically an official supporters' group directly endorsed by the sport entity.

Organizations have adapted to using photo-based platform Instagram, for instance, as part of their social media presentation strategy. This includes images meant to portray aspects including action, fans, and marketing for a program, often utilizing hashtags in a similar manner to those used on Twitter, to help media consumers identify the content more readily (Bowles, 2016). Still, Facebook and Twitter also remain a primary aspect of a sport organization's social media strategy, as Blaszka *et al.* (2018) found in an examination of collegiate sports.

The following sections of this chapter will feature discussion of social media use by different stakeholders involved in major sports.

These groups include athletes, coaches, teams and clubs, leagues, practitioners working for sporting events, and sports governing bodies.

LEARNING ACTIVITY 2

Think about an athlete who you believe uses social media well, note their overall number of followers, interaction with fans, and the types of messages they choose to disseminate. Examine their social media platforms and determine what types of posts are effective and what posts are not as effective. Discuss your findings with your classmates.

ATHLETES AND SOCIAL MEDIA

In terms of individuals utilizing social media, fans seem to be most interested in athletes and coaches. While the tweets by Chad Johnson and Cardale Jones had different goals, neither led to long-term negative effects. High-profile athletes have utilized social media as endorsers for products, though unlike the usual celebrity endorsers, the athlete's perceived knowledge of and potential actual usage of the product may carry more importance for consumers than just fame and relative attractiveness (Agnihotri and Bhattacharya, 2020). In addition, the opportunity to respond to push notifications from friends and Facebook connections can offer an opportunity for an athlete to engage in positive self-presentation and a potential reduction of sports-related anxiety (Encel *et al.*, 2017). In a similar fashion to the average social media user, that connection also can come with unwanted distractions for athletes on social media, which can be solved by simply disconnecting or ceding control of the accounts to others, as a study based on interviews with Australian athletes found (Hayes *et al.*, 2019). Further, athletes have shown that they will engage with newer technology, with short-video platform TikTok proving to be a location for fan engagement (Su *et al.*, 2020).

All of this is to say that athletes engage on social media for tangible reasons in terms of financial compensation as well as intangible reasons for engaging with supportive individuals. In addition, just as non-athletes might use social media to discuss a sporting event in real time, athletes also take the opportunity to reach for their phones. In their study of 298 athletes' social media behaviors, Encel *et al.* (2017) discovered that athletes not only use social media within hours before competing, but also during a competition when they are on the sidelines. This type of frequent usage of social media has incited various sports governing bodies to enact rules and guidelines for the use of social media by athletes, including specifics regarding the proper times to use the various platforms.

CASE STUDY 1

You are the head football coach at a Power Five university whose football team is consistently bowl eligible but rarely competes for a conference championship or participates in a New Year's Six bowl game. After last season's bowl game, the previous head football coach was fired, and that decision was met with positive reactions from your school's fan base. You are a favorite with football fans all across the country whose active social media presence played a huge role in how you landed the job in the first place. During the offseason, you posted a picture on Twitter that offended some student-athletes and fans because it was deemed racially insensitive. Two student-athletes have left the program, three more have threatened to transfer to another university, and some committed recruits have considered re-opening their recruitment. You have not posted on social media since and the athletic director as well as the university president are concerned about the effect on the team's and university's image.

Discussion: What do you do? Explain how you would use social media to repair your image, interact with fans and new potential student-athletes, and not lose the dynamic presence that makes you popular with fans. What reassurance would you give to the athletic director and university president about your social media use for the future?

COACHES AND SOCIAL MEDIA

When discussing coaches' use of social media, coaches in professional sports do not have nearly the presence compared to the individuals tasked to lead collegiate teams in the major moneymaking sports, football and men's basketball. As the continuous face of their respective programs, these coaches are largely responsible for tens of millions of dollars in athletic revenue, with their use of the platforms a paramount aspect of building a program's image (Jensen *et al.*, 2014). In addition, the use of social media can be an effective and obvious tool as part of the process of recruiting athletes (Zimmerman *et al.*, 2016) as the use of digital social media platforms increases among the younger demographics (Pedersen, 2016). In contrast to athletes' Twitter usage but similar to social media use by organizations, coaches tend to practice a more transactional approach, posting more often to inform the public and promote their program, as opposed to tweeting about personal events or information (Zimmerman *et al.*, 2016). Social media's decade as part of the communication landscape means that organizations seeking connections cannot post haphazardly. Rather, it is paramount for them to enact social media plans in order to entice potential fans and consumers to make the connection (Blaszka *et al.*, 2018).

However, if fans perceive that an organization's social media connections are intended to lead to sales, that may hinder those sales due to fan resistance (Hull *et al.*, 2017). The contrast between a departmental strategy for interest in an organization's actions and ideas — and eventual sales — and individual coaches using their feeds to post messages about events and efforts connected to the organization, might at times cause sports social media practitioners moments of frustration. If an athletic department carefully curates its social media with timed posts, a coach can still go the route of posting more individualized messaging that might run counter to the athletic department's planned strategy, which even if the content is sound can lead to some diminishing of a program's overall messaging. The possibility of a coach going off-script can be explained in an examination of athletes, who also tend to go off-script at times. Through a series of in-depth interviews, Geurin (2017) found that athletes tend to seek connections and interaction, but often do not have a specific strategy in mind. Even while enacting a social media plan, practitioners must always be cognizant of the ability — and sometimes, tendency — of the individual users to go off script and express viewpoints that are not part of the organization's intended messaging.

Regarding the use of hashtags and photos, coaches tend to utilize them as a supplement to the tweet rather than introducing different ideas in the images to maximize Twitter's limited space for messaging (Zimmerman *et al.*, 2016). Still, the use of hashtags for promotions that may lead to purchase intent does not need to be constant in order to be effective. One study found that at the University of Houston, the hashtag for the Cougars' football program disseminated positive news for the team, but was not utilized as often to inform fans of how they could purchase tickets or team merchandise (Hull *et al.*, 2017). And even if a coach's social media usage does not quite match the program's overall strategy, it can still yield a positive effect. By utilizing social media to promote their programs, individuals can engage in a relationship marketing (Abeza *et al.*, 2013; Abeza *et al.*, 2017) paradigm meant to indicate to fans that their values dovetail with each other, thus potentially inspiring long-term loyalty and possibly a purchase intention (Zimmerman *et al.*, 2016). As coaches are forming relationships in order to promote their programs, the use of social media during events can also support existing traditional media.

Even with many individuals involved and coaches often going off the preferred script, team and organization usage of social media can be similar to that of coaches and athletes. In an examination of NBA teams' use of Twitter, Wang and Zhou (2015) found that building relationships with fans and target publics through information sharing was a key component of social media usage. Still, coaches and athletes remain the most out-front representatives of an organization. With that understanding, it is important to note that the coaches at the two most consistently successful college football teams in the College Football Playoff era (i.e., 2014–present), Nick Saban and Dabo Swinney, do not have personal Twitter feeds. However, Alabama and Clemson football each have robust social media followings for their official accounts, an indicator that name brand still matters. While individual coaches might be expected to inspire a large following, often it is program history and prestige that dictates whether coaches' and official program social media feeds gain a large amount of attention (Jensen *et al.*, 2014). However, this is not to say coaches should eschew the notion of displaying an interesting personality. Just as with athletes, engagement, charisma, and humor can increase a coach's following (Jensen *et al.*, 2014). In addition, NCAA rules enacted in 2016 expanded which engagements college coaches can utilize on social media. They had been allowed to follow and send private message to recruits on social media, but the new rules expanded to mention more public acknowledgments. The NCAA specifically said that athletic department staff members could "Like" or Retweet posts by individuals who were not part of the athletic program or representatives of the academic institution (Elliott and Kirshner, 2016).

LEARNING ACTIVITY 3

Identify a major sports league and analyze its social media sites (Facebook, Twitter, Instagram) by looking at number of followers or likes, types of posts, and content. Then attempt to determine the league's motivation for using social media and its target audience.

SPORTS LEAGUES AND SOCIAL MEDIA

For the most part, the rules leagues made to limit players' social media use were not about content, but rather about prohibiting and limiting the use of social media by organizations and representatives of organizations under certain circumstances. The National Football League, Major League Baseball, National Basketball Association,

England's Premier League, and the National Hockey League are five of the top six most lucrative professional team sports leagues worldwide (Willis, 2020), and each enacted and developed social media policies during the last decade. In the wake of Periscope becoming a popular platform for live streaming, in 2015 the NFL added to its existing rules prohibiting players and coach posts before, during, and immediately after games, new language banning organizations from posting highlights during games (Wallace, 2017). Perhaps as a reaction to a bit too much personality being displayed, for example, the NBA expanded its existing social media policy beyond mandating when players cannot tweet (45 minutes before each game through the post-game media availability) to add prohibition of team officials and representatives "mocking or ridiculing" opponents or game officials on social media (McMahon, 2010).

Major League Baseball's social media policy includes advice regarding which types of posts are most (and least) appropriate, with appropriate behavior defined as sharing information about the team or charity events the players or organizations might be involved with, while inappropriate content included any unauthorized use of MLB-related logos or promoting the use of substances that are banned by MLB's Drug Prevention Program (MLB, 2012). In addition, MLB mandated that nothing will be posted on social media by players, managers, or coaches from 30 minutes prior to a game and throughout the game (Thurm, 2012). The National Hockey League enacted a social media policy in 2011, stipulating that players could not post on social media for two hours prior to every game, and similar to the rules for other professional leagues, this social media blackout lasts until the end of post-game media availability (Shoalts, 2011). Though some individual clubs already had social media guidelines in place, England's Premier League also set rules in 2012 (BBC, 2012). As opposed to specifying times when players could post, the PL's guidelines provided guidance regarding content in terms of branding, endorsements, and which types of communication (e.g., abusive, threatening, indecent) were prohibited. In the early days of these guidelines, multiple players found themselves fined for violations of the new policies, including sending unfriendly — and public — tweets to each other (Heyes, 2014).

LEARNING ACTIVITY 4

Think about the last professional or collegiate sporting event that you attended. How did you interact with the event on social media before the event started? During the event? After the event ended? Think about your motivations to interact with the event on social media.

SPORTING EVENTS AND SOCIAL MEDIA

As previously mentioned, social media is not replacing traditional media in mega-event viewing (Tang and Cooper, 2018), but as it is growing in users and content, it can serve as a complimentary avenue to traditional media efforts. During the 2016 Olympics, games-related content was spread across multiple platforms including traditional and social media. Due to the monetary value of television rights, traditional television media took the lead in how Olympic content was distributed across different media, however, social media services were able to provide different but congruent content for consumers (Hutchins and Sanderson, 2017). A similar interaction between social media and television was also observed during the 2014 World Cup, where Finnish fans live-tweeted during the event in order to interact with the broadcast (Salomaa and Lehtinen, 2018). Based on the findings of these two studies, when sporting events in major sports, specifically mega-events, use social media, they should be working in conjunction with as opposed to in competition with traditional media. As a pertinent example, ESPN is regarded as the self-proclaimed "Worldwide Leader in Sports" with sports news disseminated on platforms including multiple television networks and a robust online presence. In addition, similarly to NBC's Olympics deal mentioned earlier in this chapter, ESPN has shown that it will utilize newer forms of media as well. In 2017, ESPN launched SportsCenter on Snapchat, designed for quicker hits of stories for a younger audience (Esposito, 2018). The endeavor into a special SportsCenter for Snapchat made sense for ESPN, as a survey of 125 social media users nationwide revealed that the usage of the short-video platform was comparable to Facebook and ahead of Twitter and Instagram (Billings *et al.*, 2017). The network also utilizes TikTok (Sirabella, 2020), with these strategies illustrating the fact that traditional media can coexist with newer and evolving platforms.

It is also important to remember that while the mediums can coexist, there are always people behind the postings on social media platforms. Social media conversation can tend to coalesce around a major event, during which social media use by fans and organizations tend to overlap (Yan *et al.*, 2019). With so many individuals and their viewpoints pervasive in the dialogue around an event, competing interests can adversely affect some of the flow of information (McGillivray, 2017), further putting a burden onto official social media practitioners to retain some level of control. However, as fans utilize social media around sports fandom of, for instance, an event, fan groups in smaller conversations can form, but ultimately the larger sport entity retains influence over the masses (Yan *et al.*, 2019).

The Olympics provides an opportunity for athletes to be exposed to millions of viewers across the globe, which athletes could use to market themselves and their sponsors on social media. While the International Olympic Committee (IOC) encourages athletes to use social media in order to promote the Olympic Games, they also want to protect their own sponsors. Therefore, they enacted Rule 40 to limit athletes from publishing Olympic content related to their sponsors during the two-week period of the Olympic Games (Schlereth and Frederick, 2017). However, a recent push for an expansion of athlete's rights has led to a relaxation of Rule 40 that was planned to be implemented at the Tokyo Olympics. This lifting of harsh restrictions will provide athletes a greater ability to use social media, as well as their name image and likeness to generate income based on their Olympic participation (SportsBusiness Staff, 2019).

Social media also has an important presence at major international sporting events such as the Olympic Games. At the time of the broadcast, the 2012 London Olympics were not only the most-watched television event in U.S. history, but also the largest social media event (Tang and Cooper, 2013). During the Games, the @London2012 Twitter account was primarily used to disseminate objective information covering a variety of sports, athletes, national teams, and results. However, the account also engaged in self-promotion including commenting on how well London served as a host city for the Games (Frederick *et al.*, 2015). The 2016 Olympic Games in Rio de Janeiro also saw a large uptick in social media interaction. On Twitter alone, the Games stimulated 187 million tweets and 75 billion total impressions (Akhtar, 2016). In addition, Facebook reported more than 1.5 billion interactions and Instagram had 916 million interactions from more than 130 million people (Hutchinson, 2016). This marked increase in consumption of social media content during sport mega-events, however, has not significantly altered the viewing of the Olympics on television (Tang and Cooper, 2018). The rise of YouTube and Facebook video — in addition to platforms which have yet to emerge — may soon enough herald a change in viewing habits. Perhaps anticipating this, NBC renegotiated its Olympics broadcasting deal in 2014 with specific language that the network would hold exclusive rights to broadcast the Games through 2032 on whatever happens to be the preferred viewing medium of any particular time (Sandomir, 2014). While social media may not yet be replacing traditional media viewing of the Olympic Games, it provides an opportunity for organizations associated with mega-events to improve their prominence within major sports. In addition, social media utilization assists the organizations officially associated with the Olympics through Rule 40 (Abeza, 2020). First introduced into the Olympic Charter in 1991 (IOC, 1990), Rule 40 prevents non-official Olympic sponsors from associating themselves with the Olympic brand, as well as the Games' commercialization, without authorization.

CASE STUDY 2

You are the communications director for USA Swimming. After the postponement of the 2020 Olympics, the schedule of events has changed including the rescheduling of qualifying events and sponsorship appearances. With the Olympics as the height of your organization's quadrennial calendar, you previously designed your entire social media plan based around that single event. With no competitions to promote and the date for resuming contests still unknown, the motivation for how you use your organization's social media has changed and you need now to establish new goals and objectives that can still promote the mission and vision of USA Swimming.

Discussion: With a classmate, create a new social media strategy that works to highlights current USA Swimming athletes, gains followers and grassroots members, and also generates excitement for the Olympics Games in 2021. Explain what mediums you will focus on and why and create sample posts for each medium that will be effective and interesting to your followers.

GOVERNING BODIES AND SOCIAL MEDIA

Sports governing bodies are sports organizations that have a regulatory or sanctioning function at national (e.g., USA Swimming) and international levels (e.g., International Swimming Federation — FINA). **National governing bodies** (NGBs), sometimes called National Sport Organizations (NSOs), regulate the individual sports at a national level and support national teams that compete in international events. Some NGBs represent niche sports, and therefore can use social media during major sporting events like the Olympic Games to increase their visibility within the market (Greenhalgh *et al.*, 2011). Particularly, for athletes in niche sports, the Olympic Games are the most important time of their professional career.

During the highest moments of their careers, Olympic athletes in niche sports can use social media to engage in real-time and direct one-to-one dialogue with their existing and new audiences. The exposure and the spotlight, in turn, can provide them the opportunity to endorse brands and generate financial rewards. Li *et al.* (2018) examined how the 2016 Olympic Games affected the followers of American NGBs (e.g., USA Tennis, USA Wrestling, USA Track & Field). The researchers examined 33 NGBs and found that team performance as well as overall Twitter usage helped increase the number of followers the accounts received. Specifically, they found that the Twitter accounts of women's soccer, basketball, gymnastics, golf, swimming, and beach volleyball attracted the greatest number of followers during the Rio Olympics (Li *et al.*, 2018). Ultimately, the governing bodies and power brokers for these sports found that social media brings attention and a wider fan base.

PRACTITIONER PERSPECTIVE

Practitioner: Kassidi Gilgenast, Chief Marketing Officer, USA Volleyball
Education: University of Colorado, Bachelor of Business Administration

Kassidi Gilgenast began her tenure as Chief Marketing Officer for USA Volleyball (USAV) in January 2020. In that role, she

(*Continued*)

oversees all marketing, communication, and creative services at USAV including their social media presence. Gilgenast first started at USAV in 2014 in the High-Performance division, before moving into the marketing department in 2018. USAV is the national governing body (NGB) of volleyball in the United States which supports the national indoor, beach, and sitting volleyball teams at sanctioned regional and international competitions. In addition, it is responsible for the growth and development of volleyball among 40 Regional Volleyball Associations and has one of the highest memberships of any NGB within Team USA with a total membership of over 375,000 youth participants.

Why is social media important for your work and your organization's mission?

Social media is one of the most critical forms of media for our organization and to the operations of our Marketing, Communications, and Creative Services department. It provides an important means of communication with our members and enables us to share the stories of our athletes with our global fan base and grow awareness for the sport of volleyball.

How do you use social media each day?

We post content on a daily basis including announcements about events, original videos, and feature stories about athletes, coaches, and clubs. We create opportunities for shareable and interactive content for the volleyball community and occasionally share and repost content from other organizations or individuals that may be relevant to our audience. Social media is a major source of information on organizational updates and initiatives, event highlights, and storytelling for USA Volleyball.

How does your organization interact with followers via social media?

We actively engage with followers on social media via likes, comments, and reposts of individuals and organizations who interact with our posts and offering opportunities for interactive

(*Continued*)

(Continued)

engagement in our content such as stickers, polls, quizzes, and shareable templates for social media fans.

What is USAV's primary social media site and why?

Our largest following on social media is Facebook, but our primary social media platform is Instagram because it far exceeds all other platforms in measures of reach and engagement.

How has USAV's social media strategy evolved in the last few years?

Our social media strategy has evolved significantly in the last few years to be much more driven by rich media. We have a heavy focus on video content and are much more data driven in our approach to social media overall. We've also become much more intentional about use of branded short URLs, increased engagement as a brand with fans and other accounts, and shifted our focus from Facebook to Instagram. We have also expanded and tested opportunities to engage with SnapChat, LinkedIn, and are considering including TikTok in our overall strategy.

How has the postponement of the Olympic Games in Tokyo affected your social media strategy?

Overall the postponement has primarily postponed the content that we had lined up to help fans get to know our National Team athletes and prevented us from launching into countdown and Olympic celebration content. In general, one of our main concerns is now lack of access to athletes due to changes in budget, safety protocols, and travel restrictions so we'll have fewer opportunities to gain access to fresh content moving forward and we're unsure how media access will look at the Games in 2021.

KEY SKILLS FOR PRACTICE

Practitioners in Social Media for Major Sports Organizations can be expected to handle multiple platforms as well as multiple mediums. For instance, if an individual works as a social media coordinator for a team in Major League Soccer, it is likely they will manage the team Twitter and Instagram feeds, create press releases and game reports, as well as keep the statistics for the games and players. It goes without saying that time management is essential, as well as the ability to handle multiple platforms. Long past are the days when students could master writing or visual content production and call it a day. In addition, learning graphic design and being able to utilize more than just photographs, video, or the written word have become essential for success in social media usage. For instance, Major League Baseball utilizes Facebook and Twitter for game broadcasts and highlights with an opportunity for fans to comment, and has further engaged fans through polls in which they can vote for highlights on Twitter (Sirabella, 2020). This also brings up an important point that might be less obvious for many social media practitioners. The ability to create and utilize data from polls to enhance and determine the level of user engagement has become paramount for successful social media campaigns.

Concurrently, with the ability to manage multiple platforms in terms of time and skill, students and practitioners should also create schedules for their social media usage as part of a sport organization's media and public relations strategies. As this chapter discusses, the opportunity to reach the target publics for an organization can be hindered without a concrete — though flexible — plan for posting. This includes the frequency of posting, the type of content, the type of platform or platforms, and whether there will be cross-posting with the same or similar content across multiple platforms. This can include an eye to what makes the organization unique among its peers and competitors. In Philadelphia, the Flyers utilized popular team mascot sensation "Gritty" in social media messages and parodies, for instance (Sirabella, 2020). The results of forging such connections manifest in fans appreciating and interacting more with the sport organization as a brand that offers gratifications for its followers (Anagnostopoulos *et al.*, 2018).

Ultimately, it is very likely that each sport organization with which students might seek employment will be interested in social media skills. Students should already be utilizing their Twitter and Instagram feeds at minimum in order to create and cultivate a persona and skillset that make them stand out as someone clever enough to represent a major sports organization.

CHAPTER SUMMARY

Social media platforms have proven to be viable and effective outlets for disseminating information and engaging with sports entities' target publics. As social media gained popularity among individual athletes and sports organizations, the potential for gaffes and challenging public relations situations led the major sports entities to enact rules and guidelines pertaining to the use of social media. Concurrently, organizations have sought to develop social media practices that best convey what they wish for potential fans to know and perceive about them. Research has shown that providing information and an opportunity for interaction with other fans, as well as the organization, is an effective approach.

KEY RESOURCES

- U.S. Pro Sports Original Social Media Policies, http://www.espn.com/espn/page2/story/_/id/7026246/examining-sports-leagues-social-media-policies-offenders.
- NCAA Social Media Strategies and Regulations, https://www.ncaa.org/documents/social-media-ncaa-strategies-and-regulations.
- The Journey of Cardale Jones, https://bit.ly/3hgenPB.
- Shorty Awards for Sport Social Media, https://shortyawards.com/category/6th/sports.
- The Most Popular Social Media Accounts in Sport, https://www.90min.com/posts/6546643-30-biggest-social-media-accounts-in-sport.

TEST YOUR KNOWLEDGE

1. What are the important distinctions that separate major from minor sports?
2. What are the unique features of the major social media sites and what primary motivations do stakeholders in major sports have for using the different sites?
3. How has social media and sports changed in the last decade?
4. Why is authenticity important for social media users in sport?

5. What are the important characteristics of a social media strategy in major sports?
6. Discuss the similar and different ways that coaches and athletes in major sports use social media.
7. Identify how social media and traditional media can be used together during major sporting events.
8. Evaluate the different social media policies of major sport leagues and governing bodies.

REFERENCES

Abeza, G. (2020). Balancing the interest of sponsors vs athletes. *Routledge Handbook of the Olympic and Paralympic Games.*

Abeza, G., O'Reilly, N., and Seguin, B. (2019). Social media in relationship marketing: The perspective of professional sport managers in the MLB, NBA, NFL, and NHL. *Communication and Sport, 7*(1), 80–109.

Abeza, G., O'Reilly, N., Seguin, B., and Nzindukiyimana, O. (2017). Social media as a relationship marketing tool in professional sport: A netnographical exploration. *International Journal of Sport Communication, 10*(3), 325–358.

Abeza, G., O'Reilly, N., and Reid, I. (2013). Relationship marketing and social media in sport. *International Journal of Sport Communication, 6*(2), 120–142.

Achen, R. M. (2016). Quantifying the Use of Relationship Marketing Tactics in the National Basketball Association. *Journal of Contemporary Athletics, 10*(1), 1.

Agnihotri, A., and Bhattacharya, S. (2020). Endorsement effectiveness of celebrities versus social media influencers in the materialistic cultural environment of India. *Journal of International Consumer Marketing,* 1–23.

Akhtar, A. (2016). Olympics was a hit on social, less so for NBC TV. *USA Today.* Retrieved from https://www.usatoday.com/story/tech/news/2016/08/22/olympics-talk-amassed-187-million-tweets-15-billion-facebook-interactions/89114052/.

Anagnostopoulos, C., Parganas, P., Chadwick, S., and Fenton, A. (2018). Branding in pictures: Using Instagram as a brand management tool in professional team sport organisations. *European Sport Management Quarterly, 18*(4), 413–438.

BBC (2012). Premier League issues social networking guidance for players. *BBC.com*. Retrieved from https://www.bbc.com/sport/football/18977631.

Billings, A. C., Qiao, F., Conlin, L., and Nie, T. (2017). Permanently desiring the temporary? Snapchat, social media, and the shifting motivations of sports fans. *Communication and Sport*, *5*(1), 10–26.

Blaszka, M., Cianfrone, B. A., and Walsh, P. (2018). An analysis of collegiate athletic departments' social media practices, strategies, and challenges. *Journal of Contemporary Athletics*, *12*(4), 271–290.

Bowles, J. (2016). Instagram: A visual view of the southeastern conference. *Journal of Contemporary Athletics*, *10*(4), 227.

Calcaterra, C. (2012, March 14). Major League Baseball's social media policy. *Baseball Almanac*. Retrieved from https://mlb.nbcsports.com/2012/03/14/major-league-baseball-releases-its-social-media-policy-and-its-pretty-good/.

Coche, R. (2017). How athletes frame themselves on social media: An analysis of Twitter profiles. *Journal of Sports Media*, *12*(1), 89–112.

Collins, D. R., Heere, B., Shapiro, S., Ridinger, L., and Wear, H. (2016). The displaced fan: The importance of new media and community identification for maintaining team identity with your hometown team. *European Sport Management Quarterly*, *16*(5), 655–674.

Doyle, J. P., Su, Y., and Kunkel, T. (2020). Athlete branding via social media: Examining the factors influencing consumer engagement on Instagram. *European Sport Management Quarterly*, 1–21.

Dubin, J. (2015). Chad Johnson shows up at fan's house to play him in FIFA. *CBS Sports*. Retrieved from https://www.cbssports.com/nfl/news/chad-johnson-shows-up-at-fans-house-to-play-him-in-fifa/.

Elliott, B. and Kirshner, A. (2016). Players like it, but the NCAA's new social media rule could be chaos for coaches. *SB Nation*. Retrieved from https://www.sbnation.com/college-football-recruiting/2016/4/14/11429908/coaches-recruits-twitter-facebook-social-media-rules.

Esposito, G. (2018). Inside ESPN's Snapchat SportsCenter strategy. *Front Office Sports*. Retrieved from https://frontofficesports.com/espns-snapchat-sportscenter-strategy/.

Encel, K., Mesagno, C., and Brown, H. (2017). Facebook use and its relationship with sport anxiety. *Journal of Sports Sciences*, *35*(8), 756–761.

ESPN (2020). 2020 sports calendar: Schedules impacted by the coronavirus. *ESPN.com*. Retrieved from https://www.espn.com/espn/story/_/id/29011029/coronavirus-impacted-schedules.

Fitz-Gerald, S. (2012). Shots fired: Kings troll Canucks fans on twitter, but later apologize. *National Post.* Retrieved from https://nationalpost. com/sports/hockey/nhl/shots-fired-kings-troll-canucks-fans-on-twitter.

Frederick, E. L., Burch, L. M., and Blaszka, M. (2015). A shift in set: Examining the presence of agenda setting on Twitter during the 2012 London Olympics. *Communication and Sport, 3*(3), 312–333.

Geurin, A. N. (2017). Elite female athletes' perceptions of new media use relating to their careers: A qualitative analysis. *Journal of Sport Management, 31*(4), 345–359.

Geurin, A. N., and Burch, L. M. (2017). User-generated branding via social media: An examination of six running brands. *Sport Management Review, 20*(3), 273–284.

Gibbs, C., O'Reilly, N., and Brunette, M. (2014). Professional team sport and Twitter: Gratifications sought and obtained by followers. *International Journal of Sport Communication, 7*(2), 188–213.

Gladden, J. M. and Sutton, W. (2014). Professional sport. In P. M. Pedersen and L. Thibault (Eds.), (2014). *Contemporary Sport Management,* (5th ed., pp. 216–239). Human Kinetics Publishers.

Greenhalgh, G. P., Simmons, J. M., Hambrick, M. E. and Greenwell, T. C. (2011). "Spectator support: examining the attributes that differentiate niche from mainstream sport". *Sport Marketing Quarterly, 20*(1), 41–52.

Hayes, M., Filo, K., Riot, C., and Geurin, A. (2019). Athlete perceptions of social media benefits and challenges during major sport events. *International Journal of Sport Communication, 12*(4), 449–481.

Heyes, S. (2014). Social media governance in the English Premier League. *8ms.com.* retrieved from https://8ms.com/blog/social-media-governance-english-premier-league/.

Hull, K., Lee, J., Zapalac, R., and Stilwell, M. (2017). H-Town Takeover: Social media agenda setting and branding efforts at the University of Houston. *Journal of Issues in Intercollegiate Athletics,* 10, 162–181.

Hutchins, B. and Sanderson, J. (2017). The primacy of sports television: Olympic media, social networking services, and multi-screen viewing during the Rio 2016 games. *Media International Australia, 164*(1), 32–43.

Hutchinson, A. (2016). How the 2016 Rio Olympic dominated social media [Infographic]. *Social Media Today.* Retrieved from https://www.socialmediatoday.com/social-networks/how-2016-rio-olympics-dominated-social-media-infographic.

Jensen, J. A., Ervin, S. M., and Dittmore, S. W. (2014). Exploring the factors affecting popularity in social media: A case study of Football Bowl Subdivision head coaches. *International Journal of Sport Communication*, 7(2), 261–278.

Kassing, J. W. and Sanderson, J. (2010). Fan–athlete interaction and Twitter tweeting through the Giro: A case study. *International Journal of Sport Communication*, 3(1), 113–128.

Kucharska, W., Confente, I., and Brunetti, F. (2020). The power of personal brand authenticity and identification: Top celebrity players' contribution to loyalty toward football. *Journal of Product & Brand Management*, 29(6), 815–830.

Lesmerises, D. (2017). Cardale Jones — from playing school to graduating from Ohio State — got it right. *Cleveland.com.* Retrieved from https://www.cleveland.com/osu/2017/05/cardale_jones_-_from_playing_s.html.

Li, B., Scott, O. K. M., and Dittmore, S. W. (2018). Twitter and Olympics. Exploring factors which impact fans following American Olympic governing bodies. *International Journal of Sport Marketing*, 19(4), 370–383.

McGillivray, D. (2017). Platform politics: sport events and the affordances of digital and social media. *Sport in Society*, 20(12), 1888–1901.

McMahon, T. (2010). Post on NBA social media policy memo. *ESPN.com.* Retrieved from https://www.espn.com/espn/now?nowId=21-0621451155481828036-4.

Moran, E. (2019). How TikTok is helping sports leagues and teams better engage with female fans. *Front Office Sports.* Retrieved from https://frontofficesports.com/tiktok-women-sports/.

Ordway, D. (2020). Power Five colleges spend football, basketball revenue on money-losing sports: Research. *Journalists Resource.* Retrieved from https://journalistsresource.org/studies/society/education/college-sports-power-five-revenue/.

Park, J. A. and Dittmore, S. (2014). The relationship among social media consumption, team identification, and behavioral intentions. *Journal of Physical Education and Sport*, 14, 331–336.

Pedersen, B. (2016). College football coaches who are social media geniuses. *Bleacher Report.* Retrieved from https://bleacherreport.com/articles/2625566-college-football-coaches-who-are-social-media-geniuses.

Salomaa, E. and Lehtien, E. (2018). "Congratulations, you're on TV!": Middle-space performances of live tweeters during the FIFA World Cup. *Discourse, Context & Media, 25*, 132–142.

Sandomir, R. (2014). NBC extends Olympic deal into unknown. *New York Times.* Retrieved from https://www.nytimes.com/2014/05/08/sports/olympics/nbc-extends-olympic-tv-deal-through-2032.html.

Schlereth, N. G. and Frederick, E. (2017). Going for gold: Social media and the USOC. *Journal of the Legal Aspects of Sport, 27*, 19–31.

Sharpe, S., Mountifield, C., and Filo, K. (2020). The Social Media Response From Athletes and Sport Organizations to COVID-19: An Altruistic Tone. *International Journal of Sport Communication, 13*(3), 474–483.

Shoalts, D. (2011). NHL unveils social-media policy. *Toronto Globe and Mail.* Retrieved from https://www.theglobeandmail.com/sports/hockey/nhl-unveils-social-media-policy/article594514/.

Sirabella, C. (2020). 4 top sports brands on social — and what we can learn from them. *Likeable.com.* Retrieved from https://www.likeable.com/blog/2020/4-top-sports-brands-on-social-and-what-we-can-learn-from-them/.

Snel, A. (2018). Voice behind Golden Knights' Twitter account leaves NHL club before playoffs. *LV SportsBiz.* Retrieved from https://lvsportsbiz.com/2018/03/27/voice-behind-golden-knights-twitter-account-leaves-nhl-club-before-playoffs/.

SportsBusiness Staff. (2019). IOC relaxes Rule 40 ahead of Tokyo 2020. *Sport Business.* Retrieved from https://www.sportbusiness.com/news/ioc-relaxes-rule-40-ahead-of-tokyo-2020/.

Su, Y., Baker, B. J., Doyle, J. P., and Yan, M. (2020). Fan Engagement in 15 Seconds: Athletes' Relationship Marketing During a Pandemic via TikTok. *International Journal of Sport Communication, 13*(3), 436–446.

Tang, T. and Cooper, R. (2013). Olympics everywhere: Predictors of multi-platform media uses during the 2012 London Olympics. *Mass Communication and Society, 16*(6), 850–868.

Thurm, W. (2012). MLB moving in right direction with new social media policy, but questions remain. *SB Nation.* Retrieved from https://www.sbnation.com/2012/3 /16/2874753 /mlb-players-social-media-policy-twitter-facebook.

Vale, L. and Fernandes, T. (2018). Social media and sports: Driving fan engagement with football clubs on Facebook. *Journal of Strategic Marketing, 26*(1), 37–55.

Wallace, B. (2017). Tackling Tech: Inside the NFL's new social media rules. *Patriots.com*. Retrieved from: https://www.patriots.com/news/tackling-tech-inside-the-nfl-s-new-social-media-rules-304986.

Wang, Y., and Zhou, S. (2015). How do sports organizations use social media to build relationships? A content analysis of NBA clubs' Twitter use. *International Journal of Sport Communication, 8*(2), 133–148.

Willis, Z. (2020). America only has four of the most profitable sports leagues in the world. *Sportscasting*. Retrieved from https://www.sportscasting.com/america-only-has-4-of-the-most-profitable-sports-leagues-in-the-world/.

Yan, G., Watanabe, N. M., Shapiro, S. L., Naraine, M. L., and Hull, K. (2019). Unfolding the Twitter scene of the 2017 UEFA Champions League Final: Social media networks and power dynamics. *European Sport Management Quarterly, 19*(4), 419–436.

Zimmerman, M., Johnson, J., and Ridley, M. (2016). Twitter Use by College Football Coaches: An Examination of the Football Bowl Subdivision. *Journal of Contemporary Athletics, 10*(1), 33.

https://doi.org/10.1142/9789811237669_0005

Chapter 5

Social Media Use in Minor Sports

Andrew C. Billings*, Norm O'Reilly†, and Elisabetta Zengaro‡

*The University of Alabama, United States
†University of Maine, United States
‡The University of Alabama, United States

CHAPTER OBJECTIVES

- To understand the use of social media in minor sports
- To be able to discern major sports from minor sports media entities
- To understand the use of social media by minor sports athletes and events
- To identify the role of social media in minor sports relationship building efforts
- To delineate the role of influencers in minor sports
- To comprehend revenue generation using social media within minor sports
- To evaluate how two forms of minor sports currently utilize social media

KEY TERMS

Click-through rate   Micro-influencers
Three-click rule   Engagement rate
Influencers   Social media presence

111

INTRODUCTION

Social media has dramatically changed the game for all sports entities. One could argue that change has been even more dramatic for minor sports. Long before Mark Zuckerberg ushered in the more formal era since the mainstreaming of social media via Facebook, FC Barcelona, the Toronto Maple Leafs, the Indian cricket team, and the Los Angeles Lakers could still reach millions of fans in a variety of ways. The same was not the case for most local sports organizations, nor could it be said for many national and international associations that nevertheless struggled with traditional media companies convinced that what they offered were of minimal or niche interest.

Thus, the beginning of a chapter on minor sports must include at its outset a definition of what is meant by "minor." In this chapter, we include sports entities (including teams, leagues, governing bodies, athletes, coaches, and beyond) that would have received minimal to no focus in a pre-digital landscape. We do not wish to imply that these sports are "minor" in and of themselves, as the players and coaches within them tend to be just as dedicated and the followings just as avid as any sports one would dub "major." However, in the mere sense of eyeballs focused on the sports entitities themselves, these sports have followings that are smaller. Sadly, this includes many women's sports that struggle for consumer focus due to a confluence of historical, cultural, and hegemonic practices. The same could be said for the national federations who represent low profile Olympic sports, such as equestrian, table tennis, and triathlon. They also include examples, such as programs from Division II (DII) of the NCAA. These American college sports programs would otherwise queue behind the largest Division I (DI) college sports programs. "Minor" also includes sports that differ in popularity in a given nation, such as the case we will advance later in this chapter about the Italian Fencing Federation. Undergirding the entire chapter will be the central opportunity afforded to minor sports within social media platforms. Now that there is a mechanism to reach fans and followers, how can minor sports leverage social media platforms effectively to reach fans and followers?

SOCIAL MEDIA USE IN MINOR SPORTS: KEY CONCEPTS

One could rightly contend that many of the minor sports received the opportunity to become media producers not with the social media era, but in the 1990s with the expansion of the Internet and cable television broadcasting. While technically true, the sports operating under the moniker of our "minor" definition were none-theless relegated and harder to find. The real and significant costs of production made television still a long shot for most minor sports organizations. Such struggles might initially seem negligible, but, in effect, become incredibly limiting for organizations to reach audi-ences. For instance, a Google search might yield millions of results, yet 71% of all websites visited come from the top 10 results of that search (Jacobsen, 2017), making an organization on the third page of a search the functional equivalent of the organization on the 78th page of that search (not to mention the 1104th page), as those sites are rarely visited. Similarly, if a sport, team, or result is not on a web homepage, opportunities for virality become limited.

Reflect on the fact that industry leaders consider 2% to be a good "click through rate" (CTR, defined as the number of people who click on a site during search). Combine that with a tacit "three-click (or tap)" rule, meaning that those 2% of people who visit a site are likely only willing to click a maximum of three times to find what they are looking for (Kasavana, 2001). Suddenly, the prospects for minor sports in these offerings seem negligible. The same can be said for the expansion of cable TV offerings. One could find all sorts of sport offerings once the number of channels expanded to hun-dreds. Still, the average American would only seek out and watch 17 of these channels (Nielsen Insights, 2014), meaning the rest were relegated to the less accessed parts of a television programming guide. So, even if one may pull off finding the dollars for produc-tion, who would find or watch your content?

Here is where social media altered that equation dramatically for minor sports. If one was willing and able to find the initial account to follow, the information from that account would appear in a feed in the same prominence and manner as larger entities. Yes, paid and promoted social media will now be elevated ahead of organic content (Canham, 2020), yet a minor sport is otherwise on equal footing with all other sports entities with social media outlets. Particularly, social media has a built-in feature of aggregating users with common needs. Along with that feature, a sport organization posts content on its social media account that addresses the needs and interests of those users, further drawing more followers to the account and, thereby, helping pull together the target audiences of a specific sport to the account. Assuming National Basketball Association (NBA) star Kevin Durant has not paid money to an external agency to boost the visibility of his post, one can surmise it will reach more followers, yet will appear alongside a disc golf star who also posted un-boosted content if one has opted to follow them. Engagement rate becomes the crucial metric for minor sports, and reports show one can garner just about the same rates of engagement regardless of the size of following. Case in point, the National Hockey League's (NHL) Carolina Hurricanes have about one-eighth of the Instagram following of Major League Baseball's (MLB) Los Angeles Dodgers, yet they have an engagement rate (assessed by clicks, likes, and shares) that is slightly higher (1.58 vs. 1.52; Zoomph, 2020). In this regard, the three following sections discuss social media related to minor sports athletes, minor sports events, and minor sports relationship building effort.

MINOR SPORTS ATHLETES AND SOCIAL MEDIA

There are only a few athletes who are celebrities that can generate hundreds of millions of followers. For the rest, the world is very different. They make very little from sponsorship and endorsements. They may not be included in television interviews. They are not avatars in video games. They may not get appearance fees to show up at parties. They number in the hundreds of thousands globally, and this is the group we are referring to here. The 33rd ranked beach volleyball player in the world or the 19th place finisher in the Olympic marathon. This is the focus of this chapter, those for whom social media may represent their only way to reach larger audiences.

Of course, athletes are media producers in social media spaces. In these environments, there is the potential for more engagement between athletes and a higher percentage of their fans. After all, it would be virtually impossible for a major sports athlete receiving tens of thousands of accolades after a game to thank each fan individually; however, a minor sports athlete receiving a dozen such accolades might find it much more plausible to at least "like" or interact with each one or most of their followers.

Geurin-Eagleman and Clavio (2015) found differences in the social media pages of niche athletes, concluding that these types of accounts were more likely to offer fan-generated content than on major athlete social media pages. The authors also found that fans engaged with niche athlete status updates more than other content directly relating to past or future competitions. Such findings show a desire to get to know the athletes' personalities much more intimately. Given the higher chances of a response from the athlete, fans seemingly see more potential for a parasocial interaction to move into a social and/or interactive space.

Other studies have found social media presences for lower-profile sports, albeit with different levels of frequency and effectiveness. For instance, Mackova and Turkova (2019) examined Facebook posts by female skiers, finding that this was a common practice of four Czech skiers, but that skiers participating in para alpine skiing were less likely than able-bodied skiers to post about their accomplishments. Indeed, minor sports participants and organizations (see Vooris and Achen, 2019) are less likely to post and, when they do, are less likely to utilize audio-visual elements when doing so. This presumably occurs because of lower budgets and smaller (or even non-existent) media content teams. Nevertheless, as the ability to post content in the audio-visual domain gets increasingly easier (see Clavio, 2020), the opportunity for enhanced minor sports athlete social media engagement becomes larger.

LEARNING ACTIVITY 1

Seek out an athlete that you believe is either part of a minor sport or is minor within their major sport (someone who perhaps does not garner much playing time). When you interacted or posted with that account, did you get a response? How do you think this response unfolded (or didn't) because the athlete had a smaller following?

MINOR SPORTS EVENTS AND SOCIAL MEDIA

Minor sports events include a set of events that are small in terms of budget, human resources, spectators, staff, media attention, sponsorship, merchandise, and just about any other marketing-related benefit a major event accrues. Think of a North American state or province level championship in a minor sport, such as table tennis, sailing, orienteering, or bowling. Or, any master's level pay-to-play tournament (e.g., ice hockey, basketball, chess, billiards) where adult recreational players or teams pay a registration fee to play for a trophy that holds no jurisdictional title. In any of these cases, social media becomes a targeted, inexpensive, and efficient way to initiate and nurture relationships.

One area in which minor sports can often compete on relatively the same footing as major sports pertains specifically to event promotion, as most fans do not find themselves formally following the social media accounts for such events, instead opting to follow them once fans determine they will spend time seeking information about an upcoming event. Yes, the @Olympics Twitter account has a noteworthy six million followers, yet the large majority of these are added before and during the opening days of a given Games rather than consistently built over time. As such, short time frames become the key opportunity windows for minor sports to thrive, particularly when using event specific hashtags to drive fans to their accounts through search features.

For example, Vann *et al.* (2015) examined Twitter usage within two events: the Commonwealth Games and the Netball ANZ Championship. They note a key struggle was the establishment of clear, consistent hashtags that fans could follow. Yet, they still found the platform was useful in bolstering promotion of the event and fostering kinship among like-minded fans. Moreover, they provided minute-by-minute analyses, showing that Twitter seemed to be something that fans were more likely to participate in during breaks in matches and, most particularly, once a victor has been determined. As such, one could conclude that social media use within such events does not happen concurrently as much as it happens intermittently. Just as in major sports, when the game has breaks and lulls, social media usage spikes to pick up the slack for minor sports as well.

MINOR SPORTS RELATIONSHIP BUILDING AND SOCIAL MEDIA

Relationship building through social media is a key indicator and driver of success. Relationship building via social media includes a few important aspects for a minor sport organization to consider. First, in terms of initiating new relationships, social media enables a relationship marketing-based approach where the minor sport organization can use any touch point to seek to achieve a new follower (the first stage in a social media relationship). For example, a local 5 km run can post race results on its Facebook page and require a participant to join a Facebook group to view their results. Second, once a relationship is established on a social media channel, regular, relevant, and shareable content needs to be created so that the follower starts to move towards being an influencer to others, by posting, tagging, and sharing content about the minor sport organization. An example would be a NCAA Division III women's soccer club who hires a graduate assistant to post daily video, pictures, and GIFs of the players and coaches in-game, during practice, and in daily (outside of sport) life to the page, including things like predictions for their next game, future life plans of the student-athletes, and benefits from sponsors provided.

The psychological continuum model (PCM) (Funk and James, 2001) argues that fans must first advance through awareness and attraction stages before they can then move to larger forms of fandom such as attachment and allegiance. A foundational study of niche sports' use of social media (Mahoney *et al.*, 2013) found that a platform such as YouTube is effective for highlighting these smaller sports (e.g., slacklining, parkour, longboarding), but primarily advances content at the early stages (awareness and attraction) with little content focusing on attachment and allegiance — presumably because such sports have not yet developed to stages where enough fans would be at this end of the PCM. Thus, it is fair to conclude that minor sports use social media for early stages of sports fandom much more than later PCM elements as those stages are more easily obtained and more likely to be the places potential fans of minor sports find themselves: early, growing fandom.

Niche sports such as action sports have found homes in social media spaces, largely because traditional sports media outlets are resistant to expanding coverage to unproven audiences newer sports could provide. However, as Thorpe (2017) reported, some action sports secure social media followings largely because the athletes themselves can advance compelling media content, using GoPro cameras, GPS devices, and drones to bring the action to their fans without formally needing a media entity to secure rights to the content. Social media provides an opportunity for growth, as minor sports ultimately garner very loyal followings simply because it might have taken a bit more work to find that platform than your typical FIFA or NBA statistics, for instance.

Within cases where the goal is more about depth of relationships, sport-for-development organizations increasingly find social media as a way to bridge national (and linguistic) divides. Hambrick and Svensson (2015) identified three main uses for social media accounts in such development and peace organizations including news dissemination, event promotion, and stakeholder education.

Increasingly communities find and build networks via such social media presences, with informing serving as step one and engagement serving as step two (Anagnostopoulos *et al.*, 2017). Using CrossFit as an example for minor sports social media use, Kang *et al.* (2019) studied three social media platforms (Facebook, Twitter, YouTube), finding that Twitter was the preferred channel (62% of all posts) and that information was the primary driver of content. Meanwhile, Facebook was the platform in which organizational messages were more likely to be advanced. It was also found that a focus on information and relationship building can become a foundation within the establishment of a social media presence, arguing that the actual building of online communities or promotion of products remains a more ambitious — and thus, less frequent — endeavor.

CASE STUDY 1: SOCIAL MEDIA USE IN ITALIAN FENCING

La Federazione Italiana Scherma (Italian Fencing Federation) serves as Italy's governing body for fencing. Fencing, while popular in many European countries, is considered a minor sport because of its niche appeal globally. As a small-scale sport, fencing attracts more competitors than fans to events (Csobán and Serra, 2014), so effective social media campaigns could potentially increase outreach for those nations who dominate the sport in global competitions. Table 1 lists the social media platforms for the governing bodies of the top five minor sports in Italy: La Federazione Italiana Scherma (fencing); La Federazione Italiana Giuoco Calcio (soccer); La Federazione Italiana Nuoto (aquatic sports); La Federazione Italiana Pallavolo (volleyball); and La Federazione Italiana Judo, Lotta, Karate e Arti Marziali (martial arts).

Based on the data in Table 1, fencing reaches its biggest audience on Facebook, with 61.5% of their total social media followers being found on that platform. For La Federazione Italiana Scherma, Facebook is also used as an interactive forum because posts consist of a mixture of photos and videos, where users can interact through sharing, commenting, and reacting to posts.

Table 1. Social Media Platforms by Gulf South Conference School.

School	Sports	Instagram N = followers	Facebook N = followers	Twitter N = followers	YouTube N = Subscribers
UAH	16	4,704	6219	7998	2080
AUM	11	2337	5855	3069	225
CBU	15	404	1117	2650	580
DSU	15	2380	14632	8764	825
LU	17	4395	5811	5543	0
MC	15	5509	5768	5808	398
UM	16	2115	3200	3383	1830
SU	20	2067	3462	4877	165
UU	11	3630	4747	3845	0
VSU	12	7286	8936	12100	480
UWA	19	1604	6258	7689	1270
UWF	15	6346	15112	12200	1020
UWG	13	6028	10597	15000	705
Average		3754	7055	7148	737

Table 2. Social Media Posts by Platform and Gulf South School (January 2020–August 2020).

School	Instagram N = posts	Facebook N = posts	Twitter N = posts	YouTube N = posts
UAH	145	196	825	36
AUM	343	475	688	32
CBU	22	0	147	19
DSU	31	212	320	50
LU	178	260	819	100
MC	342	331	717	4
UM	150	35	422	38
SU	82	92	162	10
UU	221	408	587	16
VSU	11	371	423	1
UWA	37	415	770	48
UWF	58	160	776	43
UWG	32	400	801	7
Average	127	258	574	31

Therefore, posts engage in dialogue with fans, rather than simply informing them. In this instance, Facebook is not just used to share news releases as with the exemplar of U.S. sports. Table 2 lists the number of posts per social media platform since January 2020. This table provides a visual of the differences in how these organizations use social media based on the number of posts per platform for each organization.

Fencing has the top number of Instagram (N = 515) and YouTube posts (N = 615). For niche sports, YouTube can be a valuable resource because of its accessibility and ability to foster relationships with users (Mahoney *et al.*, 2013). For fencing, YouTube represents an alternative streaming platform where users can watch videos of competitions, athletes, and coaches. The Italian Fencing Federation's extensive use of YouTube symbolizes that the organization may recognize that YouTube can be used as an alternative format to cable television for broadcasting competitions and interviews where fans have unfiltered access.

However, even though fencing has the most YouTube posts of the other governing bodies, YouTube represents fencing's least number of social media followers. The Italian Fencing Federation uses Twitter primarily to inform fans of events and news about fencing. However, Instagram is fencing's second most popular platform. This is reflected through the Italian Fencing Federation's use of Instagram in engaging fans with pictures and videos of athletes and coaches to provide a more personal narrative of the sport rather than using the platform primarily to update statistics.

CASE QUESTIONS

1. How can social media streaming platforms be used to substantiate traditional broadcast coverage for minor sports, like fencing?
2. How do the differences in social media platform use among the two examples in this chapter provide insight into challenges for promoting minor sports via social media?
3. In your opinion, is the popularity on Instagram for the Italian Fencing Federation indicative of different social media strate-

gies for minor sports in Europe? In other words, how does the anticipated audience affect platform content?

Having discussed the place and value of social media in the context of minor sports athletes, minor sports events, and in minor sports relationship building efforts, it will be worth looking now at the role that social media influencers play in minor sports and the opportunity that social media provides in revenue generation for minor sports. These two topics are discussed in what follows.

INFLUENCERS IN MINOR SPORTS

As mentioned previously in this book, influencers can be characterized by three different attributes: what one knows (a contributor's level of expertise on certain subjects), whom one knows (network size including number of followers), and who one is (contributor's traits and values). The role of the influencer is very different in minor sports than in major sports. That is to say, social media is an "enabler" of influencers in minor sports, while it can better be defined as an "enhancer" in major sports. More specifically, major sports properties possess vast reach, extensive revenues from sponsorship, large media deals, and millions of fans (e.g., NHL, English Premier League (EPL), Indian Premier League (IPL), etc.). As such, there are many influencers with major reach, including leagues, clubs, star athletes, high profile coaches, and many other stakeholders. Consider, for instance, the 2019–2020 Toronto Raptors basketball club. Looking at the data related to the Raptors's use of social media from the fourth quarter of 2020, they are full of influencers, which include obvious star player Kyle Lowry (889,000 Twitter followers). However, other less direct influencers play a key role, including the musician Drake, a Raptors sponsor and superfan, who has a potential reach of more than 39 million Twitter followers.

A minor sports property, almost by definition, has no equivalent in terms of social media strategy development in sport. These properties must rely on the growing and increasingly influential group of individuals and organizations, known as micro influencers. Joe Gagliese, co-founder of ViralNation, considers a micro-influencer as anyone with at least 10,000 followers on their social media platforms and includes those with up to 50,000 followers (Leiber, 2018). However, Gagliese is also of the opinion that even smaller followings could potentially have value. As Bidin (2018, para. 3, 5, 7) advances, there are three binaries influencers can traverse, namely:

(a) digital news media's promise of legitimacy vs. influencer's premise of charisma
(b) digital news media's crisis of trustworthiness vs. influencers' burden of relatability
(c) digital news media's accessible legibility vs. influencers' niche reach (i.e., the potential audience that the influencer can reach, such as a well-known chef's following of other food-oriented social media platforms).

One could quickly see that an individual could become a micro-influencer with as few as 1,000 followers — but only if they are an intriguing niche group referred to as nano influencers.

Now, in considering this group of social media influencers with 1,000 to 50,000 followers, understanding who they are can aid a minor sport organization in leveraging their influence to improve marketing outcomes. These outcomes can be in the form of increased ticket sales (spectators), participation (memberships, participants), fundraising dollars (donations), sponsorship reach (i.e., increased interest/knowledge of sponsors and their products), awareness, and many others. Of course, the big question for the minor sport organization's management to consider is *how* to engage and work with these micro-influencers. One must first ask who they are. In general, they are individuals, associations, or organizations who are well known, have credibility, and are brands within their given (and often very specific) area of interest, work, or passion. Most importantly, they have the "ears" and "eyes" of the people and organizations within their area of interest. As noted in Chapter 1, their information is often considered to be compelling and reliable by their followers. Particularly, they are perceived as relatable, accessible, and intimate. A few examples to consider are as follows:

1. An athlete involved with your organization who has future potential (either via athletic skill, media skill, or — ideally — both) and already a strong following.
2. A connected participant in your sport or club. For spectator sports, this could be a superfan. Often you might not even realize you have a world-renowned doctor, lawyer, professor, media personality, or businessperson already connected to you. Just a re-tweet or like from this individual can have an impact.
3. A connected parent, grandparent, spouse, or sibling. This is similar to the previous example, but the individual is not formally participating in the athletic events themselves.

Secondly, as manager, the next question to ask pertains to how one could engage these micro-influencers and encourage them to support one's efforts on their social media. Tactics and ideas could include:

1. For those up-and-coming athletes, support them fully so they can continue to maximize their on-field performance. Thus, manage their social media channels, help them create and post regular, innovative, and high quality content, and use your club's social media platforms to share their content and increase their following. Specific examples of this support include capturing content (such as video recording a training session) or building content for posting (e.g., preparing an infographic) on their platforms.
2. For those who are 'connected' (e.g., parent, master athlete, superfan), this is a much different tactic than the one above. First, you must find a way to provide them value when they push out your content. How can your organization help them or their organization? Is a partnership or a collaborative effort possible? Can you celebrate a donation they make? A very simple example, and one that happens often, is when a parent of a young

athlete on a local soccer, hockey, or any community club, 'sponsors' the club under the name of their company. In most cases, this is a pure donation under the guise of a sponsorship. However, for the minor sport organization seeking to increase its social media following, this is also a potential cross-promotion opportunity. Can you create a post thanking the sponsor with tags to the company's employees, its followers, its websites, other parents in the club, etc.? If this leads to any social media traction (i.e., new followers, activity), then continue to build the partnership.

Working with micro- and nano-influencers is an example of influencer marketing on a smaller scale. Brands partner with such people because they match and reach a particular niche. They are typically well known in their particular area of interest and have high rates of engagement from their audiences.

LEARNING ACTIVITY 2

Have a friend suggest a sports club, league, team, or association that they would consider to be part of minor sports. Can you identify who that sports entities' biggest influencer is? Would you consider that influencer a "micro-influencer" or is their impact more broadly defined? Does your selection of the top influencer shift depending on the social media platform consulted?

CASE STUDY 2: SOCIAL MEDIA USE IN THE GULF SOUTH CONFERENCE (USA)

NCAA DII schools are one example of how minor sport organizations use social media to further promote their sports coverage. For example, the Gulf South Conference (GSC) serves as the primary athletic conference for NCAA DII member schools across the Southeast and Gulf Coast of the United States (GSC, 2020). Table 3 highlights the social media platforms each school uses along with their number of followers.

Table 3. Facebook, Instagram, and Twitter Followers by Gulf South School and Sport (as of September 2020).

Sport	BSB	SB	MBB	WBB	MSOC	WSOC	XC	FB	VOL
UAH									
Facebook	0	0	1358	854	457	370	0	n/a	0
Instagram	0	0	927	0	1044	351	253	n/a	0
Twitter	1063	1383	2820	1202	459	147	420	n/a	966
CBU									
Facebook	165	933	0	184	483	0	236	n/a	0
Instagram	228	160	0	155	0	0	0	n/a	0
Twitter	1178	481	504	641	205	224	130	n/a	142
DSU									
Facebook	0	0	0	0	0	0	0	0	n/a
Instagram	0	0	0	0	0	0	0	0	n/a
Twitter	6790	2619	1955	664	1072	1164	203	8069	n/a
UWF									
Facebook	0	2082	0	1389	1034	1034	92	6822	1533
Instagram	1236	1047	429	919	1624	1068	232	5880	2110
Twitter	2146	1562	1452	1734	519	366	69	17200	674
UWA									
Facebook	375	600	0	51	0	1276	259	2378	500
Instagram	0	0	0	667	531	0	0	1455	822
Twitter	2592	2757	205	1001	0	825	209	5444	485
MC									
Faccbook	0	0	0	0	0	455	0	0	0
Instagram	0	660	0	0	877	0	0	911	875
Twitter	2472	1739	600	544	7	1016	43	4747	628
UWG									
Facebook	0	0	0	0	n/a	0	148	411	0
Instagram	0	808	0	0	n/a	455	308	0	0
Twitter	1556	1309	906	173	n/a	645	136	3963	127
VSU									
Facebook	0	0	492	206	n/a	306	217	0	893
Instagram	779	435	1748	527	n/a	672	0	2028	

Table 3. (*Continued*)

Sport	BSB	SB	MBB	WBB	MSOC	WSOC	XC	FB	VOL
Twitter	674	1731	1713	1247	n/a	1164	369	15200	207
SU									
Facebook	387	0	214	0	0	0	0	0	0
Instagram	241	170	0	220	374	0	0	0	0
Twitter	854	838	408	631	293	0	0	6692	85
LU									
Facebook	1364	1463	195	52	674	595	0	n/a	0
Instagram	0	1068	173	258	3205	887	0	n/a	167
Twitter	3460	2328	2430	2139	346	734	2016	n/a	187
AUM									
Facebook	0	0	0	703	157	321	0	n/a	0
Instagram	0	0	0	447	203	0	0	n/a	0
Twitter	449	687	407	1028	152	154	91	n/a	100
UU									
Facebook	0	173	0	59	0	452	0	n/a	993
Instagram	482	173	0	496	776	0	519	n/a	927
Twitter	849	572	1288	1352	508	555	30	n/a	506
UM									
Facebook	885	4390	0	382	483	764	542	n/a	809
Instagram	1254	1873	1723	421	0	1110	559	n/a	1023
Twitter	2997	1585	122	495	110	632	349	n/a	701

Table 4. Percentage of Football-Specific Twitter Followers by Gulf South School.

School	Total followers of each sport account	Football followers	Percentage of total followers (%)
DSU	25417	8069	31.7
MC	11796	4747	40.2
UWA	13644	5444	39.9
UWF	26550	17200	64.8
UWG	8899	3963	44.5
SU	10256	6692	65.2
VSU	23546	15200	64.6

Table 5.   Social Media Platforms by Sport Organization.

Sport	Instagram N = followers	Facebook N = followers	Twitter N = followers	YouTube N = followers (est.)
Fencing	28,221	85,919	18,572	6,890
Soccer	2,799,247	213,883	83,378	275,000
Aquatic Sports	107,003	105,330	24,236	1,300
Volleyball	191,190	250,368	251,321	24,000
Martial Arts	29,987	50,930	2,176	15,900

Table 6.   Social Media posts by Platform (January 2020–August 2020).

Sport	Instagram N = posts	Facebook N = posts	Twitter N = posts	YouTube N = posts
Fencing	515	475	263	615
Soccer	416	397	149	52
Aquatic Sports	69	199	114	6
Volleyball	495	475	839	251
Martial Arts	219	506	285	56

Table 4 provides a summary of the total number of posts each school had per account during the first eight months of 2020.

To further outreach, each school also has social media accounts for each sport. Table 5 indicates the number of followers for each school on Facebook, Instagram, and Twitter, respectively.

Not every school offers football, but for those that do, it still represents their greatest fan base as shown in Table 6.

As the numbers in Table 3 show, GSC schools have twice as many followers on Facebook and Twitter, than Instagram. YouTube is used more infrequently based on the number of subscribers for each school. As shown in Tables 4 and 5, GSC schools appear to reach more fans on Twitter based on the number of posts and followers, indicating a trend that Twitter may offer more interactivity in sports consumption, a concept discussed earlier in this chapter. However, most schools still have a greater fan following for the "big three" of U.S. sports: football, baseball, and basketball (Hyre *et al.*, 2017). When compared to the total number of followers for each sport, football represents the greatest percentage of each school's total followers as shown in Table 6. The number of posts across the timeframe for Facebook and Twitter are significantly higher than those of Instagram and YouTube, suggesting these schools may put more effort into the platforms they think will achieve the greatest outreach based on their followers and provide the best chance at building relationships with fans/sponsors that could later turn into profits. Many schools do not continue to post content during the off-season, which could be limiting the return on investment from social media. Inconsistencies across platform use may not be a conscious effort, but a reflection of the limitations facing the sports information director (SID) at a smaller NCAA institution in marketing sport programs (Zullo, 2018). As shown in Chapter 6, the popularity or brand value of a sport and social media following are interrelated.

CASE QUESTIONS

1. How might challenges facing the DII Sports Information Director lead to inconsistencies in promoting minor sports on social media?
2. In your opinion, does having multiple social media platforms for each sport contribute to a lack of a unified identity in branding?
3. How can schools expand on the popularity of football in building larger fan bases for their other sports? Do you think they use the same strategies in marketing football on social media in comparison to the non-revenue sports?

REVENUE GENERATION FOR MINOR SPORTS

Generation of revenue in minor sports is challenging. In most cases, true corporate sponsorship, where the brand is seeking a specific return-on-investment (ROI) from that sponsorship, typically spends in the form of a sales increase that exceeds the total of their investment. Thus, these types of organizations often seek sponsorship/partnerships which focus on a combination of marketing benefits and philanthropic efforts from the brand's perspective. If the brand (sponsor) is also a small organization, they typically alter their objectives to be a mix of some business outcomes, along with benefits associated with being supportive of a small sport organization (Zinger and O'Reilly, 2010). The pursuit of contra or in-kind sponsorship (i.e., not cash but a needed product or service) is also highly recommended in these small organization contexts. As for social media, it is not a direct revenue generator for minor sports organizations, but it is instead a source of indirect influence on revenue generation. Social media-based sponsorship activation is, in part, about placing a sponsor in an emotional relationship between a consumer (or fan) and a sponsored activity (for example, a minor sport). Social media helps a sponsor reach a targeted niche market to achieve its objectives. Also, effective activation, promotion, or reach via social media can help support the revenue generation tactic and lead to its success.

Although sponsorship is commonly linked to revenue in professional sports, it is not the only source of revenue for minor sports organizations and, quite honestly, should not be a major priority in most cases, since sponsorship requires major effort and time commitment from the senior leader of the small sport organization (typically the executive director), as well as financial resources, athlete/coach time, and long timelines (O'Reilly and Madill, 2012). Thus, one could consider a breadth of options available to minor sports organizations in terms of revenue generation, and then determine the role that social media could potentially play in each, and build out marketing programs based on this. Many of these may not be relevant in all contexts of minor sports organizations; however, the following are included for consideration:

1. **Cash sponsorship** — As noted, in certain cases, small sports organizations can find cash sponsors who can achieve an ROI by activating the partnership that is greater than the rights fee they will pay. For example, a local restaurant sponsors a local minor professional soccer club for $1,000 USD/year, including a 10% discount at the restaurant. Over the year, the club uses the res-

taurant for functions, team meetings, and post-practice/game get-togethers, leading to new incremental revenue for the restaurant and proceeds that exceed their investment.

Role for Social Media: In the case of sponsorship, social media plays a role in the 'activation' side, as it is a way that a minor sport organization can share, or more importantly allow its sponsors/partners to reach members, fans, participants, and others. Increasing the social media following and content quality can also help on the sponsorship sales side, as it can help a potential sponsor/partner see potential reach, and how they can use the partnership for their own business objectives (e.g., sales). For instance, a post about new team uniforms builds excitement for both the designer as well as those wearing it: the athletes.

2. **In-kind (or contra) sponsorship** — In this instance, instead of cash, the sponsor provides the minor sport organization with a needed product (e.g., bottled water for volunteers) or service (e.g., security personnel onsite). For the brand, this is often considered better than cash sponsorship, as it also provides the opportunity for consumers to try their product or service. In-kind sponsorship also gives the opportunity for consumers to try a sponsor's product or service.

    Role for Social Media: This is similar to the first application above, with the distinction that social media activation ideally should involve ways to support and drive the use of the product and/or services that are the focus of the in-kind sponsorship, such as a brand offering content space on their social media platforms for the sport property to include content and their own links. For instance, local restaurant posting a game result and offering their location for a victory celebration ties the minor sport and company in a way that can bolster both sides, but without money formally changing hands.

3. **Corporate philanthropy** — Given what was noted earlier about sponsorship being challenging for many minor sports organizations, corporate philanthropy (sometimes referred to as 'public–private partnerships') is an important area of consideration. From the corporate contributor side, they are often

drawing on budgets outside of their marketing communications side, and typically under the guise of 'corporate sponsorship responsibility' (Corporate Social Responsibility [CSR]), where they want to give back to society, but in a way that garners attention (e.g., Nike and its Black Lives Matter initiatives supporting a local club in a predominately black area).

Role for Social Media: If the minor sport organization gets a chance to receive such contributions, their job is to let their stakeholders know about the corporate donor, the cause, and the CSR efforts of the corporation on all of its social media platforms, and perhaps consider developing new content that is specific to the partnership, such as including regular posts about the donor. For instance, a company donating chemical-free pesticide to treat a local athletic field provides an opportunity to show how groomed the field is all while making the CSR opportunity a place to advance company reputation as well.

4. **Fundraising program** — Social media can enable an effective fundraising program (think 'crowd sourcing' on all platforms). This can be as simple as a "Friends of..." program for the minor sport organization or a more elaborate social media property specific to the fundraising campaign.

Role for Social Media: Social media can be used to communicate the cause through short video clips and infographics, and once awareness and understanding is created, the sport organization can use the fundraising tools available on different social media platforms to raise funds. For example, sports organizations can create a Fundraiser, and use Facebook Pay to facilitate ticket sales or other sports-related social events.

5. **Fundraising events** — For many years, traditional fundraising events (e.g., bingos, auctions, dinners, awards nights, etc.) have been a very effective way for minor sports organizations to generate resources to fund their operations.

Role for Social Media: These activities have been around for years. In these cases, social media can play a role in extending their lives, by continuing to generate interest and attendance/donations. However, an important role has emerged in fundraising for social media as many organizations convert to or add digital versions of these events (e.g., online auctions, Zoom awards night, etc.), many of which were launched during the COVID-19 pandemic.

6. **Cost efficiency** — As a final point here, it is vital for the minor sport organization to consider the ability of social media to reduce other promotional expenses (e.g., advertising) which will allow for cost savings, which is often just as valuable as revenue generation.

TRENDS AND CURRENT ISSUES

In minor sports organizations, the use of social media remains a challenge in practice today. Without the volume of digital followers and social media reach, minor sports organizations were unable to continue to operate in many cases without the traditional revenues (i.e., tickets, memberships, sponsorships, entry fees, etc.) they were accustomed to receiving. The important take-away is that the current reality is that minor sports organizations need to build their digital assets considerably and pivot their operations to include a digital environment.

A good example of how one could do so comes in the case of Danish badminton Olympic medalist Viktor Axelsen. Certainly his achievements could explain part of his popularity on social media, but he forged a unique bond with the world's largest badminton market (China) by learning Mandarin. Even when the 2020 Olympics were postponed, those bonds could still be cultivated and continued on social media while the world waited. By using his social media account to, for instance, thank his supporters in three languages (Danish, English, and Mandarin), Axelsen continues to build an atypically large fan base even with his major promotional vehicle, the Olympics, on hold. Many of the sports and athletes discussed in this chapter are considered niche and/or minor, but two qualities of social media (pandemic-proof and global) allow for the opportunity to combine a series of "minor" audiences into a combined fan base that suddenly appears much more major.

CHAPTER SUMMARY

Minor sports are dealing with smaller followings and funding opportunities, yet they still can adopt many useful strategies for bolstering their presence and interaction with internal and external stakeholders through social media. Indeed, although still challenging, social media provides a platform not previously available to minor sports organizations. The primary platforms these institutions use are largely the same platforms that any major entity would incorporate. Influencers still matter, even if on smaller scales. From the smaller schools of the Gulf South Conference to the minor sport of Italian fencing, social media becomes a cost-efficient and relatively easy-to-implement mechanism for building awareness for a sports entity. One could argue that audiences for minor sports could grow in magnitude at larger pace, as the goal might be to double one thousand followers instead of one million. As such, social media in minor sports is crucial not merely for survival, but also to thrive in the evolving sports media environment.

KEY RESOURCES

- Pew Research Center: https://www.pewresearch.org/
- ESPN Department of Research and Insights (espn.com/analytics)
- Sprout Social: https://sproutsocial.com/
- Social Media Examiner: https://www.socialmediaexaminer.com/

RECOMMENDED ONLINE LINKS

- Sprout Social Media Demographics: https://sproutsocial.com/insights/new-social-media-demographics/.
- Deloitte Digital Fan Engagement: https://www2.deloitte.com/content/dam/Deloitte/us/Documents/technology-media-telecommunications/us-enhancing-digital-fan-engagement.pdf.
- Sport Techie Future of Live Streaming: https://www.sporttechie.com/future-of-live-streaming-sports-lies-with-social-media-networks.

- Global Web Index 5 Things to Know about Sport and Social Media: https://blog.globalwebindex.com/chart-of-the-week/sport-social-media/.
- Social Media HQ Social Media Impact on Sports: https://socialmediahq.com/how-social-medias-impact-on-sports-will-continue-to-grow/.

TEST YOUR KNOWLEDGE

1. What is the definition of minor sport? Should it solely be defined by the number of fans who follow it?
2. Do minor sports utilize entirely different social media strategies than major sports? Why or why not?
3. What is an engagement rate? What are some strategies minor sports social media content providers can use to bolster it?
4. What is a bounce rate? What are some strategies minor sports social media content providers can use to lower it?
5. What is the "three-click" rule? Based on your personal experience, is it valid?
6. How would one best define an influencer? Micro-influencer? What would the key difference be between the two?
7. What would you argue are the best ways to monetize social media presences for minor sports?

REFERENCES

Anagnostopoulos, C., Gillooly, L., Cook, D., Parganas, P., and Chadwick, S. (2017). Stakeholder communication in 140 characters or less: A study of community sport foundations. *Voluntas: International Journal of Voluntary and Nonprofit Organizations, 28*, 2224–2250. https://doi.org/10.1007/s11266-016-9802-4.

Bidin, C. (2019). Three opposing barometers between digital news media and influencers. *Cyborgology*. Retrieved from https://thesocietypages.org/cyborgology/2019/02/05/three-opposing-barometers-between-the-digital-news-media-and-influencers/.

Boehmer, J. (2016). Does the game really change? How students consume mediated sports in the age of social media. *Communication & Sport*, *4*(4), 460–483. https://doi.org/10.1177/2167479515595500.

Canham, S. (2020). Social media marketing trends for 2020. *Accuracast.* Retrieved from https://www.accuracast.com/articles/social-marketing/social-media-marketing-2020/.

Chen, J. (2020). Social media demographics to inform your brand's strategy in 2020. *SproutSocial.* Retrieved from https://sproutsocial.com/insights/new-social-media-demographics/.

Clavio, G. (2020). *Social media and sports.* Champagne, IL: Human Kinetics.

Csobán, K. V. and Serra, G. (2014). The role of small-scale sports events in developing sustainable sport tourism — a case study of fencing. *Applied Studies in Agribusiness and Commerce*, *8*(4), 17–22. https://doi.org/10.19041/APSTRACT/2014/4/3.

Geurin-Eagleman, A. N., and Clavio, G. (2015). Utilizing social media as a marketing communication tool: An examination of mainstream and niche sport athletes' Facebook pages. *International Journal of Sport Management*, *16*(2), 488–497. https://doi.org/10.1016/j.smr.2013.03.004.

GSC. (2020). GSC quick facts. Retrieved from on August 31, 2020: https://gscsports.org/sports/2011/8/8/GEN_0808111016.aspx.

Hambrick, M. E. and Svensson, P. G. (2015). Gainline Africa: A case study of sport-for development organizations and the role of organizational relationship building via social media. *International Journal of Sport Communication*, *8*(2), 233–254. https://doi.org/10.1123/ijsc.2014-0087.

Hyre, T., Chen, S. and Larson, M. (2017). Perceptions concerning obstacles, stereotypes and discrimination faced by female sports reporters and other female sports professionals. *Athens Journal of Sports*, *4*, 213–230. https://doi.org/10.30958/ajspo.4.3.4.

Jacobson, M. (2017). How far down the search engine results page will most people go? *Leverage Marketing.* Retrieved on March 24, 2020 at: https://www.theleverageway.com/blog/how-far-down-the-search-engine-results-page-will-most-people-go/.

Kang, S. J., Rice, J. A., Hambrick, M. E., and Choi, C. (2019). CrossFit across three platforms: Using social media to navigate niche sport challenges. *Physical Culture and Sport Studies and Research*, *81*(1), 36–46. https://doi.org/10.2478/pcssr-2019-0004.

Kasavana, M. L. (2001). eMarketing: Restaurant websites that click. *Journal of Hospitality and Leisure Marketing, 9*(3–4), 161–178. https://doi.org/10.1300/J150v09n03_11.

Leiber, C. (2018). How and why do influencers make so much money?: The head of an influencer agency explains. *Vox.* Retrieved from: https://www.vox.com/the-goods/2018/11/28/18116875/influencer-marketing-social-media-engagement-instagram-youtube.

Mackova, V. and Turkova, K. (2019). 'I have won, and I want to share it': The ways female skiers use Facebook as a communication tool. *Communication Today, 10*(1), 94–109.

Mahoney, T. Q., Hambrick, M. E., Svensson, P. G., and Zimmerman, M. H. (2013). Examining emergent niche sports' YouTube exposure through the lens of the psychological continuum model. *International Journal of Sport Management and Marketing 6, 13*(3–4), 218–238. https://doi.org/10.1504/IJSMM.2013.059717.

Nielsen Insights (2014). Changing channels: Americans view just 17 channels despite record number to choose from. *Nielsen Insights.* Retrieved on March 24, 2020 at: https://www.nielsen.com/us/en/insights/news/2014/changing-channels-americans-view-just-17-channels-despite-record-number-to-choose-from.html.

O'Hallarn, B., Shapiro, S. L., O'Reilly, N., and Madill, J. (2012). The development of a process for evaluating marketing sponsorships. *Canadian Journal of Administrative Sciences, 29*(1), 50–66. https://doi.org/10.1002/cjas.194.

Siguencia, L. O., Herman, D., Marzano, G., and Rodak, P. (2017). The role of social media in sports communication management: An analysis of Polish top league teams' strategy. *Procedia Computer Science, 104*, 73–80. https://doi.org/10.1016/j.procs.2017.01.074.

Thorpe, H. (2017). Action sports, social media, and new technologies: Towards a research agenda. *Communication and Sport, 5*(5), 554–578. https://doi.org/10.1177/2167479516638125.

Vann, P., Woodford, D., and Bruns, A. (2015). Social media and niche sports: The netball ANZ championship and Commonwealth Games on Twitter. *Media International Australia, 155*(1), 108–119. https://doi.org/10.1177/1329878X1515500113.

Vooris, R. and Achen, R. (2019). Marketing in the minors: Comparing Minor and Major League Baseball teams' use of Facebook. *Journal of Sports Media, 14*(1–2), 23–46. https://doi.org/10.1353/jsm.2019.0003.

Wenner, L. A., and Billings, A. C. (Eds.) (2017). *Sport, media, and mega-events*. Routledge.

Zinger, T. and O'Reilly, N. (2010). An examination of sports sponsorship from a small business perspective. *International Journal of Sports Marketing and Sponsorship, 11*(4), 283–301. https://doi.org/10.1108/IJSMS-11-04-2010-B003.

Zoomph (2020). A digital revolution: Social media report. *Zoomph*. Retrieved from: https://zoomph.com/a-digital-revolution/.

Zullo, R. (2018). Sports marketing & publicity efforts in Division II intercollegiate athletics. *The Sport Journal, 21*(2). Retrieved from http://thesportjournal.org/article/sports-marketing-publicity-efforts-in-division-ii-intercollegiate-athletics/.

https://doi.org/10.1142/9789811237669_0006

Chapter 6

Social Media in Sports Decision-Making

Jessica R. Braunstein-Minkove*, Ari Kim*, and
Norm O'Reilly†

*Towson University, United States
†University of Maine, United States

CHAPTER OBJECTIVES

After reading this chapter, you will be able to do the following:

- Define decision-making, including the differences between programmed and nonprogrammed decisions
- Identify the steps in the Rational Decision-Making Process
- Discuss the decision-making process from the perspective of a sport industry professional
- Identify the role that social media plays in informing the decision-making process
- Describe ways in which primary data and secondary data can inform decisions regarding social media strategies and tactics
- Compare the basic analytical approaches available to sport industry professionals to inform decision-making with and through social media

KEY TERMS

Programmed decision-making
Nonprogrammed
  decision-making
Decision-making steps
Internal factors of
  decision-making

External factors of decision-
  making
Primary data
Secondary data

INTRODUCTION

In industries that are consumer facing, social media has become an influencer and, in many cases, a driver of the decisions made by managers. By definition, decision-making is the process of identifying a problem (or challenge) and selecting the best option, from a set of alternatives, to maximize the potential for success in achieving the desired outcome (Foster *et al.*, 2020). In simpler terms, decision-making is the act of choosing among several alternative possibilities (Parent and Slack, 2006), where the selected choice is expected to be the one that offers the most predictable outcome with the highest likelihood of a positive after-effect (Oliveira, 2007). Indeed, decision-makers undertake a variety of approaches to assess a number of possible substitutions from different possible scenarios before making a choice. The evaluation of alternative choices involves gathering and analyzing facts to increase the chance of making the most accurate decision with the most desirable long-term effects (Foster *et al.*, 2020).

In sport, like any field, major decisions must factor in potential implications to the various stakeholders that are impacted by our business strategies (Foster *et al.*, 2020). This is particularly vital as a result of the growth and impact of social media in sport. Given the intense interest in and personal investment of fans, sport is an industry where social media has a strong impact on the decision-making process of those responsible. Therefore, in a space that is influenced by both the producer (i.e., the organization or the sport industry professional) and the consumer (i.e., the audience, the fan, the participant, or the consumer), many factors must be taken into account when making a decision that is in line with an organization's goals and objectives. For example, during the early stages of COVID-19, the NBA and the NHL both completed their 2019–2020 seasons and awarded championships by setting up 'bubbles' (i.e., games in central locations, played without fans in attendance) where athletes, coaches, media, and support staff were isolated for many weeks. This decision was made in a collaborative fashion by owners, leagues, players, player associations, broadcasters, host cities, sponsors, and local health authorities. Such a decision is influenced by many factors, including fan reactions on social media, which enable the league and clubs to gauge fan opinion and to track their sentiments on the topic. Social media also provided a platform for fans to participate in the happenings within the bubbles, beyond the court (or ice), and the ability to share that content (and their views) on various social media platforms.

Therefore, given the role and value of social media in sport, this chapter will focus on informed decision-making with and through social media.

SOCIAL MEDIA IN SPORTS DECISION-MAKING: KEY CONCEPTS

Decision-making, on some level, is part of our everyday experience. Ultimately, it is the results of these decisions that impact the success, well-being, and even survival of an organization, large or small. For a sports organization, particularly in regards to social media, decisions include everything from what content to include on your Facebook page to how to structure your social media team. Therefore, each decision that is made is vital to reaching an organization's goals and objectives.

Decision-making involves making choices when (a) something of value is at stake (e.g., asset, customer, revenue), (b) a decision-maker's degree of certainty regarding alternative choices is unclear, and (c) the outcome of any of the alternative options involves a certain level of risk (e.g., financial). Taking all of this into account, the act of decision-making can be either simple or complex, depending on the nature of the decision itself (Zachary and Vorm, 2016). In choosing a particular alternative, a manager's degree of certainty, and the level of risk tolerated, play a major role in making optimal decisions (Hambrick and Snow, 1977). Therefore, the consideration of the organization's environment and context is imperative to appreciate why a particular alternative is chosen (Fantino and Stolarz-Fantino, 2005). This is particularly important for organizational decision-making, which has wide and long-term implications (Hambrick and Snow, 1977).

The decisions that managers within an organization make can be categorized as programmed and nonprogrammed decisions (Parent and Slack, 2006). **Programmed decisions** are customary decisions that are based on structured, well-informed, and clearly presented organizational policies and procedures. In the case of social media, a programmed decision would be one that is a relatively straightforward routine operating decision (e.g., a daily Facebook post). Conversely, a **nonprogrammed** decision is one that is new or unique, lacking clear guidelines for reaching a decision. Related to social medial, this may be a complex, senior-level decision that happens outside of established guidelines and procedures. Given our ability to prepare for programmed decisions, that will be the primary focus of this chapter; however, continuing to encourage creative thinking and problem-solving will also be a useful tool for social media managers, as it is still important to "prepare" for nonprogrammed decisions.

Based on all available information, decision-makers assess a variety of solutions from different possible scenarios before making a choice. The selected option is expected to be the one that offers the most predictable outcome with the highest likelihood of a positive after-effect (Oliveira, 2007). An evaluation of alternative choices involves gathering and analyzing facts to increase the chance of making the most accurate decision with the most desirable long-term effects; however, not all types of decisions require data. For example, Scott and Bruce (1995) proposed four different types of decision-making styles: (a) rational, which is characterized by thorough research for and a logical evaluation of alternatives, (b) intuitive, which is characterized by a reliance on hunches, (c) dependent, which is characterized by a search for advice and direction from others, and (d) avoidant, which is characterized by attempts to avoid making decisions altogether. While social media data can inform all four decision-making styles, this chapter focuses on the role social media plays in the rational model. Specifically the rational model of decision-making is grounded in thorough research and a logical evaluation of possible options in decision-making, designed to understand and evaluate the effectiveness of nonprogrammed decisions. With this, the rational model emphasizes the process of choosing an alternative (how decisions should be made) rather than the selected alternative (how decisions are actually made) (Parent and Slack, 2006). It is a step-by-step, nonintuitive decision processing approach that assumes managers act in economically rational ways with all available information on each available alternative (Parent and Slack, 2006).

As depicted in Figure 1, the rational model of decision-making includes the following steps (Parent and Slack, 2006):

1. **Monitor the decision environment**. The first step is scanning the decision environment properly by monitoring an organization's internal and external state. Factors to consider in an internal assessment include an organization's vision and mission, financial state, human resources, technological resources, and physical resources. Just as important is an external environment

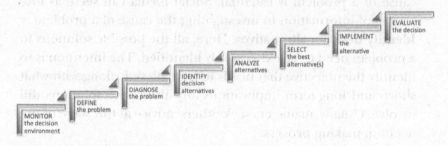

Figure 1: Steps in the (Rational) Decision-making Process.
Source: Parent and Slack (2006).

scan, including political, social, legal, technological, and economic issues. Both competitive and consumer analyses are pivotal to the assessment as well, as is social media as a platform through which to obtain the data to inform the ultimate decision.

2. **Define the problem**. It is necessary in any decision-making process to properly clarify the problem itself. As Archer (1980) stated, "If a problem is not acknowledged, it cannot be defined. If it is restrictively acknowledged, it will be restrictively defined" (p. 56). Hence, it will be necessary to acknowledge a specific decision area that will be clarified by diagnosing the problem or situation in detail. It involves delineating the elements and parameters of a problem as well as determining what the decision-maker wants to achieve. Therefore, this step involves addressing questions such as what is expected to be achieved, what constraints would be encountered to achieve the objective, and what are the risks involved in (not) achieving the objective. Objectives are expected to be specific, measurable, achievable, realistic, and time-bound. Additionally, both the short-term and long-term implications of the problem need to be identified.

3. **Diagnose the problem**. A clear identification of a problem is as good as finding a solution. Often, only a very small amount of information is visible about a problem, whereas the real problem is either unavailable or hidden. Similarly, what people in organizations often observe is the symptoms of a problem rather than the root cause and investigating and pinpointing the root cause of a problem is essential. Social media can serve as one source of information in investigating the cause of a problem.

4. **Identify decision alternatives**. Here, all the possible solutions to a problem need to be exhaustively identified. The intention is to identify the objective that needs to be achieved, along with what short- and long-term implications any alternative solutions will involve. Usually, managers seek others' advice at this stage of the decision-making process.

5. **Analyzing alternatives**. The merits of each alternative and its possible outcomes will be assessed to determine the most effective

and functional alternative. This involves predicting the possible outcome of any chosen alternative, analyzing what would happen if a given alternative is selected, assessing which alternative gives the best return against the specified objective, and weighing one alternative against another. This stage usually encounters disagreements among people who are involved in the decision-making process.

6. **Select the best alternative(s)**. This is the decision-makers' so-called moment of truth, where they select the one best alternative from the list that was narrowed down during the analyzing alternatives stage. If the above steps were implemented properly, then decision-makers are highly likely to make the proper selection in this step.

7. **Implement the alternative**. Decision-makers need to make sure that the decision is carried out according to directions. This involves planning, organizing, leading, and directing.

8. **Evaluate the decision**. In this final step, decision-makers need to determine if the best decision was made and if adjustments need to be made moving forward. Once the alternative has been implemented, social media data can serve as one source of information in informing future decisions regarding maintaining, altering, or eliminating the alternative moving forward.

INFORMED DECISION-MAKING

In considering a specific context for a decision and the environment in which it is to be made (e.g., sport), Zachary and Vorm (2016) advised that the decision be classified as a context that is either internal or external. **Internal** factors present a set of internal characteristics that impact decision-making (i.e., the context that the sport industry professional making the decision is currently situated in). This includes: historical context (the decision-maker's history in prior decisions), social context (organizational roles of the decision-maker), knowledge of context (decision-maker's expertise and experience), and internal context (decision-maker's workload, stress, etc.). **External** factors, on the other hand, consider the physical, natural, and social environment (i.e., the sport industry environment) as the context in which a decision is situated and that it constrains decisions.

From a sport industry professional's perspective, per Zachary and Vorm (2016), any sport organization facing a decision needs to be aware of the interests of each of the key stakeholders in its environment (e.g., ownership, employees, governing bodies/leagues, sponsors, partners, community, and consumers/audience). In considering these stakeholder groups, a practitioner may seek relationships that lead to new opportunities (e.g., new product, new channel, new audience), better ways to reach fans (e.g., new social media platform, new ticketing program), and/or the best way to convert the casual consumer to one that is brand loyal (e.g., new pricing structure, fan affinity program). In deciding how to seek these outcomes, a sport industry professional can follow a rational decision-making approach (Parent and Slack, 2006). As previously noted, rational decision-making style is a step-by-step, logical process, which assumes that the decision-makers for other stakeholders will act in an economical way with all available information for each alternative. With this in mind, it is vital to address the type of information, both internally and externally, that will be necessary to determine the most appropriate alternatives (Figure 2).

First, a sport industry professional must conduct an internal assessment. This will always begin with the individual factors noted by Zachary and Vorm (2016) mentioned earlier; however, as all decisions should link back to one's mission, it must also incorporate those related to the organization in general. This should, minimally, include the organization's vision, mission, objectives and goals, strategy, and culture. As these decisions involve social media, a scan of all organizational social media platforms for content, tone, and continuity of messaging should be included in the first step.

In addition to an internal assessment, it is vital that you conduct an external appraisal as well. The environment outside of the organization that must be evaluated includes the legal/political landscape, technology, culture, physical environment, and the economy. While this data will be vitally important, an environmental scan would not

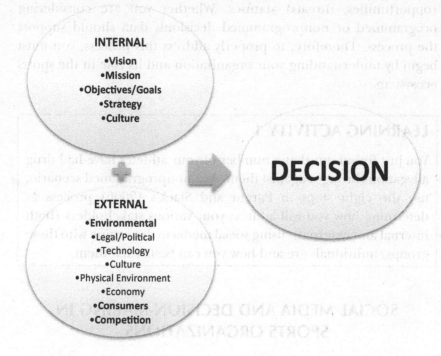

INTERNAL
- Vision
- Mission
- Objectives/Goals
- Strategy
- Culture

DECISION

EXTERNAL
- Environmental
- Legal/Political
- Technology
- Culture
- Physical Environment
- Economy
- Consumers
- Competition

Figure 2:   Internal and External Factors That Impact Decision-Making.

be complete without also addressing your consumers and competition. Due to the interactive nature of social media, an organization's external-facing side is becoming easier to assess, as audience feedback is provided via comments, likes, follows, and other readily accessible data. The type of analyses that can be conducted (noted late in the chapter) will provide you with a better understanding of who you are reaching, how you are reaching them, and what is most impactful. A competitive analysis will also be able to provide you with greater insight as to their platforms, content, and successes as well. This should be used in informing your decisions so that your brand is unique and meets the needs of your target audience.

While there are a variety of tools and mechanisms through which this can take place, a simple, yet productive, evaluation can take the form of a SWOT analysis. This assessment addresses an organization's internal (strengths, weaknesses) and external (opportunities, threats) statuses. Whether you are considering programmed or nonprogrammed decisions, data should support the process. Therefore, to properly address this process, you must begin by understanding your organization and its role in the sports ecosystem.

LEARNING ACTIVITY 1

You just found out that a number of your athletes have had drug allegations brought against them. As a nonprogrammed scenario, use the eight steps in Parent and Slack's (2006) process to determine how you will address your various stakeholders (both internal and external), using social media to determine who these groups/individuals are and how you can best reach them.

SOCIAL MEDIA AND DECISION-MAKING IN SPORTS ORGANIZATIONS

Pivotal to this chapter is the point that decision-making within the context of social media in sport is dynamic (i.e., fast changing). As it has been well described in the previous chapters of this book, social media, at its core, is different than traditional media platforms, as it evolves much more quickly. Indeed, social media platforms provide an interactive and participatory outlet through which consumers (e.g., fans, audience) themselves may both connect with and add to, by creating their own user-generated content (UGC). As a result, decisions are influenced by both the organization's and consumer's input, with each perspective factoring into the presentation of the content itself. This is a very important point with regards to the influence of social media on decisions by organizations, as input comes from both the organization itself (producer side) and the fan/consumer base (user side).

For those sports entities that only exist digitally (e.g., esports, fantasy sports, mobile sports betting), social media is their primary communication platform. Thus, the use of social media, as a communication outlet for their sports product, allows for an understanding of who their consumers are and how to best reach them. In turn, social media informs their marketing and communications decision-making. Hypothetically, Wizards District Gaming may have a different consumer base than their parent organization (i.e., the Washington Wizards), potentially pulling from Twitch or YouTube users who are already on those platforms, rather than the Wizards traditional consumer base, to inform their marketing decisions. Relatedly, sports organizations that do have the opportunity for traditional (or non-digital) experiences can learn from virtual offerings as well, using similar tactics to determine their social media strategies. In this regard, in the US, Angel City Football Club of the National Women's Soccer League (NWSL) and the Seattle Kraken of the National Hockey League (NHL) are good examples that launched their inaugural brand and name on a variety of social media platforms (for more on this, please see Chapter 9). The decision of these two sports organizations to launch in this manner allowed the organizations to broaden their reach beyond their local geographic markets. Additionally, it provided for the opportunity to assess the impact of their messaging through social media analytics, as both teams have the ability to track who is watching (e.g., age, gender, location, and other demographics), what merchandise is being purchased through official suppliers, and how people are reacting (e.g., shared posts, likes, etc.). Hence, the new brands of both clubs have been shaped, in part, by the connections made to their community via social media based on the content and channel decisions made by the clubs.

As discussed throughout this book, prior to the digital age (i.e., the time period that began in the late 21st century, coinciding with the widespread use of digital technology/the Internet), sports business professionals had full control over content creation and dispersion (e.g., through the traditional website, press releases to the media), thereby driving the image development of their brand for their consumers and audiences. At that time, communication was largely one directional (i.e., conveyance). However, with the advent of social media, particularly with UGC as an input in the consumer decision-making process, the creation of content is now multidirectional. For example, if you are looking to purchase a new pair of running shoes, may you go to the brand website to purchase them? Or, can you visit social media sites (including ones about the brands you are considering) to find reviews (e.g., blogs and Facebook), photos (e.g., Instagram), or even a video of someone wearing or showing off their new look (e.g., TikTok, YouTube)? However, the challenge in a social media environment, from the decision-making perspective of the organization, is that the organization itself is no longer able to generate every message associated with their product and/or brand. Conversely, this also allows the organization to pursue more advanced engagement via social media. Indeed, those carefully crafted messages that can be developed by the sport organization can be discussed, critiqued, supported, advocated for, shared, and/or altered by followers (users) on social media. Therefore, it is important for sport industry professionals to understand how social media content on various channels may be received when they are deciding what, when, and where to post. For more on this, please see Chapter 16.

Social media itself is an important source of data in the decision-making processes of an organization. A study conducted by Nielson (2016), global market research agency, reported that information obtained from social media accounts for 54% of the information used when consumers make decisions to purchase. Therefore, evidence exists to support that social media can significantly influence consumers' purchasing decisions. Social media also serves as a facilitator of peer influence when it comes to making purchase decisions, as 71% of consumers are likely to purchase an item based on social media referrals (Nielson, 2016). Importantly, UGC has become an expanded version of word of mouth, an avenue that is seen as more authentic than traditional advertising.

SOCIAL MEDIA TO INFORM DECISION-MAKING

Over the past two decades, social media has added to both the type and accessibility of information, which is often available through platforms that a sport organization is already using (Abeza *et al.*, 2013). Particularly, social media provides sports organizations with the opportunity to learn about their consumers based on the way that they interact with the site(s). Per the process addressed in Parent and Slack's (2006) model regarding rational decision-making, sport industry professionals need to understand their own needs and intentions, as well as those of their consumers. This is true of both programmed and nonprogrammed decisions, where the former is often proactive and standardized, allowing for continuous assessment for potential adjustments, and the latter may become a standing plan in time, but is often a single-use plan or reactive in nature. This type of decision-making process (i.e., nonprogrammed) warrants data to substantiate an organization's plan, particularly given the nature of social media and the fact that messaging is both far-reaching and everlasting. In order to do so effectively, information needs to be assessed in a holistic manner, including both primary and secondary data. **Primary data** is information (qualitative or quantitative) that is collected by the entity, directly for their own use, with a specific objective (or set of objectives) in mind. Some organizations hire staff or engage external agencies to collect and/or analyze primary data to inform decisions on a daily basis, while others contract out on an intermittent basis (e.g., annually, quarterly), or on a project-by-project basis.

Often, the decision about how much time, expertise, and energy to invest in primary data is resource-based, as many smaller sport entities do not have the funds for an in-house business analytics staff or to retain a market research agency. Consider the budget for a larger National Sport Organization (NSO) such as USA Basketball or Hockey Canada, versus a small NSO or event, like Speed Skating New Zealand or the Irish Table Tennis Championships. While one may have the resources to allocate a staff member or engage a research agency in contract work, others may be doing their best to focus efforts on understanding their reach through the limited resources they have on hand. In the latter case, primary research may be more limited. Fortunately, low-cost (often with no hard cost) resources are available with social media to begin to restructure a decision-maker's thinking process and make those informed decisions based on data collected via your organization's social media platforms in an active way (e.g., posting content with "chat now," "contact now," "comment," etc. buttons to gauge audience interest or general feedback).

In cases where primary data are not available, affordable, able to be collected in a timely fashion, or the available data do not provide the information that you need, **secondary data** will be helpful to inform decision-making. **Secondary data** are data gathered for some other purpose than the study at hand. Importantly, secondary data can complement the use of primary data, inform the collection of primary data, or validate those findings. Specifically, in situations involving social media, secondary data often provide a more robust (e.g., big data) approach to audience insight through analytics programs associated with an organization's own social media platforms (e.g., Facebook Insights, Twitter Analytics, Instagram Insights, YouTube Analytics, Google Analytics) or with the help of companies such as BuzzSumo, Sprout Social, Hootsuite. Secondary data are typically widely available, often inexpensive, and timely to acquire.

In acquiring primary data, sports organizations have adopted and applied analytical approaches to assist with both programmed and nonprogrammed decision-making. Historically, most sports-related analytical approaches have been primarily associated with on-the-field sports operations and sports performance (e.g., baseball's use of analytics to assess batting averages, pitcher selection, strategic lineup adjustments, and overall team offensive/defensive strategy). However, since the late 1900s, with the prominence of digital data, sports organizations have integrated more data-driven decision-making into core business functions (i.e., programmed and/or nonprogrammed decisions), such as ticket sales/pricing, database management, corporate partnership valuation, sponsorship, merchandising, in venue fan satisfaction, fan engagement, customer relationship management systems, and, most important to this book, social media strategy development and implementation.

In turn, organizations can track metrics online that assess their business performance (e.g., the ratio of users who click on a specific link to the number of total users who view a page, email, or advertisement, known as a click-through rate).

TYPES OF SOCIAL MEDIA DATA ANALYTICS USED IN SPORT ORGANIZATION DECISION-MAKING

A number of different types of social media data analytics (SMA) are available to sports managers seeking various approaches to analyze data gathered from their social media platforms. While these will be further outlined in Chapter 7, we would be remiss to not mention them here, as these processes allow practitioners to make sense of the data that will be used in decision-making.

Descriptive SMA addresses "what happened?" and "what is happening?" With descriptive SMA, social media data are gathered and then presented in the form of reports, visualizations, and clustering to understand a well-defined business problem or opportunity. Currently, descriptive data analytics accounts for the majority of the social media analytics landscape. However, there are many other ways that data can be used. Therefore, sport industry professionals will need to determine what metrics they will use to measure success (e.g., reach, engagement, brand sentiment). Social media metrics will be discussed further in Chapter 15.

Diagnostic SMA examines "why something happened?" For example, while descriptive analytics can provide an overview of your social media marketing campaign's performance (mentions, followers, fans, page views, reviews, pins, etc.), diagnostic analytics can distill these data to see what worked in your past campaigns and what did not. Diagnostic analytics include inferential statistics, behavioral analytics, correlations, and retrospective analysis. The outcomes of these analyses are often a cause and effect analysis of a business issue. For example, what caused a sudden boost in online ticket sales without any obvious reason? Diagnostic SMA helps you determine that a student night promo deal posted on Instagram leads to a 15% increase in sales, whereas Facebook ads did not impact the increase of ticket sales. In turn, you may shake up your action plan with a result of diagnostic analytics (i.e., cut off Facebook ads)

Predictive SMA involves analyzing social media data to predict a future event. Examples include linear and logistic regression models. Predictive analysis deals with the question of "what will happen based on past events?" In simple terms, a model is built based on past events or activities using social media data, which allows the manager to input variables to estimate the impact of a future event. For example, you may predict higher interest in and demand for your new "All-You-Can-Eat" concessions promotion by analyzing consumers' comments on your social media, and may stack up more food and staff up your concession service team in advance. Also grouped in the "future" category, you will find **prescriptive SMA**. This process suggests the best action to take when handling a scenario. For instance, if you have groups of social media users that display certain patterns of interactive behavior with your organization, this method can help optimize the organization's posts based on each group or segment of social media users.

PRACTITIONER'S PERSPECTIVE

South Korea is one of the most connected countries in the world, boasting an Internet penetration rate of roughly 96%. Additionally, approximately 87% of South Koreans between the ages of 20 and 30 use social media (Statista, 2020). Therefore, understanding the role of social media in sports decision-making is vital in a country such as South Korea. With that, Doojin Sa, Director of Digital Media for the professional soccer league (K-League), shares his perspectives as a social media expert in Korean sport.

The Practitioner: Doojin Sa, Director of Digital Media, K-League

(*Continued*)

Sa has overseen the broadcasting rights and digital content of the K-League since 2018. Prior to joining the K-League, Sa worked at leading global accounting firm PwC as a certified public accountant. In that role, he provided financial advisory services to the 2018 PyeongChang Olympic Committee. Being intrigued by the dynamics of an industry that he genuinely enjoyed working in, Sa decided to shift his career focus to sports. Consequently, he graduated from the FIFA Master's program in Management, Law, and Humanities of Sport, to learn the ecosystem of the soccer industry.

Which social media platform is your organization currently using to communicate with K-League fans?
Facebook was the first social media platform we used since 2010, and we have more than 106,000 followers as of October 2020. Instagram is a relatively new channel that has been added to our social media portfolio, but it has shown rapid growth, with current followers totaling 109,000. While most of the content that we share on Facebook and Instagram are published in Korean, to communicate with Korean fans, we run the official K-League Twitter (@kleague) fully in English, utilizing it as a platform to attract a global audience.

To respond to the increasing interest of K-League fans to consume video content, we recently added social media platforms

(*Continued*)

(Continued)

for video sharing (i.e., YouTube, TikTok) to our social media portfolio. As a result, we have a contract with a digital marketing agency to provide quality social media content and better manage the channel.

How do you utilize social media data in making business decisions? We are in the early stage of utilizing social media analytics in basic-level decision-making. At this point, we mainly use them to understand user demographics of each social media platform. For example, followers on Facebook are likely loyal soccer fans who are well aware of K-league teams and players, and therefore expect to acquire expert knowledge. On the other hand, we aim to post casual stories and soft news on Instagram because more young, female followers are on Instagram. The partner we work with for our YouTube channel has their own analytics team and share social media data analytics results with us including types of content that generate buzz and fan engagement.

LEARNING ACTIVITY 2

Select a professional sports team in your area and visit at least two of its social media platforms (Facebook, Instagram, Twitter, Pinterest, TikTok, etc.). Identify one problem (e.g., inconsistent messaging, dated content, "missing the mark" with their audience(s), etc.) and "work" as a member of their social media team to set a plan in place to solve it! Your job is to determine what type of primary and secondary data you will use to inform your decision, identifying the type of social media data analytics that you will use, and the questions that will guide your investigation.

KEY SKILLS FOR PRACTICE

This section presents a number of key skills students should focus on in order to prepare themselves to be able to use social media data in making informed decisions as a successful sport business professional. The ability to diagnose a problem is the first step in making good decisions, and one that requires asking the right questions. The intention here is to hone your **critical thinking skills**. This soft skill, which includes the ability to assess a situation in a thorough and objective manner, allows you to address issues in an organized and rational manner. The use of SMAs will be worthwhile and meaningful only when the decision-makers are able to raise the right question(s).

Second, **analytical skills** are the ability to observe, research, and interpret social media data to find solutions to complex business problems, make informed decisions, and achieve business goals. These skills include both technical skills and an understanding of data analysis and interpretation. Depending on a professional's role and responsibilities in a sports organization, they may need soft skills like analytical thinking and/or hard skills such as evaluating statistics, technical knowledge, software programming, or hardware maintenance.

Communication skills are essential to engage with multiple audiences and persuade stakeholders to contribute. Importantly, near-perfect analysis can be devalued when it's poorly communicated. To that end, completeness, accuracy, and clarity of communication are important. Completeness is the degree to which the delivered message provides all the information the receivers need in a language they understand. The ability for data visualization would be a plus, as visualizing the data is an effective way to make the audience understand. Accuracy is the degree to which the reasoning in the deliverable is logical and based on the correct information. Clarity is the degree to which the phrasing and expression of the communication are precise and to the point.

Therefore, while technical skills (i.e., analytics) are extremely helpful in the decision-making process, soft skills (i.e., critical thinking and communication) are vital in ensuring that the message is delivered clearly and in the manner it was intended. Additionally, due to the interactive nature of social media, flexibility and adaptability will need to be key elements of your decision-making process (see Chapter 16).

PRACTITIONERS' PERSPECTIVE

The Los Angeles Football Club (LAFC) is one of the most successful Major League Soccer (MLS) teams both on and off the field. This is particularly true when it comes to fan engagement and data analytics. Two practitioners from LAFC share with us their perspectives on social media management and the use of data analytics in social media decision-making.

The Practitioners: Ryan Bishara (left), Senior Vice President of Business & Data Strategy at LAFC; Colin Kelly (right), Vice President of Digital at LAFC.

Ryan Bishara, a 2020 Forbes 30 Under 30 for Sports (US & Canada) recipient, currently leads the Business & Data Strategy department for LAFC. In this role, Bishara oversees LAFCs data-driven decision-making process to optimize business across the organization.

Colin Kelly's career began at Syracuse.com, followed by stints at the National Hockey League (NHL), CBSNewYork.com, and the Jacksonville Jaguars. He started his career in MLS with the New York City Football Club (NYCFC), moving on to LAFC in 2015. As the lead of digital media at LAFC, Kelly developed the

(Continued)

digital strategy for LAFC and oversees the social media arm of the club. In this role he has curated diverse social media platforms, focusing on presence and growth through content creation and engagement.

What are the main goals of your social media strategy?

Kelly: We are a relatively new club, so our main goal with social media is to establish who we are as a team and reinforce our brand identity. Even with the relatively short history of the team, we are known for having a more engaged audience on social media than any team in the league. By communicating with our fans and followers on social media, this helps us to establish emotional connections between our team and our fans, driving the choices we make to reach them in the future.

How do you collaborate with the league in creating a social media strategy?

Bishara: MLS sets the integrated social media framework and provides general guidance for which social media platforms might be utilized in communicating with our fans. Additionally, they ask us to promote not only the team but the league as a whole, as best we can. In terms of the team's social media strategy and specific content creation, though, each team can decide what would be the best practice for them, creating content in a way that best meets organizational goals.

How do you evaluate your social media strategy?

Bishara: To do that, we rely heavily on consumer surveys to see the impact of our marketing communication strategy including social media. These surveys are sent to our database, many of which are our followers on social media. On those surveys, we ask what social media platforms they follow us on to get a sense where the interest and excitement comes from. We also look at the sentiment about the club on social media in specific areas. For example, how much

(Continued)

(Continued)

do they feel that the club represents the city, whether we support the community, if we provide the best in-person sport experience in Los Angeles, etc.

Do you track and analyze the social media metrics to evaluate your social media practices?

Kelly: Although there are metrics to capture the outcome of social media strategies — like number of followers for reach and number of likes for engagement – we are not yet tracking the social media metrics on a regular basis nor using an analytics system. There are certain types of social media posts to generate high engagement that can be measured. For example, we recently got high engagement for postings to wish a player happy birthday, wishing other LA teams — like the LA Lakers — good luck with their season. But we have yet to systematically track those metrics. Our social media goal is to build long-term relationships with our fans and generate emotional connections between us and the fans. Therefore, we use our metrics to create quality content, which helps us in creating strong relationship with fans, rather than trying to jump on a trendy topic. In terms of measuring 'brand identity and customer relationship,' our digital team tries to read every story posted about the club, yet we have not been utilizing social media analytics tool to the fullest extent.

How does social media data analytics impact your organization and other stakeholders in making business decisions?

Bishara: Like most professional sports teams, we have corporate partners that support the club (i.e., sponsors). Because the majority of engagement and impressions toward the partnership are coming from social media, we do analyze the exposure of the partner brand through the social media and share sponsorship outcomes with those entities. To do that, we work with a social media analytics agency called Zoomph to capture the reach and exposure on social media and create a dashboard for reporting

(Continued)

using the Tableau program. The data is a performance indicator for us, allowing us to recognize areas to improve as well as for our partners to attribute the value of the sponsorship. In turn, this becomes a basis for our business decisions and how both parties can derive the best return on investment (ROI) together with the partnership.

LEARNING ACTIVITY 3

Go to your LinkedIn account and sign in. Create a new account if one does not exist. Next, use LinkedIn to contact a social media specialist of your choice in the sport industry (e.g., a social media manager of a local sports organization). If you are unable to reach a social media specialist, seek to interview any professional working in the sport industry. Conduct a brief informational interview to learn how they use social media data in making business decisions. Discuss your findings with your classmates and address both differences and similarities in the various industry segments.

TRENDS AND CURRENT ISSUES

In addition to delving into the topic of decision-making in sport specific to social media, a review of a few important trends and current issues in sports decision-making will provide some helpful context. Furthermore, while the role and value of data in the decision-making process is important, as noted in this chapter, the interviews presented here indicate that many organizations may not yet be using these metrics or tools to their fullest advantage. While this is the case, there are many examples of organizations that are successfully implementing strategies to use data in their social media decision-making. The NBA, for example, is one of the most successful American leagues in this category, using data from their various social media platforms to determine the type of content that best resonates with their audience. As a result of their intentional use of their teams and athletes on various platforms, the NBA was named on Fast Company's Most Innovative Companies list for "giving a fan a courtside seat" through their use of social media (Fast Company, 2021). Therefore, while the trends presented here address the role of data in decision-making in social media, we encourage the first step of becoming comfortable with the data itself so that you can use it to the best of your ability to support the development and adjustment of your social media strategies.

REACTIVE, NOT PROACTIVE

Considering the magnitude of sports communication though social media, sports organizations are becoming increasingly interested in analyzing the information they have collected on social media platforms and utilizing it towards making better business decisions. However, the use of SMA is still in the early stages in many parts of the industry, with the main focus often on descriptive analysis related to social media. Yet, sports organizations do not actively use SMA in larger business decisions to build and measure overall organizational goals and objectives. Therefore, the implications here are to be proactive in maximizing the use of social media to inform decisions for the organization overall.

GARBAGE IN, GARBAGE OUT

The quality of social media data could become more important by introducing the notion of garbage in, garbage out (GIGO). GIGO, which implies that the quality of output is determined by the quality of the input, has been a universal concept in computer science and information technology to authenticate the validity of the data and programming. For social media practitioners in the sport industry, the concept of GIGO highlights the importance of data mining. If the data used are incomplete, incorrect, or irrelevant, the output (i.e., data-driven business decision) is unlikely to be informative or beneficial.

SOCIAL MEDIA INTELLIGENCE OUTSOURCING

The sheer volume of the social media data available for data analytics is beyond the capacity of most sports organizations, leading many sport industry leaders to go with outsourcing. In this, they opt to contract with companies who provide social media management and monitoring services for sports entities (e.g., MarketCast — formerly known as Turnkey Intelligence). This provides organizations with the opportunity to work with experts to conduct social media audits (e.g., presence, tactics, and accounts), using the findings to make strategic decisions moving forward.

CASE STUDY: ABERDEEN IRONBIRDS

The Aberdeen IronBirds. a minor league affiliate of Major League Baseball's Baltimore Orioles, founded in 2002 by retired Oriole and Major League Baseball Hall of Famer Cal Ripken, Jr. (inducted in 2007). Thanks to the love and support of local fans, who feel a sense of nostalgia towards Cal Ripken Jr., the team had immediate success for the first ten years of their existence. However, ticket sales and home attendance have exhibited declining trends in recent years, potentially due to their aging fan base. Therefore, the general manager of the IronBirds wants to attract the younger consumers (18–25 yrs. old).

As a minor league team, with a limited marketing budget, the IronBirds want to know which social media platform(s) would be the best to use in communicating with their target market(s) so that they can focus their efforts and resources in the most efficient way.

Discussion: Based on the IronBirds stated objectives, your job is to select the specific social media platform(s) that you recommend

---

(*Continued*)

(Continued)

the IronBirds focus on, adhering to the eight steps in the rational decision-making process. Additionally, list the primary and secondary data that the Aberdeen IronBirds should review to help increase ticket sales and home game attendance among younger consumers, explaining why you would use these data sources and how they would help you determine your final decision/recommendation(s).

CHAPTER SUMMARY

Social media not only provides an effective platform to reach consumers, it also provides the resources that we need to support our efforts — as long as we know the best way to use it! The hope is that, after reading this chapter, you now realize both the role and value of social media in informed decision-making. For sport industry professionals, social media provides access to and information about your audience members and the way that they choose to "consume" your content. Therefore, as you now have a better understanding of the type of analysis that can assist you in this decision-making process, we believe that you can use this knowledge to determine who to reach, what platforms to reach them on, the best way to keep them engaged, and, ultimately, how to reach your organizational goals and objectives.

KEY RESOURCES

- Zoomph:
  - Social media intelligence and sports sponsorship measurement platform: https://zoomph.com/solutions/sports-sponsorship-measurement/.
- Data Visualization (example):
  Texas Rangers boost attendance and optimize marketing spend with 360-degree view of ballpark operations: https://www.tableau.com/solutions/customer/season-texas-rangers.

- Expert Insights: How sports analytics is empowering better decision-making: https://hub.packtpub.com/sports-analytics-empowering-better-decision-making/.
- What Sports Analytics Can Teach Business Managers: https://mitsloan.mit.edu/ideas-made-to-matter/what-sports-analytics-can-teach-business-managers.
- Social Media in Sports Marketing: https://opendorse.com/blog/social-media-in-sports-marketing/.

TEST YOUR KNOWLEDGE

1. What is the difference between programmed and nonprogrammed decision-making?
2. What internal and external contingencies impact an organization's decision-making process?
3. What role does social media play in the sport industry professional's decision-making process?
4. Why is it important to use data in decision-making?
5. How would you use social media analytics to generate an informed decision as a sport industry professional?
6. Provide an example of how a sport entity can implement the eight steps of the rational decision-making process.

REFERENCES

Abeza, G., O'Reilly, N., and Reid, I. (2013). Relationship marketing and social media in sport. *International Journal of Sport Communication, 6*(2), 120–142.

Fantino, E. and Stolarz-Fantino, S. (2005). Decision-making: Context matters. *Behavioural Processes, 69*(2), 165–171.

Fast Company (2021, February 20). *The World's 50 Most Innovative Companies 2019.* Retrieved from https://www.fastcompany.com/most-innovative-companies/2019.

Foster, G., O'Reilly, N., and Dávila, A. (2020). *Sports Business Management: Decision Making Around the Globe, 2nd edition.* Routledge.

Hambrick, D. C. and Snow, C. C. (1977). A contextual model of strategic decision making in organizations. In R. L. Taylor, M. J. O'Connell, R. A. Zawacki, and D. D. Warrick (Eds.), *Academy of Management Proceedings*, 1977, 109–112.

Nielson (2016). *Social media report.* Retrieved from https://www.nielsen.com/wp-content/uploads/sites/3/2019/04/2016-nielsen-social-media-report.pdf.

Oliveira, A. (2007). A discussion of rational and psychological decision-making theories and models: The search for a cultural-ethical decision-making model. Electronic *Journal of Business and Organization Studies, 12*(2), 12–17.

Scott, S. G., and Bruce, R. A. (1985). Decision-making style: The development and assessment of a new measure. *Educational and Psychological Measurement, 55*, 818–831.

Parent, M. M., and Slack, T. (Eds.). (2006). International perspectives on the management of sport. Amsterdam, The Netherlands: Elsevier Butterworth-Heinemann.

Statista (2020). *Social media usage in South Korea — Statistics & Facts.* Retrieved from https://www.statista.com/topics/5274/social-media-usage-in-south-korea/.

Zachary, W. and Vorm, E.S. (2016). Approaches to context-based proactive decision support. *Proceedings of the Human Factors and Ergonomics Society 56th Annual Meeting, 60*(1), 238–240. http://doi.org/10.1177/1541931213601053.

Chapter 7

Social Media and Data Management in Sport

Yoseph Mamo*, Yiran Su[†], and Gashaw Abeza[‡]

*Tennessee State University, United States
[†]University of Georgia, United States
[‡]Towson University, United States

CHAPTER OBJECTIVES

After reading this chapter, you will be able to do the following:

- Assess the nature of social media data in the sport industry
- Identify the different methods of mining social media data
- Evaluate the different data analytics approaches in social media data management
- Describe the three social media analytics approaches
- Describe the role of data warehouse in social media data management
- Evaluate data governance in social media data management
- Identify the key skills necessary in social media data management

KEY TERMS

Data governance

Data management

Data mining

Data warehouse

Multimodality

Sentiment analysis

Social media

Social network analysis

Statistical analysis

INTRODUCTION

Social media, as discussed in Chapter 1, includes blogs, social network sites (e.g., Facebook), content communities (e.g., YouTube), and discussion sites (e.g., Reddit). This section introduces the "what" of social media data. Before delving into the nature of social media data, it is important to recall what constitute data in any business environment. Data refer to information about an object that is often represented as a set of values of variables, either quantitatively or qualitatively. When people and organizations engage in social media activities on sites such as Twitter, Facebook, and Instagram for varying reasons, such as posting, liking, and retweeting, they constantly produce social media data. These digital footprints can be broadly classified under the following typology.

Text: Text data refer to the written contents of social media messages. Text data can be derived from a standalone message without any other content or from the message accompanying an image or a video on social media, such as image captions on Instagram. Most social media platforms impose character limits on the text components, and such limits change constantly. In addition to the body of the message, hashtags, a type of metadata tag used on social networking services, can be used as text data. Hashtags provide unique value in a wide variety of social media data analytics, such as data classification, clustering, searching, indexing, and social network analysis. Hashtags can be used as the search query to collect tweets. For example, to analyze the real-time reaction of social media users' pertaining to Super Bowl ads, the Twitter application programming interface (API) can be used to crawl tweets with the hashtag

#SuperBowlAds over a period of one-week beginning on game day. Researchers and practitioners can subsequently clean the data by eliminating exact duplicates copied by individuals from other Twitter users. The resulting corpus of tweets is ready for sentiment and thematic analysis to yield consumer insights. Text data in Twitter, for example, includes tweets, emojis, retweets, replies, mentions, and hashtags.

Image: Social media users often post pictures on their platforms. Such image data are instrumental in social media analytics because they reveal rich information within a single post, as well as interesting patterns when aggregated. Notably, each image is associated with metadata, including geographic location (latitude, longitude), user-provided hashtags, timestamps, likes, reports, and comments. By capturing different types of metadata, sports organizations can generate a holistic view of the patterns and themes underlying users' posting behaviors. Examples of image data include photos, infographics, GIFs, icons, and stickers.

Video and Audio Files: Video and audio files are becoming ubiquitous on social media sites such as YouTube, Snapchat, Tik Tok, and Instagram, which fall under a social media platform category of content community. Notably, a number of dedicated smartphone apps have been developed to support the creation, hosting, and sharing of videos, such as Tik Tok and Instagram Reel. The ubiquity of smartphones, the Android ecosystem, data storage capacity, Internet speed, and Wi-Fi networks make it easy to create and share video and audio files across multiple devices and then cross-share them across multiple platforms. In the sports industry, social media users generate and share video and audio content for both professional and personal use. For example, sport teams use in-house videos as promotional materials and tools for fan engagement.

Collectively, the integration of different types of data sources is often called **multimodality**, which, in our context, means the application of multiple literacies or modes on social media. The term multiple literacies refers to social media users' ability to interpret the varying formats of media content through which they obtain information. Particularly, in the social media environment, multiple literacies can include textual literacy, video literacy, and technological literacy. Sporting teams post video clips on social media with captions, tweets, and emojis. Cristiano Ronaldo's social media accounts (Facebook, Twitter, Instagram) are good examples of multimodality communication being applied in the content that an athlete communicates. Ronaldo's postings usually include written text, mentions, hashtags, and weblinks to video clips and pictures. According to published research in sport business journals, social media posts by sporting leagues, such as the National Basketball Association (NBA) and National Football League (NFL), have been viewed and shared more than 10 billion times (Broughton, 2017). Furthermore, the engagement of these leagues with their fans through such posts involves spoken language in the videos, audio files, written language, and symbols. Each team's account has its own brand identity and personality that it exhibits across platforms by means of multimodality. From the data perspective, a vast amount of data with rich meanings (text, numeric, image, and video data) are generated by users. Such data are unstructured, semi-structured, or structured data, and, therefore, systematic data management procedures are required to manage these data.

The common characteristics of structured data are that they emerge from a single source or multiple sources in numeric format (e.g., attendance figures, ticket prices, sales records, buyers' demographic and contact data). In addition, survey responses, such as items on a Likert scale (e.g., intention to purchase), provide another example of uni-faceted data through which respondents indicate their degree of intention to purchase on a scale of 1 to 7. Semi-structured data includes email, Extensible Markup Language (XML), and other markup languages. By contrast, unstructured data originate from diverse sources (e.g., social media, online and mobile users' behaviors in real time, and customer service records), and they are nonnumeric, multi-faceted, and concurrent in nature. Data management involves the process of data mining, data warehousing, data analytics, and data governance. Put differently, it involves data acquisition, mining, storing, cleaning, integration, aggregation, query processing, analysis, interpretation, and presentation. In the following sections, the major social media data management practices will be discussed, namely, data mining, data warehousing, data analytics, and data governance.

SOCIAL MEDIA AND DATA MANAGEMENT: KEY CONCEPTS

SOCIAL MEDIA DATA MINING PRACTICES

Social media **data mining** is, "the process of acquisition or extraction of data from social media that result from users' interactions". The popularity of sport and the rapid development of social-media-based communication have changed the means of discovering hidden patterns and information from large datasets. Social media mining applications (e.g., NCapture, Python) use machine learning and statistical techniques to identify patterns and structures in data.

Coding and programming skills are methods and processes to give computers instructions to solve problems. Coding is a subset of programming. Coding includes machine-readable inputs, language and syntax, and writing lines of codes. Programming includes creating and developing an executable machine program, debugging and testing, translating requirements, and documentation review and analysis. Although coding and programming skills are gaining traction within the sport industry, many sport organizations are turning to easy-to-use analytics tools that provide one-click data-driven insights and visualizations at a cost. Although not all of these tools are widely used in sport management, a growing number of software companies are making inroads into the sport business. For example, Orlando Magic utilizes SAS to collect data and produce data visualizations to help team decision-makers; in the NFL, teams and players use Catapult, an innovative data-analytics wearable technology to help players minimize injuries (Statistical Analysis System, n.d.). In the sport business, the pattern can be extracted through user profiling, analysis of user engagement rates, and analysis of fan comments. The results are often used for ticket promotions or mar-

Table 1. Data Mining Software List.

No.	Name	Introduction	Examples	Sports Examples
1	Sisense	The Sisense data and analytics platform accelerates the time it takes to build, embed, and deploy intelligent analytics apps that unleash user creativity and engagement.	Sisense was used to predict COVID-19 pandemic growth by performing social network analysis.	NetBet Sports uses Sisense to analyze the consumption patterns of its customer base.
2	SQL Server Analysis Services (SSAS)	SQL Analysis Services is a viable and useful tool for the most common predictive analysis for companies. SQL Analysis Services provides multiple data sources, integrated data cleansing, and other features supporting integrated data mining solutions.	SQL Server Analysis Service could be connected with SQL Server Big Data Cluster to perform sentiment analysis on live streaming data yielded from social media.	Sports organizations could use SQL Server to host their database. They could then further use SQL Analysis Services for predictive analysis, gaining insights from social media data.
3	Oracle Data Mining (ODM)	ODM and Oracle big data tools to analyze social media activities that involve their brands and products.	ODM could perform sentiment analysis using social network data retrieved from Twitter.	Sports organizations could use Oracle Data Mining to build the audience attribution platform by using social media data.
4	RapidMiner	RapidMiner can extract insights from unstructured content such as online reviews, social media chatter, call center transcriptions, claims forms, research journals, and patent filings.	RapidMiner offers a specialized operator named *Search Twitter*, which allows organizations to crawl targeted users' tweets and visualize the results of text mining within a simple working environment	Sports organizations could use RapidMiner to analyze spectators' comments on social media by text mining.

keting campaigns targeted at specific segments. Table 1 provides a summary of the most popular data mining software applications currently available on the market. Note that as shown in the examples, the functionalities of the listed software go beyond social media data mining, such as churn analysis and inventory management. However, social media data mining involves collecting user-generated information from social media platforms, extracting valuable data from consumers, identifying patterns and trends, and shaping business decisions that are the next frontier of these analytic tools.

SOCIAL MEDIA DATA WAREHOUSE PRACTICES

With expansive reach and use of social media in the sport industry, many managers are interested in retrieving data to a central repository system (i.e., a storage place for the data where it can be accessed and analyzed) so that they can make better decisions. Unlike a database designed to handle structured data with a defined schema, a **data warehouse** involves cleaning, sorting, annotating, validating, integrating and aggregating, and preparing the data for analysis (Wang *et al.*, 2018). In other words, a data warehouse is a type of database that integrates data from various data sources to perform analytics. For example, it is common practice among sport organizations to record transactional and operational data from customers in various departments (e.g., customer relationship management system, sales, operations, and marketing). Such data are often stored in internal databases and, at times, across dispersed geographic locations. By contrast, social media data consist of fan-generated content and are mainly stored in public and community sources. Thus, a central repository that integrates data from different databases is important to make effective decisions.

Consequently, data warehouses have emerged as important assets for sport organizations to retrieve data from both internal and external databases. For example, sport managers are interested in running promotions for season ticket holders, and they need to know the loyalty levels of fans by examining their purchase histories, word of mouth, membership durations, and donation amounts from their internal databases. Moreover, fans' social media posts are valuable inputs for selecting the most loyal fans. The former types of information are often available within the company's internal database as structured data, whereas individual social media interactions are stored in service providers' servers and are mostly unstructured. In this case, organizations should implement a system that cleans and stores social media data in the central repository and retrieves it when needed by using various matching algorithms (e.g., name, phone, locations, profile pictures). Database management systems commonly used in sport include Microsoft SQL Server, Core e-business solutions, Amazon Redshift, and SSB Data Management Software. Thus, the data warehouse is vital because it stores data from private and public sources and provides rich information to organizations so that they can make optimal decisions. In the next section, we will discuss some analytical techniques that can help managers obtain critical business insights.

An example of a data warehouse is TruMedia. TruMedia provides custom developed sports data warehousing and analytics solutions to professional teams and sports media. With the ability to handle a large volume of data, TruMedia designed its data warehouse to be user friendly, and can be accessed through the sports SQL language. TruMedia also helps sports analysts and commentators display position data through graphics such as heat maps to enhance the interpretation of athletes' performance.

INTERVIEW WITH NORBERT HERMAN, DIRECTOR — CONSUMER & TRAVEL SOLUTIONS LEADER, IBM

In this short interview, Mr. Herman shares with us IBM's perspective and the state of data management in sport.

Question: Can you tell us how important sport industry is to IBM?

Norbert Herman: Let us start by specifying the lens that we look through and what we measure for? From a revenue perspective, the sport business is microscopic. We make our big money from the financial sector, public sector, health sector and other big industry. Brand wise, sport is very important. That is why we have many sponsorships worldwide. Our sponsorship of the Wimbledon is one example. We have a deep and rich tradition of sponsoring many large sports events. Mainly because sport communicates with the human and leaves an emotional impact, therefore, it is critical to brand value. We are also constantly and heavily devoted to research into technology that impacts human experience in any vertical. We have done some great work with the Toronto Raptors, where we used artificial intelligence to help with the recruiting mechanism of what kind of players do you bring in the team, how does the team form dynamics of performance as a team, how do you increase the odds of being a great performing franchise. So, I would say sports play a critical role in our business, but it is by no means through the lens of just revenue.

Question: Can you share about the state of big data and sport industry today?

Norbert Herman: I would say, in the broader world of entertainment as well as in the narrow space of sports, big data will play a key role for both the fan and the sport athlete. A couple of reasons: One is the volume of data that is available and two is the quality of data about the human psyche. For example, we do not write about things until we are extremely happy or extremely mad. I mean, there are many other feelings, than that. As people create digital content, along the transactional data, we can capture the insights related to how they feel towards a particular product or experience. The ability to understand and to be able to pause that data, means that we can take a picture or upload a video, do commentary on it, and figure out which part of the world and what human psychology has influenced that piece of data. A key contribution in this space is the science of psycholinguistics. What we write provides a level of unguarded transparency.

(Continued)

(Continued)

What we say and how we say it provides a great view into our heads and hearts.

At IBM, we are comfortable with the mountains of data that are being generated. One could spend massive amounts of time on the wrong dataset because one does not understand how to very quickly piece together what one is after, based on what is available to one. Good AI tools and processes allow you to maneuver those mountains of data to pull them through and to piece out the insights that you are after with your hypotheses. They allow you to quickly validate and invalidate with your hypotheses by going at the activation point and testing out your theories. I usually use the framework of the discover, decide, automate, activate for such experimentation. This is a very common framework that we use in the marketing technology side of things. But I think it is very applicable to big data because until you activate that insight, you don't know whether you wasted your time or not. And we get typically over-enamored with discovering the right datasets or maybe running very complex and sophisticated ensembles of AI or we might get very enamored with the throughput and automation of how quickly we can surface these insights. While all of that is meaningless until you get to the activation touchpoints to know whether your hypotheses is correct and now you are starting to see a trend, that trend is shifting to another domain.

SOCIAL MEDIA DATA ANALYTICS PRACTICES

The analysis of social media content has become a core activity owing to the availability of enormous amounts of data through web-based application programming interfaces. Analytics refers to, "the practical application of data analysis to real-world problems to inform the choice of decision-makers in sport organizations" (Bill Gerrard, 2021). The science of analyzing and interpreting social media data has been propelled by various computational and methodological advances. Some of the commonly used general analytical approaches include audio analytics (e.g., speech analytics), video analytics (e.g., edge-based analytics, server-based analytics), and text analytics (e.g., computational linguistics, machine learning, sentiment analysis). Although these different data analytics approaches are available, we find that sentiment analysis, social network analysis, and statistical analysis (e.g., predictive modeling) are the most widely used social media analytical approaches in sport management. In addition, while video and image analysis are in the early stages of development and are rarely used for purposes other than on-field performance analytics, the capability to be able to analyze video and image data could significantly impact the sport business by providing additional data points to better understand consumers. The approaches described in the following sections have been selected, as an example, from among a few existing social media analytics approaches. The descriptions of each of these approaches are not comprehensive. Instead, they serve to encourage further exploration of the use of the underlying techniques in sport-related research.

Sentiment Analytics

Because social media are diverse and contain noise, managers aim to uncover subjective information to inform their business decisions, also referred to as opinion mining. Sentiment analysis is an ideal technique to identify and extract subjective information from user-generated content. At its core, sentiment analysis mainly uses two methods: machine learning and lexical-based learning. Moreover, sentiment analysis uses supervised, semi-supervised, and unsupervised machine learning models. Supervised machine learning models infer a function from given labeled input data assigned by the researcher, whereas unsupervised learning allows the computer to find its own structure without human guidance. Moreover, sentiment analysis mainly relies on machine learning techniques (e.g., Naïve Bayes, support vector machine, matrix factorization) to categorize contents as negative and positive by assigning weighted sentiment scores to themes and topics within a text data. The tools that are often used to compute sentiment analysis include but are not limited to Lexalytics, SentiWordNet, SentiStrength, Social Mention, and Trackur. In the case of Lexaytics, it provides sentiment and intent analysis to gain the richest possible insights from complex text documents by using deep learning (e.g., natural language processing) ability. For example, this analytics tool allows sport managers to automatically categorize how fans feel about the game and/services.

Within the sport management domain, sentiment analysis is a fast-growing trend, and extant studies have employed this approach to generate domain-specific knowledge (Burton, 2019; Chang, 2019; Fan *et al.*, 2020). Chang (2019) examined 328,000 tweets in real-time to measure spectators' emotional responses during the 2016 Super Bowl. Data were collected through Twitter search application program from the Panthers and the Broncos fans during the Super Bowl game. Change (2019) used a lexicon-based text mining approach to categorize tweets into five different emotions. The findings indicated that fans expressed positive emotions when their team scored, whereas they expressed negative emotions when the opponent's team scored.

Sentiment analysis can provide important information about organizational changes (e.g., strategies, structure, and culture), as well as individual and group behaviors, thereby enhancing decision-making in terms of informing sport organizations about fans' experience, brand reputation, public opinion, etc. This technique is important in sport management research to process and communicate complex insights to quickly absorb their meaning and make decisions. The growing availability of social media and modern analytical techniques represents an essential resource for sport managers, analysts, policymakers, and other stakeholders to evaluate aggregated data and generate effective infographic reports that highlight the organic relationships among variables to explain complex phenomena. This is important for evaluating sport organizations' performances at the macro (e.g., social change/impact, group dynamics), meso (e.g., reputation and image), and micro (e.g., fans' attitude toward services) levels, as well as increasing manager ability to make effective decisions.

Social Network Analytics

Social network analysis is the process of analyzing the structures of social networks to explain how these networks operate and analyzing the complex set of relationships within a network (Wasserman and Faust, 2019). Social network analysis has emerged as a key technique in sport management, suggesting that an understanding of the structures of networks provides important insights to sport organizations. Given that sport fans communicate and interact through social media, it is unsurprising that many studies have examined the informal relationships among fans, athletes, teams, and sport governing bodies. Social network analysis can be used to perform statistical and visual analyses of the individual relationships within a network based on measures such as network density, network centrality, and network flow.

One of the primary benefits of social network analysis is that it illustrates various invisible patterns of interaction to identify and assess important groups within a network.

By using social network analysis, Yan *et al.* (2019) investigated patterns of attention and power in the data associated with the European Football Championship League final match. By retrieving data from various Twitter networks associated with the Champions League's hashtag #UCL, they collected 19,869 pre-match posts, 3,276 halftime posts, and 5,691 post-match posts. The authors used a data scraping software, NodeXL, to collect content attached to #UCL during the pre-match, halftime, and post-match periods. The findings suggested that large sport teams and superstar athletes have a stable and privileged status in the organization of these networks.

To help facilitate social networking analysis, sentiment analysis, and other types of analysis as shown in Table 2, there are a number of data mining and analytics software programs that make possible the data scraping and acquisition as well as data analysis processes.

Table 2. Data Mining and Analytics Software Programs and Web Sources Used in Published Works.

Data Mining/Analytics Software/Web Sources	Description of the Tool
DiscoverText	used a text analytics solution called DiscoverText — http://discovertext.com
ck	used HTTrack, an offline browser software, to capture the main page of blog posts the authors investigated
NVivo10	used text analytics software NVivo10
Omniture	used Omniture, an online marketing and web analytics tool that tracks website referrals
Pajek (PAY- yek)	used Pajek (PAY- yek) software program to conduct a social network analysis
sportsfangraph.com	used sportsfangraph.com, a site that tracks the number of fans that like teams on Facebook and who follow them on Twitter
Searchtastic	Used the online tool Searchtastic, to download tweets
Twazzup	used Twazzup (the Twitter search engine) that identifies key Twitter users who actively tweet about a given key word, denoting them as "influencers" on that specific topic
Twitalyzer	Used Twitalyzer, a Twitter analytics tool

LEARNING ACTIVITY 1

Go to Google Scholar and search for articles using the keywords "Sport," "Social media," and "Social Network Analysis," and identify two articles that you find from your search. Make sure that those two articles are (a) published in the last five years and (b) the articles have actually used social network analysis. For the latter, the abstract of the articles on Google Scholar can help you find out the specific type of method that the articles employed. Then, download the articles or ask your librarian to find the articles for you, and read the method sections of the articles. Summarize how the articles used social networking analysis in their study in a maximum of two paragraphs for each article.

Some of the data mining and analytics software programs and web sources used in published scientific works are presented in Table 2.

CASE STUDY: SPORTS PERFORMANCE PLATFORM

Microsoft has developed a Sports Performance Platform (SPP) for data mining and customized sports analytics solution projects. The SPP helps both athletes and sport teams make better, faster, and more data-driven decisions. The SPP not only collects historical data to help it gain a competitive edge, but it also bridges the gap between collecting and organizing data and predicting trends and making faster decisions. Teams such as the Seattle Reign FC, Real Sociedad, and Sport Lisboa e Benfica are using the SPP's predictive outcome modeling and analytics capabilities to improve player performance.

The SPP gives athletes and teams access to advances in cloud computing, data aggregation, machine learning, and predictive analytics. These actions would modify the decisions they make based on new data-driven methods, whether in the locker room or in the athletic performance laboratory. Furthermore, coaches could have aggregate insight into an athlete's performance, recovery, and readiness. The SPP also helps coaches run predictive modeling for injury prevention, make clutch decisions about game-day availability, and design practice regimens that can keep athletes play at their optimum. Moreover, SPP creates customized solutions that will deliver the next generation of sports performance for athletes and teams everywhere. The rapid growth of machine learning techniques is likely to enhance the application of SPP in various sport settings substantially.

QUESTIONS FOR DISCUSSION

1. What are the major challenges of implementing data mining tools in sports businesses?
2. What statistics are deemed as more important than others?

(*Continued*)

(Continued)

3. Do you see any adverse consequences of using data mining in sports? If so, what?
4. If a venture capitalist funded you to create a competitor to the SPP, how would you go about doing that? What data mining approach might you offer to potential customers?

Statistical Analytics

Statistical analytics methods have been widely applied to structured data to explain the relationships between two phenomena in the sport management domain. A few of these statistical techniques are regression models, correlation analyses, structural models, factor analysis, trend analyses, and Markov Chain Monte Carlo method. However, thus far, studies that used statistical techniques to gain insights from social media data have been limited in practice and in published research due to the fact that social media data are typically unstructured and need to be transformed into a coded format that is suitable for forecasting various possibilities. Statistical analytics uses both supervised and unsupervised learning models to provide answers to questions such as what is likely to happen, what is going to happen, and why it will happen (Gandomi and Haider, 2015). The following are some additional social media data collection and analytics tools along with YouTube or Vimeo tutorials.

LEARNING ACTIVITY - 2

Identify a Twitter account of a player or a team that you usually follow. Watch three of your preferred videos from Table 3 and try to apply the data mining or analytics tool discussed in your preferred tutorial. Describe your learnings in one paragraph for each of the three tutorial videos that you have selected.

Table 3. Social Media Data Collection and Analytics Tools/ Software Programs.

Social Media Collection & Analytics Tools	Purpose	YouTube Tutorials
NCapture	Helps to quickly and easily capture content like web pages, online PDFs and social media for analysis in NVivo 10	https://youtu.be/ hcU7LvfMQr8
DiscoverText	Collects, cleans, and analyzes text and social data streams	https://vimeo. com/55175059
DataSift	Online tool that collects live data, as well as a comprehensive cache of past contributions, from a variety of social media sites	https://youtu.be/ Wng1M8sEYpw
IssueCrawler	An academic tool for discovering linked content on the web	https://youtu.be/ qMlYhyyLQaU
NodeXL	Helps collect data from a variety of sites about organizations that are connected to your accounts	https://youtu.be/ pwsImFyc0lE
Pajek	Conducts a social network's analysis	https://youtu.be/ PRrKo0maZ8Y
33Across	Helps analyze how audiences interact with the brand's social media interactions. Helps to get insight into how people view, consume, and share content across devices	https://youtu.be/ FGve4JYJV7k
Brandwatch	Monitors conversations across various social networks. Helps conduct sentiment analysis	https://youtu. be/6k8wRGjSAK8 https://youtu. be/4Pwk3Edruuo
Google Analytics	Can be used to determine the conversion value of visitors from social sites as well as see how visitors from different social sites behave on an organizations' site	https://youtu.be/ D7S4KmM204w

(Continued)

Table 3. (*Continued*)

Social Media Collection & Analytics Tools	Purpose	YouTube Tutorials
Moz Analytics	Helps visualize data. It collects, and offers insights into how one measures up to the competition	https://youtu.be/ mnPUfiIj7u4
Salesforce Analytics	Helps to gather and analyze social media chatter	https://youtu.be/ vfu29tVREzc
Social Mention	Aggregates user-generated content from across social media sites	https://youtu.be/ YQp8i5EUEWs
SentiStrength	It estimates the strength of positive and negative sentiment in online texts	https://youtu.be/ JE-5Nd6dzGU

SOCIAL MEDIA DATA MANAGEMENT AND GOVERNANCE

While social media is widely available, its complexity and its usefulness for business purposes is highly dependent on governance, policies, and the way social media operates across different jurisdictions. Data governance refers to the overall management of the availability, usability, quality, privacy, ownership, ethical issues, and security of data. In other words, data management and governance can be considered as both organizational processes and structures. Data governance is an extension of IT governance, and it targets the process of leveraging of different types of information systems, including data mining, data warehousing, and analytics, as well as the proper use of data. Therefore, organizations often look for standards, processes, and control mechanisms to ensure the accessibility and protection of data. For example, the NBA's (2020) Privacy Policy states that:

"When you interact with us through the Services, we may collect data from you or from other sources. This "data" may be information that you directly provide to us, such as personal information you provide when you visit the Services, or information that is passively or automatically collected from you, such as anonymous information collected from your browser or device. The categories of other sources from which we collect personal data include our affiliates, partners, vendors, data brokers and public sources. The data we collect consists of personal identifiers, commercial information, Internet/other electronic network activity information, geolocation data, professional or employment-related information, characteristics of protected classifications, and inferences drawn from this information."

Moreover, the NBA's social media policy outlines social network usage guidelines for players, coaches, and teams. More specifically, the NBA prohibits players from using social media 45 minutes before game time.

Extant documents indicate that regulatory requirements, access to data, privacy issues, and ethical issues are among the primary factors that must be controlled to achieve robust data management and governance within organizations. For example, while China is the world's second-largest digital economy and it accounts for 40% of global e-commerce, access to digital information is heavily regulated and restricted (Meltzer, 2020). The four main steps toward the development of an effective social media governance policy are as follows: (a) develop a formal data governance policy or refine the existing policy, (b) involve all stakeholders when developing a policy, (c) comply with legal and regulatory requirements, and (d) evaluate new technologies to support data governance. A comprehensive social media management and governance strategy within a sport organization should be created by following the aforementioned steps to address the organization's objectives.

The issue of effective data management and governance of social media usage is vital for the success of sport organizations. Good governance enhances the capability of the stakeholders from individual business units. Researchers and practitioners should be prepared to overcome multiple challenges in the pursuit of understanding and using social media. Because social media is considered a major source of big data and has massive monetary value associated with it, it is heralded as the New Raw Material of the 21st

Century (Berners-Lee and Shadbolt, 2011). Along this line of thought, perhaps the most challenging steps in the management of social media data are identifying the owner of the data and outlining the extent to which third parties can use the said data.

KEY SKILLS FOR PRACTICE

Technical skills are of utmost importance in social media data management. Data management professionals need to have skills such as dealing with real-time data (to help inform timely decisions), enhancing data quality (know-how of technological tools to screen out valuable data), managing data warehouse architecture (know-how in identifying compatible warehouse from the several options available), and data security skills (a few short-term data security certificate programs are available).

Change management skills are required in data management. In the world of digital media, technological advancements are being introduced on an on-going basis. To cope with and effectively manage the constantly changing technology, one needs to improve her/his change management skills. A skilled management and implementation of changes within a data management department is not only essential but a must. For this, a professional needs to be proactive in the management of change by continuously keeping oneself up-to-date (about the current situation), recognizing trends, and anticipating future occurrences based on trends, and then preparing oneself to design a timely solution that fills the gap.

Decision-making skill is another skill a data management professional needs to develop. The top management relies on a data management professional when it comes to recommendations about new data technologies. In this regard, one needs to develop strong decision-making skills. Decision-making skills involve identifying problems, generating alternative solutions, evaluating the alternatives, and selecting the best alternative. In this regard, technological innovations vary in terms of their complexity, compatibility to the existing system, and technological readiness of the organization. Therefore, one cannot adopt and utilize all the technological innovation introduces to the sport industry. However, based on your decision-making skills, you can define needs, identify alternatives, evaluate them, and decide if the new technology is usable, compatible, and valuable to your organization.

Communication skill is an essential in social media data management. In fact, in data management, the most important thing is making sense of data, interpreting it, and reporting the findings in one or two pages of summary to inform the top managements' decisions. Simply put, your job is to turn complex data into actionable insights, and present it in the most comprehensible way. However good one is in data mining and analytical skills though, unless the person communicates the findings effectively, the hard work that is put into data mining and analytics will be greatly degraded. Therefore, you need to work on your communication skills, which include writing skills and making speeches. Remember that data are meaningless without people to interpret and report them.

TRENDS AND CURRENT ISSUES

It is commonly known that the top management are reluctant to adopt new technological innovations, understandably because they involve uncertainty (risks as well as rewards). In the same way, social media and the management of the data have not been any different. Top management have been reluctant to invest in social media as discussed in Chapter 15. However, the top managements' view towards social media and digital data is changing gradually and becoming part of normal business practice in most sport organizations.

One of the challenges that data management faces today is the issue of data integration. At present, we are in the age of data abundance, but what good does data do unless it is manageable? In this regard, data integration becomes important. For example, one might be able to mine a one-year Twitter data from a professional sport team's account. But it is not easy (although possible) to identify those conversations specifically related to ticket sales, merchandise sales, parking, tech related comments, etc. Hence, there are multiple data points within the massive data available, and linking those data points and assembling them to have a structured valuable dataset that produces actionable insights is not an easy task.

Data security is another issue in the area of data management. The question of who owns social media data, who should access it and who should not, and the ethics behind its use are concerns voiced over the past few years. The concerns are not only related to access to consumers data that the companies who own social media platforms have, but also possible cyber-attacks by hackers. LinkedIn's 2012 massive cyber-attack is one example. In fact, social platforms have stringent platform security, and also have bug bounty programs and their own security blogs. Yet, users' security concerns remain.

CHAPTER SUMMARY

With the rise of social media and digital data in the past decade, a variety of unstructured, semi-structured, and structured digital data have been generated on different social media platforms (e.g., Facebook, Twitter, YouTube, Instagram) by various entities (e.g., athletes, coaches, teams, fans, governing bodies) in different form of data (e.g., text, images, and video and audio files). These social media data are being used to inform both on-the-field (e.g., scouting) and off-the-field (e.g., customers service) decisions. Having covered the basics of data (e.g., text, image, video and audio files), this chapter provided an overview of four specific topic areas related to social media data management. These topic areas are data mining, data analytics, data warehousing, and data governance. The chapter also discussed the key skills necessary for social media data management including technology skills, decision-making skills, communication skills, and change management skills. In its last section, the chapter discussed trends and current practices in data management related to data integration, data security, and top management support.

KEY RESOURCES

- MIT Sloan Sports analytics conference: www.sloansports conference.com.
- Big Data in Sports Analytics (SSAC17): https://youtu. be/2PHWyat3Tw8.
- Transforming Big Data Into Compelling Insights: https://youtu. be/c4vsfzGzSMg.

TEST YOUR KNOWLEDGE

1. Identify the three data types discussed in this chapter and briefly describe them.
2. How do you describe multi-modality? Provide examples.
3. Define data mining and identify two examples of data mining software programs.
4. Define data analytics and identify two examples of data analytics tools.
5. Define data warehouse and provide two examples of data warehouse used in sport.
6. Define data governance and describe issues associated with it (at least, two issues).
7. Identify the four key skills necessary in social media data management, and briefly describe each.

REFERENCES

Bill Gerrard, D. (2020). In T. Slack, T. Byers, & A. Thurston. (Eds). *Understanding Sport Organizations: Applications for Sport Managers* (pp. 394–408). Human Kinetics Publishers.

Broughton, D. (2017). How the research was conducted, surprises you may find. *Sport Business Journal.* https://www.sportsbusinessdaily.com/ Journal/Issues/2017/07/17/Research-and-Ratings/Social-sidebar.asp x?hl=social+media+posts+by+NBA+and+NFL+&sc=0.

Burton, N. (2019). Exploring user sentiment towards sponsorship and ambush marketing. *International Journal of Sports Marketing and Sponsorship, 20*(4), 583–602, 687–705.

Chang, Y. (2019). Spectators' emotional responses in tweets during the Super Bowl 50 game. *Sport Management Review, 22*(3), 348–362.

Fan, M., Billings, A., Zhu, X., and Yu, P. (2020). Twitter-based BIRGing: Big Data analysis of English national team fans during the 2018 FIFA World Cup. *Communication and Sport, 8*(3), 317–345.

Gandomi, A. and Haider, M. (2015). Beyond the hype: Big data concepts, methods, and analytics. *International Journal of Information Management, 35*(2), 137–144.

Golfarelli, M. and Rizzi, S. (2009). *Data warehouse design: Modern principles and methodologies.* McGraw-Hill, Inc.

NBA.com. (2020). NBA Privacy Policy. Retrieved September 4, 2020, from https://www.nba.com/news/privacy_policy.html.

Meltzer, J. (2020). China's digital services trade and data governance: How should the United States respond? Retrieved November 28, 2020, from https://www.brookings.edu/articles/chinas-digital-services-trade-and-data-governance-how-should-the-united-states-respond/.

Statistical Analysis System (n.d.). Predictive analytics and AI deliver a winning fan experience. SAS. https://www.sas.com/en_hk/customers/orlando-magic.html.

Slack, T., Byers, T. and Thurston, A. eds. (2020). *Understanding Sport Organizations: Applications for Sport Managers.* Human Kinetics Publishers.

Wang, Y., Kung, L., and Byrd, T. A. (2018). Big data analytics: Understanding its capabilities and potential benefits for healthcare organizations. *Technological Forecasting and Social Change, 126*, 3–13.

Wasserman, S. and Faust, K. (2019). *Social Network Analysis: Methods and Applications.* New York, NY: Cambridge University Press.

Yan, G., Watanabe, N. M., Shapiro, S. L., Naraine, M. L., and Hull, K. (2019). Unfolding the Twitter scene of the 2017 UEFA Champions League Final: Social media networks and power dynamics. *European Sport Management Quarterly, 19*(4), 419–436.

Zafarani, R., Abbasi, M. A., and Liu, H. (n.d.). *Social Media Mining.* 299–314. https://doi.org/10.1017/cbo9781139088510.013.

Chapter 8

Social Media and Relationship Marketing in Sport

Rebecca Achen* and Gashaw Abeza†

*Illinois State University, United States
†Towson University, United States

CHAPTER OBJECTIVES

After studying this chapter, you will be able to:

- Define the concept of relationship marketing
- Describe relationship marketing as a business approach
- Explain the application of relationship marketing in sport
- Describe the intersection between social media and relationship marketing in sport
- Identify the three core components of relationship marketing
- Identify the benefits of social media in building relationships with customers
- Apply the principles of relationship marketing to social media content creation
- Create a plan for addressing contemporary issues using social media to build relationships

KEY TERMS

Communication
Customer retention
Engagement
Interaction
Long-term relationship

Relationship marketing
Social listening
Value
Value co-creation

INTRODUCTION

Social media's expansive reach in society has presented a variety of opportunities for stakeholders in the sport industry. Sports teams, leagues, athletes, events, fans, sponsors, and other sports entities use social media platforms for multiple purposes. For example, sports marketers employ social media as a medium to carry out marketing communications such as news updates, sales, advertising, public relations, internal communications, and relationship marketing (Abeza *et al.*, 2020). While social media platforms serve as an important tool for achieving marketing communication goals, they appear particularly valuable for realizing relationship marketing objectives.

Relationship marketing is the process of establishing, maintaining, and enhancing relationships between an organization and its stakeholders with the central goal of retaining a stakeholder through long-term mutual satisfaction (Grönroos, 2004). As a process, relationships are to be maintained and enhanced on an ongoing basis, and two or more parties are required to communicate, interact, and engage in dialogue. Because of this, entities need to employ effective communication mediums, and social media platforms arc effective platforms for ongoing multi-way dialogue. This notion is primarily based on the nature of social media, which is inherently relationship-centric.

In adopting a relationship marketing approach, businesses are able to listen to and understand customers' needs, deliver a co-created product, build long-term relationships, and, eventually, secure long-term profit through continuous dialogue (Grönroos, 2000). By extension, the dialogue enables businesses to achieve goals such as increased loyalty, reduced marketing costs, increased profitability, and increased financial stability and security (Abeza *et al.*, 2020). In the sport industry, relationship marketing can be an effective marketing approach, considering the challenges that sports organizations and fans are facing today (Achen, 2019). For sports fans, for instance, ticket prices and merchandise costs are rising faster than inflation over the course of time, and at the same time, alternative entertainment options are becoming increasingly available to them (Lawrence *et al.*, 2020). Such factors are discouraging fans from continuing to monetize their loyalty to a sport team (Abeza *et al.*, 2020). Additionally, the COVID-19 pandemic altered sports consumption significantly by pausing the majority of in-person sports events. Social media allowed a channel for sports organizations to maintain communication and interaction with fans during the pandemic.

The operational costs for sports organizations also are on the rise (Čečević *et al.*, 2020), thus, preserving a sport team's fan base while increasing fan loyalty are the primary challenges facing sports marketers today (Lee *et al.*, 2020). Further, there are some unique relational features in the sport industry (e.g., fans attachment to a sport team) that offer a conducive environment for applying a relationship marketing approach. In embracing the approach, sports organizations can listen to and communicate with customers (i.e., build a relationship) and address customer needs and desires, while maintaining and enhancing their fan base (Achen, 2014).

The purpose of this chapter is to discuss the use and value of social media as a relationship marketing tool. Specifically, the chapter covers the concept of relationship marketing, its application as a business approach, its implementation in the sport industry, and the intersection between social media and relationship marketing in sport. The chapter also discusses social media content management and platform use in sport.

HISTORY AND BACKGROUND

While relational approaches to marketing have existed for as long as the history of trade and commerce (Ballantyne *et al.*, 2003), relationship marketing started to attract the attention of a great number of marketing researchers and practitioners beginning in the 1980s

(Payne and Frow, 2017). In academia, relationship marketing dominated the business management research in the 1990s, receiving coverage in a number of academic books, journals, and conferences. The prominence of a relational perspective in business management research has also been reflected in the 2000s in the definition of marketing that was released by the American Marketing Association (AMA). Marketing is, "the activity, set of institutions, and processes for creating, communicating, delivering, and exchanging offerings that have value for customers, clients, partners, and society at large" (AMA, 2020, p. 1). The AMA issued, revised, and renewed the definition of marketing that had been used since 1938. It incorporated relational concepts in its successive revisions released in 2004, and maintained those concepts in updates in 2007, 2013 (O'Malley, 2014), and 2017. With its widespread application in academic research and practice, research has been conducted on the topic over the past 50 years.

In practice, relationship marketing rose in popularity as shifts in consumer profiles and business goals revealed a lack in traditional marketing models for businesses, especially those in the service industry (Egan, 2004). Today, relationships are a common part of everyday business talk, language, activity, and purpose. The traditional marketing models, which focused on increasing transactions, were not sufficient in an environment where customers expected businesses to meet their individual needs and businesses had shifted their main focuses to customer retention. Relationship marketing offers strategies and tactics more congruent with the needs of the service industry, which is characterized by intangibility, inseparability, variability, and perishability (Egan, 2004). The following section discusses the key concepts for understanding relationship marketing as a business approach and its application in the sport industry.

RELATIONSHIP MARKETING AND SOCIAL MEDIA IN SPORT: KEY CONCEPTS

It is important to mention that relationship marketing is a diverse field with no single best explanation, clear domain, and scope. This chapter adopts the definition and understanding of relationship marketing as a management approach, as proposed by the Nordic school of thought. The central concept behind the relationship marketing approach is the management of a shared relationship between an organization and its stakeholders. The shared relationship is maintained and enhanced through communication and interaction, with the intent of producing mutual value. In maintaining and enhancing the communication and interaction process on a continuing basis and by fulfilling the promises made, companies will be able to deliver a co-created and customer-valued product (Gronroos, 2004). Tactically, the relationship marketing approach is designed to connect closely with customers and to gain more information about them, which enables businesses to deliver greater value to them (Peppers and Rogers, 2011). In maintaining a closer relationship with customers, learning about them, communicating and interacting with them, and developing a mutual understanding, companies become valuable to customers.

There are a number of benefits that result from a relationship marketing approach for companies and their customers. For companies, customer retention and loyalty are major concerns with the ever-changing customer expectations in competitive markets. Studies report that increasing customer retention rates by 5% results in a profit enhancement of 2580% (Feinberg and Kadam, 2002). Related studies (e.g., Kim and Trail, 2011) also state that attracting new customers can be up to five times more expensive than maintaining existing customers. In other words, losing an existing customer results in losing a long-term revenue stream and not just the loss of a single encounter or the particular sale that the customer represents. Hence, as noted above, a relationship marketing approach can result in increased profitability, stability, and security. These benefits can be realized in communicating positive word of mouth, fostering loyalty among customers, and reducing the cost of serving customers over time.

In traditional business transactions, each stakeholder may act to satisfy its own interest. However, in a relational exchange, partners are given special recognition of their interest, and such previous recognitions inform an exchange that takes place at a particular time and influence future actions. Thus, within the context of the relationship, neither party acts entirely independently of the other. A relationship marketing approach provides a list of benefits to customers including minimized searching costs, familiarity with service offerings, reduction of perceived risks associated with future purchase choices, greater efficiency in decision-making, and cognitive consistency in decisions (Abeza *et al.*, 2019). For example, a sport organization adopting a relationship-marketing approach would focus their efforts beyond making an initial sale. On social media, this would involve providing content that gives fans an inside look into the organization, for instance, during a team practice or at a community-service event. Season ticket holders may be given opportunities to meet and interact with the players and coaches to get added value from their partnership with the team. Another example could be assigning a relationship executive to a slate of ticket accounts whose sole job is to check-in with their list of customers periodically to ask for feedback, search for issues that can be resolved, and build a connection with them. This type of pre-emptive customer service makes customers feel valued and addresses their concerns proactively while helping an organization solve problems before they cause customers to avoid making a future purchase.

APPLICATION OF RELATIONSHIP MARKETING IN SPORT

As noted, relationship marketing is a customer-focused strategy that includes any marketing activity used to establish, develop, enhance, and maintain customer relationships. In sport, all marketing transactions involve relationship marketing to some degree. To help sports marketers advance from the transactional end of marketing to the relational end, Shani (1997) was the first to present a framework for relationship marketing in sport. The first step in his framework is to segment the market and break those segments into smaller niches, which can be targeted more effectively. Then, teams can build customer databases to identify core customers and tailor personalized communications to each customer, a strategy that moves them toward relationship marketing. Finally, once a sport organization has fully adopted relationship marketing, it can start to implement strategies aimed at building bonds with fans.

Sports marketers should shift from a transaction-based to a relationship-marketing-based orientation because sport is an ideal setting for relationship marketing (Achen, 2014). Partially, this is because it is very similar to the service industry. At its core, relationship marketing focuses on serving customer needs by collaborating with them through mutually beneficial and participatory relationships. Additionally, relationship marketing is more effective in competitive markets where consumers continually desire and demand the product (Buhler and Nufer, 2010). Thus, shifting marketing strategy from methods meant to drive transactions to those aimed at building customer relationships will make sports organizations more prosperous in the competitive environment. Customer retention is also an essential business outcome in the sport industry because creating a loyal fan base leads to repeat attendance, more merchandise purchases, and increased interest from sponsors. While a number of relationship marketing benefits are available both for companies and their partners, its effectiveness depends on the tool(s) a company uses to carry out communications and interactions on an ongoing basis. For this, social media is increasingly becoming an accepted set of digital tools that enable parties to engage in real-time communication, interaction, and multi-way dialogue.

SOCIAL MEDIA AND RELATIONSHIP MARKETING IN SPORT

As discussed, the central intent of relationship marketing is retaining consumers through the long-term mutual satisfaction between businesses and consumers. The retention of customers is maintained and enhanced through communication and interaction, with the intent of producing a co-created and a mutually valued product. In this regard, social media includes valuable channels for the practical implementation of relationship marketing approaches. Particularly, the features of social media such as its speed, ubiquity, instantaneity, network, participation, collaboration, and real-time play a significant role in facilitating the building of meaningful relationships. Hence, connecting with customers through social media gives marketers the opportunity to engage with them in a more direct, effective, and timely manner, thereby, providing opportunities for sports organizations and consumers to participate in value co-creation. Moreover, social media allows sports organizations to encourage interactions with fans outside of their home market, thus building relationships with customers across the globe.

For instance, a sport organization can post a content on its Facebook page and followers may comment on the posted content. Then, the organization may respond to the comments and start to engage in back-and-forth exchanges. Such interaction allows an organization to listen in real-time directly to users, address consumers' constantly changing needs and desires, fulfill promises, gain a commonly shared understanding, and, over time, co-create a commonly shared value. For this, sports organizations have to be willing to commit resources to social media to effectively interact and connect with consumers.

The use, place, and significance of social media as a vehicle for relationship marketing value creation from an organization, platform, and consumer domain have been investigated by Abeza *et al.* (2020). Please see Figure 1 for a summary of the reported findings. With an understanding of relationship marketing as a three-stage process, the authors investigated the value of social media as a relationship marketing tool. The three stages they describe are communication, interaction, and value/co-created value, which are commonly referred to as CIV.

- Communication refers to an act of broadcasting content by a sport organization that is meant to inform the consuming public about a good or service.

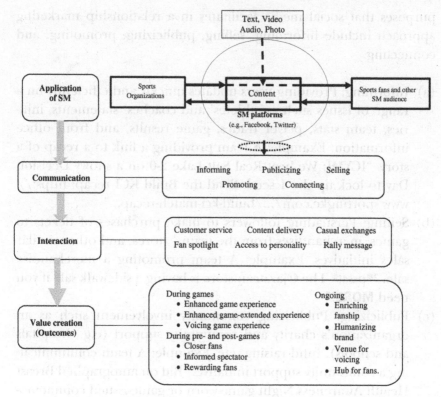

Figure 1. Social Media Use as a Relationship Marketing Tool in Sport

- Interaction refers to a multi-way reciprocal exchange of content, where two or more parties acquire access to shared information through interaction.
- Value/co-created value refers to adding greater or extra value, on top of the core product offering (i.e., the game), that emerges through the process of communication and interaction.

Communication

While the extent to which sports organizations use their different social media platforms for varied communication purposes fluctuates, five commonly intended purposes can be identified. The purposes that social media facilitates in a relationship marketing approach include informing, selling, publicizing, promoting, and connecting.

(a) Informing: Providing users updates quickly and efficiently on a range of issues such as athletes' and coaches' statements, injuries, team stats, player trades, game results, and front office information. Example: A team providing a link to a recap of a story. "ICYMI: We beat Real Salt Lake 2-0 on a snowy Decision Day to lock up the 1 seed. Read the Build KCI recap: https://www.sportingkc.com/.../build-kci-match-recap..."

(b) Selling: Persuading followers to make purchases of tickets to games, merchandises from the teams' stores, and other similar sales initiatives. Example: A team promoting a merchandise sale. "*pssst* The @jazzteamstore is having a sidewalk sale if you need **MORE**!"

(c) Publicizing: Publicizing community involvement such as an organization's charity and community support (e.g., hospitals and schools), fund raising, etc. Example: A team communicating a community support initiative. "Bid on autographed Breast Health Awareness Night game-worn or game-issued commemorative jerseys! Proceeds benefit Mayo Clinic Cancer Center to further breast cancer research and breast health awareness."

(d) Promoting: Stimulating sales through contests, sweepstakes, giveaways, lottery, raffles, and communicating these opportunities. Example: A team communicating promotional offers. "Season tickets on-sale today! RT this tweet for your chance to win a pair of tickets to the first game of the season!"

(e) Connecting: Recognizing fans' through content such as birthday and holiday wishes, or video and photograph contents, and providing non-sports-related information about players or behind-the-scenes looks at the organization. Example: A team personalizing its social media communication. "An unbreakable bond. Fighting Irish Tommy Tremble talks about growing up with Eric. A childhood friend whom he considers a brother."

LEARNING ACTIVITY 1

Find a social media account for your favorite sports team and examine the recent posts from that account.
1. Which of the above intended purposes (i.e., informing, publicizing, etc,) are you able to identify? Give an example of each from those posts.
2. Which one of the purposes that you identified has been most frequently communicated? And, why do you think that specific purpose was communicated most frequently by your favorite team?

Interaction

Interaction is the second component of the relationship marketing process. Interactions that are carried out on different social media platforms by sports organizations can be varied in nature. Some could simply be a two-way interaction between an organization and a follower or multi-way between an organization and its different followers. Some interactions could be frequent, others occasional, and some others irregular. While sports organizations may exhibit interactions that are not included in the following list, six commonly observed interaction types can be identified that are facilitated by social media. The types include customer service, fan spotlight, access to personality, casual exchanges, rally message, and content delivery.

(a) *Customer service.* In *customer service,* interactions can take place to address users' varied questions about the organization (from front office to a coaching staff) and troubleshooting technical issues such as online access. This type of interaction particularly involves addressing concerns and requests. Example: A customer sends a direct message to ask about the clear bag policy, which the organization answers via direct message.

(b) *Fan spotlight*: In *fan spotlight*, conversations will be initiated by followers related to event experiences, often using pictures during or after live events. For instance, fans posting about their appearance at an event, and the sport organization replying by recognizing their event attendance. Example: A fan tweets a picture of him/herself during the game and tags the sport organization. The sport organization replies to the fan thanking him/her for attending and retweets his/her message.

(c) *Access to personality*: In *access to personality*, sports organizations invite their followers to submit questions that a player will answer in real time. While interactions can take place between the player and the follower, it will be facilitated on the sport organization's social media platform. Example: Sue Bird, Seattle Storm's professional basketball player, answers questions from fans during a one-hour Twitter chat on Seattle Storm's Twitter page.

(d) *Casual exchanges*: In *casual exchange* interactions, conversations center around aspects of consumers' relationship to a sport organization (sharing enthusiasm for players and team, discussing concerns about team performance or roster moves, being followed back by the team account, receiving a birthday wish from the team, etc.). Example: A fan comments on a Facebook post about a player trade, exclaiming their excitement for the new player, and the organization responds to their comment.

(e) *Rally message*: In *rally message*, conversations are carried out around team campaign messages, which serve as a connection point where users come to interact, express their support, and engage in conversation with other followers. Some of these include the hashtag #ChiefsKingdom — Kansas City Chiefs — and #cowboysnation — Dallas Cowboys. Example: The Kansas City Chiefs send out a tweet asking fans to send pictures of where they are watching the game and include the hashtag #ChiefsKingdom.

(f) *Content delivery*: In *content delivery*, brief conversations are carried in response to followers' request for organization-related digital content, such as a video or GIF for a play made during the game or the request for a live stream of a practice session. Example: A Duke Basketball fan requests the organization stream their exhibition game.

Value

The value created by sports organizations via social media may vary depending on the level of communication and interaction taking place on a given platform. In the case of more than one organization working together on social media (e.g., a sponsor activating with a sport organization on a channel), we could call this co-creation of value. Despite the variation, social media platforms facilitate the (co-) creation of value in the process of followers' communication and interaction with an organization. As noted, communication and interaction are the first two stages in the relationship marketing process. The three (co-) created values include events, pre-and post-events, and on an ongoing basis.

(a) *During events.* Organizations can keep followers up-to-date (e.g., giving live play-by-play updates, scores, highlights), provide real-time customer service (e.g., problem fans encountered at a venue on game day), and serve as an avenue where fans come together to celebrate victory or discuss a loss. For example, fan expressing a game experience on Twitter and a team replying to the fan's tweet: @melycutie: Coincidence? I am wearing my Gallagher Tshirt and we have a 4-1 lead!!! @canadiensMTL, and @CanadiensMTL replied: @melycutie Not a coincidence. #GoHabsGo

(b) *Pre- and post-events.* The value created in pre- and post-events is usually initiated by sports organizations. Some of the value that can be (co-) created during these periods include bringing fans closer to an organization (e.g., offering an exclusive behind-the-scene information to fans such as backstage video, players injury update), enabling followers to be informed fans (e.g., providing information about upcoming or past games through contents such as event highlights, athletes training), and presenting rewards to fans (e.g., communication contests, prizes, and discounts). For example, a team providing access to behind-the-scene activities before games by interacting with fans: [a fan] @ScalabrineBrain: @STLLouisRams Can we see @MichaelBrockers locker? #ForeverLSU, and @RamsNFL replied: @ScalabrineBrain You got it! Big @MichaelBrockers [Picture of Brockers and Donald's locker]

(c) *Ongoing.* Sports organizations can use social media to facilitate the co-creation of value on an ongoing basis. The four commonly identified values are: enriching fanship (e.g., posting pictures of fans' families and friends on an organization's Facebook page), humanizing the brand (e.g., providing a personality to an organization through jokes and funny pictures), venue for voicing (e.g., allowing followers to voice their concerns, complaints, and questions, and responding to them), and hub for fans (e.g., serving as a venue where followers gather outside of live events to have content to react to and bond over). For example, giving a team a personality (e.g., jokes and funny pictures), engaging in a friendly interaction with fans: @chicagobulls: SO MUCH IS HAPPENING; @nataliaromnovaa replied: @chicagobulls STOP YELLING; @chicagobulls replied: @nataliaromnovaa WE CAN'T CONTROL THE SOUND OF OUR VOICE RIGHT NOW; and @ nataliaromnovaa replied: THIS IS SO WILD.

SOCIAL MEDIA CONTENT MANAGEMENT IN SPORT

If sports organizations are going to use social media from a relationship marketing perspective, then the goal should be to engage consumers in interaction and two-way communication. As such, the content posted by organizations should be designed to encourage engagement, discussion, and conversation, moving beyond information dissemination, to build deeper connections with customers. Engaging content is more likely to reach social media followers and be shared, which will ultimately increase the number of consumers that follow teams' social media pages. Engagement also has the ability to improve customer relationships and encourage customers to act as ambassadors by sharing content, which extends an organization's reach. While the term engagement has many meanings in marketing research, this chapter focuses an engagement as interaction with a brand on social media, based on the definition provided by Hudson *et al.* (2016), who state that interaction on social media is the, "proactive engagement with the brand on social media platforms such as following, replying, tweeting, sharing, liking, participating, and so on" (p. 3). Using this definition, the goal for sports marketers should be to encourage interaction by posting content that fans want to interact with and value.

Sports fans are interested in engagement and have been found to view social media as opportunities to interact, communicate, and connect with sports brands. They are interested in doing so because they want to portray their passion and connection to the team, demonstrate the hope they have for organizational success, meet their individual need to demonstrate their knowledge or share their experiences, and demonstrate a desire to belong to a group and build camaraderie. Thus, sports teams can encourage fans to interact by embracing these motivations. Additionally, sports fans are motivated to create content to show their love of the brand, contribute to content by interacting with it on the page because they want to influence the organization or others, and consume content to meet informational needs. In general, engagement with sports social media is also motivated by the need for integration and social interaction, that is, sports consumers will engage with the team on social media to feel like they are a part of something and to engage in discussions with others like them.

As mentioned previously, nurturing and encouraging engagement between sports customers and organizations is essential to social media strategy. Therefore, it is important to look at the strategies that are effective for building relationships and encouraging interaction with customers through social media. It is obvious that the type of content posted on social media platforms is essential for building relationships. However, there is no consensus in terms of what types of posts drive interaction. Research reports discuss that posts with social elements, social relevancy, or posts highlighting social causes show an increase in comments but a decrease in likes (Gutiérrez-Cillán *et al.*, 2017). Posts designed to entertain result in an increase in likes, comments, and shares in some studies but a decrease in likes in others (Tafesse, 2015). Posts that are focused on encouraging interaction, such as those that ask questions or request responses, do increase interaction, especially comments, however, there is some evidence that this strategy can decrease likes and shares (Schultz, 2017). Posts that promote contests have shown increases and decreases in likes (Gutierrez-Cillan *et al.*, 2017). Sales promotions, coupons, discounts, and product promotion posts can increase comments, likes, and shares (Coelho *et al.*, 2016), but they can also decrease likes (Cvijikj and Michahelles, 2013). Studies have found that informative posts can increase comments and likes or have no impact on likes or interactions in general (Kim and Yang, 2017). Content that is topical, humanized, and humorous can encourage likes and comments, and educational content can increase likes (Malhotra *et al.*, 2013). Customers are more likely to interact with posts that include videos, contests, and questions (Tafesse, 2016).

The above-mentioned research highlights an important fact for sports organizations — what encourages interaction is likely context-dependent, and potentially even organization-dependent. However, one over-arching theme in the research is that social media should be used to build relationships with customers instead of directly asking customers to make a purchase, especially since asking customers to purchase on social media does not generate likes (Swani *et al.*, 2013). More specifically, some studies in sport reported posts that posed questions were effective in getting individuals to interact (Thompson *et al.*, 2014). Additionally, behind-the-scenes content seems to be effective at encouraging interaction between fans and sports organizations (Achen, 2015; Thompson *et al.*, 2017). Sports consumers are also likely to engage with content that promotes players or team personnel, thus making it an effective type of content for building relationships (Achen, 2015). Using polls or creating contests that encourage fans to show their love for the brand can also increase engagement (Vale and Fernandes, 2018). For sports marketers, this means that designing content that will foster interactivity is essential to using social media to encourage consumer-brand engagement and improve relationships. Differences in content types support the notion that social media can be used in sport to build relationships, and that fans prefer this. Achen (2015, 2018) found that based on interaction data, fans prefer to use social media networks to connect directly to players and are not as interested in receiving traditional marketing messages on these platforms.

An important consideration for sports marketers is the off-season, when researchers suggest relationship-building content may be even more important because there is less direct contact with fans and fewer traditional marketing opportunities (Stavros *et al.*, 2014). Using social media to create dialogue and interaction opportunities in the off-season can help build stronger relationships year-round. Fans have even agreed, stating that interaction with a sporting event year-round is important to them (Thompson *et al.*, 2017). Player and personnel promotional content has also been found to encourage the highest levels of interaction in the off-season (Achen, 2018). This type of content includes behind-the-scenes content or human-interest stories about players. As Achen (2018) points out, fans are interested in the lives of players outside of the sport and enjoy connecting with them in this way.

Sports teams that desire to build relationships with customers via social media should move beyond disseminating information about the team and focus on posts that encourage interaction and provide customers with added value that connects them to the sport organization. While teams and organizations should still post informative content, such as trade announcements, injury reports, event promotions, and game results, strategy should move beyond these basic types of posts. Regardless of the content type, posts should be high quality. In conclusion, the types of content that consumers want are context-dependent. Thus, marketers need to assess the content needs and desires of their target market(s) on social media.

LEARNING ACTIVITY 2

Let's check your understanding of what types of posts can build relationships with customers! Take the time to visit three sports organizations' social media sites (and make sure to pick sites with lots of activity) and find a post on each site that you think is designed

(*Continued*)

(Continued)

to build relationships with customers by encouraging interaction and dialogue. Then answer these questions for each post.

1. Does the content of the post provide the customer with something more than they would find on the organization's website or on a news site?
2. Does the post avoid selling something to the customers or focusing on promoting purchases?
3. Are customers engaging with the post (commenting or sharing)?
4. Is the organization participating in the discussion by responding to comments on the post? If the answers are yes, you likely have a piece of content that is focused on relationship-building.
5. Are any other organizations tagged or associated with the post? If so, do you see it as evidence of the co-creation of value?

LEVERAGING THE RIGHT PLATFORMS

While there is not much academic research regarding which platform type might be better for building relationships, sports marketers should consider how sports fans might use social media platforms differently when creating content strategy meant to drive interactions. Research in the general business literature has compared consumers' uses of Twitter and Facebook. Logan (2014) found that consumers follow brands on Twitter to get information, but this was not a reason for following brands on Facebook. In fact, Logan (2014) suggested that Facebook might be more useful for starting conversations with customers that connect them with each other, instead of posting advertising or corporate messaging. Using Facebook and Twitter in these ways was also supported by Kwon *et al.* (2014) who revealed that Twitter was used to share and find information and Facebook was used to build social connections. Additionally, Facebook might be a better network for two-way dialogue with customers (Kim *et al.*, 2014). However, if a brand was proactive and responsive, Twitter could be a good network for engaging in conversation with consumers (Smith *et al.*, 2012). While research has not specifically compared how organizations use Instagram in relation to other networks, Instagram is widely regarded as a photo-sharing network and thus sports organizations could use this network to provide high-quality photos and videos for behind-the-scenes looks into the organization or report on game highlights. For more on identifying the right platform for a specific purpose and target market, please see Chapter 16.

Specifically in sport, Thompson *et al.* (2018) suggested that news and information were most common on Twitter, such as game information, and Facebook was used more for relationship-building content like fan polls and behind-the-scenes information. These differences in networks are also supported by research that found college sports entities use Facebook for interactivity (Wallace *et al.*, 2011), while Twitter is used for information dissemination (Doran *et al.*, 2015). Pinterest can also be a site for engaging with customers and interacting, especially by posting user-generated content or content that focuses on the fans to encourage interaction (Hambrick and Kang, 2015). Sports marketers should carefully consider their use of social media as part of their content strategy and focus on platforms that allow them to build relationships with customers.

PRACTITIONER PERSPECTIVE

Practitioner: Emily Wade, Social Media and Digital Marketing Manager with Kroenke Sports & Entertainment
Education: B. S., Sport Management, University of Kansas

(*Continued*)

(Continued)

What goals drive your social media strategy?
If I were to list three goals of our social media strategy, they'd be: creating a community, creating a personality, and creating revenue opportunities that fit the social media presence. My number one goal was always to create a community. I truly believe that, above all else, to have a dedicated and loyal fan base on social media will always be the best strategy. I went about creating a community in two ways: by responding to fans and my "inside joke" strategy, which gave our content a life of its own. If you didn't get the joke, you wanted to get the joke. It created conversation within our fan base and drew fans in from other teams. It was an organic way to grow a following and eventually increase the fan base.

Creating a personality was important for the Avalanche Twitter account and individual players. By giving players' their own unique, distinct traits through our social media coverage, fans felt that they could better relate to players. Fans would cheer for the player, even if he wasn't playing his best, because they loved who he was off the ice, too.

Creating revenue opportunities, while less exciting from a creative perspective, was essential to continue to grow our department. However, my goal was for our sponsored content to be so well-integrated into our organic content that it received the same engagement. I knew that fans didn't want to see promotional graphics and enter to win contests, they want to see content they love that just happens to be sponsored.

For these three goals to work, I had to get the higher-ups to buy in to the idea that you create good content first and then revenue comes after. You can't force people to be fans; you have to create a presence on social media that fans want to be a part of. I truly believe having a look and voice that is unique to your brand is so, so valuable.

What have you seen work well for building customer relationships on social media?
Responding, responding, responding. I made it a goal to respond to every single fan who mentions the team or uses the team hashtag.

(Continued)

Every single time a response was sent from a team account, the fan would respond something like: "whoa! I can't believe the Avs actually responded to me!!" And then they kept tweeting at us. And then their friends starting tweeting at us. And then the more that the team-facing engagement grew, the more fans engaged with the content.

What outcomes of social media use are important to your organization(s)?
The organization wants views, retweets and link clicks. The organization wants more followers. The organization wants to sell sponsorship content on social platforms. The organization wants people to click to buy tickets from social media. And while, in general, if we can accomplish those things, we are a successful social media presence, I believe that the number of replies to tweets and the number of social mentions are much, much more valuable.

What would you tell young professionals who want to work in social media in sport?
Be a content creator. Learn how to take photos, make graphics, and produce videos. If graphic design or videography is truly your passion, then focus on those. But if you just like social media + marketing in general, being able to create content that fits into a strategy is so important. Practice with your own social media. So much of social media is adapting, that the better you are at seeing trends and utilizing features, the more valuable you'll be.

KEY SKILLS FOR PRACTICE

As sports professionals, there are many skills that will help you use social media to build relationships with customers. This section will discuss some of the skills that have been deemed to be most important.

CONTENT MANAGEMENT

In communicating content on social media platforms, one must be able to balance accuracy and speed. Breaking news on social media is currency for recognition, but breaking accurate news is much more rewarding. As much value frequent news-breaking may generate over time, communicating unsubstantiated news can be damaging, so balancing speed when breaking news while still double-checking the facts is important. Staying up-to-date with current issues and popular culture also serves to humanize the brand. When brands can make posts about issues their consumer base cares about, they are building relationships by connecting with fans outside of sport. It is important to note that this does not mean sports organizations should post about every current event or issue that is happening. Instead, organizations should focus on posts that highlight their personality and the things their consumer base cares about. Using effective listening skills will ensure that organizations are posting about things their base cares about. Also, one needs to expand their contact and network within an organization and industry. Having a wider professional network can be one way to fact-check news on a timely basis and minimize the chance of communicating inaccurate information. For more on content management, please see Chapter 16.

CONTENT GENERATION

For a social media account to be appealing to its audiences, the content that one generates needs to be fresh, topical, friendly, creative, and entertaining. Communicating content that is personalized, humorous, and presented with a friendly tone is essential for the meaningful use of social media as a relationship marketing tool. As research indicates, sport consumers value and interact with content that highlights players outside of the game and content that provides fans an inside look into athletes' lives, and the organization. Thus, the organization needs to embrace human-interest stories that show the personality of the brand. The effectiveness of content can also be increased if it includes different media types such as embedded short videos, pictures, GIFs, and links.

CONSTANT ADAPTATION

In the past few years, new social media platforms have emerged and existing ones have advanced their features. Such change and evolution demands that a social media professional be someone who is ready to constantly adapt with such constant changes. While planning a content strategy is important, social media managers should also be flexible and avoid becoming complacent and relying on what has worked in the past. To be successful at constant adaptation, you must proactively seek out new platforms, content types, and media options. Also, as part of this adaptation, students should start following professionals and blogs that will help them learn new trends and be connected to changes being made by networks. There are many blogs and web sources published by companies who work in this space, such as HubSpot, and professionals on Twitter who work in social media marketing inside and outside of sport.

FOCUSED LISTENING

Taking time to actively listen to customers on social media is an essential skill. There are multiple ways an organization could choose to do this. First, you can use the analytics of each platform to identify the types of content that are being viewed and interacted with most often. Sports marketers should also review the comments on posts to determine user sentiment, as well as to learn more about how fans are evaluating the content posted by the organization. Marketers, however, need to look even deeper into how fans are discussing the organization online and even set up social media management software solutions, such as Agorapulse, Hootsuite, Sprout, Sendible, Buffer, and Meet Edgar. Reviewing how fans are talking about you can provide ideas about content you may not have known was of value otherwise. Truly listening to customers requires you, as a sport marketer, to seek out any conversation happening about your product online, not just those that you facilitated.

Two final sources of listening to customers include periodic customer surveys and face-to-face conversations with customers. The content you post might not always be interacted with on social networks but might be of significant value to your fan base. Asking customers directly what they find value in on your social media networks, then using their feedback to improve strategy, is a great way to show that you want to provide value to your customers. These strategies also help you stay tuned in to what your fan base wants, especially as social media and content strategy evolve.

LIVELY INTERACTION

Having a social media platform with rare or limited interaction will take away the basic essence of social media and its potential as a relationship marketing channel. Therefore, one would be expected to engage in frequent and regular interactions such as casual exchanges, appreciating fans support, etc. It is not enough to encourage discussion between fans, you must also take the time to respond to fans, ask questions, and be a part of the discussion. You can do this by remembering to review comments. You can also do this by responding to direct messages, tagged posts, or user-generated content. This interaction is supported by humanizing the brand, which requires the social media manager to create a personality that consumers can connect to. It is difficult to have two-way discussions with fans if they don't feel the organization is authentic, personable, or approachable.

USE CUSTOMIZATION

One must understand the unique features of individual platforms and tailor their use in a way that fits the distinct attributes of a given platform. For example, using Twitter for breaking news, and Instagram for merchandise sales. Similarly, recognizing an individual platform's appeal to a certain user demography and psychography is vital, which allows the framing and customization of content that resonates with a target consumer.

TRENDS AND CURRENT ISSUES

MEASUREMENT OF EFFECTIVENESS

An ongoing issue with using social media has been measuring its effectiveness. Outside of advertisements or sales posts that directly link consumers to purchasing options, there is little tying the consumption of or interaction with social media content to traditional business outcomes. Thus, it has not been easy to connect an organization's investment in social media marketing to business outcomes. Most importantly, it is difficult to connect social media marketing to its impact on customer relationships. This is rooted in the "attribution" challenge, a key aspect of all evaluations in marketing, where it is difficult to attribute the decision of a consumer to one specific action (e.g., a social media post or membership). It is also impacted by the difficulty in ascertaining if social media followers are primarily highly identified fans whose consumer behavior is unlikely to be effected by social media interactions and communications, or if they are a mixture of low and high identified fans who can be influenced by sports organizations on social media platforms. There are ways to estimate the impact of a social media activity, but it is challenging (for more on this, please see Chapter 15). Partly, this is because looking at engagement metrics does little to tell one the depth of the relationship between an organization and its customers. In addition, it is due to the difficulty in connecting specific content types to their impacts on relationships without surveying customers before and after the use of the content. As measurement tools and software continue to be developed, social media managers may find this easier and more fruitful. Additionally, as the conceptualization of return on investment evolves with the ever-changing nature of social media, managers may be able to adjust how they value social media effectiveness, focusing solely on how using social media meets specific organizational goals.

ENCOURAGING INTERACTION AND DISCUSSION

The majority of this chapter discussed the need for sports social media marketers to engage customers in interaction and communication. However, doing so can be difficult. Much of the research on social media suggests that most people who follow businesses online are consumers of content, but not necessarily active and engaged users. This presents a challenge for sports marketers who must ask questions that will actually spark debate and discussion with fans. Generally, this requires a good understanding of what fans are interested in and the kinds of discussions followers might be willing to have. Often, this might mean posing questions that push the organization out of their comfort zones. For example, after a team's tough loss, it might be advantageous to ask fans to identify areas of improvement that will lead to victory. While it is not likely that a coach or general manager will utilize these suggestions, it makes fans feel heard and brings conversations that they are having anyway directly to the organization. Another example might be asking fans what they thought of a pre-game video, uniform combination, or community activity. Social media managers could even curate opinions prior to creating a new t-shirt design or trying a new charity event. Opening up these conversations on social media allow the organization to create a natural focus group where novel ideas can be created and co-creation can be encouraged. Although the organization may have some negative comments and posts to respond to, being willing to give fans a voice can build stronger relational bonds that connect fans more deeply with an organization, even those who are making the negative comments. Additionally, sports organizations need to remain vigilant in their research of trends that foster engagement and take the aforementioned advice to connect with fans and ask them what they are interested in engaging around on social media.

SOCIAL MEDIA INFLUENCERS

Social media has given ordinary people the ability to accumulate cultural capital by sharing information with members of their digital communities on a regular basis. These users often respond to the needs and interests of their digital community and their followers consider them both sources and guides. By extension, the users evolve as influencers of their community on social media. As such, social media influencers have persuasive power and likely shape audience attitudes. Particularly, elements of cultural capital such as relatability, accessibility, and intimacy give rise to authority, leading consumers to value social media influencers' recommendations. Hence, social media influencers do not rely on formal power (e.g., celebrity athletes) or prestige (e.g., social class), but rather, on their role as a connection point between peers and 'what matters' in their community. Hence, empowering these opinion leaders would be a beneficial tactic to improve social media use towards relationship objectives. Sport organizations should actively search social media networks to find individuals who are fans of the organization, who often speak about the organization, and have strong followings. Reaching out to these individuals and asking them to help grow the brand and shape its image can provide a bridge between the organization and its fans that is fostered through authentic collaboration with ambassadors. It provides an opportunity for a third-party endorsement. Constructing relationships with influencers that are mutually beneficial can be time-consuming, but ultimately this would improve the credibility of the information that the organization is distributing on social media. Influencers can also be used as a test market for new content types or networks that the social media manager is considering utilizing. Organizations can enhance their relationship with influencers by providing resources such as behind-the-scenes access and fresh stories.

CHAPTER SUMMARY

Understanding how to use social media from a relationship marketing perspective allows sports organizations to build relationships with customers through interactions and communications, while providing added value. To do so, sports managers should balance different content types that appeal to fans, while also meeting organizational goals. In a crowded space, it is important for sports organizations to connect with customers through quality, consistency, and fresh content that encourages dialogue and positive word-of-mouth publicity. For those who want to work in this space, it is important to seek out opportunities to learn about content management and creation and build a professional network that keeps them connected to the industry and stay up-to-date with news.

KEY RESOURCES

- Sprout social discusses building relationships on social media networks: https://sproutsocial.com/insights/build-customer-relationships/.
- Hubspot discusses using relationship marketing on social media and gives some examples: https://blog.hubspot.com/marketing/relationship-marketing.
- Relationship marketing examples: https://inbound.human.marketing/the-top-4-relationship-marketing-examples.
- Social media listening tools: https://marketingland.com/6-of-the-best-social-listening-tools-for-2019-249953.
- Pulizzi, J. (2013). *Epic content marketing*. McGraw-Hill Publishing.
- Recommendations for other books on social media marketing: https://blog.hootsuite.com/books-social-media-manager-read/.

TEST YOUR KNOWLEDGE

- What is relationship marketing and why would an organization choose it as a marketing strategy?
- How does social media marketing meet relationship marketing goals?
- What is the most important skill for a marketer to use social media to build relationships? Why?
- How can social media managers in sport build relationships with customers on social media networks?

- As a sports professional, do you see value in using a relationship-marketing approach to social media content and management? Why or why not?
- How would you train your social media managers to create content and engage customers on social media networks?
- How would you capitalize on relationships built through social media to enhance your business outcomes?

REFERENCES

Abeza, G., O'Reilly, N., and Séguin, B. (2019). The sequential-funnel-based focus group design: Adapting the focus group for research in sport management. *Journal of Global Sport Management*, 1–28. https://doi.org/10.1080/24704067.2018.1550621.

Abeza, G., O'Reilly, N., Finch, D., Séguin, B., and Nadeau, J. (2020). The role of social media in the co-creation of value in relationship marketing: a multi-domain study. *Journal of Strategic Marketing*, 28(6), 472–493.

Abeza, G., O'Reilly, N., Seguin, B., and Nzindukiyimana, O. (2017). Social media as a relationship marketing tool in professional sport: A netnographical exploration. *International Journal of Sport Communication*, 10(3), 325–358.

Achen, R. M. (2014). Relationship marketing in United States professional sport: Attitudes, opinions, and viewpoints of sport professionals. *Global Sport Business Journal*, 2(3), 14–27.

Achen, R. M. (2015). Likes, comments, and shares: A multivariate multi-level analysis of Facebook engagement. *Global Sport Business Journal*, (3), 1–16.

Achen, R. M. (2019). Re-examining a model for measuring Facebook interaction and relationship quality. Sport, Business and Management, 9(3), 255–272. doi:10.1108/SBM-10-2018-0082.

Achen R. M., Kaczorowski, J., Horsmann, T., and Ketzler, A. (2018). Exploring content and interaction on Facebook in the off-season: A comparison of United States professional sport leagues. *International Journal for Communication and Sport*, 11, 389–413.

AMA (2020). Definitions of marketing. Retrieved from https://bit.ly/3pQJFyZ.

Ballantyne, D., Christopher, M., and Payne, A. (2003). Relationship marketing: Looking back, looking forward. *Marketing Theory*, 3(1), 159–166.

Buhler, A. and Nufer, G. (2010). Relationship marketing in sports. Oxford: Elsevier.

Čečević, B. N., Antić, L., and Spasić, K. (2020). Cost accounting and performance measurement with the purpose of increasing the competitiveness of sports organizations. *Economic Themes, 58*(2), 235–253.

Coelho, R. L. F., de Oliveira, D. S, and de Almeida, M. I. S. (2016). Does social media matter for post typology? Impact of post content on Facebook and Instagram metrics. *Online Information Review, 40*(4), 458–471.

Cvijikj, I. P. and Michahelles, F. (2013). Online engagement factors on Facebook brand pages. *Social Network Analysis and Mining,* (4), 843–861.

Doran, A. J., Cooper, C. G., and Mihalik, J. (2015). A content analysis of NCAA Division I track & field teams' Twitter usage: Defining best practices in social media marketing. *Journal of Contemporary Athletics,* 9, 227–247.

Egan, J. (2004). Back to the future: Divergence in relationship marketing research. Marketing Theory, *3*(1), 145–157.

Feinberg, R. and Kadam, R. (2002). E-CRM web service attributes as determinants of customer satisfaction with retail web sites. *International Journal of Service Industry Management,* 13, 432–451.

Grönroos, C. (2000). Creating a relationship dialogue: Communication, interaction, value. *Marketing Review, 1*(1), 5–14.

Grönroos, C. (2004). The relationship marketing process: Communication, interaction, dialogue, value. *Journal of Business & Industrial Marketing, 19*(2), 99–113.

Gutiérrez-Cillán, J., Camarero-Izquierdo, C., and San José-Cabezudo, R. (2017). How brand post content contributes to user's Facebook brand-page engagement: The experiential route of active participation. *BRQ Business Research Quarterly, 20*(4), 258–274.

Hambrick, M. E. and Kang, S. J. (2015). Pin it: Exploring how professional sports organizations use Pinterest as a communications and relationship-marketing tool. *Communication and Sport, 3*(4), 434–457.

Hudson, S., Huang, L., Roth, M. S., and Madden, T. J. (2016). The influence of social media interactions on consumer — brand relationships: A three-country study of brand perceptions and marketing behaviors. *International Journal of Research in Marketing, 33*(1), 27–41.

Kim, Y. K. and Trail, G. (2011). A conceptual framework for understanding relationships between sport consumers and sport organizations: A relationship quality approach. *Journal of Sport Management,* 25, 57–69.

Kim, C. and Yang, S-U. (2017). Like, comment, and share on Facebook: How each behavior differs from the other. *Public Relations Review*, *43*(2), 441–449.

Kim, D., Kim, J.-H., and Nam, Y. (2014). How does industry use social networking sites? An analysis of corporate dialogic uses of Facebook, Twitter, YouTube, and LinkedIn by industry type. *Quality and Quantity*, 48, 2605–2614.

Kwon, S. J., Park, E., and Kim, K. J. (2014). What drives successful social networking services? A comparative analysis of user acceptance of facebook and twitter. *The Social Science Journal*, 51, 534–544.

Lawrence, H. J., O'Reilly, N., Speck, A., Ullrich, C., and Robles, K. (2020). The determinants of season ticket holder advocacy in the NCAA football bowl subdivision. *Sport, Business and Management: An International Journal.*

Lee, D., Walsh, D., Maeng, L. S., and Lee, M. (2020). BIRFing and CORSing of sport fans. *Sport Business in the United States: Contemporary Perspectives.*

Logan, K. (2014). Why isn't everyone doing it? A comparison of antecedents to following brands on Twitter and Facebook. Journal of Interactive Advertising, 14, 60–72.

Malhotra, A., Malhotra, C. K., and See, A. (2013). How to create brand engagement on Facebook. *MIT Sloan Management Review*, *54*(2), 18–20.

O'Malley, L. (2014). Relational marketing: Development, debates and directions. *Journal of Marketing Management*, *30*(11–12), 1220–1238.

Payne, A. and Frow, P. (2017). Relationship marketing: looking backwards towards the future. *Journal of Services Marketing*, *31*(1), 11–15.

Peppers, D. and Rogers, M. (2011). *Managing customer relationships: A strategic framework*. Hoboken, NJ: Wiley.

Schultz, D. E. and Peltier, J. J. (2017). Social media's slippery slope: Challenges, opportunities and future research directions. *Journal of Research in Interactive Marketing*, 7(2), 86–99.

Shani, D. (1997). A framework for implementing relationship marketing in the sport industry. *Sport Marketing Quarterly*, *6*(2), 9–15.

Smith, A. N., Fischer, E., and Yongjian, C. (2012). How does brand-related user-generated content differ across YouTube, Facebook, and Twitter? *Journal of Interactive Marketing*, 26, 102–113.

Stavros, C., Meng, M. D., Westberg, K., and Farrelly, F. (2014). Understanding fan motivation for interacting on social media. *Sport Management Review*, *17*(4), 455–469.

Swani, K., Milne, G., and Brown, B. P. (2013). Spreading the word through likes on Facebook: Evaluating the message strategy effectiveness of Fortune 500 companies. *Journal of Research in Interactive Marketing, 7*(4), 269–294.

Tafesse, W. (2015). Content strategies and audience response on Facebook brand pages. *Marketing Intelligence and Planning, 33*(6), 927–943.

Tafesse, W. (2016). An experiential model of consumer engagement in social media. *Journal of Product and Brand Management, 25*(5), 424–434. doi:10.1108/JPBM-05-2015-0879.

Thompson, A. J., Martin, A. J., Gee, S., and Geurin, A. N. (2018). Building brand and fan relationships through social media. *Sport, Business and Management: An International Journal,* 8, 235–256.

Thompson, A. J., Martin, A. J., Gee, S., and Eagleman, A. N. (2014). Examining the development of a social media strategy for a National Sport Organisation. *Journal of Applied Sport Management, 6*(2), 42–63.

Thompson, A. J., Martin, A. J., Gee, S., and Geurin, A. N. (2017). Fans' perceptions of professional tennis events' social media presence: Interaction, insight, and brand anthropomorphism. *Communication and Sport,* 5, 579–603.

Vale, L. and Fernandes, T. (2018). Social media and sports: Driving fan engagement with football clubs on Facebook. *Journal of Strategic Marketing, 26*(1), 37–55.

Wallace, L., Wilson, J., and Miloch, K. (2011). Sporting Facebook: A content analysis of NCAA organizational sport pages and Big 12 conference athletic department pages. *International Journal of Sport Communication,* 4, 422–444.

Chapter 9

Social Media and Brand Management in Sport

Matt Blaszka* and Beth A. Cianfrone†

*Indiana State University, United States
†Georgia State University, United States

CHAPTER OBJECTIVES

After studying this chapter, you will be able to do the following:

- Understand the importance of using social media to develop a sport brand, for a team as well as an individual athlete.
- Evaluate the various ways organizations, teams, and athletes use social media to enhance their brand and create brand equity.
- Recognize the role of brand associations and brand personality in social media strategies.
- Discuss the strategies of using social media to aid in rebranding of a sport organization.
- Identify strategies that may work best for particular organizations in brand management.

KEY TERMS

Brand   Brand management
Brand ambassadors   Engagement
Brand associations   Influencers
Brand equity   Like-gating

INTRODUCTION

Since the early 2000s, the reach of sports brands has become more global than ever because of the increased use of social media platforms, such as Facebook and Instagram. Through social media, sports teams, leagues, coaches, and players have a voice to enhance and bring their brand to life through millions of fans across the globe. As a result, some sports organizations, events, and professional athletes have become lucrative international brands. Forbes reports the financial values of sports entities annually. According to the Forbes 2020 reports (*Most Valuable Brands, Most Valuable Sports Teams,* and *Highest Paid Athletes in the World*), the following examples provide some context around the top sports brands and their social media:

- Nike is the top sports business brand, valued at US$39.1 billion in 2019 (Swant, 2020). It has more than 10 different Twitter accounts and the main one (@Nike) has 8.2 million followers.
- The NFL's Dallas Cowboys are the most valuable team brand at US$5.5 billion (Badenhausen, 2020b). The team has 8.5 million likes on Facebook, 3.9 million followers on Twitter, and 3.5 million on Instagram (@Dallas Cowboys).
- Real Madrid was the top international brand valued at US$4.24 billion and has more than 250 million followers on social media as the most followed sports team in the world (Badenhausen, 2020b). They have 110 million followers on Facebook and 93 million on Instagram (@RealMadrid). They have multiple Twitter accounts to reach their fans in different languages: Spanish (@RealMadrid), English (@RealMadridEn),

Arabic (RealMadridArab), French (@RealMadridFra), and Japanese (@RealMadridJapan).

- Tennis star Roger Federer is the most valuable individual athlete brand with earnings of US$106.3 million (Badenhausen, 2020a). Federer has 18 million followers on Facebook, 12.7 million on Twitter, and 8 million on Instagram, more than double the Cowboys.
- The third most valuable individual athlete brand is soccer player Christiano Ronaldo, with US$105 million in earnings in 2020 (US$45 million in endorsements and US$60 million in salary). In 2020, he was the most followed athlete (and person) on both Instagram, with 238 million followers, and Facebook (122 million). He also has over 86.9 million followers on Twitter.

It is not surprising that each of these brands has a strong social media presence, which acts as an extension of their brand and helps fortify their brand value. Sports marketers, social media managers, and athletes use social media to launch, grow, develop, change, cultivate, and enhance their sports organizations' brand or personal brand. Because more than half of the world's population utilizes some form of social media (Kemp, 2020), the sheer growth and access to social media has provided organizations and athletes with the opportunity to market and improve the value of their brand. Those who leverage their social media platforms most effectively are likely to reap greater financial gains for their brand and thus develop and cultivate a larger fan base.

It has become increasingly important for sports organizations/ teams, coaches, and athletes to use social media to "tell their story" to the world. In doing so, sports entities utilize social media to connect directly with both their current fan base and potential new fans. The importance of social media as part of the overall sports marketing or branding campaign cannot be understated. For example, the Chicago Bulls (@chicagobulls) have 4.1 million followers on Twitter, 5.7 million followers on Instagram, and 17 million likes on Facebook. Each platform has unique features to amplify their brand message and different audiences. Teams and leagues use their social media toolbox in unique ways to reimagine the connection between organizations and fans, thus the importance of having clear brand messaging. A **brand** can be defined as a product or service that has unique components (e.g., name, symbol, or design) that are distinguishable from that of its competitors (Keller, 1993). In sports marketing, it has been noted that building and maintaining a strong brand is beneficial to the organization (e.g., Gladden and Funk, 2001; Kunkel *et al.*, 2014). The overall scope of social media provides athletes, teams, and organizations the platform to highlight various unique aspects of their brand. With the continued evolution of social media, it is critical for organizations to have a consistent strategy in managing the brand. This chapter will provide an overview of sports brands and social media, as well as a review of key concepts related to the brand, including brand management and building brand equity. Finally, the chapter will highlight the related trends and describe the skills needed to work in this area.

SOCIAL MEDIA AND BRAND MANAGEMENT: KEY CONCEPTS

Social media has developed into a branding tool for sports entities. Athletes, organizations, and leagues have spent the last 10 years building, sustaining, and evolving social media branding strategies. One of the many challenges as it relates to branding a product via social media is the continued change in the usage pattern by social media users. As noted in Chapter 1, many social media sites have come and gone (e.g., MySpace, Vine, Google+), while others have sustained a foothold (e.g., Facebook and Twitter) over the last decade. This can be attributed to changing demographics, advent of newer technology, and trends, as well as the need for short and quick bursts of information in today's society. Additionally, some popular social media sites among millennials and Gen Z in 2020 (e.g., Instagram, Snapchat, TikTok) did not exist in 2010, and may not exist in 2030. As such, teams and organizations need to evolve their social media branding strategy as the platforms' usage and the demographics shift when new platforms are released. To be proactive, teams and organizations often create an account of an up-and-coming social media site, just in case it becomes mainstream. This is critical for organizations as they develop various plans around their social media strategy.

An example of this is TikTok, the recently launched and increasingly popular social media site. Leagues, teams, and players partner with TikTok to allow their brand to reach younger audiences, specifically Generation Z, as well as international audiences. The NBA was one of the early adopters of TikTok, starting a league account on Musical.ly in 2016. At that time, Musical.ly was "an opportunity to grow our fan base and reach a unique audience…the platform skewed female and the content was substantially different than what we were doing on other platforms", noted Bob Carney, NBA Senior Vice President, Digital & Social Content (Feldman, 2018). The Musical.ly platform turned into TikTok, leading the NBA to partner with TikTok in 2018, where they used to show custom highlights and local language clips in more than a handful of countries. By 2020, the @NBA account had more than 11 million followers. The ability to connect directly with Generation Z is critical for the organization to develop fans. The NBA and NFL are leading this charge, and some examples of their league TikTok efforts are listed as follows.

- #NBAHandshake — The NBA asked fans to show their coolest handshake at the beginning of the 2018 season.
- During the early parts of the COVID-19 pandemic, while many fans were placed on stay-at-home mandates by local governments or working/schooling from home, the NBA created the #HoopsAtHome Challenge to encourage fans to post their best at-home basketball skills.
- During the 2020 NFL Draft, the NFL had a #GoingPro Challenge. TikTok live streamed the event.

As noted, sports entities use different social media platforms for different messages. From a marketing perspective, a sport organization needs to have a specific plan in place for each of the platforms they intend to utilize (Blaszka *et al.*, 2018). This strategic marketing management takes purposeful effort from the sport organization. For example, the New York Mets can host their pre- and post-game press conference on Facebook, utilize Twitter to keep fans up-to-date on the latest scoring plays, pitching changes, or hits, and use Instagram to share a short clip of a big home run. All three of these platforms use the same branding marks by including the New York Mets logo, their team hashtag (#lgm, which stands for "Let's Go Mets"), and the apple emoji, symbolizing the "Big Apple". This consistency across platforms provides the team with a strong brand presence and encourages those marks to be used by their social media followers (i.e., fans). Additionally, the organization changes the profile picture (e.g., Pride Month) and can provide sponsorship opportunities with various posts (e.g., Delta and "Climbing Up the Leaderboard" Mets Instagram post), as a way to leverage the brand in both social and economic terms.

Each of these social media platforms provide different content to their varied demographics. While some of the content may overlap, because every platform has its own styles, purposes, and technical features (e.g., Instagram is picture-centric, while TikTok is video-centric), it is important that the brand messaging remains consistent. Additionally, all of these are part of the brand attributes or associations, which help support the team brand. Thus, a strategic approach to organizational brand management, including a formalized plan, is needed. The brand management plan defines and outlines the organizational marketing goals with respect to growing, maintaining, highlighting, or changing the brand, brand image, or other brand attributes, and how different facets of the organization will implement the plan is also necessary. This strategic brand management plan can be implemented across social media, advertising, ticketing, and other marketing elements, such as in-game experiences and signage.

In order to fully incorporate a branding strategy with social media, there needs to be a plan to manage the brand. **Brand management** can be defined as a process that communicates and transfers the advantages associated with a brand to its goods and services (Kotler and Keller, 2016). What makes social media unique in brand management is the constant communication between the brand and consumers, including a two-way dialogue. Each social media brand manager needs to develop a strategic social media marketing plan that differentiates its entity from the social media clutter. It is important to note that a good strategy is more than just targeting fans, but rather connecting and creating an emotional connection to establish loyal fans. As such, having elements of the brand that are easy to identify, endure change, and provide meaning to a sports consumer can help provide a positive and competitive advantage on social media.

An ultimate goal of brand management is increased **brand equity**. Brand equity is "a set of brand assets and liabilities linked to a brand, its name, and symbol that add to or subtract from the value provided by a product or service to a firm and/or to that firm's customers" (Aaker, 1991, p. 15). When used effectively, social media can contribute to a stronger brand equity. A high level of brand equity can lead to many benefits, such as increased media exposure, television deals, ticketing sales, and sponsorships (Gladden *et al.*, 1998). Brand equity is often measured by consumers' levels of brand awareness, established brand associations, perceived brand quality, and consumers' brand loyalty (Aaker, 1991), so we will examine how these aspects of brand equity can be enhanced through social media.

BRAND EQUITY COMPONENTS

BRAND AWARENESS

Brand awareness is often the first step in any consumer behavior model. If people are unaware of your organization, then they will not be able to consume the product. Therefore, efforts to drive individuals to your social media platform would help people learn more about your team. It would also help current fans become more engaged and loyal. To reach a specific potential target market, organizations may purchase advertisements on social media platforms.

Facebook shares information with advertisers, allowing advertisers to target according to demographics, such as age, gender, or location, or similar profile 'likes'. Another tactic to generate awareness and followers is "like-gating", where teams require individuals to "follow us on social media for a chance to win" or "retweet/share to be entered to win (Brison *et al.*, 2015). Initially, "like-gating" was tied to a third-party app, which prevented individuals from seeing particular parts of the Facebook page until they "liked" the page or winning a contest. Facebook made policy changes to stop this, but the concept of using retweets or shares to garner more followers is still a common tactic on other platforms. For example, during the 2020 holiday season, the PGA Valspar Championship (@valsparchamp) had a social media contest to raffle off various golf items related to their event. The tournament utilized their social media accounts (Facebook, Twitter, and Instagram) in order to promote their "12 Days of Giveaways" contest. As part of the daily giveaways, they asked for you to follow/like the account, like the individual post, and tag a friend in order to be eligible to win the prize for that day. This contest created excitement and engagement for the followers, allowed the organization to garner new followers, and may have provided an opportunity for organic original content from the followers who won prizes and shared about it on their personal accounts. Along those same lines, asking current followers to create and promote content can be helpful.

User-Generated Content (UGC) is a great way to create a connection between an organization and fans. Additionally, it is a great way to learn the story of a brand. UGC also serves as promotion or electronic word-of-mouth (eWOM) publicity to drive brand awareness, creates perceived value, and confidence in the product. For example, the Texas Rangers can host a Bark-in-the-Park theme night, where fans are encouraged to dress up their dogs in Rangers gear and post the pictures or videos on social media and tag the team, with the possibility to be featured on the Rangers' social media platforms. This engages a segment of the fan base, creates brand awareness among those who may not follow the Rangers but follow the dog owner's account, all while creating interesting and entertaining content.

BRAND ASSOCIATIONS

In order to increase brand equity through social media, the organization must understand what parts of a brand are relatable to fans. A consumer's image of a brand is based on the **brand associations**, the unique meaning or characteristics of the brand to the consumers (Keller, 1993). Brand associations can be brand attributes, such as brand mark/logo, rivalry, concessions, or organizational attributes, like team history, nonplayer personnel, stadium community, team success, socialization, commitment, and team characteristics. Associations could also be brand benefits ascertained by the fan or brand attitudes from the consumers (Keller, 1993). All of these factors help develop and measure brand equity.

When you think of the Dallas Cowboys, what brand attributes come to mind? Perhaps the club's history, star logo, silver and blue colors, Super Bowls, America's Team, current or past players, cheerleaders, owner Jerry Jones, the stadium, rivalry with The Washington Football Team, or watching the team on Thanksgiving Day, come to mind. These are all brand attributes that help the fan connect with the brand and assets contributing to the strongest brand value in sports. The Cowboys highlight each of these associations on their social media accounts to reaffirm their identity to their fans and continue to enhance the brand value. Organizations can use their social media platforms to build and enhance their connection with consumers by highlighting any of these brand associations. Because some demographics of fans may relate more to a specific brand association than others, the organization can adjust different brand attributes accordingly.

LEARNING ACTIVITY 1

Identify a sport organization and think of its brand associations. Then, review its social media accounts and feeds to determine if and how the brand associations are reflected in its posts. Find examples to support each association. Compare and contrast the different associations being disseminated on each platform.

BRAND QUALITY

Social media provides sports media personnel with an opportunity to reiterate the quality of their brand. The "like-gating" mentioned earlier is a way to enhance brand awareness, but also perceived brand quality (Baker *et al.*, 2013; Brison *et al.*, 2015), as a team, athlete, or product with many 'likes' or followers is deemed reputable or popular. Similarly, the eWOM created via fan engagement activities, like Twitter retweets or Facebook shares, offer more support for the quality of the organization or the individual athlete.

For example, in November 2020, Buffalo Bills QB Josh Allen's grandmother died and the response on social media from the fan base of the Bills known as the "Bills Mafia" shows the power of eWOM. The #BillsMafia took to Twitter to honor her and donate to the local children's hospital that Allen supports. This fan-generated content was a reflection of the fandom and quality of the QB brand, and subsequent eWOM spread to social media followers from across the globe and even fans of other teams contributing to the cause. The Bills shared Allen's thankful response, and as of November 21, 2020, the fans had raised over US$675,000 for Oishei Children's Hospital and the west wing part of one of the floors of the hospital building will now be known as the 'Patricia Allen Pediatric Recovery Wing'. It was an opportunity for fans across the world to show their support of the team and the quality of their fan base.

Consumers, especially fans of players and teams, want to believe the brand they support is superior to others, which is developed through the emotional connections (McQueen *et al.*, 1993). Good storytelling that provides insight and behind-the-scenes content helps those connections. Finally, as part of the two-way communication and instantaneous nature of social media, social media managers can play a major part in the service quality of their organization. The customer service aspect between sports organizations and fans is one that cannot be overlooked for a brand. A brand needs to be able to respond to disgruntled fans or answer questions when fans have questions about game day logistics or other satisfaction-based queries. With sport being a customer service industry, it is critical for organizations to respond to the masses swiftly and to individuals who may need assistance. Notre Dame Football has a specific Twitter account (@gamedayND) and app to answer game day inquiries, such as parking, concessions, and lost and found. While this may be a separate account, it is still consistent with the main team Twitter account and is a representation of their brand quality.

BRAND LOYALTY

In an effort to be fan-centric and provide fans a way to connect to the brand, learn more about the brand, and develop connection to their fan base, sports teams need to be creative and purposeful when creating brand loyalty. As noted earlier, in order to gain trust and develop a fan base, athletes and organizations use their platforms to become a "must-follow". To target these followers, organizations craft their messaging encouraging engagement in their online community and providing followers a chance to display their loyalty. Loyalty can be displayed in many ways, including conversation/engagement and showing off team brand associations via a social media profile picture of a team logo or picture of a favorite player. In order to successfully engage with fans, organizations need to talk with their fans and not at them. In general, fans are participatory in nature. Facebook groups allow organizations to engage with their fans uniquely. Some organizations use private Facebook groups to show exclusivity to those most loyal. The Chicago Bulls have private Facebook groups for their season ticket holders and the Atlanta Basketball Host Committee used a Facebook group for NCAA Final Four volunteers. Members of these groups share in their commitment to their organization and discuss team/organization-related information or stories. This community-feel helps foster their brand loyalty.

National College Colors Day (the Friday before Labor Day in the United States) is an excuse for college athletic teams and fans from across the United State to celebrate their teams and show their loyalty by wearing their school colors and posting it on social media.

This highlights the brand messaging and positioning, provides UGC that gets people excited, interested and engaged. Fans can bring back vintage logos or brand marks, which can, in turn, be highlighted on social media and connect generations through this nostalgia, as well.

STRATEGIC BRAND DEVELOPMENT WITH SOCIAL MEDIA

INDIVIDUAL ATHLETE BRAND DEVELOPMENT

Individual athlete's personal brand can grow through social media and athletes can develop personal relationships with fans (Kunkel *et al.*, 2019; Su *et al.*, 2020). These relationships may be back-and-forth communication or merely parasocial interaction, where fans feel like they have a relationship with an athlete because they feel that they know so much about them. The athletes who share more personal information and everyday life situations often do the best with their brand presence.

One example of an athlete's breakout success on social media was NFL wide receiver, JuJu Smith-Schuster of the Pittsburgh Steelers. His social media content is authentic, displays his humorous personality, and provides insight into what he likes to do for fun. His popularity began organically in 2017, when he was a rookie on the team. He posted funny tweets (@TeamJuJu) about his disappointment when his bike, which he rode to and from practice, was stolen. He posted videos of him riding the bike home from practice (with football helmet on) and saying he was going to miss it. Other more prominent players chimed in on Twitter supporting him. A day later, the bike was returned, but by then there was a hashtag about #jujusbike because so many people joined in the online conversation about the situation. Smith-Schuster is active on multiple social platforms and popular for his 'everyday life' type posts:

- In 2018, Smith-Schuster shared a video of himself, dressed as himself in full Steelers uniform for Halloween, trick-or-treating with kids and handing out candy to people in Pittsburgh.

- He has his own YouTube channel, JuJu TV, with over a million followers, with fun-filled content, like him going to Steelers tailgates before games, watching his own highlight reel, or videos of him playing Call of Duty. He also shows himself in everyday life, such as family vacations, or him going back to his alma mater, the University of Southern California, for Homecoming.
- He participated in the "Ask Me Anything" section of Reddit in August 2020, with more than 2,300 comments.

His accessibility and openness helped him grow his brand and, now, maintain it. His brand will also help the Steelers' brand, as well as the NFL. A study by Su *et al.* (2020) found that individual brands (such as an athlete's brand) are often sub-brands, related to their teams, leagues, and break-out events. The spillover of fans and brand presence from leagues, teams, and athletes to and from each other provide ways for the young athletes to gain prominence, such as if a player is drafted to a team with a strong social media following. Sometimes, it can go the other way, and the team and league benefit from the player's social media presence and spillover to their brand/accounts.

For example, when University of Oregon star basketball player Sabrina Ionescu was drafted first overall by the New York Liberty in 2020, the Liberty benefited from Ionescu's strong social media presence. At that point, Ionescu had 600,000 followers on Instagram, ten times the Liberty's 60,000, as well as twice as many Twitter followers as the team. Certainly, some Ionescu fans suddenly started following the Liberty, showing the spillover effect. This exemplifies the importance of social media brand managers working with their athletes to benefit both the team's and individual's brand. This relates to what Shannon Gross, Director of Content Strategy for the Dallas Cowboys, noted in Chapter 1. As the Director stated, more behind-the-scene stories are being put out these days by players than teams. Teams are, in a way, competing with their own players over content. According to Gross, players that have been coming into the league in the past few years have been raised on social media and have been using the platforms since they were in junior high and high school. Before 2016, players were not in the same position and might not have even bothered with it that much. Recently, however, players that are joining teams have their own social media management teams that follow them around, and teams are competing over content with their own players. The 2020 Name, Image, and Likeness (NIL) changes in college athletics can further impact these dynamics.

ORGANIZATIONAL BRAND DEVELOPMENT

It is critical for a sport organization's social media staff to know the brand associations that the organization represents, as well as the brand values, to reflect in communications. Creating consistency on social media platforms should be a fluid extension of the overall marketing and communication plan of the organization. As a result, the social media efforts should follow the brand values. For example, the independent baseball organization Savannah Bananas's marketing platform is "We Make Baseball Fun — Fans First. Entertain Always. All Inclusive". Given the brand personality of the organization is fun and family-oriented, the team-related social media communication and voice should represent these values. They have posted videos or pictures of their players and fans dancing down the streets of Savannah with bananas and wearing their yellow uniforms. This shows consistency with the brand for both the in-person audience and the social followers. Conversely, this brand management style, while effective for the Bananas, may not work for the MLB New York Yankees, who have a rich history and, as a professional team, brand values may not reflect the silly fun that the Bananas exude. The Yankees should stay true to their brand values and associations and display those through social media accounts. Certainly, social media has an entertainment component, so the team would still showcase fun fan engagement. However, when teams shift personalities too much on social media, they run the risk of alienating their core fans.

Sometimes teams use ancillary figures as new brand attributes to increase brand equity. The Philadelphia Flyers are a well-established NHL team, but saw an opportunity to grow their brand by creating a new mascot, Gritty, in 2018. At first, like many changes to the team's brand, the large googly eyed orange furry creature was not well received. The Flyers wanted to reengage their younger audience. Typically, mascots are a marketing asset targeting families and children, and seen only at athletic or local events. The Flyers marketing team created individual Gritty social media accounts: TikTok, Twitter, and Instagram, where he became a fan favorite because he was fun, engaging, and developed into a true character with antics on short videos. As of December 2020, Gritty has more than 297,000 Instagram followers, 353,000 Twitter followers, and 142,000 followers on TikTok. In 2020, he was voted the best mascot by the NHL Players Association.

Two special cases for brands are a brand release and rebranding efforts. These are described in the following sections.

Brand Release. The 32nd franchise in the NHL, the Seattle Kraken, used social media to unveil the team name, colors, and logo in 2020. The team officials had conducted numerous market research activities and listened intently on social media to their new audience, before deciding on a final name. The day before the brand was to be released, the team account used Twitter to send out a short video to let fans know the release date was upon them. The team announced the Kraken on Facebook Live, YouTube, and Twitter using a dramatic movie-quality level video, which brought to life the team's name, logo, and colors, and new mantra "Release the Kraken". Many of the city's biggest stars and sports brands, such as Russell Wilson and the Seattle Storm, tweeted out in support of the new brand. More importantly, input was given from fans of the organization. Additionally, the CEO, Tod Leiweke stated, "The Kraken is a name born of the fans. It was suggested and championed by the fans (Booth, 2020)". This reiterates the importance of fan engagement with the brand. On the announcement date, the team worked with the entire NHL team social media managers, so it looked like many supportive social engagements, including a 'group chat' video that featured every other team welcoming the team. There was also a series of open sessions with the team on social media, called "Brand Deep Dives", which included topics like "Inside the Logo" and "Seattle Hockey History" to engage the fans and immerse them with the new brand associations. In less than a week after the announcement, the Kraken increased their Twitter followers from 140,000 to 200,000 and brand merchandise quickly sold out.

Rebranding. Sports organizations are turning to social media to announce rebranding efforts. **Rebranding** consists of changing or modifying some brand aspects. The NFL's Los Angeles Rams rebranded their team logo in 2020, using social media to reveal the logo and interact with fans. In February 2020, the team's Chief Operating Officer, Kevin Demoff, announced there would be a new color scheme, logo, and uniform. When fans asked him for hints on

Figure 1: Example of Brand Management from LA Rams' Rebranding and Kevin Demoff's Tweet

Figure 2: Kevin Demoff's Follow up Tweet

Twitter, he responded with fake images to get people interested. With much excitement, on March 23rd, 2020, the Los Angeles Rams unveiled their new logo. The initial comments on social media were mostly negative. In fact, the fans' response was so harsh, that Demoff announced, via Twitter, that if the Rams fans raised US$2 million at the most recent Rams telethon to benefit their local United Way and Food Bank, he would do a "Mean Tweets" segment, where he read the mean Tweets about the logo.

As promised, when the fans raised more than US$2 million, Demoff recorded himself reading the Mean Tweets, and posted it on social media (See Figure 1). The mean Tweets reflected how the fans were attached to the old logo and the importance of a logo for the brand. Some of the comments that he read included:

> *Rams fans: 2020 can't get any worse/Rams: Hold my beer*
> *This is actually embarrassing. Looks like some freshman college students in Graphic Design 101 made it in about 6 minutes.*
> *Don't need you to read them, they're pretty much everywhere you look.*

The Rams response to the negative brand change was engaging, self-aware, and self-deprecating (See Figure 2). The response reiterates the importance of including your loyal fans in the decision-making process through market research, such as the Kraken. While it may take the fans time to adjust to the new logo, it would seem a new season would shift the fans' focus.

Some brand changes are not as drastic or more seasonal, including a brand refresh or new marketing slogan. A **brand refresh** is a minor form of rebranding, such as when a team unveils updated uniforms, but not major changes to the logo or word marks. In 2020, many NFL teams underwent a brand refresh and used social media as the main media outlet to distribute this information. Sometimes brand changes can be centered on a new marketing slogan, to reflect a new season. The Atlanta Braves historically used "ChopOn" as a branding mark, in reference to their Tomahawk Chop, in which fans would be encouraged to cheer and chant with their foam tomahawks. This language was used on digital and traditional signage throughout their stadium encouraging fans to cheer and chant with their tomahawks. On social media, "#ChopOn" was their social media hashtag to unite fans. In what may have been a strategic move away from the negative Native American term, the Braves shifted their marketing slogan to "#FortheA" before the 2020 season. After initial postings of this marketing slogan and hashtag on social media, fans voiced a lot of negative feedback on social accounts. This is not unique to the Rams or Braves, as it sometimes takes time for new brand marks or slogans to gain foothold within teams with long-standing traditions. It highlights the importance of brand components to fans. Organizations often need to build upon the new branding for fans to feel comfortable with the change. Utilizing social media to build these new marketing slogans or marks helps reach a wide variety of users.

LEARNING ACTIVITY 2

Research to determine the recent rebrands in professional sports in the last two years. Examine one of these and how they utilized at least two social media platforms (e.g., Facebook, Twitter, and Instagram) to release the brand. How did the organization announce the rebrand on social media and their organization's website? How uniquely were each of the social media platforms utilized in order to promote their rebrand? What was the overall reception of these rebrands on social media? Feel free to use popular press web articles to help locate rebranding information.

SKILLS FOR PRACTICE

Whether working on an established brand or trying to release and grow a new brand, a social media manager should be cognizant of the greater brand management plan and organizational brand, and develop a social media plan to support the desired outcomes. Some of these skills are discussed as follows.

Organization Skill. From a brand management standpoint, a social media staff member should be very organized. This organizational skill set will be helpful to manage multiple social accounts and ensure that the brand strategy is consistently implemented, personality shown, and that quality posts reiterate the brand message. Working in social media is fast-paced, timeliness is important (a post about something that happened yesterday can seem stale and old news), as is accuracy. Organization provides a foundation to succeed given these constraints. As part of this organization, a social media manager would have a strong understanding of brand equity and the brand assets that the team may possess. A manager can create a running list of the brand assets, including the coach, players, mascot, special interest groups, fans, color scheme, logo, or stadium. These assets provide the groundwork for utilization and consistency of the brand. An organized social manager would also have social media calendars or a clear plan on how to effectively deploy multiple platforms with the varying goals and content on each platform. As such, the plan must be easily understood by the co-workers and brand message understood by the fan base.

Communication Skills. To aid in the clarification of these goals, a social media staff member should be a good communicator. Both written and oral communication skills are important to effectively express the brand content and social media brand strategy, as well as make sure that co-workers, marketers, and athletes are communicating the same brand goals. As an extension of this skill, social media staff may need the skill of storytelling, given the fans desire for more team and athlete access and the need for original and compelling content to gain attention.

Social Awareness. Paired with communication skills, social media staff members must have social awareness and be well-read with contemporary culture to help create an online brand that is fresh, relevant, and appropriate. They should follow cultural trends, social cues, and stay current with an understanding of cultural phenomena such as pop culture television programs, music, and general timely related news. If it is national dog day, and that 'holiday' makes sense for your team or athlete, then there should be social media posts that match the day. However, the social media manager should have the social awareness to keep their finger on the pulse of what is happening in society; if there are major catastrophes or critically negative events occurring in the world that day, then posting a dog picture may seem insensitive or lacking in understanding of the temperature of society. As such, it may be better to 'go dark' until it seems appropriate to return to sports-related posts. Organizations have received criticism for posting irrelevant material and not "reading the room" during times when social media posts from a sports franchise or player may be seen as commercialization or insensitivity. As such, the skill of being socially aware is an important soft skill.

Editing Skills. Video production, graphic design, and technology knowledge are necessary, as noted in the other chapters. To aid in storytelling, social media staff may necessarily have to gain some knowledge of video production or photography. Having the ability to tell stories with short videos or photos on game day without having to rely on others can be beneficial in being timely and relevant in social posts. Graphic design skill also plays a pivotal role in producing content. Typically, graphic design skill includes artistic ability and creativity. The artistic ability may include design elements, like composition or color, as skills that would aid in creating content that matches the brand and is visually appealing. Additionally, social media staff needing the technical skill of using the latest editing and content creation software (e.g., Quark Xpress) and the Adobe Suite (e.g., Photoshop, Lightroom, etc.) has become critical. These skills would allow a social media staff member to create their own gifs, images, and videos to share and promote the brand. Lastly, having the latest technological advancements at the user's fingertips can benefit an organization. Organizations are hiring social media staff that are able to not only think of the unique content, but also produce it.

Summary. An example of a way to utilize the various skills mentioned earlier can be noted in the recent trend in the NFL schedule release on social media. In 2019, the Atlanta Falcons released their schedule with a video, which was based off the Games of Thrones introduction (a nod to their pop culture knowledge) and the video was high quality production that brought to life the schedule, as well as the teams and stadiums they played in. The visuals made it feel like it was a Game of Thrones introduction and the storytelling made something that is typically uneventful, appear compelling.

CASE STUDY 1

The NBA's Atlanta Hawks (@ATLHawks) provide a unique case for social media branding. The Atlanta Hawks Basketball Club owns the operating rights of State Farm Arena, and both are managed by CEO Steve Koonin. Because of this, the two organizations consider themselves one brand. Additionally, the management team also runs the College Park Skyhawks (G-League) and Hawks Talon Gaming Club (NBA 2K League). These teams serve as brand extensions of the Hawks. We sat down with Alicia McNease, Brand Communications Manager for the Atlanta Hawks and State Farm Arena, to learn more.

The organization's brand mantra is "True to Atlanta" and the goal for the Hawks social media staff is to always highlight that for the Atlanta community. McNease indicated that "this is executed in the players' efforts, team marketing, and attention to community needs". Internally, the brand mantra is "True to You", as the Hawks staff equally supports their employees. Their brand strategy relates everything back to the culture of Atlanta — "we are a mecca for music, arts, fashion, and the Hollywood of the South. We use social media to facilitate this brand mantra", notes McNease. The social media staff are key contributors in showcasing the brand from the hashtag #TruetoAtlanta to developing community-centric content. On the court, last season's city-edition Peachtree uniforms theme was carried over on social media.

(Continued)

Player-based social media content, such as culture brackets, where they choose between local artists or restaurants, are popular and keep the community involved. McNease stressed the importance of knowing that your audience comprises different segments and not being afraid to cater to these different segments — a social post about voting may interest one group of fans, while a player fashion update may interest another. During the beginning of the COVID-19 pandemic, one of the goals of the Hawks's organization for the Gen Z and millennial market was providing virtual summer camp programs on the website that were promoted on social media that went beyond basketball, with dance tutorials and talks about different culturally relevant topics such as social justice and the importance of voting. From a corporate partnership perspective, the Hawks sponsoring partnerships are also activated on the Hawks, State Farm Arena, College Park Skyhawks, and Hawks Talon social media accounts.

The five person social media team, which is housed in the Marketing department, is responsible for creating this content. The social team uses Facebook, Instagram, Twitter, Snapchat, and LinkedIn to grow the Hawks/State Farm Arena brand. They are also responsible for the social media content of State Farm Arena, the Skyhawks, and the Hawks Talon GC. Branding-wise, after the last Hawks jersey release, now each team has the same color scheme, making branding consistent across all platforms. Finally, influencer engagement on social media plays an important role in affirming the "True to Atlanta" brand. The talent that is associated with the organization, such as artist 2 Chainz (part owner of the Skyhawks) and Real Housewives of Atlanta star Shamea Morton (Hawks in-game host), offer national brand exposure with their social followers. The social media team also sets up interviews or creates videos/interviews of celebrities who attend games and behind-the-scenes information from the talent that may be performing during the in-game concerts. It is clear that through all of these branding efforts, the Hawks stay True to Atlanta.

TRENDS AND CURRENT ISSUES

With the ever-changing platforms, sports marketers can utilize social media as part of a greater marketing campaign and use targeted advertisements to get in front of specific groups of consumers. The organizations can use highlights from games and featured stories to help ticketing, sell merchandise, promote sponsored content, public relations, sports information, and sweepstakes/promotions, regardless of developing or maintaining a brand. This all helps drive traffic to their social media pages as well as the website and the team app. In order to do this, the brand must be consistently highlighted. In this regard, we note the following trends.

THE USE OF HUMOR AND RIVALS

Non-sports social media, such as fast-food chains Wendy's and Popeyes Chicken, are known for their savvy social media humor, which aids the brand in generating awareness and affective response. You may recall the media storm in 2019 when Popeyes Chicken announced via Twitter their new chicken sandwich, prompting a Twitter war between Popeyes and Chick-fil-A. The brand awareness for Popeyes in selling a new product was so high, they quickly sold out of sandwiches across the country. Similarly, it is becoming common for sports teams and rivals to interact more frequently on social media, such as on Twitter — due to its real-time ability. This trend began with 'Twitter wars' and/or jests at each other, but then the trend moved to more humorous ways to troll each other. Even mascots can partake in this rivalry, such as in the Fall 2019, when the University of Oregon Duck and rival University of Washington's Harry the Husky mascots had a humorous Twitter battle. The brand manager for the mascots knew pop culture, as things like "@HarrytheHusky only watched season 8 of GOT" a reference to *Game of Thrones*, while Harry responded "@TheOregonDuck doesn't order fries, but eats some of yours". This back-and-forth provided fans with entertainment and helped garner brand awareness, as it became a story in national news outlets. Similar to knowing the brand values, when some clubs become too 'snarky' or not 'self-aware' and it doesn't fit their organization's brand, it can lead to backlash from the team's players or fans. Sports media staff members should work with their counterparts on other teams to establish rapport and dialogue that is entertaining for fans and aids both brands.

INFLUENCERS

Another trend in social media and branding is the increased role of athletes or celebrities as **brand ambassadors** or **influencers**. Because athletes and celebrities are widely recognized and reach many different audiences with their millions of followers on social media, they can influence a brand. Leagues frequently use both athletes and celebrities for brand promotion on social media. In August 2020, the WNBA worked with broadcast partner ESPN to develop a social media campaign promoting the season on ESPN. ESPN sent the official WNBA orange hoodie to celebrities, like LeBron James, who then posted pictures of it with #orangehoodie on their personal social accounts. The hoodies sold out, game viewership increased, and the league's brand profile was elevated, in part due to the influencer actions and the social media campaign. For teams, they can leverage celebrities who are fans of their teams, such as the Kansas City Chiefs and Paul Rudd. For non-sports organizations, companies can partner with athletes who have large social media followings to enhance their brand, such as Papa John's Pizza benefiting from Shaquille O'Neal, the former NBA star, (also Papa John franchise owner) being a major content contributor on social media. Finally, some athletes are such worldwide brands that they have their own companies. Tennis great Serena Williams, who has over 12 million followers on Instagram alone, owns a fashion brand — S. During the launch of the company, she released a sequin jacket for purchase through Instagram which drove more than 50% of her sales the first week.

LEARNING ACTIVITY 3

Using the Key Resources — Athlete Influencers, listed at the end of the chapter, research an athlete influencer from each of the following five sports: NBA, NFL, WNBA, LPGA, and an

(Continued)

international soccer player. For each athlete, select a social media platform and analyze the 10 most recent social media posts.

- Is there anything in their profile page that mentions brands, charities, social causes, or political passions they influence? If so, how are they listed?
- What specific products/brands or events were they promoting in the social media posts, if any, and how do they promote them?
- What social causes or political passions do they support on social media, if any?
- In your mind, do you feel there is a connection between the athlete and the brand(s) they are promoting?

COLLEGE ATHLETE BRAND MANAGEMENT

With the 2020 NIL changes in college athletics, the management of student-athletes' brands will be a challenge and a trend for both the student-athletes, universities, and partner brands. Many universities are hiring athlete brand management personnel so athletes know how to position themselves on social media. For example, Indiana University hired Opendorse in 2020, which has established the Ready program. The Ready program creates opportunities for student-athletes to understand NIL and receive assistance in maximizing their value while on campus. In 2020, Opendorse had 15,000 athletes across the NCAA involved. Other schools are working with INFLCR to promote the university's brand, as well as student-athletes' brands, on social media communications.

As of July 2020, more than 22,000 athletes were using the INFLCR app. For example, in 2019, Georgia State University (GSU) Athletics partnered with INFLCR for three sports (football, men's and women's basketball). The INFLCR app allows GSU sports communications staff to develop personalized photo galleries, videos, and graphics for student-athletes, coaches, or brand ambassadors for distribution on their personal accounts. The platform was very successful in creating new impressions and followers, and, in 2020, GSU signed on for a 5-year deal for all of their student-athletes to have access to the platform (Georgia State Athletics, 2020). It should be noted, these platforms may offer a competitive advantage in recruiting also, as schools with these contracts can provide student-athletes a way to grow their personal brands, as well as aiding the overall athletic department's brand. Issues may arise as lower revenue programs may not have the resources to aid students in their brand management, creating challenges for these programs to keep pace.

CASE STUDY 2

Organizations are quick to receive feedback on their brand changes on social media. In 2020, both the NFL's Atlanta Falcons and Tampa Bay Buccaneers unveiled their new uniforms via social media. While the Bucs were seen mostly positive, the Falcons received more negative feedback. Both the Falcons and Bucs received their fair amount of negative feedback after the online release.

Tampa Bay Buccaneers ('Bucs'). This was the Bucs fourth uniform change and their first since 2014 when they released infamous "alarm clock" jerseys, which were often considered the NFL's worst uniforms. The Bucs owner, Ed Glazer, mentioned the importance of "valuable feedback" from their fans while working on the new uniforms. The Bucs released their uniforms, which paid homage to their lone Super Bowl victory, on social media. While seen as mostly positive and being a more popular team with Tom Brady, fans online were still somewhat negative of the new brand.

Atlanta Falcons. This was the Falcons's first uniform redesign in 17 years. The rebrand took information gleaned from fan focus groups and research collected from former and current players.

After a series of online leaks, the Falcons released their uniforms one day after the Bucs. From the research, the main takeaway was to "own" the black color in the uniforms and to incorporate the red. As owner Arthur Blank noted, the "black has been a part of our history since 1966 and both our fans and players have asked us to bring it back". The Falcons's major change was swapping the wording "Falcons" across the chest to "ATL". Blank noted, "The 'ATL' moniker is known around the world" and represents their "unity, diversity, and togetherness" (Bergman, 2020). The feedback from fans was mostly negative and the uniforms were seen as amateurish.

Discussion. Both teams took similar approaches when rebranding uniforms, which included an online release, a connection to the past, and fan feedback. As we learned in this chapter, rebranding is always a tough endeavor and often can be negative. With the trend of online releases becoming more regular, teams must be creative and unique when releasing a new brand mark or uniform.

- In case study 2, what made each of these situations unique?
- What were some of the factors that led to negative feedback for the Falcons?
- Explain how teams can be more effective with online releases?
- What can organizations do to have a unique online release?

CHAPTER SUMMARY

Having a brand strategy on social media is an important tool for athletes, teams, and organizations. As social media continues to influence the consumer, it will be important to have a staffed social media team that coexists with the marketing team. For all sports entities, building brand equity through brand awareness, brand associations, brand loyalty, and brand quality through their online platforms will be critical as social media continues to evolve into the latest platforms. The use of social media should be as a tool that provides more avenues for engagement and brand building as part of the organization's marketing strategy.

In summary, this chapter provided a road map to understanding the use of social media as a component of brand management strategy for teams and individual athletes. Throughout this chapter, we discussed the ways organizations, teams, and athletes use social media to enhance their brand images through various assets such as brand associations, brand personality, and a rebranding. Organizations use these strategies to assist in their brand management. Likewise, social media managers need to have specific skills in order to manage these brands. Specifically, they must be organized, good communicators, have a skillset that involves graphic design, video production, and up-to-date knowledge of technology, as well as cultural acuity.

KEY RESOURCES

Branding Overview Websites:
- Brandswinchampionships.com
- Dsmsports.net — Digital and Social Media Sports
- socialnsport.com

Branding Overview Industry Executives:
Twitter Follows
- Jess Smith (@warjesseagle)
- Jeremy Darlow (@JeremyDarlow)

Outsourcing Social Media:
- www.Opendorse.com
- www.inflcr.com

Athlete Influencers/Instagram Accounts:
- Odell Beckham (@obj)
- Brittany Griner (@brittneyyevettegriner)
- Sabrina Ionescu (@ASabrina_i)
- LeBron James (@king james
- Leo Messi (@leomessi)
- Shaquille O'Neal (@shaq)
- Cristiano Ronaldo (@cristiano)

- Lexi Thompson (@lexi)
- JJ Watt (@jjwatt)
- Serena Williams (@serenawilliams)
- Russell Wilson (@dangerusswilson)

TEST YOUR KNOWLEDGE

1. Why is branding important as it relates to sports entities?
2. What is brand equity and what are its four components?
3. Explain the importance of brand association as it relates to a team. Provide five different brand associations for your favorite team.
4. What role do brand endorsers play on social media? Explain how this can effect an athlete.
5. Why is it important for organizations to adapt to new social media platforms?

REFERENCES

Aaker, D. A. (1991). *Managing Brand Equity: Capitalizing on the Value of a Brand Name*. New York, NY: The Free Press.

Badenhausen, K. (2020a). Highest-paid athletes in the world. Retrieved from https://www.forbes.com/athletes/#786381f355ae.

Badenhausen, K. (2020b). The world's most valuable sports teams 2020. Retrieved from https://www.forbes.com/sites/kurtbadenhausen/2020/07/31/the-worlds-most-valuable-sports-teams-2020/?sh=220ebf683c74.

Blaszka, M., Cianfrone, B. A., and Walsh, P. (2018). An analysis of collegiate athletic department social media practices, strategies, and challenges. *Journal of Contemporary Athletics, 12*, 271–290.

Booth, T. (2020). Release the Kraken: Seattle unveils name for NHL franchise. Retrieved from https://www.1011now.com/2020/07/23/release-the-kraken-seattle-unveils-name-for-nhl-franchise/.

Brison, N. T., Baker, T. A., and Byon, K. K. (2015). Facebook likes and sport brand image: An empirical examination of the National Advertising Division's Coastal contacts' decision. *Journal of Legal Aspects of Sport, 25*, 104–122.

Demoff, D. [@kdemoff]. (2020, April 3). Love the new logo, great! Donate to @LAunitedway @lafoodbank during @Abc7 to "LA" Thon today. Want to vent about the new [Tweet] Twitter. https://twitter.com/kdemoff/status/1246222594107310080

Feldman, J. (2018). NBA looks to grow global fan base with TikTok, custom highlights. Retrieved from www.si.com.

Gladden, J. and Funk, D. (2001). Understanding brandy loyalty in professional sport: Examining the link between brand associations and brand loyalty. *International Journal of Sport Marketing and Sponsorship, 3*(1), 67–94.

Gladden, J., Milne, G., and Sutton, W. (1998). A conceptual framework for assessing brand equity in Division I college athletics. *Journal of Sport Management, 12*, 1–19.

Georgia State Athletics. (2020). Georgia State extends partnership with INFLCR. Retrieved from https://georgiastatesports.com/news/2020/7/7/athletics-georgia-state-extends-partnership-with-inflcr.aspx.

Keller, K. L. (1993). Conceptualizing, measuring, and managing customer based brand equity. *Journal of Marketing, 57*, 1–22.

Kemp, S. (2020). More than half of the people on earth now use social media. Retrieved from https://wearesocial.com/blog/2020/07/more-than-half-of-the-people-on-earth-now-use-social-media.

Kotler, P. T. and Keller, K. L. (2016). *Marketing Management: Analysis, Planning, and Control,* (15th ed.). Prentice-Hall.

Kunkel, T., Biscaia, R., Arai, A., and Agyemang, K. (2019). The role of self-brand connection on the relationship between athlete brand image and fan outcomes. *Journal of Sport Management, 34*(3), 201–216.

Kunkel, T., Funk D. C., and King, C. (2014). Developing a conceptual understanding of consumer-based league brand associations. *Journal of Sport Management, 28*, 49–67.

McQueen, J., Foley, C., and Deighton, J. (1993). Decomposing a brand's consumer franchise into buyer types. In D. Aker and A. Biel (Eds.), *Brand equity & advertising: Advertising's role in building strong brands* (pp. 235–245). Hillsdale, NJ: Lawrence Erlbaum Associates, Inc.

Su, Y. S., Baker, B. J., Doyle, J. P., and Kunkel, T. (2020). The rise of an athlete brand: Factors influencing the social media following of athletes. *Sport Marketing Quarterly, 29*(1), 33–46.

Swant, M. (2020). Forbes The World's Most Valuable Brands 2020. Retrieved from https://www.forbes.com/the-worlds-most-valuable-brands/#5654b70b119c.

Chapter 10

Social Media and Sponsorship in Sport

Petros Parganas* and Christos Anagnostopoulos†

*Adidas, Germany
†UCLan Cyprus & Molde University College, Norway

CHAPTER OBJECTIVES

After reading the chapter, you will be able to do the following:

- Understand the implications of social media on sponsorship
- Discuss the sponsorship activation process in the social media environment
- Recognize the role of social media in ambush marketing
- Discuss the recent developments in celebrity endorsements
- Identify the different forms of influencers and their role in sponsorship and athlete endorsement

KEY TERMS

Ambush marketing	Social ambush
Endorsements	Social media activation
Influencer marketing	Sponsorship activation
Instafamous	Vloggers
Micro-celebrities	

INTRODUCTION

While social media dates as far back as the late 1990s with the launch
of Six Degrees, it has become a phenomenon that has grown exponentially across different industries, including the sport industry,
since the early 2000s. In the past decade, social media has touched
different aspects of the sport industry, and, most importantly, it has
greatly impacted sports marketing. The different social media platforms have been used by sports teams, players, leagues, and
federations for a range of marketing purposes such as branding,
sponsorship, endorsements, ambush marketing, relationship marketing, and more. In this chapter, the use of social media in relation
to sponsorship will be discussed. Specifically, the chapter discusses
the implications of social media on sponsorship, and most notably
the sponsorship activation process where social media plays an
important and ever-growing role. Further, the impact of social
media on ambush marketing, and the recent developments in celebrity endorsements, are discussed.

SPORT SPONSORSHIP AND SOCIAL MEDIA: KEY CONCEPTS

Sponsorship as a concept was first observed in ancient Greece
(called "choregia") and the first scholarly work related to sponsorship was done by the ancient Greek historian and philosopher
Xenophon who discussed the contribution of sponsorship to the
development of private–public finance and the political economy at
the time. However, academic interest in sponsorship is a compara-
tively recent phenomenon with Meenaghan (1983) providing the
first widely used definition of modern sponsorship: *The provision of
assistance either financial or in-kind to an activity by a commercial organization for the purpose of achieving commercial objectives* (p. 9).

Nowadays, sponsorship is viewed as one component of the
wider marketing communications mix. Sponsorship can be executed at a local, regional, national, or international level, and
examples of sponsorship can be seen in sports, culture, arts, festi-
vals, fairs, events, municipalities, music, venues, and entertainment.

Recent reports have shown that global sports sponsorship spending has increased each year since 2009, reaching a total of 65 billion dollars in 2019 (TwoCircles, 2020). In the United States, sports sponsorship receives the majority with around 70% of all sponsorship expenditure and is applied on sports associations, leagues, teams, athletes, facilities, events, venues, and recently, e-sports. In Canada, this number is closer to 50% (Canadian Sponsorship Landscape Study, 2020). Regardless of the magnitude of the expenditure, any type of sponsorship aims to address a variety of objectives, among others, such as:

- increasing sales
- increasing brand awareness
- enhancing brand image
- providing entertainment to clients
- improving customers' relations
- developing business and trade relations
- reaching (new) target markets
- increasing purchase intention

While companies seek tangible benefits from the sponsorship programs that they invest in, sports sponsorship differs from advertising in that consumers perceive corporate messages delivered via an association with sport as less obtrusive and direct. In becoming involved in sponsorship, companies are buying the right to associate themselves with sports teams or sports events and exploit the opportunities offered by the accompanying media exposure and public interest. Also, sponsorship is a three-way relationship, which is about placing a sponsoring brand in an emotional relationship between a consumer (for example, a fan) and a sponsored activity (for example, a sports team). Due to the emotional involvement of fans when attending sports events or watching/streaming their team play, a sponsor's investment in a sport generates a goodwill effect among fans, which in turn influences their attitudes and behaviors toward the sponsor.

Research findings report a positive correlation between a sports team's revenues (matchday, broadcast, and commercial/sponsorship) and online followers (Parganas *et al.*, 2017). The utilization of social media represents a promising avenue for businesses to reach global audiences, enhance the fan experience, engage with and receive timely feedback from customer groups, and build relationships with consumers. Specifically, social media is viewed as having a particularly strong ability to enhance and render more efficient (i.e., less costly) the activation of a sponsorship. Given their exponential growth among sports entities and fans, social media can help spread sponsorship messages to reach a large and emotionally driven audience faster than traditional marketing messages such as print or television advertisements.

SPONSORSHIP ACTIVATION AND SOCIAL MEDIA

In any sponsorship, acquiring the sponsorship rights to a property is only part of the job as it does not guarantee the aspired return on investment. Efforts to support one's sponsorship with additional strategic initiatives are referred to as sponsorship activation which is defined as, "communications that promote the engagement, involvement, or participation of the sponsorship audience with the sponsor" (Weeks *et al.*, 2008, p. 639). Without activation, the sponsorship could be considered an advertisement. Activation investments are often measured using the 'activation ratio', which is the ratio of amount invested beyond rights fee to what was spent on the rights fee itself (O'Reilly and Lafrance Horning, 2013), including any associated activities that allow sponsors to promote the sponsorship and engage with fans and consumers. The activation ratio can range from 0 to very high, with some studies showing ratios as high as 7:1 (O'Reilly and Lafrance Horning, 2013).

Regardless of the activation method used, there are several factors that need to be considered during the activation process:

- the sponsor's business objective(s) (i.e., what a sponsoring party is trying to achieve with the sponsorship)
- the strategic fit between the sponsor and the sponsored entity

- the amount of activation spending and the activation ratio
- the timing of activation activities (e.g., before, during, or after an event)
- Country- and culture-specific elements (e.g., using country-specific language when supporting a team or athlete or using the local language)
- integration with the overall marketing strategy of the sponsor to deliver a consistent message across all platforms

In recent years, the traditional marketing activation tactics such as billboards, ads (TV, Radio, Newspaper), public relations, hospitality, etc., have decreased in focus with digital activations, social media, and branded content emerging as the most common techniques (Canadian Sponsorship Landscape Study, 2020). Notably, social media features such as speed, easy access, real-time functioning, network, and public forum are providing sponsors the opportunity to reach out directly to sponsorship audiences, to have frequent conversations with them, and humanize their brands. Indeed, traditional advertising has been in decline since 2009 and social media platforms nowadays not only form the biggest part of many sponsorship activation strategies but also increasingly generate their biggest value (Hurst and Plastiras, 2017).

From a sponsorship activation perspective, sponsors aim to deliver social media content which aligns with consumers motivations, as it will increase their interaction and engagement with the sponsors' posts and thus add more value to the sponsorship in terms of awareness, positive experience, and associations and, finally, sales. Through the use of social media, a sponsor aims to provide consumers with a sense of what it is like to be at an event, especially for those who are unable to attend. For this, sponsors use pictures and videos from event venues, and behind-the-scenes content or resharing of fans' social media posts are part of these efforts. In this regard, social media serves two main purposes during the activation of the sponsorship, namely, providing information and entertainment (Gillooly *et al.*, 2017).

Airbnb ✔ @Airbnb · Nov 18, 2019   ᴏᴏᴏ
We're excited to be partnering with the IOC and our Airbnb hosts for the
next 5 Olympic and Paralympic Games, providing travel experiences that
benefit the global sporting community as well as local communities.
Together, we can host the world. #Olympics airbnb.com/olympics

Figure 1: Example of Informative Sponsorship Post on Twitter (Deal Announcement) for its Partnership with the Olympic Games.

Social media also appears to be used as a support tool for offline sponsorship activations or an online application of their offline sponsorship activations. Sponsorship content posted in social media can be very factual and take the form of the sharing of information about the sponsor itself (e.g., promoting its products and services), the relevant sponsorship activities (e.g., announcement of the sponsorship deal, see Figure 1), or the details about the sponsored property (e.g., live updates about the event). In this context, sponsorship-related social media has the ability to provide valuable content to followers.

At the same time, sponsors need to include creative and entertaining content in their social media sponsorship activation efforts to reach their potential consumers: Online competitions and sales promotions (e.g., Q&A sessions, polls, prizes, sales promotions, etc.), "behind-the-scenes" or "fun facts", informal use of language to encourage sponsored athletes or teams, direct involvement in conversations with followers (e.g., replying to fan comments, providing clarifications, etc.), or efforts to facilitate interactions between sponsored athletes with the sponsor's followers serve this purpose well (see Figure 2). With regards to the latter, sponsors can involve other sponsors (i.e., co-sponsors), other properties that they sponsor, as well as engage individuals and celebrities in the same conversation. Thereby, they use social media as a platform to engage in ongoing conversations with followers that can reach beyond the traditional forms of activation in sponsorship.

The PUR Company Inc. @ThePURCompany · Feb 21, 2018
Tonight is the goal medal game for Women's Olympic Hockey between
#TeamCanada and #TeamUSA! Comment which team you are rooting
for using the hashtags!

♡ 7   ⟲ 2   ♡ 8   ⬆

Figure 2: Example of Entertainment Sponsorship Post (Facilitate Interactions Between Sponsored Athletes with the Sponsor's Followers) During PyeongChang 2018 Games.

LEARNING ACTIVITY

First, identify a major sporting event in your area or that you have interest in that has a title sponsor. Then, examine the Twitter page of the title sponsor during the time of the event. How did the title sponsor use its Twitter account before, during, and after the event that they sponsored (related to the sponsored event)?

SOCIAL MEDIA ACTIVATION MEASUREMENT

This section presents measurement approaches adopted in relation to sponsorship activation via social media. In fact, measuring return on investment on social media and key performance indicators are discussed in reasonable detail in Chapter 15. In the sponsorship industry, there is a lack of agreement as to what constitutes success, what exactly to measure, and how to benchmark. Different sponsors may have different objectives and therefore different criteria for their success. In addition, different social media platforms provide their own individual ways of tracking, analyzing, and reporting on traffic and engagement metrics. For instance, social media platforms are among the different marketing communication mediums that are used for brand awareness and image building. These, however, are difficult to accurately trace back to the sponsor's activities: How much of the added followers or the increased engagement should be associated with the actions of the sponsor? Nevertheless, some key performance indicators (KPI) that help inform the effectiveness of an activation in the social media environment (see also Meenaghan *et al.*, 2013) include:

- **Reach.** This refers to the number of users who have come across a particular content on a social media platform. It essentially tells how many people have seen a post. Often — and perhaps misleadingly — this is also referred to as "noise" or "buzz." This is because, similar to the traditional oral communication, it refers to the level of interaction of consumers of a product, service, or event which amplifies or alters the original marketing message. For instance, a brands' Facebook message can be seen by its followers in the news feed of the brand but also in a story published by a friend. In order to measure the "buzz" of a sponsorship, only relevant social media posts should be considered, i.e., posts on which the brand (sponsor) is featured either (depending on the social media tool used) as a mention, hashtag, link, or keyword.
- **Engagement.** This is any kind of interaction that users have with a particular post on social media other than just viewing it. That is, engagement involves taking action beyond viewing or reading a sponsor's post. Depending on the social media tool, engagement metrics include 'liking' a brand's post, viewing a video, adding a comment to a brand's post, or sharing a brand's post with other users. Voting on activation (e.g., Kraft Hockeyville, where hockey fans in Canada and the United States vote on candidate cities who want to be Hockeyville via social media) is a great example of an engaged measurement. The amount of time

investment contributes to the quality of the engagement metric. That is, clicking on the "Like" button shows approval or agreement with a post without verbal expression, while inserting a comment on a post is the expression of a textual opinion and is seen as a higher level of engagement because it requires more effort by the users to directly respond to organizational messages (Anagnostopoulos *et al.*, 2018). The collection and quantitative analysis of all engagement metrics provides the sponsor with an overview of the success of an activation.

- **Sentiment analysis.** It is categorizing a post based on its tonality (negative, positive, in favor of the sponsor, etc.). It is important for brands to listen carefully to what is being said about their business online as well as the tone of all relevant expressions. Sentiment analysis includes the opinions, attitude, and feelings that people have about a sponsoring brand on social media. It delves deeper into the "buzz" in order to add context and qualitatively examine the positivity or negativity of all the mentions, comments, or shares.

For all the KPIs noted above, the **quality** aspect is of great importance. Many factors influence the quality of a post, starting from selecting the most appropriate social media tool with respect to the features of each tool (e.g., Twitter for real-time game updates or Instagram for pictures), the targeted audience of the sponsorship (Snapchat for younger audience or LinkedIn for business professionals), the timing of the post (e.g. when are Facebook users more active?), the adherence to the best practices for each tool (appropriate size of picture, proper length of video), as well as the promotion quality of the sponsor's logo or hashtag (e.g. appearance, clarity, size and/or position of the sponsors logo in a post or its co-appearance among other brand logos, the memorability of a hashtag). Nevertheless, sponsors can nowadays choose between a number of sophisticated tools (e.g., Hootsuite, Brandwatch, Talkwalker, NodeXL, Gephi, etc.) that offer them a variety of options to monitor, track, and visualize the performance of their social media activations.

AMBUSH MARKETING

Some companies try to find other (and cheaper) ways to be implicitly associated with an event for different reasons. Some of these reasons include: situations where the cost of sponsorship and activation are expensive, an event's pre-existing exclusive deal with a competing sponsoring company, and the desire to reap the benefit of the goodwill and popularity stemming from sponsored events' wider media coverage and extensive audience (Abeza *et al.*, 2020). **Ambush marketing**, also called pseudo-sponsorship, is the practice of non-sponsors' association with an event without having an official or direct commercial connection with that event (Chadwick and Burton, 2011). Ambush marketers, without being contractually tied to an event, can significantly lower the value of legitimate sponsorship. Using communication techniques, ambushers can divert attention away from the event, weaken the link between the event and the official sponsor(s), and catch the attention of the audience by spontaneous, creative, and out-of-the box messages.

An intriguing and important development for ambushers to execute their creative marketing initiatives was the emergence of social media platforms. Ambush marketing via social media (known also as "social ambush") exploits the inherent characteristics of social media: Fast and low-cost dissemination of information (and therefore difficult to control); huge visibility due to the sheer number of social media users worldwide; and new levels of creativity by featuring text, pictures, and videos in posts and including a range of online activities from visual trickery to witty wordplay and sly jokes. As a result, ambush marketing campaigns are often a lot more memorable than typical posts or ads, precisely because they are unusually entertaining or clever. Therefore, such posts are highly likely to be liked, shared, or retweeted more often by social media users, thus spreading the word instantaneously and adding to the confusion of the audience. For example, retail brand Wish came up with a social media campaign during the FIFA World Cup 2018. The campaign focused on placing their products along with the activities of some big players who would not be present at that tournament.

Players such as Gareth Bale and Gianluigi Buffon were joking about missing the tournament and used the company's products to get involved in completely unrelated activities than their profession (see Figure 3). Besides the company's own social media channels, all involved players have been posting their spots across their social media feeds — a massive distribution network considering the multi-million online following of such athletes. Within few hours, several million people viewed and interacted with the funny posts, assisting Wish in using sport as a vehicle to spread the company's message instantly to a worldwide base.

Ambush marketing is not a new phenomenon and numerous instances of it have been reported in several major sporting events, such as Olympic Games or FIFA World Cups (Abeza *et al.*, 2020; Burton and McClean, 2020). The objectives of non-sponsoring companies include taking advantage of the attention and goodwill associated with the events and capitalizing on the large audiences

I had some time on my hands, so picked up a new hobby. Thanks @WishShopping #timeonyourhands

Figure 3: Retail Company Wish Featuring Football Star Gareth Bale in a Video Tweet to Promote its Products During the FIFA World Cup 2018.

created around the event (Wolfsteiner *et al.*, 2015). In addition, ambush marketers are usually direct and close competitors to an official sponsor of an event and through ambush tactics they aim to weaken the public's perceptions of a competitor's official association with the event.

The ambush tactics and strategies however have been changing over the years and adapting to new circumstances and environments. In general, three different types of ambush marketing exist, which can be further divided into 11 specific ambush marketing strategies (Chadwick and Burton; 2011):

- direct (i.e., a non-sponsoring agency using protected intellectual property), including predatory, coattail, and property infringement strategies,
- indirect (i.e., a non-sponsoring agency using suggested references to an event), including sponsor self, associative, distractive, values, insurgent, and parallel property,
- incidental (i.e., a non-sponsoring agency gaining the benefits of association without clear intention of ambushing), which include unintentional and saturation strategies.

As a result of the changing nature of the ambush tactics over time, from the above-mentioned 11 strategies, only six are adaptable to the online medium (Abeza *et al.*, 2020): Coattail ambushing, property infringement, associative ambushing, values ambushing, unintentional ambushing, and saturation ambushing (Table 1):

With the rapidly evolving nature and use of social media, anti-ambushing regulation centered around these medium remains a challenge during the events (Finlay, 2018; Hoskins, 2018). The three most common counter-ambush strategies include (per O'Reilly *et al.*, 2015) legislation (law to punish parties found involved in ambushing practice), communication (increasing public awareness about event properties, including trademarks), and surveillance (identifying intellectual property infringement). From a sponsors' perspective, one additional counter-ambush strategy is to increase

Table 1. Ambush Strategies in Social Media.

Ambush strategy	Description	Social media example
Coattail ambushing	Direct association with a property using a legitimate link, such as participating athletes or official sponsors	English football player Wayne Rooney, sponsored by Nike, tweeted about the Nike #Makeitcount campaign during the Euro 2012 tournament. The tweets were regarded as hidden advertisements, connecting Nike to the English national team playing at the Euro 2012 soccer tournament, the official sponsor of which was Nike's main competitor, Adidas (marketingweek.com)
Property infringement	Intentional unauthorized use of protected intellectual property, such as a logo, a name, and words	Usually congratulating messages from ambushers to athletes and teams with the mention of the name of the event
Associative ambushing	Use of imagery or terminology to create a suggestion that an organization has links to the event	"We've taken a look at the top 10 snowboarding videos on the internet!" Michelin tweeting during the 2018 PyeongChang Winter Olympic Games with a picture of a skier on a field covered with snow (Figure 4)
Values ambushing	Use of an event or property's central value or theme to imply an association	"Whopper, from the Greek word meaning tasty" Burger King ambushing McDonald's during Olympic Games of Rio 2016 by indicating the Greek origin of the Whopper and thereby making a direct connection to the Greek origins of the Olympic Games (Figure 5)

(*Continued*)

Table 1.　(*Continued*)

Ambush strategy	Description	Social media example
Unintentional ambushing	Incorrect consumer identification of a non-sponsoring company as an official sponsor, unknowingly based on a previous association with an event	A sports apparel brand (e.g., Nike, Puma), even though not being the official sponsor of an event (e.g., FIFA World Cup, official sponsor Adidas), earning considerable attention as a result of athletes wearing its products during the event.
Saturation ambushing	Increasing advertisements at the time of an event with no reference or association to the event. Saturation ambushing merely capitalizes on the increased broadcast media attention and audiences that are around an event	During the Beijing 2008 Olympics, Lucozade had indulged into aggressive marketing of its products, much above its standard marketing, featuring athletes and many sports significantly

sponsorship activations to limit opportunities for potential ambushers (Brownlee *et al.*, 2018).

To adapt to the new challenges offered by social media, governing bodies such as the Olympic Committee have formulated social media guidelines and policies for competing athletes and other credentialed officials (Rule 40) since the Olympic Games in Beijing 2008, which have been updated ever since up to the Tokyo 2020 Games. Monitoring of the social media environment and providing athletes with clear instructions on how to use words, symbols, and official sponsorships has proven to be successful to some extent (Abeza *et al.*, 2020). However, despite the strategies and guidelines in place, the nature of ambush marketing has evolved over time with innovative, creative, and very responsive posts, making any protection efforts very challenging (Nufer, 2016). The distinctive

Michelin ✓
@MichelinTyres

The UK snow has got us in the mood, so we've taken a look at the top 10 snowboarding videos on the internet! - sole-power.com/skiing-snowboa...

6:31 PM · Feb 27, 2018 · TweetDeck

Figure 4: Michelin's Associative Ambushing During the PyeongChang 2018 Winter Olympic Games.

← **Tweet**

Burger King ✓
@BurgerKing

Whopper, from the Greek word meaning tasty.

8:05 PM · Jun 5, 2016 · Sprinklr

47 Retweets   **177** Likes

Figure 5: Burger King's Values Ambushing During Rio 2016 Olympic Games.

features of social media (e.g., easy and free access, wide availability, border- and timeless) make it hard to fight ambush marketing.

SPORTS CELEBRITY ENDORSEMENTS IN SOCIAL MEDIA

A **celebrity endorser** is defined as, *any individual who enjoys public recognition and who uses this recognition on behalf of a consumer good by appearing with it in an advertisement* (McCracken, 1989, p. 310).

Celebrity endorsement as a marketing strategy dates several decades back and the main aim is to increase the awareness of the endorsed products and strengthen the consumers' perceived association between the celebrity's attributes and the endorsed product. Sports celebrities are individuals who work in the sport industry and benefit from great recognition in their respective sports. In most cases these individuals are either athletes or a coaches. And, in all cases, they are high profile celebrities.

Celebrity athletes (and coaches) have embraced social media to interact with friends and fans and keep current with the latest news. In fact, famous sports personalities have become among the most followed online individuals. Football stars such as Ronaldo, Neymar, or Messi have a worldwide online follower base of above 250 million people (Football Benchmark, 2020). Traditionally, the athlete–fan relationship was one-way, with athletes giving an interview in a newspaper or TV channel and fans able to see or read them but often unable to respond directly to the athlete. Social media however lowers these barriers to communication: Within an online social network, sports fans can send messages to their favorite athletes, who can in turn read and respond to them.

This direct communication between athletes and their fans represents a vehicle whereby athletes can promote not only themselves, their sport, organization, and team but also their sponsors (Kassing and Sanderson, 2010). That is, athletes frequently use their social media accounts to post about non-sports-related issues. Such posts vary from music and television shows, to charities and favorite restaurants, and even posts about their personal lives. They also invite their followers to check out pictures, blogs, and websites. Several athletes can even praise or recommend a particular product or service through posts on their social media accounts. Such promotional messages present the sponsor in a positive light and create a call to action, by encouraging consumers to check out the sponsor's website or directly to purchase the product. This is the benefit that sponsors seek when partnering with celebrity athletes to create endorsements. In turn, the athletes' social media followers interact with such posts and get involved in conversations and perhaps provide similar positive feedback about a product. Such online exchange of information and thoughts between followers provides the endorsed company with free advertising through online word of mouth and offers an additional venue to promote their products to millions of online fans instantly. As with traditional advertising mediums, meanings are also transferred from the athlete to the brand and then to the consumer, the magnitude however being at a totally new level now.

Equally important, such online discourse may even reach consumers who are not following the athlete and thereby offer unsolicited product testimonies to an additional number of consumers to learn about or purchase the product. While such an online social network with millions of followers and interactions represents an effective way for the endorsed companies to market their products to a wider audience, sports celebrities need to find the right balance among the variety of topics they choose to post about. On top of this, sports celebrities are usually involved in endorsements of various products and they are contractually required to allocate enough frequency to the respective endorsement posts. A balanced mix of posts from different categories gives a more genuine feel and maintains the interest of their followers. Therefore, it is in the interest of the endorsed company to ensure that the relevant posts of their celebrities appear in a believable, heartfelt, and timely manner, reflecting the characteristics of expertise and trustworthiness, in order to capitalize on the popularity of their accounts and transform such a huge consumer base into revenue streams.

On the other hand, sponsors need to consider and understand that the use of social media for promotional purposes comes with a number of caveats. The very nature of social media opens the door for two-way communication that offers several advantages for sponsors, but at the same time, this unfiltered communication can turn against the sponsor very quickly. Companies and celebrities have increasingly been facing the impact of negative online word of mouth and complaint behavior. Such instant waves of criticism, commonly referred to as online (social) firestorms, are characterized by a high number of posts with an enraged, emotional tonality, spreading extremely fast through social media. Usually, reacting to an online firestorm is difficult as companies have no control over their customers and cannot censor what users post online. On top of this, the level of aggression is not only influenced by the original content, but also by comments and responses of other users, which can have an amplified and negative effect that turns against the endorsed company and product. For instance, if an athlete expresses his or her discontent for a company, it reaches millions of consumers instantly, which can have a negative impact on the company's image and reputation and might lead to a significant loss of revenue streams.

CASE STUDY: MERCEDES-BENZ RIDES TWITTER TO SUPER BOWL

The Super Bowl is one of the most attractive platforms for sponsorship and advertising. On a yearly basis, it usually represents the most-watched TV show in the US and one of the most watched worldwide. To prepare for the premiere of its first ever Super Bowl commercial, car manufacturer Mercedes-Benz developed a Twitter campaign and event in the days leading up to the event to capture consumer interest. Mercedes-Benz incorporated social media and celebrity athletes into its marketing strategy, creating four automotive teams around the country and holding a "tweet-race" to the 2012 Super Bowl in Dallas.

Each team was assigned a celebrity coach: Tennis star Serena Williams, rock singer Pete Wentz, baseball player Nick Swisher, and hip-hop artist Rev Run, who also raised funds for charities during the process. The four coaches encouraged users to follow them on Twitter and tweet for their favourite teams. For instance, one of Serena Williams's post read as *Don't forget to include #MBteamGL in your tweets today! I need your help to win the #MBtweetrace! Follow @Hoo_de_Hoo for more details.* The goal was to generate as many tweets and retweets, or "tweet fuel," as possible. Points or "tweet fuel" could also be gained through a series of established road challenges. These included "Meet the Family," where the teams tweeted photographs of other Mercedes-Benz vehicles spotted on the road, and "America's Game," where they took photos of themselves in front of high school, college, or professional football stadiums. The team that reached the finish line with the most points/"tweet fuel" would be declared winner.

Mercedes-Benz hoped to attract new customers by promoting its products through this creative social media initiative, linking the campaign to a major sporting event and using celebrity athletes to generate interest in the promotion (Hambrick and Mahoney, 2011). According to Stephen Cannon, VP of marketing for Mercedes-Benz USA, *Tweet Race represents a strategic leap of faith into social media. You have to do it by participating. I can't sit on the sidelines and read white papers. That was the insight that drove us to focusing resources, dollars, and effort on social marketing.*

CASE QUESTIONS

1. What sponsorship objectives would Mercedes-Benz try to achieve in its Twitter campaign presented above? Which ones rely on social media activation to be successful?
2. Identify the endorsement that Mercedes-Benz employed in the case presented above. What are the social media elements?
3. If you work for the Ferrari or BMW Group, which are competitors of Mercedes-Benz, how would you use social media to ambush its Twitter campaign?

INFLUENCER MARKETING

What does it mean to be a celebrity in the 21st century? On Instagram or YouTube, some of the most popular accounts are not owned by celebrity athletes or Hollywood actors/actresses, but by ordinary consumers who are largely unknown to the offline general public. These individuals have managed to build a strong following through sharing interesting, original, and entertaining content. A famous example is "The F2Freestylers", also known as "The F2", a British freestyle football duo comprising former semi-professional footballers Billy Wingrove and Jeremy Lynch. Both had been rejected by academies of professional football clubs in their youths before creating videos about football skills and tricks and posting them in their respective Instagram and YouTube channels. At the time of writing, they are regarded as global football infuencers with their YouTube channel counting over 12.6 million and their Instagram account with more than 8.8 million subscribers (Figure 6).

The term "instafamous people" is used to account for the fact that their fame is limited to the online space (mainly Instagram and YouTube) with a much lower level of attention offline compared to traditional celebrities. In the online world, instafamous celebrities possess visibility and popularity similar to traditional celebrities, and at the same time, they appear more relatable to consumers because they are regarded as "down-to-earth", ordinary people in the real world (Schouten *et al.*, 2020). In addition, they are regular content

Figure 6:   The F2 Using Instagram to Showcase one of Their Football Skills.
Source: Instagram.

creators and continuously feed that image by posting not only within a specific (usual niche) area but also about ordinary, everyday events like grocery shopping, doing sport exercises, or simply lounging on the couch (Lou and Yuan, 2019). Such online celebrities, usually referred to in the literature as "influencers", "micro-celebrities," or "vloggers", have become one of the hottest marketing trends for product endorsements, while numerous influencers transgressing into more 'traditional' celebrities have found their way to the general public and mass media.

Celebrity endorsements were the original form of influencer marketing. Recently, brands have turned to online celebrities to distribute information and influence consumers' product perceptions. Influencer marketing is becoming ubiquitous and spending is increasing on a yearly basis (Mediakix, 2018). Influencers are viewed as reliable information sources by their followers and directly influence their purchasing decisions (Schouten *et al.*, 2020). The rationale of influencing consumers through influencer product endorsements remains basically the same as described for celebrity endorsements: meanings are transferred from the influencer to the brand and then to the consumer. Like celebrity endorsers, influencers post (professional) photos of themselves to remind us of their physical attractiveness or videos showcasing the mastery of a skill to position themselves as experts in a particular field. Through that mix of posts, they become public figures who bridge the gap between star (sport) celebrities and ordinary people.

The F2 mentioned previously is such an example with global appeal. On a more local level, examples include "Street Style Society" (S3) in France or Munya Chawawa in London, football freestyler and comedian, respectively, and at the same time associated with the apparel sports brand Adidas (see Figures 7 and 8). Whether or not associated with (paid by) a particular brand, a popular influencer post featuring a brand contributes to online brand conversations and awareness. Studies have found that influencer marketing has the ability to trigger 11 times more return on investment (measured in terms of reach, engagement, and ultimately sales) than other forms of traditional advertising annually (Kirkpatrick 2016).

Figure 7: S3 Performing on Instagram and Wearing Adidas Apparel and Shoes.
Source: Instagram.

Figure 8: Munya Chawawa Talking in Instagram About a New Collection of Sportswear Apparel Company Adidas.
Source: Instagram

Such behavior has not remained unnoticed by brands and many of those online celebrities are nowadays used as ambassadors for brands who want to increase their following and awareness in the social media sphere. The goal of several brands is to build a network of influencers with a view to impact the behavior of their consumers. The influencer is placed at the center of the campaign and all marketing activities are oriented around him or her. The influencer marketing trend started roughly a decade ago on blogging platforms and has gradually transferred to social media such as Twitter, YouTube, and Instagram (Abidin, 2016). Paid collaborations between brands and social media influencers are commonly realized in the form of sponsored content. As mentioned, many of these influencers exist within niche online social circles wherein they disseminate influential messages to their followers, containing both informational and entertainment value. That is, they offer detailed descriptions about and comparisons of products, while at the same time cover such posts with personal touches to create an enjoyable and entertaining experience for their audience and not least to disguise the underlying commercial message.

It is important to understand the thin line that separates real influencer marketing from a simple, "innocent" product endorsement from an individual in social media. Whether or not a brand is behind an influencer's post is not always clear. Imagine for instance the following situation: You log into your Instagram account and a micro-celebrity you are following posts a picture clearly depicting him or her strolling through the park enjoying a famous chocolate bar. A few posts below you see one of your friends (also with a fairly big number of followers) posting an image holding a cup of coffee from a famous coffee shop. While both are examples of influencer marketing, they differentiate themselves in the fact that the first one is paid by the chocolate brand and the second is a spontaneous post from your friend (perhaps to make you jealous!). It is exactly this blurring of lines between paid and genuine endorsement what makes influencer marketing so powerful.

However, the blurred influencer marketing environment creates some potential ethical and legal implications. For instance, we can classify under unethical a behavior where in an influencer does not believe in the product (or does not even use it at all), but still posts a positive review of it (because they are getting paid to do so). If the association between the influencer and the brand is not disclosed properly, it is misleading for the consumers as they are receivers of, practically, a lie. Besides losing their credibility to their followers, there might be legal implications as well, since the influencer could get into trouble with recent policy regulations. To avoid any ethical or legal troubles, social media influencers must disclose their relationship with the brands they endorse and communicate this paid endorsement by including the words or hashtags such as #ad or #sponsored in the post.

While the use of influencers in campaigns is increasing (Mediakix, 2018), brands need to find the correct balance in the amount and type of influencers they use and understand more about who they may want to partner with in order to promote their brand or products. Building on Heinze *et al.*'s (2020) classification, four different types of influencers can be identified, based on the size of their follower base (Table 2): Nano, micro, macro, and mega. Usually, nano

Table 2. Types of Social Media Influencers.

Influencer Type	Followers	Description
Nano	1000	• Very active on social media • High level of engagement with and trust from their audience • Very influential for complex engagement
Micro	1001– 10,000	• Developed subject expertise in a particular domain • Usually enthusiasts for a particular topic • Longer term popularity and trust from their audience • Tend to have a good tone of voice and a style of communication which resonates with their followers.
Macro	10,001– 100,000	• Professionalized approach to their social media management • Have agents and are very interested in paid engagements and promotions. • Might be more difficult for them to show real affinity with a brand as they might already work with multiple brands in your area.

Table 2. (*Continued*)

Influencer Type	Followers	Description
Mega	100,000+	• Often celebrities who have the followers because of who they are and not what they do on social media • Can be occupied by social media stars and social media personalities who engage on social media as a way of making a living. • High exposure but low engagement with their audience

Source: Adapted from Heinze *et al.* (2020).

influencers have a small but very engaged online following. As the number of followers increase, the engagement ratio decreases. Nano or Micro-influencers are usually individuals with a following of a few thousands or less, which sometimes need to "apply" to become influencers for a brand. Macro-influencers on the other hand are usually individuals with a large social media following (in the region of tens of thousands) and are usually approached by a brand to endorse its products. A mega or star-influencer should be considered a person with a very large online following who in several cases can be also famous offline. Sport celebrities for instance are considered part of this type of influencers. The characteristics of the "down to earth" individual may be more evident on the micro-influencer, where the engagement with and impact on their following base is high, while their relatively small audience is located within a geographical area that makes them more suitable for local brands. However, a brand that needs a global appeal might opt for a macro-influencer, counting on the global profile of the influencer. Other considerations include the cultural aspect of an influencer. The impact of some sectors of a society might be more evident for some cultures than for others. Similarly, what works for some consumers in some cultures might not work for others. Brands need to take such factors into consideration when selecting their influencers to endorse their products.

LEARNING ACTIVITY

Pick up two Macro social media influencers. One should be a professional athlete, and the other one an entrepreneur from outside sport. Have a look at their 10 most recent posts on Twitter or Instagram. What is the nature of their posts? Do you discern similarities and/or differences? Why? Explain.

Since micro influencers maintain a closer relationship with their followers, influencer marketing strategies target more niche communities allowing a new type of influencers to be tailored for specific communities, body types, or industries in mind. Indeed, the latest trend for companies is to use fictional characters as spokespersons for their products. Virtual influencers, that is, computer-generated human avatars with a social media presence, have been used lately by companies to promote their products online, addressing especially younger audiences (Moustakas *et al.*, 2020). Seraphine, for instance, created by Riot Games Inc. — the studio behind the Esports game "League of Legends" — has a social media follower base of more than 400,000 real people (Figure 9).

Virtual influencers are being given human traits (e.g., struggles, conflicts, goals, and aspirations), while often an engaging storyline is built around them to develop an emotional connection with their followers. For instance, Alex Hunter, a fictional character in the FIFA game series made by EA Sports, is supposed to be a footballer, growing up in London, with parents, friends, and goals like real humans. Alex Hunter has been used by sports apparel company adidas to endorse football shoes (Figure 10). Besides human-like appearances, there are other virtual influencers which are fantastical creations like Janky and Guggimon (Figure 11). Nevertheless, they also have an increasing online following (Bloomberg, 2020), while all virtual characters wear real clothing labels, eat real food, and drive real cars, which makes them attractive to companies to endorse their products. While the success and longevity of such endeavors remains to be seen, it represents the most recent trend in the field of social media influencers.

Figure 9: Virtual Influencer Seraphine Enjoying the Sun by the Beach.

Source: Instagram.

Figure 10: Fictional Character Alex Hunter Endorsing Adidas Football Shoes.

Source: Twitter.

Figure 11:   Virtual Influencer and Fantastic Creation Guggimon Endorsing Red Bull.

Source: Instagram.

KEY SKILLS FOR PRACTICE

In this digital age, working in the social media sponsorship area in the sport industry is a demanding job. It needs **organizational skill**, which involves planning, executing, measuring, and reporting — and doing it all over again for another campaign. Therefore, those working in similar positions need to be strategic planners, understand the bigger picture, and recognize how social media fits in the overall objectives. While there are similarities to the "offline" sponsorship manager, the social media manager needs to make sure that online sponsorship activation is executed consistently with offline activation as well as with the overall business strategy. In this regard, **environmental scanning** skills will be essential, involving collecting, reading, and interpreting data, which are key in order to report the most relevant metrics and derive the most appropriate insights for your stakeholders.

Additionally, a relatively strong sales acumen with good **communication skills** is also needed. That is, how to approach a sponsorship sale in order to be as effective and successful as possible, for both parties. For this, understanding customer needs and developing solutions to those needs is necessary. This in turn requires proper understanding of the different social media platforms to target the right audience. In addition, the ability to sell a sponsorship and understand the sales process is essential. This involves preparing and presenting accurate and comprehensive sales pitches/presentations and establishing close business relationships with all levels of clients.

TRENDS AND CURRENT ISSUES

Sports sponsorship has grown considerably during the past decade. Sponsors spend on sponsorships and activations at all levels and on all platforms, athletes have been valuable partners in endorsements, and influencer marketing is booming. Although the onset of COVID-19 globally has changed the previously promising forecasts for the future of the sponsorship business. Indeed, after the world was suddenly hit by a pandemic and while its impact is difficult to be evaluated currently, there are already discussions and research on the amount of (immediate) losses sponsorship will suffer. One set of industry studies (SponsorshipX, 2020) suggested that sponsorship investment in rights fees would decline about 50% overall in 2020, with activation expected to experience a more than 60% decrease. Clearly, sponsorship has been hit very hard.

The impact of COVID-19 on sport and social media is massive. First, consider that the two largest global sporting events planned for 2020 (i.e., Tokyo Olympic Games and EURO 2020 in Italy) have been postponed, and — at the time of writing — the future is very uncertain for all events anywhere. Most major events where sponsorship is common have been canceled or postponed, with a few playing in front of empty (or reduced capacity) venues. That means that the foundations on which sponsors have planned their marketing activities have changed and as the underlying product does not hold the same value for them, renegotiations of sponsorship contracts are inevitable.

However, besides the losses, organizations attempt to come up with a strategy for any similar incident in the future. Even if matches are played in ghost stadiums and thus impacting one revenue stream, the broadcasting figures might not be affected or even increased. Sponsors need to re-evaluate their objectives, fans to re-evaluate the offerings. Technology and social media in particular could play an even more important role for people to follow, engage, and stay in touch with their favorite sport or team and this in turn might create new opportunities, both from a playing and a viewing perspective. In addition, brands have gone one step further by "hiring" digital spokespeople (virtual influencers) for their products. While their success needs to be assessed in the following years, initial results suggest their acceptance and applicability, especially in times during which interacting safely with other humans can no longer be taken for granted. Going back to ancient Greeks, they used to say that out of every disadvantage one can draw an advantage. At the end, sports matches are a great example of how to capitalize on disadvantages.

CHAPTER SUMMARY

Social media plays a leading role in the wider sports sponsorship landscape. Given that sports organizations, companies outside sport as well as high profile athletes see value in utilizing various social media platforms for meeting sponsorship-related objectives, the importance of studying the social media–sponsorship nexus has become clear. To help you better understand this nexus, the present chapter offered the necessary conceptual background and covered topics around the implications of social media on sponsorship, the sponsorship activation process in the social media environment, the role of social media in ambush marketing, the recent developments on celebrity endorsements, as well as the different forms of influencers and their role in sponsorship and athlete endorsements. The chapter, however, provides only the foundational concepts for understanding this nexus, so — as a current or future sport administrator — it is imperative to keep up with the fast changes that constantly occur in relation to the way social media impact sports sponsorship.

KEY RESOURCES

The Benefits of Sports Sponsorships in the Digital Age of Visual Data: https://visua.com/the-benefits-of-sports-sponsorships-in-the-digital-age-of-visual-data.
Social Media in Sports Marketing: https://opendorse.com/blog/social-media-in-sports-marketing/.
Social media and sports sponsorship: a legal perspective: https://www.sportspromedia.com/opinion/social-media-and-sports-sponsorship-a-legal-perspective.
The Surprisingly High Sports Sponsorship Value of Unofficial Social Media Accounts: https://www.sporttechie.com/high-sponsorship-value-of-unofficial-social-media-accounts-gumgum-sports/.

TEST YOUR KNOWLEDGE

1. What differentiates sponsorship from other marketing communication approaches?
2. What is sponsorship activation and what is the role of social media?
3. How is success measured in social media activations?
4. What are the effects of social media on ambush marketing?
5. Discuss the advantages and disadvantages of celebrity endorsements in social media.
6. Explain the reasons behind the success of influencer marketing.

REFERENCES

Abeza, G., Braunstein-Minkove, J., Seguin, B., O'Reilly, N., Kim, A., and Abdourazakou, Y. (2020), Ambush marketing via social media: The case of the three most recent olympic games. *International Journal of Sport Communication*. DOI: https://doi.org/10.1123/ijsc.2020-0266.

Social Media in Sport

284

Social Media in Sport

Abidin, C. (2016). Visibility labour: Engaging with influencers fashion brands and #OOTD advertorial campaigns on Instagram. *Media International Australia, 161*(1), 86–100.

Anagnostopoulos, C., Parganas, P., Chadwick, S., and Fenton, A. (2018). Branding in pictures: using Instagram as a brand management tool in professional team sport organisations. *European Sport Management Quarterly, 18*(4), 413–438.

Bloomberg (2020). Virtual Influencers Make Real Money While Covid Locks Down Human Stars [online] https://www.bloomberg.com/news/features/2020-10-29/lil-miquela-lol-s-seraphine-virtual-influencers-make-more-real-money-than-ever, [accessed 16 November 2020].

Brownlee, E., Greenwell, T. C., and Moorman, A. (2018). An experimental approach to assessing the effectiveness of official sponsor designations in an ambush marketing scenario. *Sport Marketing Quarterly, 27*(3), 145–153.

Burton, N. and McClean, C. (2020). Exploring newsjacking as social media — based ambush marketing. *Sport, Business and Management: An International Journal,* DOI: 10.1108/SBM-12-2019-0116.

Canadian Sponsorship Landscape Study (2020). 13th Annual Study Report. Downloaded September 29th, 2020 from www.sponsorshiplandscape.ca.

Chadwick, S. and Burton, N. (2011). The evolving sophistication of ambush marketing: A typology of strategies. *Thunderbird International Business Review, 53*(6), 709–719. doi:10.1002/tie.20447

Finlay, C. J. (2018). National proxy 2.0: Controlling the social media of Olympians through national identification. *Communication and Sport, 6*(2), 131–153.

Football Benchmark (2020). [online] www.footballbenchmark.com [accessed 5 May 2020]

Gillooly, L., Anagnostopoulos, C., and Chadwick, S. (2017). "Social media-based sponsorship activation — a typology of content", *Sport, Business and Management, 7*(3), 293–314. https://doi.org/10.1108/SBM-04-2016-0016.

Hambrick, M. and Mahoney, T. (2011). 'It's incredible — trust me'. *International Journal of Sport Management and Marketing, 10*(3/4), 161–179.

Heinze, A., Fletcher, G., Rashid, T., and Cruz, A. (2020), Digital and Social Media Marketing — A Results Driven Approach. 2nd Edition. Abingdon: Routledge.

Hoskins, J. R. (2018). Silence is golden: Olympic property protection in the age of social media. *Capital University Law Review,* 46, 125–157.

Hurst, C. and Plastiras, A. (2017). The rising importance of social media for football clubs. [online] Nielsen Sports. https://nielsensports.com/rising-importance-social-media-football-clubs/ [accessed 30 April, 2020].

Kassing, J. W. and Sanderson, J. (2010). Fan-athlete interaction and Twitter tweeting through the Giro: A case study. *International Journal of Sport Communication*, 3(1), 113–128.

Kearney, A. T. (2012). 'Olympic advertisers study can't find a social media gold medallist', Marketing Blog, 13 August [online] http://www.marketwired.com/press-release/at-kearney-olympicadvertisers-study-cant-find-a-social-media-gold-medalist-1688658.htm [accessed 10 November 2020].

Kirkpatrick, David. "Influencer Marketing Spurs 11 times the ROI over Traditional Tactics: Study." *Marketing Dive. Industry Dive, 6 Apr. 2016.* [online] http://www.marketingdive.com/news/influencer-marketing-spurs-11-times-the-roi-overtraditional-tactics-study/416911 [accessed 30 April 2020].

Lou, C. and Yuan, S. (2019). Influencer marketing: How message value and credibility affect consumer trust of branded content on social media. *Journal of Interactive Advertising*, 19(1), 58–73, DOI: 10.1080/15252019.2018.1533501

Marketingweek (2012). Nike launches London campaign [online] https://www.marketingweek.com/nike-launches-london-campaign/ [accessed 13 November, 2020].

McCracken, G. (1989). Who is celebrity endorser: Cultural foundations of the endorsement process. *Journal of Consumer Research 16*(3), 310–321.

Mediakix (2018). The influencer marketing industry global ad spend: A $5–$10 billion market by 2020 [online] https://mediakix.com/blog/influencer-marketing-industry-ad-spend-chart/ [accessed 25 April 2020].

Meenaghan, T. (1983). Commercial sponsorship. *European Journal of Marketing, 17*, 1–74.

Meenaghan, T., McLoughlin, D., and McCormack, A. (2013). New challenges in sponsorship evaluation actors, new media, and the context of praxis. *Psychology and Marketing, 30*(5), 444–460.

Moustakas, E., Lamba, N., Mahmoud, D., and Ranganathan, C. (2020) Social Media Conference ©2020 IEEE Blurring lines between fiction and reality: Perspectives of experts on marketing effectiveness of virtual influencers [Social Media 2020]. DOI: 10.22619/IJCSA.

O'Reilly, N. and Lafrance Horning, D. (2013). Leveraging sponsorship: The activation ratio. *Sport Management Review, 16*(4), 424–437.

O'Reilly, N., Pound, R., Burton, R., Seguin, B., and Brunette, M. (2015). *Global Sport Marketing: Sponsorship, Ambush Marketing, and the Olympic Games.* Morgantown, WV: FIT Publishing.

Parganas, P., Liasko and Anagnostopoulos, C. (2017). Scoring goals in multiple fields: Social media presence, on-field performance and commercial success in European professional football. *Sport, Business and Management,* 7(2), 197–215. https://doi.org/10.1108/SBM-11-2016-0072.

Schouten, A., Janssen, L., and Verspaget, M. (2020). Celebrity vs. Influencer endorsements in advertising: The role of identification, credibility, and Product-Endorser fit. *International Journal of Advertising, 39*(2), 258–281, DOI: 10.1080/02650487.2019.1634898.

TwoCircles (2020). [online] https://twocircles.com/gb-en/articles/projections-sponsorship-spend-to-fall-17-2bn/ [accessed 13 November 2020].

Weeks, C. S., Cornwell, T. B. and Drennan, J. C. (2008). "Leveraging Sponsorships on the Internet: Activation, Congruence, and Articulation". *Psychology and Marketing, 25*(7), 637–654.

Wolfsteiner, E., Grohs, R., and Wagner, U. (2015). What drives ambush marketer misidentification? *Journal of Sport Management, 29*(2), 137–154. doi:10.1123/JSM.2014-0122.

Chapter 11

Social Media and Sports Media

David Cassilo

Kennesaw State, Georgia

CHAPTER OBJECTIVES

After reading this chapter, you should be able to do the following:

- Understand the impact of social media on traditional sports media
- Discuss the concepts of social media within a sports journalism context
- Recognize techniques to engage in personal branding as a sports journalist
- Identify strategies to gather information using social media as a sports journalist
- Describe how social media can enhance an online broadcast of sport
- Understand the role of social media in contemporary sports media
- Apply social media strategies to a variety of contexts within sports media

KEY TERMS

Content aggregation

Engagement

Gatekeeper

Live streaming

Personal branding

Second-screen viewing

Self-commodification

User-generated content

INTRODUCTION

Since the dawn of the printing press, new technology has reshaped the journalism industry. Social media is one of the latest of those technologies, which has significantly impacted news production and journalism practices (Pedersen, 2014). Originally designed for sharing content and engaging in conversation, social media has quickly become a vital part of a journalist's job (Lee and Ma, 2012). Social media affords journalists the ability to provide constant, instant, and live updates to their audience that prior technologies could not (Li *et al.*, 2017). Additionally, social media has become such a popular news source that nearly two-thirds of Americans get their news from it (Matsa and Shearer, 2018). Practically, social media allows journalists to easily and efficiently connect with industry experts for input on their stories. In particular, Twitter has become a live news feed, making it near essential that journalists not only have a presence on the platform but also the skills to effectively communicate information.

In sports media, the ability to communicate news nearly instantaneously is just one of the many ways the industry has been reshaped by social media. Athletes and teams now use social media to bypass journalists and disseminate information directly to fans, meaning that the sports journalist is no longer the gatekeeper of all news on his or her beat (Pederson, 2014). In some cases, bloggers have become more influential than journalists (ideally the journalist is also a blogger). While the ability to break news may be diminished, social media has afforded journalists with a plethora of new job responsibilities including personal branding (Brems *et al.*, 2017), audience engagement (Guzman, 2016), aggregating content (Coddington, 2020), and utilizing new forms of social media as they develop. Balancing these duties comes with the simultaneous navigation of credibility issues (Lecheler and Kruikemeier, 2016) and increased competition. Thus, while social media has allowed sports journalists to reach a wider audience than ever before, that is only possible when that journalist develops the necessary skills to effectively use these platforms. The chapter ahead will discuss how social media has changed the sports media industry as well as introduce some of the social media skills needed to succeed as a sports journalist today.

HISTORY AND BACKGROUND

In 2015, 59% of all adults in the US claimed to be sports fans (Gallup, 2019). Thus, as users seek sports information on social media platforms, media organizations have to provide the content to match that interest. As sports news has shifted to a digital format, that news is commonly disseminated on social media. Thus, sports fans need social media to keep up with their favorite teams and leagues. As discussed in Chapter 1, contemporary social media had its rise in early 2000s, but for sports media, perhaps the more important moment was the debut of Twitter in 2006. Twitter, in particular, has affected the news routines of the sports newsroom due to its ability to easily communicate information to a wide audience at a near instantaneous rate (English, 2016). Due to these capabilities, social media has evolved as a go-to source for sports information. A 2019 UK survey found that 64% of young sports fans prefer social media sports content to traditional sports television content (Friend, 2019). In recent years, newer social media platforms such as Instagram, Snapchat, and TikTok have become popular among consumers as well.

Viewing social media as a new tool to reach and expand audiences, sports networks and media organizations adopted the platform in a variety of different ways. **Second-screen viewing** has encouraged the sports audience to interact with the broadcast they are watching by using social media (Rubenking and Lewis, 2016), a practice which has become commonplace (Schultz and Sheffer, 2010). Meanwhile, social media leads to increased competition for the sports writer. Athletes and teams quickly identified social media as a way to directly communicate information like retirements, free agency decisions, and trades to fans (Sanderson and Kassing, 2011). Thus, since its advent, social media has provided information more quickly to sports fans, but it has also changed the media sources from which the information comes.

The next section of this chapter discusses some of the key concepts that demonstrate the dynamic and interrelated relationship between social media and sports media. These concepts include personal branding, engagement, information gathering, and credibility.

SOCIAL MEDIA AND SPORTS MEDIA: KEY CONCEPTS
JOURNALISTS' PERSONAL BRANDING

In the age of social media, there is great importance for journalists to build their own brands. Social media sites have created an environment where the audience largely follows journalists because of their content and not because of their media organization. Gone are the days of the Houston Astros fans going to the *Houston Chronicle* website to get their baseball fix. Now fans follow all of the team's top beat reporters on Twitter, regardless of what publication they write for. Thus, the ability to create one's own area of expertise or niche in social media can lead to a dramatic increase in exposure. Take NBA journalist Adrian Wojnarowski, for example. While at *Yahoo! Sport*, he became the go-to source for all NBA news. His posts on Twitter were referred to as "Woj Bombs" as he quickly demonstrated an ability to break NBA news before all other journalists. In 2011, Wojnarowski had 90,000 followers on Twitter. As of 2020, he had more than 4 million.

In order for a journalist to engage in **personal branding** on social media, it is essential that he or she can identify his or her own skills and be able to "present them on a well-arranged platter" to the media consumer (Brems *et al.*, 2017, p. 445). In the case of

Wojnarowski, his skill is breaking credible NBA news, and he presents that skill on Twitter (@wojespn) by posting breaking news frequently in a clear and concise manner for the audience. By creating this personal brand, Wojnarowski is engaging in **self-commodification**, a practice essential to journalism in the digital age (Jerslev and Mortensen, 2016). In the tumultuous field of journalism wrought with economic uncertainty, journalists skilled in personal branding have established themselves as commodities worth having. Journalists with a large social media following theoretically bring their audience to a news organization's website, thus increasing traffic and revenue. The journalist with a small social media following has little evidence to point to that he or she can grow an audience.

Personal branding, though, is not solely about what skills journalists possess or how they report via social media platforms. It is also about how they present themselves on social media. This begins with the aesthetic parts of a social media account. Take a journalist's Twitter page, for instance. The bio, profile picture, samples of work, publications associated with, and banner image should all be part of a coordinated effort for the journalist to create a crafted image of themselves (Brems *et al.*, 2017). Presentation also includes content the journalist posts that is not their own reporting or their own opinions. As an example, NFL journalist Adam Schefter posts content from the league, teams, and other journalists on his account — making his Twitter page (@AdamSchefter) its own NFL news feed and a one-stop shop for all NFL fans. Other sports journalists may use their social media accounts to discuss politics or social justice issues, which becomes a part of their online brand and creates an expectation of certain types of content from the audience. Regardless of what the brand is, through social media, a sports journalist is defined by more than what they report; the other choices they make on those accounts construct how the online world views them. For instance, a poll from Darren Rovell on Twitter in July 2020 asked users if, based on sports journalists' Twitter feeds during the coronavirus pandemic, they were rooting against sports coming back. Of the more than 33,000 voters, 47.5% said they believed that to be true.

In some cases, personal branding can cause a journalist to become a celebrity, and different strategies can generate this result. With the advent of social media sites, much like athletes themselves, sports journalists possess a new area of exposure. They are able to easily connect directly with readers and reveal to the world a behind-the-scenes look at both the reporting process and their own personal lives. In an analysis of the tweets of a popular Swedish journalist, Olausson (2018) found celebrity constructed on social media through practices such as fame by association and live streaming, or documenting one's own daily experiences through social media, often aided by the journalist's ability to frequently post photos and videos. Through such practices, journalists can build enough social capital to become a social media celebrity and do so more through displays of their life or perks of the job rather than by reporting ability. Whether it is through posting glimpses into their journalist celebrity, sharing content related to a certain subject matter, or routinely showing off their best media skills, a journalist focused on growing a strong personal brand can take their reach and audience to new levels.

CASE STUDY — ESTABLISHING YOUR PERSONAL BRAND

The sports editor of *The Philadelphia Star* is having trouble growing the social media presence of its high school sports coverage and brings you in as a consultant. The publication currently has one high school sports journalist, and he runs a Twitter account with the handle @PhillyStarHSS. The journalist's name and face do not appear anywhere in the account. In its current state, the account only tweets links to articles from the publication's website and game scores for all football and basketball contests within the publication's coverage area. The editor is concerned with growing the reach of the Twitter account as well as helping create a personal brand for the journalist who runs it.

Discussion: What social media recommendations do you make for the editor? What recommendations do you make specific

(Continued)

> to high school sports and social media? Explain the strategies you would implement to grow the social media presence of the account as well as how you would use social media to enhance the personal brand of the journalist.

AUDIENCE ENGAGEMENT

Sports journalists once worked in relative isolation from their audiences. Aside from a picture in their articles, the reader had little idea who the writer was, and there was no way to communicate directly with that writer outside of a letter and, later, an email. Today, social media has changed that relationship. By following that writer on Twitter, every reader has a chance to be in constant contact with their favorite beat writer. Fans have a continuous direct line to ask writers questions, give them feedback on articles, and make comments about the sport(s) they cover. And while writers cannot respond to everyone, many make an effort to engage with their readers. The endless debate and discussion that is fostered by social media led *Toronto Star* columnist Bruce Arthur to describe Twitter as, "the best sport bar in the world" (Aguilar, 2017, para. 14).

For **engagement**, there is a greater purpose for sports media organizations. One of those aims is to connect with a younger audience. A 2019 study by Hootsuite found that 80% of all global Twitter users are under the age of 50 (Sehl, 2020). Additionally, successful engagement strategies on social media allow news organizations to spread their content to a wider audience, including people who do not normally visit that publication's website (Orellana-Rodriguez *et al.*, 2016). Furthermore, by engaging with an audience via social media, journalists and media organizations will foster a relationship with their audience (Guzman, 2016). By creating that relationship, it helps generate the public support that media outlets are looking for. Finally, engagement helps sports journalists do their reporting. Through social media, they are able to find sources and information that aid in the reporting process. The journalist who does not engage is cutting off a crucial source of information.

Social media allows for a variety of techniques to create engagement. The simplest form is replying to audience-created communication. In these instances, an audience member on social media will engage with the journalist by asking a question or providing a comment, and by responding, the journalist has fostered a relationship. The sports journalist or media outlet can also spark engagement by posing questions to their social media audience like, "What player is having the most underrated season in the NHL?" or "It's MLB Opening Day! What is your favorite Opening Day memory?" While conversing via text can be an effective way to interact with an audience, each social media platform offers a variety of tools to foster engagement. Whether its live streaming, hashtags, Instagram stories, likes, or GIFs, each strategy has a unique way of connecting with an audience and driving traffic to a sport media organization's website.

While audience engagement does have its benefits, it also has its drawbacks. Direct communication between sports journalists and readers includes negative comments and feedback. Female sports journalists are often the target of harassment and vulgarity on social media. Julie DiCaro, a writer for Deadspin and former Chicago sports radio anchor, says of that harassment, "Women are still fighting a war against rampant sexism in the industry, with Twitter and Facebook serving as the new frontlines" (DiCaro, 2015, para. 7). To combat these "trolls" on social media, the sports media industry used another Twitter engagement strategy — hashtags. In 2016, the Just Not Sport organization launched the #MoreThanMean hashtag to raise awareness of online harassment of women (Antunovic, 2019). This campaign successfully accomplished its goal and even earned a Peabody Award for its effort, showing another utility of social media — allowing journalists to engage their audience on social issues.

LEARNING ACTIVITY 1

Watch a recent broadcast of a studio show on a sports television network. Identify the strategies the show uses to promote engagement with social media. Pay attention to things the broadcasters say, graphics on the screen, and any segments devoted to social media. Evaluate and share your assessment with your classmates on the effectiveness of those strategies.

INFORMATION GATHERING

While social media can help sports journalists market themselves, it also has become a near requirement for doing their job properly. With college commitments, free agency decisions, and retirements routinely announced by the athletes themselves on social media, journalists now must check their social media feeds around the clock to ensure that they have not missed any breaking news. Social media also has proven to be greatly beneficial in gathering sources. Through direct messaging on these sites, journalists now have a direct line to athletes and other key players in the sports world. In a sense, social media serves as a digital phone book, providing contact information and connectivity to every member on these sites.

Reed (2011), in one of the early studies on the topic area, interviewed sports journalists about how they use Facebook and Twitter for news gathering practices. Aside from using these sites to break news or pull direct quotes from posts, responses included that social media sites were often used for compiling background information about a subject in advance of an interview. Kian and Murray (2014) and Li *et al.* (2017) echoed most of these sentiments in their research focused on sports journalists and their social media use, saying that news gathering has become easier with these tools. This is not surprising, as social media has allowed athletes a way to disseminate their own information, bypassing sports media and team media relation departments entirely (Pedersen, 2014).

In addition to gathering information to include in the story, social media can also be used to find sources for stories. Journalists can use social media accounts to connect with people that they may not have an email address or phone number for that are easily accessible. Interviews through social media direct messaging has become commonplace within reporting. For example, a story from *The Washington Post* about Adderall, a prescription stimulant, used by esports athletes included an interview with one athlete that was conducted over direct messages on Twitter (Hamstead, 2020). While some sports journalists find these sources by initiating conversations with specific users, they can also use social media to find good sources for their story that they did not know existed. In the esports story just discussed, the journalist could have posted a message on Twitter like, "I'm doing a story about Adderall use by esports athletes and am looking for athletes who can discuss the topic." By using this strategy, the journalist now greatly expands his or her base for who can be interviewed from sources he or she knows to all Twitter users.

Yet, the increase in news gathering ease is not without its professional drawbacks. Li *et al.* (2017) surveyed Chinese sports journalists on why they used social media. Responses indicated that news gathering was a primary motivation for engaging in these platforms. However, almost half of the participants suggested that needing to frequently monitor social media increased their workload and job-related pressures. Kian and Murray (2014) also found in their interviews with sports journalists that demands of the profession increased with the advent of social media. In other research, sports journalists also indicated that while information can be found on social media, it typically requires additional time in verifying whether that information is correct (Reed, 2011).

LEARNING ACTIVITY 2

Pretend that you are a journalist for an online sports blog, and your editor has informed you that the football coach has been fired at your high school alma mater. The school is not returning any phone calls about the matter. Compile a list of sources from social media that you could use to gather information for the story. Provide details on each source and give an example of the types of content you could use from that source.

INFORMATION CREDIBILITY

A key issue facing not just sports media but all media since the advent of social media is credibility. According to Pew Research Center, in 2017, only 5% of web-using US adults placed significant trust in information they saw on social media (Bialik and Matsa, 2017), yet in 2018, Pew found that one in five adults said they often get news on social media (Matsa and Shearer, 2018). Social media is for many fans the first stop to read sports news. Providing reliable and credible information — both from original and aggregated content — remains a top priority for any sports media members to build a strong reputation and to differentiate themselves from the many other social media accounts that are out there. Furthermore, evaluation of the factual reliability of sources becomes a key part of any journalist's practices (Coddington, 2020); yet inaccurate information from social media occasionally makes its way to a national sports media outlet. In one case in 2014, MLB Network broadcasted a tweet from an account pretending to be MLB journalist Ken Rosenthal that had incorrect information regarding a baseball trade (Maloy, 2014).

One issue that journalists face with credibility via social media is information origins. In a 2016 study, researchers found that news consumers viewed information that journalists sourced from Facebook and Twitter as non-credible (Lecheler and Kruikemeier, 2016). Despite this finding, using information from social media has become nearly unavoidable for a sports journalist. With athletes and coaches on these platforms, part of reporting comes from monitoring those accounts. Additionally, some sports fans have broken stories from their individual social media accounts that journalists then have to source for their own content. For instance, the Twitter account @Jomboy_ — run by a New York Yankees fan — was instrumental in providing video evidence related to the Houston Astros sign-stealing scandal (Lee, 2020). This is a form of citizen journalism, as social media users have occasionally become the newsmakers and breakers in the sports world. Yet, such user-created journalism is not without risk, as the lack of training of these users makes fact-checking a priority for any media outlet planning to use citizen journalism.

In the sea of social media accounts purporting to have reliable information, it is important that a journalist establishes his or her own credibility to stand out. One tactic here is negotiating and sometimes separating personal and professional identity on social media (Bossio and Sacco, 2017). Such strategies for a sports journalist can include mentioning their publication in their bio or social media handle, sharing media content that shows the journalist performing their job, such as interviewing or attending events, or sharing stories they have written. Additionally, information reliability has always been an important aspect of source credibility, and that does not change on social media. Part of the reason the social media accounts of journalists like Adrian Wojnarowski, Ken Rosenthal, and Adam Schefter are so popular is that the news they break and share on their respective sport is almost always accurate.

Some issues of credibility are not unique to social media. Avoiding bias has always been an important part of being a journalist as audience perceptions of journalist bias are somewhat inevitable (Gil de Zúñiga *et al.*, 2018). This is particularly true in sport, where every fan is convinced that certain journalists or media outlets hate their team. Such claims largely stem from how journalists frame their stories and that carries over into social media content as well (Sanderson and Hambrick, 2012). It is not always possible for journalists to be completely neutral within a story, as even without intention, framing a news story a certain way is an essential form of news making (Tuchman, 1978). It is the intentional attempt at showing favoritism or bias on social media that sports journalists should avoid because it calls into question their ability to be neutral, which can raise credibility concerns. Through avoiding bias, creating a professional identity on social media, and fact-checking other social media sources, journalists can still establish their own credibility to stand out from the sea of misinformation that exists on social media.

LEARNING ACTIVITY 3

Conduct an online search for a social media platform that is currently rising in popularity. Develop a plan for how a sports media outlet (ex: ESPN, Fox Sports, *The Athletic*, etc.) could use that platform to grow its audience. Share your plan with your classmates.

KEY SKILLS FOR PRACTICE

LIVE STREAMING

With the versatility of digital media, a sports journalist needs to continually adjust their skills to engage with an audience in new ways. This can range from creating memes and GIFs to adding humor and reaction to reporting to creating one's own podcast so that the audience can consume the journalist's content in a different format. One strategy that is growing in popularity is **live streaming**. Facebook, Instagram, and YouTube are among the social media platforms that best allow journalists to connect with their audience through real-time broadcasts. Common ways that live streaming is used in sports media is the broadcasting of press conferences or interviews, reporting from live events, and hosting of structured sports shows. In all of these areas, engagement is key, as a skilled live streamer can react in real time to what is being shown in the video content, while also getting involved in the conversation. However, live streaming does bring its own issues to the sports journalism industry. First, with the ability to create and disseminate live video content from anywhere through a mobile device, there can be privacy violations due to a lack of consent from all parties being recorded (Cassilo, 2019). Relatedly, as sports networks and journalists use newsworthy live-streamed content created by non-journalists, it can also raise questions of taste, decency, and copyright (Cooper, 2019).

Live streaming is now entering another area — live sporting events. This trend began in 2016 when Twitter paid between US$10 to US$15 million to stream Thursday night NFL games (Selyukh, 2016). A few years later, Facebook and Major League Baseball agreed to a deal worth approximately US$35 million that allowed the social media giant to exclusively broadcast 25 regular season games during the 2018 season (Soshnick, 2018). The NBA has even agreed to let Twitter broadcast some playoff games and the All-Star Game (Meadows, 2020). In live-streamed events like these, engagement is paramount, as part of the NBA deal includes Q&A sessions on Twitter with players during the postseason. Whether the live stream is a game or a journalist's individual broadcast, it is important that any sports journalist develops the skill of simultaneously live broadcasting content while also engaging with a social audience.

CONTENT AGGREGATION

While social media has provided great opportunities to grow the audience of sports media outlets, it has also changed their role. Gone are the days when media outlets were the **gatekeepers, or people who decide what news is covered and published**, of news in the sports media industry. Now, news often directly comes from players or teams through social media, as they no longer need media outlets to reach a wide audience. For instance, in March 2020, Tom Brady posted to his Twitter and Instagram account that he would be leaving the New England Patriots, thus breaking the news himself. While much news continues to be broken by sport media outlets, they are also taking on new roles as curators and aggregators to account for that decline in gatekeeping responsibilities. In recent years, journalists are now required as part of their job to aggregate content from social media (Coddington, 2020). In the case of Brady, sport media members sourced his social media posts in their reporting of his decision and often embedded them directly in the story.

With **content aggregation**, there are some questions of credibility that arise. Before journalists can include a social media post as a source within their article, a round of fact-checking is a necessity.

An announcement like Brady's may not require much fact-checking other than double-checking that the information came from his official account. However, when information on social media comes from a source like a fan or a lesser known media outlet, a journalist is required to check the validity of that information before allowing it to compromise their own credibility or that of the media outlet. In 2018, a columnist from the *Boston Herald* was suspended after posting false information in a story that came from a Twitter account pretending to be Tom Brady's agent (Rapaport, 2018). Aggregation done right has little effect on perceptions of journalist credibility (Molyneux and Coddington, 2020), making it a near must-have skill for any journalist in the social media age. Thus, a journalist who wants to be a skilled content aggregator needs to be able to identify information that is worth aggregating and also identify whether that information is coming from a credible source. After that, journalists must be able to disseminate that content in their own words while also properly giving credit to the original source.

BALANCING SPEED AND ACCURACY

With social media's reach and ease of dissemination, sports journalists are under pressure to get their content up online as quickly as possible so they can become the first source to share a story and, thus, get the first round of clicks. However, social media also has provided a direct line for the audience to the journalists, meaning that if a journalist makes a mistake, he or she is likely to hear about it…fast! What results is a Catch-22 for today's journalists: get your content up as quickly as possible, but make sure it's also as accurate as possible. It's a conundrum the sports journalist is all too familiar with, which has only been heightened by social media. For decades before the advent of social technology, sports journalists in particular were always racing to finish stories in order to hit deadlines, as the sports beat often featured more night-time events than other beats at the media outlets. Now, that pressure is on all stories at any time of day due to the short lifespan of news on social media. The goal becomes to get your content out there on Twitter before the rest of the outlets do so that your site can enjoy the high levels of traffic that come with it. Wait too long, and you're destined to become old news, and in today's social environment, old news can mean being just minutes behind other sites.

This system puts pressure on editing and fact-checking. Copy editors are often the step between the story being written and published. People in these roles check content for grammar mistakes as well as accuracy issues. But in the economic turn of the journalism industry, these are some of the first jobs to go. From 2007 to 2013, nearly one-third of all copy editors in the journalism industry were let go of (Beaujon, 2013). Major publications, including *The New York Times*, have restructured their copy desk, both eliminating positions and reassigning roles (Russiel, 2017). Now the responsibility often falls on the journalist, who in the midst of writing a story as quickly as possible must also edit that story just as quickly, even if they were never trained to edit in the first place. Thus, in today's journalism industry, a journalist with strong writing and editing skills is an important commodity.

LEARNING ACTIVITY 4

Choose a topic that is receiving a large volume of coverage this week in national sports media outlets. Identify five content items from five different media outlets that you could use from social media if you were aggregating information for a story. Compare and discuss your choices with classmates.

PRACTICAL PIECE

BILL LANDIS, *THE ATHLETIC*

Bill Landis has been an Ohio State beat writer for *The Athletic* since 2018. Working for a fully digital sports news publication, he knows the importance of using social media to share stories and connect with an audience.

(Continued)

"Working at a strictly online medium, I need that vehicle to get my stories out to people," Landis said. "I don't have my byline showing up on a printed paper that's tossed on some one's doorstep every morning."

Yet, Landis says social media isn't just about story promotion or connecting with an audience. Within his reporting, he often uses direct messaging through Twitter and Instagram to connect with sources that he would not have access to otherwise.

"It's easier to access sources now than it ever has been before," Landis said. "I have a hard time envisioning what people did before this."

While social media can be extremely beneficial to many areas of a sports journalist's job, Landis admits that there can be times when it may disrupt your work–life balance due to the non-stop nature of social media feeds.

"It almost feels like you're never putting your phone down," Landis said. "Every 10 minutes, especially when you're in season, something could pop up on Twitter that can be worthy of doing a post about."

(Continued)

(Continued)

> Overall, Landis believes that how sports information gets disseminated has changed, with the athletes, teams, and leagues more often directly communicating their message to an audience and going around the media, but he feels that the media must play an important role in this process.
>
> "A lot of it is public relations — it's getting the message that they want out there," Landis said. "Our job as journalists now shifts beyond dissemination of information to asking the proper questions and providing the context."

TRENDS AND CURRENT ISSUES

One current popular trend within sport and social media is the use of **Instagram Stories**. As noted in Chapter 1, Instagram trails only Facebook and YouTube in popularity among social media sites not primarily focused on messaging, which gives journalists a large audience to connect with. Instagram Stories allow users to create a slideshow of photos and videos that users can scroll through and interact with. Sports media outlets have taken advantage of this popular platform to drive traffic to their site. *Sport Illustrated* (@sportsillustrated) includes the option in their stories to swipe up on any slide to be taken directly to a written article about the content. ESPN (@espn) attempts to create interactivity for its users through stories, as its slides commonly include the ability to rate content or take quizzes on ESPN's website. Elsewhere, Bleacher Report (@bleacherreport) commonly uses the function as a way to tell stories through the slideshow of photos and videos.

While the technology is nothing new, **video** itself remains a trend that dominates social media use. Video is incorporated in nearly all social media platforms from the video-centered sites like YouTube to the networking-centered sites like Facebook to the sites rising in popularity like TikTok. With easy-to-use video-editing software out there like iMovie, any user can create professional-looking video packages to grab the attention of the social media audience.

A Cisco study suggested that by 2022, 82% of all online content will be video content (Cisco, 2020), making it an essential skill for all sports journalists to master.

Although new and innovative social media platforms pop up all the time, a journalist looking to grow their audience must remember that, at least currently, Facebook remains king. In the United States, 69% of adults use Facebook compared to 37% for Instagram and 22% for Twitter (Gramlich, 2019). That significant gap between social media use means that it is important for all sports media sites to continue to target Facebook users. These outlets try varying strategies to connect with the Facebook audience beyond just sharing news articles. In 2020, ESPN partnered with Facebook to create a weekly top-10 highlights show relying on **user-generated content** from the social media site (Impey, 2020). Meanwhile, local sports outlets can use Facebook to engage with the community in creative ways. For instance, NJ.com's high school sport Facebook page runs live broadcasts of games. Regardless of the strategy, engaging Facebook users would likely remain a priority in newsrooms for years to come, as 79% of 18-to-29-year-olds use the platform (Gramlich, 2019).

While the reach and engagement possibilities of social media can boost the audience of any sports media outlet, those features of the platform can also have negative effects. A 2019 survey with UK journalists found that they believed the biggest issue with social media was that users were able to bypass traditional media outlets to get news (Tobitt, 2019). With fan, team, and league accounts breaking news and sharing content from events, there is less of a need to visit traditional sports media outlets. This is seen in the aforementioned example of highlights appearing nearly instantaneously on social media, thus impacting the content of televised sports highlight shows (Maese and Boren, 2015). Additionally, fans are turning to social media to find out what happened at games rather than reading journalists' stories, which has led to the near death of the journalist-generated game story. This has many sport media outlets pondering what type of content they should create with an increase on programming that focuses on debate and opinion rather than highlights and recaps (Barron, 2017).

CHAPTER SUMMARY

Social media has had a major impact on the sports media industry, and there is one important thing to still keep in mind — it is just getting started. Our society is not even two decades into the social media era of news, meaning that its utility is still being figured out. Teams, players, journalists, and news organizations will continue to develop new and exciting ways to use social media. Meanwhile, new technology will continue to pop up, changing how content is created and sports news is consumed. However, some changes appear permanent. Sports journalists will no longer be the gatekeepers of news and must adapt to the new media environment that exists. As social media allows all players, teams, and leagues to have a direct line to their fans, sports media organizations must find new ways to create content that audiences want. Thus, what lies ahead is both great opportunity and change in the sports media field. How these media organizations incorporate social media will dictate how sport is consumed going forward.

KEY RESOURCES

- Adrian Wojnarowski, ESPN Senior NBA Insider. Host of The Woj Pod, his Twitter account: https://twitter.com/wojespn.
- Video from the #MoreThanMean campaign addressing harassment towards female sports reporters: https://www.youtube.com/watch?v=9tU-D-m2JY8.
- Story from ESPN about how social media users helped expose the Houston Astros' sign-stealing scandal: https://www.espn.com/mlb/story/_/id/28476354/how-internet-helped-crack-astros-sign-stealing-case.
- Instagram account for Bleacher Report: https://www.instagram.com/bleacherreport/?hl=en.
- A discussion on Sports Illustrated's website about how Twitter influences NBA reporting: https://www.si.com/media/2017/10/22/twitters-influence-nba.

- Article from Medium about how Twitter changed all aspects of sports journalism: https://medium.com/bryann-paul/disrupt-how-twitter-changed-the-rules-of-sport-journalism-2474497df967.

TEST YOUR KNOWLEDGE

1. Define personal branding and give three examples of how a sports journalist could engage in this process.
2. Identify and briefly discuss three ways that social media has changed the job responsibilities of the sports journalist.
3. Explain three different forms of engagement for a sports journalist on social media. Discuss what makes each technique essential to the journalist's job duties.
4. What are some of the obstacles for sports journalists when gathering information from social media? In what ways, if any, can those obstacles be avoided?
5. Explain why credibility is a concern for sports journalists on social media. Discuss how these concerns can be remedied.
6. What role should a journalist's personal interests and beliefs play in their social media accounts? When is it appropriate to include these things and when is it not?
7. Describe the role of video in social media reporting. How is it impacting televised sporting events and shows?
8. What are some of the negatives and professional drawbacks that come with the increased role of social media use as part of a sports journalist's job?

REFERENCES

Aguilar, B. P. (2017). Disrupt: How Twitter changed the rules of sport journalism. *Medium.* Retrieved from https://medium.com/bryann-paul/disrupt-how-twitter-changed-the-rules-of-sport-journalism-2474497df967.

Antunovic, D. (2019). "We wouldn't say it to their faces": online harassment, women sport journalists, and feminism. *Feminist Media Studies, 19*(3), 428–442.

Barron, D. (2017). On sport television, a trend toward opinion and volume over highlights and news. *Houston Chronicle*. Retrieved from https://www.houstonchronicle.com/sport/article/On-sport-television-a-trend-toward-opinion-and-11124566.php.

Beaujon, A. (2013). Copy editors 'have been sacrificed more than any other newsroom category'. *Poynter*. Retrieved from https://www.poynter.org/reporting-editing/2013/asne-survey-there-are-about-half-as-many-copy-editors-today-as-10-years-ago/.

Bialik, K., and Matsa, K. E. (2017). Key trends in social and digital news media. *Pew Research Center, 4*.

Bossio, D. and Sacco, V. (2017). From "selfies" to breaking tweets: How journalists negotiate personal and professional identity on social media. *Journalism Practice, 11*(5), 527–543.

Brems, C., Temmerman, M., Graham, T., and Broersma, M. (2017). Personal branding on Twitter: How employed and freelance journalists stage themselves on social media. *Digital Journalism, 5*(4), 443–459.

Cassilo, D. (2019). Privacy violations and mobile streaming video: Examining organizational social media policies and Antonio Brown's Facebook live stream. *Sport in Society*, 1–17.

Cisco annual internet report (2018–2023) white paper. (2020). *Cisco*. Retrieved from https://www.cisco.com/c/en/us/solutions/collateral/executive-perspectives/annual-internet-report/white-paper-c11-741490.html.

Coddington, M. (2020). Gathering evidence of evidence: News aggregation as an epistemological practice. *Journalism, 21*(3), 365–380.

Cooper, G. (2019). Looking Back to Go Forward: The Ethics of Journalism in a Social Media Age. *Next-Generation Ethics: Engineering a Better Society*, 411.

DiCaro, J. (2015). Threats. Vitriol. Hate. Ugly truth about women in sport and social media. *Sport Illustrated*. Retrieved from https://www.si.com/the-cauldron/2015/09/27/twitter-threats-vile-remarks-women-sport-journalists.

English, P. (2016). Twitter's diffusion in sport journalism: Role models, laggards and followers of the social media innovation. *New Media and Society, 18*(3), 484–501.

Friend, N. (2019). 64% of young people prefer social sport content to TV, study claims. *SportPro*. Retrieved from https://www.sportpromedia.com/news/social-media-sport-content-instagram-youtube.

Gallup (2019). Sports. Retrieved from https://news.gallup.com/poll/4735/sports.aspx.

Gil de Zúñiga, H., Diehl, T., and Ardèvol-Abreu, A. (2018). When citizens and journalists interact on Twitter: Expectations of journalists' performance on social media and perceptions of media bias. *Journalism Studies, 19*(2), 227–246.

Gramlich, J. (2019). 10 facts about Americans and Facebook. *Pew Research Center.* Retrieved from https://www.pewresearch.org/fact-tank/2019/05/16/facts-about-americans-and-facebook/.

Guzman, M. (2016). What exactly is engagement and what differences does it make? *American Press Institute.* Retrieved from https://www.americanpressinstitute.org/publications/reports/strategy-studies/what-is-engagement/.

Hamstead, C. (2020). 'Nobody talks about it because everyone is on it': Adderall presents esport with an enigma. *The Washington Post.* Retrieved from https://www.washingtonpost.com/video-games/esport/2020/02/13/esport-adderall-drugs/.

Impey, S. (2020). ESPN partners Facebook to air home videos on SportCenter. *SportPro.* Retrieved from https://www.sportpromedia.com/news/espn-facebook-home-videos-sportcenter-coronavirus.

Jerslev, A., and Mortensen, M. (2016). What is the self in the celebrity selfie? Celebrification, phatic communication and performativity. *Celebrity Studies, 7*(2), 249–263.

Kian, E. M., and Murray, R. (2014). Curmudgeons but Yet Adapters: Impact of Web 2.0 and Twitter on Newspaper Sport Journalists' Jobs, Responsibilities, and Routines. *# ISOJ Journal, 4*(1).

Lecheler, S. and Kruikemeier, S. (2016). Re-evaluating journalistic routines in a digital age: A review of research on the use of online sources. *New Media and Society, 18*(1), 156–171.

Lee, C. S. and Ma, L. (2012). News sharing in social media: The effect of gratifications and prior experience. *Computers in Human Behavior, 28*(2), 331–339.

Lee, J. (2020). How the internet helped crack the Astros' sign-stealing case. *ESPN.* Retrieved from https://www.espn.com/mlb/story/_/id/28476354/how-internet-helped-crack-astros-sign-stealing-case.

Li, B., Stokowski, S., Dittmore, S. W., and Scott, O. K. (2017). For better or for worse: The impact of social media on Chinese sport journalists. *Communication and Sport, 5*(3), 311–330.

Maese, R. and Boren, C. (2015). Sport video clips are now ubiquitous on social media. Can the NFL put the genie back in the bottle? *The Washington Post.* Retrieved from https://www.washingtonpost.com/sport/sport-video-clips-are-now-ubiquitous-on-social-media-can-the-nfl-put-the-genie-back-in-the-bottle/2015/10/13/e986f34c-71c9-11e5-8248-98e0f5a2e830_story.html.

Maloy, B. (2014). MLB Network fell for a fake Ken Rosenthal Twitter account. *Sport Illustrated.* Retrieved from https://www.si.com/extra-mustard/2014/07/31/mlb-network-fake-ken-rosenthal-twitter-david-price.

Matsa, K. E., and Shearer, E. (2018). News use across social media platforms 2018. *Pew Research Center, 10.*

Meadows, B. (2020). NBA, Twitter deliver basketball's ultimate showcase. *NBA.* Retrieved from https://www.nba.com/article/2020/01/08/nba-twitter-turner-partnership-extension.

Molyneux, L. and Coddington, M. (2020). Aggregation, clickbait and their effect on perceptions of journalistic credibility and quality. *Journalism Practice, 14*(4), 429–446.

Olausson, U. (2018). The celebrified journalist: Journalistic self-promotion and branding in celebrity constructions on Twitter. *Journalism Studies, 19*(16), 2379–2399.

Orellana-Rodriguez, C., Greene, D., and Keane, M. T. (2016). Spreading the news: How can journalists gain more engagement for their tweets? In *Proceedings of the 8th ACM Conference on Web Science* (pp. 107–116).

Pedersen, P. M. (2014). The changing role of sport media producers. In *Routledge Handbook of Sport and New Media* (pp. 119–127). Routledge.

Rapaport, D. (2018). Boston Herald columnist suspended after being 'catfished' by person posing as Brady's agent. *Sport Illustrated.* Retrieved from https://www.si.com/media/2018/02/09/ron-borges-boston-herald-tom-brady-catfish-don-yee.

Reed, S. (2011). Sport journalists' use of social media and its effects on professionalism. *Journal of Sport Media, 6*(2), 43–64.

Rubenking, B. and Lewis, N. (2016). The sweet spot: An examination of second-screen sport viewing. *International Journal of Sport Communication, 9*(4), 424–439.

Russiel, J. (2017). By dismantling its copy desk, The New York Times is making a mistake that's been made before. *Poynter.* Retrieved from https://www.poynter.org/reporting-editing/2017/by-dismantling-its-copy-desk-the-new-york-times-is-making-a-mistake-thats-been-made-before/.

Sanderson, J. and Hambrick, M. E. (2012). Covering the scandal in 140 characters: A case study of Twitter's role in coverage of the Penn State saga. *International Journal of Sport Communication*, 5(3), 384–402.

Sanderson, J. and Kassing, J. W. (2011). Tweets and blogs. *Sport Media: Transformation, Integration, Consumption*, 114.

Schultz, B. and Sheffer, M. L. (2010). An exploratory study of how Twitter is affecting sport journalism. *International Journal of Sport Communication*, 3(2), 226–239.

Sehl, K. (2020). Top Twitter demographics that matter to social media marketers. *Hootsuite*. Retrieved from https://blog.hootsuite.com/twitter-demographics/.

Selyukh, A. (2016). Twitter wins NFL deal to stream 2016 Thursday Night Football. NPR. Retrieved from https://www.npr.org/sections/thetwo-way/2016/04/05/473099436/twitter-wins-nfl-deal-to-stream-2016-thursday-night-football.

Soshnick, S. (2018). Facebook signs exclusive deal to stream 25 MLB games. *Bloomberg*. Retrieved from https://www.bloomberg.com/news/articles/2018-03-09/facebook-says-play-ball-in-exclusive-deal-to-stream-25-mlb-games.

Tobitt, C. (2019). Journalists see social media as biggest challenge to news industry in 2019, survey finds. *Press Gazette*. Retrieved from https://www.pressgazette.co.uk/social-media-biggest-challenge-for-journalism-in-2019-cision-state-of-the-media-survey-finds/.

Tuchman, G. (1978). *Making News: A Study in the Construction of Reality*. New York: Free Press.

https://doi.org/10.1142/9789811237669_0012

Chapter 12

Social Media, Social and Legal Issues in Sport

Melinda Weathers* and Jimmy Sanderson[†]

*Sam Houston State University, United States
[†]Texas Tech University, United States

CHAPTER OBJECTIVES

After reading this chapter, you should be able to do the following:

- Evaluate the differences between traditional media and social media
- Identify areas of legal risk that social media poses for sports organizations
- Assess how athletes, coaches, and other team personnel use social media to advocate for racial, gender, and other forms of social change
- Describe how social media use by athletes, coaches, owners, other team employees can fracture sports organizations' relationships with their fans and other stakeholder groups
- Identify four types of abuse and maltreatment that athletes can experience on social media
- Identify the key skills necessary to manage organizational risk on social media platforms

KEY TERMS

Active audience	Maladaptive parasocial interaction
Burner accounts	Parasocial interaction
Cancel culture	Self-presentation
Finstas	Title IX
Hashtag hijacking	Trolling
Live-tweeting	Virtual maltreatment

INTRODUCTION

Social media platforms are prominent tools in the sport industry. As described in earlier chapters, sports organizations employ social media as a tool to enact and enhance organizational functions such as marketing and public relations. While social media is certainly embedded in the operation and functionality of sports organizations, it also poses legal risk and liability for sports organizations. Additionally, athletes, coaches, and other sports figures have increased their use of social media for advocacy and activism around racial and social justice issues, further adding to the sensitivity of social media. As one example, in 2019, members of the United States Women's National Soccer Team (USWNT) advocated for pay equity and circulated the #EqualPayForEqualPlay hashtag on Twitter (Moran, 2019). In 2020, amidst racial tensions in the United States, multiple athletes, coaches, and sports organizational personnel took to social media to address police brutality against the Black community. Importantly, due in part to social media, the impacts of this movement were global.

In particular, a tipping point occurred on May 25, 2020, when Minneapolis, Minnesota, police officers arrested George Floyd, a Black man who was reported to have purchased cigarettes using counterfeit money. Floyd was handcuffed and pinned to the ground and one officer knelt on Floyd's neck which resulted in Floyd's death from suffocation. This incident was documented by video and circulated quickly across various social media platforms (What We Know About the Death of George Floyd, 2020). Floyd's death came on the heels of the police shooting of Breonna Taylor in Louisville, Kentucky, in March 2020. Here, police entered Taylor's boyfriend's apartment and her boyfriend (who was there at the time) thought an intruder had entered the home and subsequently fired a gun, resulting in the police opening fire and killing Taylor (Breonna Taylor: What happened, 2020; Reinking, 2020). In response to public protests and advocacy for police reform in the United States, athletes and sports organizations have become active participants. For instance, on July 24, 2020, as the Tampa Bay Rays participated in their opening day game after the Major League Baseball season had been postponed due to the COVID-19 pandemic, the team's Twitter account posted, "Today is Opening Day, which means it's a great day to arrest the killers of Breonna Taylor" (Varn, 2020).

These events signaled a shift in sports social media operations as previously, sports organizations had been reticent to post about social and political issues on their social media platforms. Perhaps one reason for such trepidation is that when athletes, sport figures, and sports organizations post about such topics on social media, they can generate intense backlash from social media users. As one example, in 2015, University of Missouri football players joined in a campus-wide protest centered on racial injustices on campus, including threatening to boycott playing if University President Tim Wolfe did not step down. While Wolfe ultimately resigned, many people posted on social media that the Missouri players had no business protesting against racism and suggested that the football players deserved to have their scholarships revoked (Frederick *et al.*, 2017).

Social media is much different from traditional media in that it possesses an **active audience** as opposed to passive ones found in traditional media. On social media, audiences can circulate messages and shift the intended meaning, all of which can happen very quickly. Thus, sports organizations cannot control how audiences will interpret messages or campaigns that are well-intentioned. For example, in 2014, Florida State University decided to make quarterback Jameis Winston available for a Twitter Q&A. Florida State fans were encouraged to use the #AskJameis hashtag to pose questions to

Winston; however, once this campaign was made public on Twitter, it quickly spiraled out of control (Sanderson *et al.*, 2016) since Winston had been plagued by legal problems at Florida State, including allegations of sexual assault and allegedly shoplifting crab legs from a grocery store. Consequently, when the Twitter Q&A started, people engaged in **trolling** behaviors (i.e., creating discord and causing contention and upsetting audiences through inflammatory comments) through **hashtag hijacking** (i.e., a hashtag that is set up for PR purposes is hijacked by social media users and employed to make the organization look bad). Instead of asking questions of Winston related to his role as quarterback, or the Florida State football team, questions centered on his legal issues, along with posing sarcastic questions that made fun of Winston's intellect (Sanderson *et al.*, 2016a). Some Twitter users also criticized Florida State communications personnel, suggesting that they should have known that such a campaign would be met with backlash (Sanderson *et al.*, 2016a). The questions regressed so quickly that the Q&A was stopped after only a few minutes, yet the sarcastic questions continued to flood Twitter with the hashtag #AskJameis.

In another illustrative example, after a video surfaced in 2014 of NFL running back Ray Rice striking his then girlfriend, Janay Palmer, the Baltimore Ravens held a press conference where Rice and Palmer addressed the incident (Sanderson and Freberg, 2016). During the press conference, Rice made several speaking mistakes (e.g., referencing that life was about getting knocked down and getting back up). The Ravens Twitter account **live-tweeted** (i.e., sending updates on Twitter as an event unfolds) the press conference and reported Rice's comments verbatim. While Rice clearly misspoke, Twitter users were quick to criticize both Rice and the Ravens, and news headlines surfaced such as, "It was not a good idea for the Ravens to live-tweet Ray Rice's press conference" (Yoder, 2014). A number of Twitter users also interpreted the press conference as the Ravens condoning domestic violence and sentiments of this nature circulated on Twitter (Sanderson and Freberg, 2016).

Sports organizations also face risks on social media since they cannot control what athletes, coaches, and other team employees post, which can lead to major crises and public relations incidents. Perhaps one of the most noteworthy examples here is the incident involving former Houston Rockets General Manager Daryl Morey. In October 2018, Morey tweeted support for protestors in Hong Kong by posting a graphic to his Twitter account that stated, "Fight for Freedom, Stand for Hong Kong." Reaction to Morey's tweet was instantaneous and soon both the Rockets and the National Basketball Association (NBA) had an international crisis on their hands. The Rockets were expected to lose US$20 million dollars in sponsorship agreements from Chinese organizations (Dubose, 2019) and the NBA was projected to lose between US$150–200 million dollars as a result of lost sponsorship revenues (Dubose, 2020). NBA commissioner Adam Silver reported that the Chinese government requested that Morey be terminated, and perhaps the league's most identifiable player, LeBron James, stated that Morey was, "misinformed or not really educated on the situation" (Cohen, 2019, para. 1). Several United States politicians, including Texas Senator Ted Cruz and Beto O'Rourke, who in 2018 had unsuccessfully challenged Cruz for his Senatorial seat, took to Twitter to voice their opinions on Morey's tweet and the NBA's response.

Although Morey was not dismissed by the Rockets, he did resign in October 2020, and media reports speculated that Morey was never able to recover from the after-effects of his tweet (Baer, 2020). This example illustrates how one tweet can cause a massive public relations issue that sports organization personnel can have no warning about. Certainly, athletes, coaches, club executives, and other sports figures can create public relations issues through commentary in game-related environments such as pre-game interviews or post-game press conferences. However, sports organizations generally have more control in these contexts and can perhaps minimize any public relations issues (e.g., communicating that a player was misquoted). Importantly, with social media, a post can be sent at any time from any location by a person with a mobile device, a risk situation that is too large for the sports organization to manage. It also becomes more difficult to refute what an athlete, coach, or team employee has said on social media, as the message comes from their personal account, which makes it difficult to claim that the statement was made erroneously or was taken out of context.

In summary, social media possesses many benefits for sports organizations, accompanied with a significant amount of risk. These risks and challenges can be monitored through measures like social media policy (Sanderson *et al.*, 2015), but there is no guarantee that policy, training, and education will eliminate a risk. Sports organizations also have to be mindful of and monitor the effects of social media. For example, there are growing concerns about athletes experiencing mental health issues from reading the abusive comments they receive on social media (Sanderson *et al.*, 2020). Sports organizations also are faced with challenges with how to respond to the growing trend of athletes, coaches, and other organizational affiliated personnel engaging in activism and advocacy on social media. Most sports organizations tend to be supportive of these efforts, but in doing so, they also have to manage resistance from stakeholders such as fans, who may disagree or have differing views about activism efforts. In some cases, a given stakeholder may not want any non-sport content on these social media platforms.

LEARNING ACTIVITY 1

Find an athlete or sports organization who has recently posted on one of their personal social media channels about a social or political issue in their country. Spend some time reading and analyzing the responses to their message. How was the message received by the audience? Why do you think the message was received in that way? In your opinion, do you think the athlete or sports organization should have posted the message? Why or Why Not?

SOCIAL MEDIA, SOCIAL AND LEGAL ISSUES: KEY CONCEPTS

One area where sports organizations face risk with social media is when the content pertains to race and racism (Kilvington and

Price, 2019). As athletes and other sports stakeholders are increasingly using social media to more actively engage in activism and advocacy related to race and social justice issues, this topic is increasing in importance. A high presence of racist comments has been observed on social media platforms with organizations ranging from the English Premier League (EPL) to National Collegiate Athletic Association (NCAA) sports in the United States (Frederick, *et al.*, 2017). For instance, Kilvington and Price (2019) identified 95,000 discriminatory posts directed at EPL teams, with 39,000 of those targeted specifically at players.

Sports organizations may also encounter racism and racist comments through the actions of players, coaches, and other team personnel. For example, in 2014, fans of the St. Louis Rams took to Twitter to protest four players coming out for pre-game introductions displaying a "hands up" gesture (Sanderson *et al.*, 2016). The players' action was in response to the killing of a Black teenager, Michael Brown, by police in Ferguson, Missouri, in August of that year. Researchers found that in response to this gesture, some fans had tagged the Rams' corporate sponsors on Twitter, requesting them to cancel their financial support of the team (Sanderson *et al.*, 2016). In another example, in July of 2020, the Boston Red Sox constructed a "Black Lives Matter" banner on the exterior of Fenway Park (Rose, 2020). After the Red Sox posted a picture of the sign on Twitter, their account was flooded with reaction, including comments such as, "I will not support an organization that supports Marxism and uses destruction to implement it" (Rose, 2020, para. 2).

As athletes, coaches, and other sports figures become more involved in speaking out on racial and social issues, social media also becomes a platform where these activism and advocacy efforts are debated and discussed. Consequently, sports organizations need to be mindful of the conversation on these platforms and be ready to respond if warranted, which is a topic that is discussed more in Chapter 13. For example, a sports organization personnel may feel that supporting athletes is the right decision for their organization, and they then use social media to offer support for athletes, coaches, and other administrative personnel. An instance of such a decision was made by the Milwaukee Bucks organization on August 26, 2020, as a response to the growing racial tensions in the United States, which were magnified by the police shooting of Jacob Blake, a Black man, in nearby Kenosha, Wisconsin, a few days earlier. Following the incident, the Milwaukee Bucks players made the decision to not play their scheduled playoff game that night. As news of this action circulated across both traditional and social media channels, the Milwaukee Bucks organization used their Twitter account to affirm their support for the players (Kalinic, 2020).

Athletes, coaches, and other sports figures speaking out on racial issues also brings potential consequences in terms of public reactions to those posts. While sports organizations may act in solidarity with the activism and efforts of players, coaches, and other team personnel, risk may arise through public reactions, particularly when stakeholders such as politicians become involved. During the 2017–2020 period in the United States, there were a number of issues involving minority athletes and President Donald Trump, which played out publicly over Twitter. For instance, in 2019, USWNT player Megan Rapinoe made public comments that she would not visit the White House if the team won the FIFA Women's World Cup. In response, President Trump posted on Twitter that Rapinoe should not disrespect the White House, the United States, or the American Flag — interestingly, Trump tagged the wrong account in his response to Rapinoe — (Rapp, 2019). Trump has also criticized NBA player LeBron James on Twitter, including sending the following tweet in 2018, after James opened up a school for at-risk youth in his hometown of Akron, Ohio: "Lebron James was just interviewed by the dumbest man on television, Don Lemon. He made Lebron look smart, which isn't easy to do. I like Mike! — a reference to former NBA player Michael Jordan, whom James is often compared to — (Stewart, 2018). As these examples illustrate, sports organizations are placed in precarious positions — do they support their players and risk upsetting politicians, including the President of the United States? Or, do they appease the politicians and, thereby, potentially risk upsetting the players? Consider the following example to illustrate the actions of one particular sports organization.

In September 2017, NBA star player Steph Curry of the Golden State Warriors publicly commented that he did not wish to attend the White House as is customary when an NBA team wins a championship (Trump Rescinds White House Invitation, 2017). In response, President Donald Trump tweeted, "Going to the White House is considered a great honor for a championship team. Stephen Curry is hesitating, therefore invitation is withdrawn!" (Trump Rescinds White House Invitation, 2017). The Warriors then subsequently released a statement affirming support for Curry and indicating that the team would not visit the White House, but instead, visit Washington D.C., and learn about history. This series of events also prompted NBA celebrity athlete LeBron James to tweet, "U bum, @StephenCurry30 already said he ain't going! So therefore ain't no invite. Going to White House was a great honor until you showed up!" (Trump Rescinds White House Invitation, 2017). For the Golden State Warriors, they made the decision to support their players and not the politician(s). Other sports organizations have been faced with similar situations since that time with how to react when their players speak out on racism and need to decide if they too want to support the athletes or another group or stakeholder.

Athletes, coaches, owners, and other sports figures may have very prominent platforms with social media. Whereas these individuals can and do use these platforms for marketing and branding purposes, these sports stakeholders are more and more often actively using their social media platforms to promote social change. As they do so, their social media platforms become spaces where social media users contest and debate these topics (Frederick *et al.*, 2019). Those who work in sports organizations, as well as those who advise athletes (e.g., agents) will need to be informed about how athletes, coaches, and other sports figures use social media to talk about race and racism. They also need to be aware of potential pushback and how racism as a topic can quickly flourish on social media platforms. Being aware of these trends will help sports organization leaders and athlete advisors better understand how to support these individuals as well as how organizations will respond to issues such as police brutality, discrimination, hate crimes, voter registration, and political leaders commenting on organizational decisions.

SOCIAL MEDIA, SPORT, AND GENDER

Sports organizations also encounter risk with gender-related issues and social media. One way this can occur is by female athletes receiving hateful and abusive comments specifically tied to their gender. Litchfield *et al.* (2018) examined comments made about tennis player Serena Williams on Facebook and Twitter. They found that one of the main ways people talked about Williams was by questioning her gender, while other comments "questioned whether Williams should be playing against women" (p. 162). As another example, when Women's National Basketball Association (WNBA) players announced that they would be featured in the *NBA 2k20* video game, some social media users responded with **misogynist** (i.e., dislike of or prejudice against women) statements and attacks (D'Anastasio, 2019). For example, one person posted an image with a PlayStation controller and imposed commands for controllers such as, "Wash vegetables," "Move vacuum," and "Make sandwich" (D'Anastasio, 2019, para. 3).

Social media and gender issues also surface with how athletes engage in **self-presentation**. In other words, through social media, athletes have the ability to construct how they want to present themselves to the public. Some athletes may choose to focus more on their athletic identity, while others may tend to focus on traits or characteristics unrelated to sport, such as their family, hobbies, and interests. With traditional media, researchers have found that most of the coverage is focused on men's sports with women's sports receiving little coverage (Cooky *et al.*, 2015). Consequently, with the advent of social media, some researchers have suggested that these platforms might allow for an increase in coverage of women's sports through the athletes, coaches, and other affiliated personnel using various social media platforms to promote the organization more

(Litchfield and Kavanagh, 2019). In addition to an increase in coverage, it also has been suggested that social media may allow female athletes to challenge some of the common stereotypes with which female athletes are often portrayed such as being overtly sexualized (Clavio and Eagleman, 2011). However, results here appear to be mixed. For instance, Weathers *et al.* (2014) analyzed the Twitter accounts of college football media figures Kirk Herbstriet (male) and Erin Andrews (female). They found that both tended to self-present in stereotypical ways with Herbstriet providing more commentary and football-specific related content, while Andrews posted more content about shopping and entertainment. Smith and Sanderson (2015) analyzed self-presentation of both male and female athletes on Instagram and found that female athletes were more likely to post pictures showing them touching another person or object, but also found that female athletes portrayed more active, athletic poses, which diverged from how female athletes are typically portrayed.

Social media also has the ability to foster more conversations and discussions about women and sport, which can lead to more inclusion and equity. Toffoletti, Pegoraro, and Comeau (2019) found that through conversations on Instagram during the 2015 FIFA Women's World Cup, sports fans were generating more support for women's sports, thereby legitimizing women's participation in sport. Sanderson and Gramlich (2016) examined Twitter conversations around the San Antonio Spurs decision to hire Becky Hammon as an assistant head coach and giving her head coaching responsibilities for the organization's summer development team. They found that Twitter provided a space where cultural change in sport was discussed and advocated for as people talked about women coaching men in sport. While there has yet to be a professional sports team that hires a female as a head coach to a team of men, more sports organizations are bringing women into assistant coach and other advisory capacities. November 2020 also brought a major advancement in this area as the Miami Marlins hired Kim Ng to be the organization's general manager, making Ng the first woman hired as a General Manager in Major League

Baseball (Connley, 2020). Ng's hiring was lauded in the media and positioned as a tipping point that could signal more women being hired into these kinds of leadership positions.

As the Marlins hiring of Ng illustrates, sports organizations are opening up avenues and opportunities for inclusion and diversity in sport to be discussed and showcased. In this regard, social media also becomes a platform where the sport industry can facilitate conversation around gender issues. Weathers, Sanderson, Neal, and Gramlich (2016) examined Twitter conversations using the hashtag #WhyIStayed, which emerged in response to the Ray Rice case mentioned earlier. Specifically, Janay Palmer decided to stay with Ray Rice and marry him, which led to people taking to Twitter to question her decision. In response, many women took to Twitter, using the #WhyIStayed to talk about why they decided to stay in abusive relationships. Through these narratives and lived experiences, these women were able to find community and share experiences with others, which brought more understanding to this particular topic.

Gender-related issues also surface on social media in response to allegations of sexual assault by athletes. This particular topic warrants close attention by sports organizations, as people have very strong opinions on this topic, and sports organizations can receive significant criticism if they are perceived to be enabling or protecting athletes or other team employees who engage in this behavior. Further, unlike racist or sexist commentary, sexual assault is against the law. Here, given the instantaneous nature of social media, sports organizations may have little idea these issues are coming until a post has been made, immediately requiring a reactive response. To illustrate, in 2018, Chicago Cubs player Addison Russell's ex-wife Melisa Reidy used Instagram to link to her blog, wherein she described domestic violence committed by an unnamed ex-husband. While Russell was not specifically named, friends of Russell's ex-wife had commented on social media that Russell had abused Reidy (Caron, 2018). Major League Baseball (MLB) conducted an investigation and Russell was suspended for 40 games in accordance with the league's domestic violence policy (Arnold, 2018). In another case, in 2016, NFL player Ezekiel Elliott was reported to have abused his girlfriend (Block, 2016). After the woman filed a police report, she then made several posts to Instagram depicting bruises which described abuse she had suffered, and tagged Elliott's account (Block, 2016). The NFL investigated and Elliott was assessed with a six-game suspension, which he initially appealed, and after litigation between Elliott, the NFL Players Association (NFLPA), and the NFL, he served his suspension (Hardy, 2017).

Sports organizations must be aware of gender issues, both that occur on social media and which are discussed on social media. Sports leaders will have to make decisions about the alleged evidence that an athlete, or other sports figure, engaged in domestic violence, as well as how to respond to misogynistic comments directed at female athletes. Social media also provides a platform where female athletes can counteract stereotypes and bring more attention to their sport and further legitimize women's participation in sport. Social media also is a venue where gender-based decisions in sport can be openly challenged. As a result of the worldwide coronavirus (COVID-19) pandemic which significantly impacted the sport industry in 2020 and 2021, some intercollegiate programs in the United States have cut sports to deal with the financial shortfall stemming from the loss of revenues from canceled events such as the 2020 March Madness Men's and Women's Basketball Tournaments, and reduced offerings, including the 2020 NCAA College Football season. In response to these decisions, some athletes and others have questioned the **Title IX** (i.e., federal program in the United States that protects people from discrimination based on sex in education programs or activities that receive financial assistance from the United States Federal Government) implications (Leistikow, 2020), where social media offered an open forum that fostered discussion about these critiques, and in turn, put pressure on sports organizations to provide more transparency regarding their decision-making.

LEARNING ACTIVITY 2

Select one female professional athlete and one male professional athlete who are active on social media. Then, identify two of their social media platforms, such as Snapchat and Instagram. Visit each of these athletes' profiles and note how they present themselves by browsing their posts from the last 30 days. What kinds of things are they saying about themselves? What is similar and different about each athlete? Did you observe any gender-related differences? If so, describe the differences in detail.

SOCIAL MEDIA, SPORT, AND ABUSE

Social media has opened up unique opportunities for communication between athletes and fans. While there are still ways to interact with athletes face-to-face, these have always been rare and are becoming increasingly difficult over time. However, through social media, athletes are much more accessible to fans. For example, Sanderson *et al.* (2020) found that athletes were posting their Fortnite handles in their social media profiles, accepting challenges to play this popular video game with fans. In another example, in 2012, prior to a Tampa Bay Rays MLB game, some fans at the game tweeted at player Elliot Johnson, inviting him to come out to the parking lot and play catch with them, which Johnson did (Zaldivar, 2012). While the outcomes of these examples are positive, there also have been a number of unfortunate examples where athletes have been subjected to abusive behavior. For instance, Litchfield *et al.* (2018) discussed derogatory comments made on social media about tennis player Serena Williams about her race and gender. Specifically, people suggested that Williams was really a man and conveyed racist terms (e.g., "Gorilla," "Black Beauty" p. 163) to describe Williams's appearance.

Kassing and Sanderson (2015) discussed the concept of **maladaptive parasocial interaction** to illustrate this abusive behavior by fans toward athletes. This term grew out of **parasocial interaction**, which is a concept that describes how media consumers interact with media figures (a.k.a. celebrities) in ways that resemble actual (i.e., in person) social relationships, but differ because they are mediated and one-sided (Horton and Wohl, 1956). This can be illustrated through people who become invested in soap opera or reality television characters. Some people interact with these individuals by giving them advice and worrying about their decisions, yet, they have no real interaction or relationship with these individuals. Parasocial interaction has largely been considered constructive, in that media consumers were displaying positive behaviors (e.g., sympathy, support, praise) to media figures. Kassing and Sanderson (2015) found that media users were engaging in parasocial interaction with athletes via social media, but were doing so in harmful and relationally inappropriate ways, which gave rise to the maladaptive parasocial interaction construct.

Several examples illustrate how the maladaptive parasocial interaction concept works. Sanderson and Truax (2014) investigated the Twitter mentions about University of Alabama placekicker Cade Foster following the 2013 Iron Bowl game against Auburn University. During the game, Foster missed three field goals, which played a role in Alabama losing to Auburn in the game. In the 24-hour period after the Iron Bowl, Foster was tagged over 12,000 times. Sanderson and Truax (2014) found that fans engaged in maladaptive parasocial interaction through sarcasm and mocking, but more seriously, through death threats and other hostile statements wishing harm on Foster and his family and which encouraged Foster to commit suicide. Similarly, Sanderson *et al.* (2020) analyzed comments on Twitter about then Chicago Bears kicker Cody Parkey after he missed a potential game-winning field goal in the 2019 NFL playoffs. They found that Parkey was subjected to death threats as well as anger-filled statements from Twitter users. For example, one person posted, "hope you get stabbed in the heart tonight and die a slow death @cparkey36" (p. 229).

The Internet and social media are largely unregulated spaces, meaning that people are generally free to post anything they want with little fear of repercussion. Through anonymous accounts and the sheer volume of people participating and conversing on social media, some social media users may feel empowered to behave in ways online that they would not act offline. Thus, a person may be very unlikely to say something critical directly to an athlete in person, yet on Twitter or Instagram or other social media accounts, where there is no threat of physical confrontation, people may feel emboldened to engage in abusive behavior toward athletes. Kavanagh and Jones (2014) conceptualized **virtual maltreatment**, which they defined as, "direct or non-direct online communication that is stated in an aggressive, exploitative, manipulative, threatening, or lewd manner and is designed to elicit fear, emotional or psychological upset, distress, alarm, or feelings of inferiority" (p. 156). Virtual maltreatment/abuse can take four different forms:

- Physical — this type of abuse/maltreatment includes threats of violence and/or negative comments which focus on an individual's attributes, or hostile wishful thinking. For instance, some people will post comments on Twitter or other social media platforms when they are upset with how an athlete has performed, a trend that is likely influenced by the growth and popularity of fantasy sports and sports betting. Consider this message toward former NFL player Mark Sanchez prior to a game: "@mark_sanchez kill yo self tonight! or imma do it for you Wednesday at practice" (Kavanagh *et al.*, 2016, p. 789).
- Sexual — this type of abuse/maltreatment includes threats of rape and sexual assault, or sexual acts to which the victim would not consent, or comments regarding sexual behavior with or of an individual. These comments can be stated aggressively and in a manipulative or lewd manner. For instance, many female athletes are often subjected to these kinds of comments on social media because of their appearance. Consider the following comment about tennis player Marion Bartoli: "Bartoli wouldn't get raped let alone fucked #wimbledon" (Kavanagh *et al.*, 2016, p. 790).
- Emotional — this type of abuse/maltreatment includes comments designed to elicit negative emotional or psychological

reaction. Examples include spreading rumors, ridiculing the victim, humiliation, isolation, belittling, and scapegoating. For instance, consider this comment about soccer player Raheem Stirling after he left Liverpool to join Manchester United: "Raheem Stirling is a cunt and waste of space @MCFC enjoy and good riddance" (Kavanagh *et al.*, 2016, p. 790).

- Discriminatory — this type of abuse/maltreatment includes comments that refer to a person's membership in a particular social group based on gender, race, religion, nationality, disability, and/or sexual orientation. As noted earlier, women athletes often are targeted on social media because of their looks. For example, this comment toward NASCAR driver Danica Patrick is representative of the abusive statements made toward women athletes: "@DanicaPatrick you will never win a race they only got you in sport because you look good now go back to the kitchen" (Kavanagh *et al.*, 2016, p. 791).

LEARNING ACTIVITY 3

Spend some time on the social media profiles of high-profile athletes and try and locate an example of each of the four kinds of maltreatment/abuse: physical, sexual, emotional, and discriminatory. In each case, in your opinion, how should the athlete and one of the sports organizations involved (e.g., the event host, the national sport organization or league responsible, etc.) respond?

Unfortunately, as the four examples provided in the previous section illustrate, high-profile athletes are subjected to what seems like a constant stream of very negative abuse via social media. In response, athletes report having different strategies for dealing with this behavior (e.g., ignoring it, using it for motivation, responding; Browning and Sanderson, 2012). Whereas some athletes may be able to ignore these comments and not be bothered by them, for others the constant barrage and nature of these messages may impact their well-being (Sanderson, 2018). With society in general and many sports organizations increasingly prioritizing mental health, it is imperative that sports organizations understand how athletes respond to abusive messages on social media and provide ways for them to counteract the psychological and emotional toll such messages can inflict.

In addition to abusive messaging, sports organization leaders also need to be aware of other ways that abuse can occur. Sexual abuse, for example, is easily enacted on social media, and while this is an issue for all sports organizations, it becomes increasingly important for organizations that serve child athletes (under the age of 18) (e.g., high schools, club sport teams). Social media platforms like Snapchat and TikTok are particularly prone to sexual abuse (Sanderson and Weathers, 2020). Sanderson and Weathers (2020) analyzed coaches who were arrested for sexual abuse with child athletes that occurred via Snapchat. They found that coaches used Snapchat to start innocent communication that then evolved into more sexual conversation. They also discovered that coaches sent graphic sexual photos and images to entice child athletes to send nude pictures to the coach. In some cases, this involved the coach creating a fake Snapchat account and posing as a teen to trap the child to send the coach a nude picture or video. They also discovered that Snapchat was used to geo-locate child athletes so abuse could be carried out. For example, the authors found that one coach went to a young woman's house and walked into her pool area because he saw that she was at her home. Another coach went to a child athlete's place of work and engaged in sexual intercourse at her workplace, while several other coaches used Snapchat to invite child victims to their homes where sexual intercourse occurred. Sanderson and Weathers (2020) discuss that sports organizations needed to provide social media policies that clearly outline acceptable behavior between adult coaches and child athletes through technology such as social media platforms. They also advocate for sports organizations to provide education and training for athletes, parents, and coaches to prevent sexual abuse from occurring and enhance youth protection and safeguarding.

At the professional level, sports organizations should educate athletes about social media and potential abuse outcomes. An example from October 2019 is when Pittsburgh Pirates player Felipe Vasquez was arrested on child solicitation charges. In the course of investigation, it was reported that Vasquez had been carrying on a sexual relationship with a 13-year-old girl for two years (Chiari, 2019). The investigation also indicated that Vasquez and the victim had first corresponded on social media before meeting up in person where Vasquez attempted to have sexual intercourse. Vasquez had also sent sexually explicit images to the victim, and law enforcement personnel were able to identify Vasquez by matching the tattoos on his body with those in the sexual images (Bumbaca, 2019).

Social media has afforded fans with unique opportunities for fans to communicate and engage with high-profile athletes. While social media provides the opportunity for positive interactions, it also opens up avenues for abuse to occur. Sports organization leaders need to make sure there are policies in place to help support athletes who are recipients of social media abuse, and to ensure that athletes' mental health is being protected. Sports organization leaders also have to be mindful of the potential for sexual abuse to occur, particularly those that work with child athletes. Policies and education are important tools that will help sports organizations manage this challenging area.

KEY SKILLS FOR PRACTICE

RISK ASSESSMENT

As was clearly outlined in this chapter and supported by many sometimes deplorable examples, social media poses a number of challenges for sports organization leaders. One of the first key skills to understand is risk assessment. As some of the examples in this chapter illustrate, social media affects every organizational level from ownership, to the General Manager, to the coaching staff, athletes, and other team employees. That is, "what happens on social media" does not stay on social media, it can cause significant consequences for the entire sports organization. Going back to the Daryl Morey case used earlier in the chapter, Morey's one tweet launched an international crisis for the Houston Rockets and the NBA that resulted in millions of dollars in revenue loss and which necessitated the Rockets ownership and NBA Commissioner Adam Silver to publicly address Morey's tweet and job status. Another area that sports organizations need to consider with risk assessment is the emergence of **burner accounts** (i.e., social media accounts that a person operates under a fake name, which allows them to post things they may not be willing to post from their identified account). For example, NBA player Kevin Durant has admitted to using burner accounts on Twitter to defend himself against criticism (Shiller, 2020). Burner accounts also extend to organizational leaders. For instance, Bryan Colangelo, the former President of the NBA's Philadelphia 76ers resigned after it was revealed that his wife was operating a burner account on Twitter. This account was posting health-related information about 76ers players along with critical comments about the organization (Detrick, 2018). One of the beneficial aspects of these social media issues is that there are a number of cases that can be looked at and learned from. Sports organization leaders have much direction and best practices they can adopt, such as looking at a case like Daryl Morey's and Bryan Colangelo's and making decisions about guidance for employees regarding social media usage.

SOCIAL MEDIA POLICIES

Another important skill to understand is social media policies. Social media policies help guide the behavior of organizational members as it pertains to social media. Social media policies can serve as a guide to help employees understand where the boundaries are for social media use and potential consequences for violating social media guidelines. Thus, they serve as a way to use critical thinking to help guide organizational behavior. For example, a sports organization might use a social media policy to tell employees to not post private and confidential organizational information on social media. Such a policy would also communicate that should an employee post such information, consequences might range from a meeting with his/her supervisor to termination of employment. Social media policies are also helpful for employees tasked with running the organization's social media accounts and can help avoid employees posting content from these accounts that can create public relations issues. For instance, in 2015, the Houston Rockets fired their social media manager after he posted a gun emoji pointed at a horse emoji from the Rockets Twitter account after the team eliminated the Dallas Mavericks in the playoffs (Gaines, 2015). Policies can help account for evolving social media content such as emojis, memes, and GIFs and outline organizational expectations around their usage.

There are several important characteristics for social media policies that are important to remember:

- Social media policies have to be updated consistently. It is important that social media policies be current with the social media landscape. For example, a social media policy should address contemporary platforms and trends in social media, such as how content like emojis, GIFs, and memes should be used.
- Social media policies need to be relevant to the audience. For example, Sanderson *et al.* (2015) analyzed social media policies in intercollegiate athletics and found that many of the policies referenced social media platforms such as Xanga and Friendster that were not relevant to student-athletes, only a few referenced platforms that student-athletes were using regularly, such as Instagram and Snapchat. These researchers also found that only a small number of policies discussed how social media could be used positively (e.g., personal branding), and it is important that social media policies be balanced and discuss both positive uses along with risk areas.
- Social media policies should give the organization latitude, but also provide guidance to employees. For example, it is beneficial to describe things that are "inappropriate" rather than

simply stating that employees cannot post "inappropriate" content on social media. It is important to remember that what an 18-year-old athlete may find "inappropriate" is much different than what a 50-year-old General Manager may find "inappropriate." For example, a policy might state that inappropriate content includes the following: any post that contains profanity or homophobic, racist, or misogynist language, or which disparages any group of people and note that this includes the posting of song/rap lyrics. Such a policy may also define inappropriate content as text or pictures of an overtly graphic, sexualized nature.

- Social media policies should list clear consequences. What happens if an employee violates a social media policy? Keep in mind that professional athletes or other employees who are unionized may be covered with union protection for any discipline. For instance, a policy could state that any employee who violates the policy will have a meeting with Human Resources personnel and be subject to discipline up to and including termination.
- Consider having employees sign the policy to enhance the adoption and following of the policy. By signing the policy it provides documentation that the employee was given the policy and had the opportunity to read it. Signatures help to guard against employees saying they were "unaware" of a policy.

SOCIAL MEDIA EDUCATION

A final key skill to understand is social media education. Social media education helps to complement social media policies. Social media education can take many different forms. For example, an intercollegiate athletic department may contract with a consultant to talk to its student-athletes about benefits and risk areas of social media. Additionally, a sports organization may also develop a web-based social media education that employees take which informs them about the organization's expectations and policies about social media usage. Social media education can provide opportunities for employees to ask questions about social media policies, and can help the organization promote buy-in and support of policies. Some important considerations for sport leaders to think about when creating or adopting a social media education program include:

- Determining how the education will be conducted. Will the organization bring in a speaker? Will the training be in-person or automated through a webinar/self-study type of format? If a speaker is brought in, will the training be in smaller groups, or a large group setting? For instance, a Division I intercollegiate athletics department in the United States may bring in a speaker to direct all student-athletes in a large group setting, whereas a minor league hockey team may bring in a social media consultant to work directly with the marketing and promotions staff.
- What will the training cover? It is important to assess what the audience knows about social media, and what kinds of information would be most beneficial. For example, a high school athletic department could survey student-athletes and their parents/guardians to determine what social media platforms the athletes use and what questions athletes and their parents have about those platforms. The training could then be designed around those platforms and specific need areas.
- How often will the training be conducted? Will it be annually, or will it be more consistent? Should the organization provide training if major shifts occur in social media? For example, with the growth of burner accounts and "fake" accounts, such as Finstas (i.e., fake Instagram accounts), sports organizations may need to address the use of such accounts with athletes and coaches.
- How will training be assessed? What kind of feedback should be obtained from participants? For example, a sports organization could include a survey that employees take after completing the training that would help them assess how the training could be strengthened moving forward.

CASE STUDY

You have just been hired as a high school athletic director, your dream job. On your first day, one of the first things the principal has tasked you with is developing a social media policy for coaches. The school has never had such a policy.

Working in groups of 2–3, create a brief policy that can be used to train coaches. What are 3–5 things that you would put into such a policy? For example, what would you tell coaches about contact with student-athletes (who are minors) on social media? Would you allow coaches to follow student-athletes on social media? What should coaches do if they see something on social media that violates a school policy (e.g., hazing, bullying)?

TRENDS AND CURRENT ISSUES

A current trend is athletes having their old social media content reposted years after it was first posted. Athletes such as Kyler Murray, Josh Allen, Josh Hader, and Donte DiVincenzo have had old Twitter posts surface at very inopportune times. For example, Kyler Murray had his old tweets surface the night he won the Heisman Trophy, Josh Allen had old tweets become public leading up to the 2018 NFL Draft, Josh Hader had old tweets surface as he was pitching in the 2018 MLB All-Star game, and Donte DiVincenzo had old tweets reappear as he was being named most Outstanding Player in the 2018 Final Four. When these archived social media posts surface, it creates public relations issues for both the athlete, their club/team, and any other direct stakeholders (e.g., league, association, sponsor, etc.). Yet, this practice of recycling old content also raises ethical questions — why are people going back years in the past to find something an athlete posted when he/she was a teenager? This issue is indicative of a larger trend of **cancel culture** (i.e., withdrawing support for public figures after they have done something that is considered offensive and is performed on social media through shaming) and is something that sports organizations have to monitor. One potential solution, or at least a way to mitigate the risk of this happening, is for athletes or whoever manages their social channels to engage in a regular social media audit to delete old content that may be problematic. However, just because a post is deleted is no guarantee that it is gone. Thus, education is also imperative here, particularly when athletes are younger as they may not be thinking about the future impact of a social media post. Some people also believe that their content cannot be made public, particularly on platforms like Snapchat, yet this is not the case.

Another area to watch is the social function that is built into video games such as Fortnite. Many athletes have become avid video game players (for a good example, check out baseball pitcher Trevor May's YouTube channel) and use video games as a way to connect with fans. As mentioned earlier, some athletes are posting their game player IDs in their social media profiles, and post about their video game consumption, including streaming their game-playing on platforms like YouTube. While this can be a unique way for athletes to connect with fans, it can also open up issues, particularly as athletes may not think they are being recorded. For instance, in 2018, San Diego Padres player Wil Myers had to apologize after he criticized manager Andy Green during a Fortnite game with a teammate he did not know was being recorded (Evans, 2018). In 2020, NASCAR driver Kyle Larson was fired by his racing team after he used a racial slur while playing a video game that soon circulated across the Internet (Fryer, 2020).

A final recent trend is the growth in athletes' social media consumption. At what point does an issue arise that starts to impact the athlete's well-being? Hayes, Filo, Riot, and Geurin (2019) looked at athletes who used social media while at events, and found that social media use helped athletes stay connected to family and friends and helped them feel more relaxed in a stressful environment. Yet, social media use at events can also cause athletes to lose focus and is an issue that sports organizations need to monitor. For instance, in 2015, Boston Red Sox player Pablo Sandoval was benched after it was discovered he was liking Instagram photos during a game (Bonesteel, 2015). Researchers have also found that athletes check social media mentions during halftime of games (Browning and Sanderson, 2012) and there are potential concerns here about the impact on athletes' well-being, training, and on-field performance.

CHAPTER SUMMARY

Social media contains multiple risk areas that can lead to legal liability for sports organizations. Athletes, coaches, and other sports personnel have become more active in activism and advocacy on social media around social and political causes. Sports organizations have to be mindful of ways that racism, sexism, and other forms of discrimination occur on social media. They are likely to encounter divergent reactions from their fans, sponsors, and other stakeholders as athletes, coaches, and team personnel discuss social and political topics. Sports organizations also need to account for abusive behavior directed at athletes and have supports in place to help athletes as they encounter this behavior. Finally, sports organizations need to develop clear and flexible policies and education plans for social media that will help athletes, coaches, and other team employees understand organizational expectations for social media usage.

KEY RESOURCES

- USOC Social Media Policy: https://www.olympic.org/documents/social-media.
- Athletes and Old Social Media Content: https://www.washingtonpost.com/sports/2019/04/20/new-rite-passage-nfl-draft-hopefuls-scrubbing-your-social-media-history/.
- Athletes and expression on social media: https://theundefeated.com/features/athletes-and-the-quest-for-balance-on-social-media/.
- US Center for Safe Sport Social Media and Electronic Communication Policy: https://usagym.org/pages/education/safesport/pdfs/usoc_electronic.pdf.
- Trevor May YouTube Channel: https://www.youtube.com/channel/UC1uJ1_T0aUnnSNtmmuM2CSQ.

- Major League Baseball Domestic Violence Policy: https://www.mlb.com/news/mlb-mlbpa-agree-on-domestic-violence-policy/c-144508842

TEST YOUR KNOWLEDGE

1. What are three risk areas that sports organizations face with social media?
2. What are two differences between social and traditional media that impact organizations?
3. What is the difference between parasocial interaction and maladaptive parasocial interaction?
4. What are the four types of virtual maltreatment/abuse? Give an example of each.
5. What are two important considerations in a social media policy?
6. How would you structure a social media policy for professional athletes compared to high school athletes?
7. What are some of the benefits and drawbacks of athletes using social media during games or at sporting events in which they are participating?

REFERENCES

Arnold, J. (2018). Addison Russell is suspended 40 games over domestic violence accusations. Retrieved from https://www.si.com/mlb/2018/09/21/chicago-cubs-addison-russell-melisa-reidy-abuse-relationship-violence-divorce.

Baer, J. (2020). Rockets GM Daryl Morey declines to address China controversy on way out. Retrieved from https://sports.yahoo.com/rockets-gm-daryl-morey-declines-to-address-china-controversy-on-way-out-012749725.html.

Bonesteel, M. (2015). Pablo Sandoval benched for liking photos on Instagram during Red Sox game. Retrieved from https://www.washingtonpost.com/news/early-lead/wp/2015/06/18/some-are-wondering-if-pablo-sandoval-was-on-instagram-during-a-red-sox-game/.

Breonna Taylor: What happened on the night of her death? (2020). Retrieved from https://www.bbc.com/news/world-us-canada-54210448.

Browning, B. and Sanderson, J. (2012). The positives and negatives of Twitter: Exploring how student-athletes use Twitter and respond to critical tweets. *International Journal of Sport Communication, 5*, 503–521.

Bumbaca, C. (2019). Pittsburgh Pirates reliever Felipe Vasquez arrested for solicitation of a child, denied bail. Retrieved from https://bleacherreport.com/articles/2854119-felipe-vazquez-arrested-charged-with-solicitation-of-a-childcomputer-porn.

Caron, E. (2018). Addison Russell's ex-wife shares blog post detailing disturbing story of emotional, physical abuse. Retrieved from https://www.si/com/mlb/2018/09/21/chicago-cubs-addison-russell-melisa-reidy-abuse-relationship-violence-divorce.

Chiari, M. (2019). Felipe Vasquez arrested, charged with solicitation of a child, computer porn. Retrieved from https://bleacherreport.com/articles/2854119-felipe-vazquez-arrested-charged-with-solicitation-of-a-childcomputer-porn.

Cohen, B. (2019). LeBron James says tweet supporting Hong Kong protests was 'misinformed.' Retrieved from https://www.wsj.com/articles/lebron-james-says-tweet-supporting-hong-kong-protests-was-misinformed-11571107697.

Connley, C. (2020). Miami Marlins hire executive Kim Ng, making her MLB's first female general manager. Retrieved from https://www.cnbc.com/2020/11/13/miami-marlins-hire-executive-kim-ng-making-her-mlbs-first-female-gm.html.

Cooky, C., Messner, M. A., and Musto, M. (2015). "It's Dude Time!": A quarter century of excluding women's sports in televised news and highlights. *Communication and Sport, 3*, 261–287.

Dawson, P. (2019). Rockets GM Daryl Morey's controversial tweet sparks reactions from Ted Cruz, Beto O' Rourke, others. Retrieved from https://www.houstonchronicle.com/sports/rockets/article/Daryl-Morey-tweet-Rockets-Fertitta-Hong-Kong-China-14497866.php.

Detrick, B. (2018). The curious case of Bryan Colangelo and the secret Twitter account. Retrieved from https://www.theringer.com/nba/2018/5/29/17406750/bryan-colangelo-philadelphia-76ers-twitter-joel-embiid-anonymous-markelle-fultz.

Dubose, B. (2019). Report: Chinese backlash costing Rockets over $7 million this season. Retrieved from https://rocketswire.usatoday.

com/2019/11/12/report-chinese-backlash-costing-rockets-over-7-million-this-season/.

Dubose, B. (2020). Report: Daryl Morey's Hong Kong tweet costs NBA up to $200 million. Retrieved from https://rocketswire.usatoday.com/2020/01/30/report-daryl-moreys-hong-kong-tweet-costs-nba-up-to-200-million/.

Evans, J. (2018). Padres' Wil Myers apologizes to manager Andy Green for comments made in Fortnite stream. Retrieved from https://www.usatoday.com/story/sports/mlb/padres/2018/09/03/wil-myers-apologizes-fortnite-stream-comments-andy-green/1188565002/.

Frederick, E., Sanderson, J., and Schlereth, N. (2017). Kick these kids off the team and take away their scholarships: Facebook and perceptions of athlete activism at the University of Missouri. *Journal of Issues in Intercollegiate Athletics, 10*, 17–34

Frederick, E., Pegoraro, A., and Sanderson, J. (2019). Divided and united: Perceptions of athlete activism at the ESPYs. *Sport and Society, 22*, 1919–1936.

Fryer, J. (2020). NASCAR driver Kyle Larson, fired for racist slur, visits George Floyd memorial, volunteers in Minneapolis. Retrieved from http://nascar.trendolizer.com/2020/08/nascar-driver-kyle-larson-fired-for-racial-slur-visits-george-floyd-memorial-volunteers-in-minne-apol.html

Gaines, C. (2015). The Houston Rockets fired a social media manager for sending a dumb, but harmless emoji tweet. Retrieved from https://www.businessinsider.com/houston-rockets-social-media-manager-horse-emoji-tweet-2015-4.

Hardy, S. (2017). A comprehensive timeline of the Ezekiel Elliott domestic violence case. Retrieved from https://www.sbnation.com/2017/8/29/16151642/ezekiel-elliott-timeline-domestic-violence-police-report-nfl-suspension-appeal.

Hayes, M., Filo, K., Riot, C., and Geurin, A. (2019). Athlete perception of social media benefits and challenges during major sporting events. *International Journal of Sport Communication, 12*, 449–481.

Horton, D. and Wohl, R. R. (1956). Mass communication and parasocial interaction. *Psychiatry, 19*, 215–229.

Kalinic, D. (2020). Bucks owners, NBPA support players' decision to boycott games: "They will not be silent on this issue." Retrieved from

https://www.complex.com/sports/2020/07/boston-fans-called-out-over-racist-comments-red-sox-black-lives-matter-banner.

Kassing, J. W. and Sanderson, J. (2015). Playing in the new media game or riding the virtual bench: Confirming and disconfirming membership in the community of sport. *Journal of Sport and Social Issues, 39*, 3–18.

Kavanagh, E. and Jones, I. (2014). #cyberviolence: Developing a typology for understanding virtual maltreatment in sport. In D. Rhind & C. Brackenridge (Eds.), *Researching and enhancing athlete welfare* (pp. 34–43). London, UK: Brunel University Press.

Kavanagh, E., Jones, I., and Sheppard-Marks, L. (2016). Towards typologies of virtual maltreatment: Sport, digital cultures, and dark leisure. *Leisure Studies, 35*, 783–796.

Kilvington, D., and Price, J. (2019). Tackling social media abuse? Critically assessing English football's response to online racism. *Communication and Sport, 7*, 64–79.

Leistikow, C. (2020). University of Iowa cuts four sports in wake of COVID-19 pandemic, loss of fall football. Retrieved from https://www.usatoday.com/story/sports/college/2020/08/21/iowa-cuts-four-sports-programs-coronavirus-covid-19-big-ten/3412974001/.

Litchfield, C. and Kavanagh, E. (2019). Twitter, team GB and the Australian Olympic team: Representations of gender in social media spaces. *Sport in Society, 22*, 1148–1164.

Litchfield, C., Kavanagh, E., Osborne, J., and Jones, I. (2018). Social media and the politics of gender, race and identity: The case of Serena Williams. *European Journal for Sport and Society, 15*, 154–170.

Moran, L. (2019). Twitter explodes over unequal pay after U.W. Women's soccer team's record rout. Retrieved from https://bit.ly/3jNrFoB.

Rapp, T. (2019). Donald Trump tags fake Megan Rapinoe Twitter, invites UWNT to White House. Retrieved from https://bleacherreport.com/articles/2842865-donald-trump-tags-fake-megan-rapinoe-twitter-invites-uswnt-to-white-house.

Reineking, J. (2020). Sport figures react on social media to the death of George Floyd in Minneapolis. Retrieved from https://www.usatoday.com/story/sports/2020/05/29/george-floyd-sports-figures-react-situation-minneapolis/5288501002/.

Rose, J. (2020). Boston fans called out over racist comments following Red Sox Black Lives Matter banner. Retrieved from https://www.complex.

com/sports/2020/07/boston-fans-called-out-over-racist-comments-red-sox-black-lives-matter-banner.

Sanderson, J. and Freberg, K. (2016). When going silent may be more productive: Exploring fan resistance on Twitter to the Baltimore Ravens live-tweeting the Ray Rice press conference. In A. Hutchins and N. T. J. Tindall (Eds.), *Public relations and participatory culture: Fandom, social media, and community engagement* (pp. 230–242). New York: Routledge.

Sanderson, J. and Weathers M. (2020). Snapchat and child sexual abuse in sport: Protecting child athletes in the social media age. *Sport Management Review, 23,* 81–94.

Sanderson, J., Snyder, E., Hull, D., and Gramlich, K. (2015). Social media policies within NCAA member institutions: Evolving technology and its impact on policy. *Journal of Issues in Intercollegiate Athletics, 8,* 50–73.

Sanderson, J., Frederick, E., and Stocz, M. (2017). When athlete activism clashes with group values: Social identity threat management via social media. *Mass Communication and Society, 19,* 301–322.

Sanderson, J., Browning, B., and DeHay, H. (2020). "It's the universal language:" Investigating student-athletes' use of and motivations for playing Fortnite. *Journal of Issues in Intercollegiate Athletics, 13,* 22–44.

Sanderson, J., Barnes, K., Williamson, C., and Kian, E. (2016a). 'How could anyone have predicted that #AskJameis would go horribly wrong?' Public relations, social media, and hashtag hijacking. *Public Relations Review, 42,* 31–37.

Sanderson, J., Zimmerman, Stokowski, S., and Fridley, A. (2020). "You had one job!": A case study of maladaptive parasocial interaction and athlete maltreatment in virtual spaces. *International Journal of Sport Communication, 13,* 221–238.

Shiller, D. (2020). KD explains why he still uses burner account on Twitter. Retrieved from https://bleacherreport.com/articles/2733874-everything-you-need-to-know-about-kevin-durants-twitter-fail.

Smith, L. R., and Sanderson, J. (2015). I'm going to Instagram it! An analysis of athlete self-presentation on Instagram. *Journal of Broadcasting & Electronic Media, 59,* 342–358.

Stewart, E. (2018). Trump is insulting LeBron James's intelligence — and Don Lemon's — on Twitter. Retrieved from https://www.vox.com/2018/8/4/17650982/trump-lebron-james-tweet-don-lemon.

Toffoletti, K., Pegoraro, A., and Comeau, G. S. (2019). Self-representations of women's sport fandom on Instagram at the 2015 FIFA Women's

World Cup. *Communication & Sport.* Advance online publication. doi: 10.1177/2167479519893332.

Trump rescinds White House invitation to Steph Curry in tweet. (2017). Retrieved from https://www.nbcsports.com/boston/boston-celtics/ trump-rescinds-white-house-invitation-steph-curry-tweet.

Varn, K. (2020). Pinellas sheriff to Rays: Breonna Taylor tweet was 'just wrong' and 'reckless.' Retrieved from https://www.tampabay.com/ news/pinellas/2020/07/30/pinellas-sheriff-to-rays-breonna-taylor-tweet-was-just-wrong-and-reckless/.

Weathers, M. R., Sanderson, J., Neal, A., and Gramlich, K. (2016). From silence to #WhyIStayed: Locating our stories and finding our voices. *Qualitative Research Reports in Communication, 17,* 60–67.

Weathers, M., Sanderson, J., Matthey, P., Grevious, A., Tehan, M., and Warren, S. (2014). The tweet life of Erin and Kirk: A gendered analysis of sports broadcasters' self-presentation on Twitter. *Journal of Sports Media, 9,* 1–24.

What We Know About the Death of George Floyd in Minneapolis. (2020). Retrieved from https://www.nytimes.com/article/george-floyd.html.

Yoder, M. (2014). It was not a good idea for the Ravens to live tweet Ray Rice's press conference. Retrieved from https://awfulannouncing. com/2014/it-was-not-a-good-idea-for-the-ravens-to-live-tweet-ray-rices-press-conference.html.

Zaldivar, G. (2012). Tampa Bay Ray's Elliot Johnson plays catch with fans after checking Twitter. Retrieved from https://bleacherreport.com/ articles/1341568-tampa-bay-rays-elliot-johnson-plays-catch-with-fans-after-checking-twitter.

Chapter 13

Social Media and Crisis Communication in Sport

Ann Pegoraro* and Evan Frederick[†]

*University of Guelph, Canada
†University of Louisville, United States

LEARNING OBJECTIVES

- Identify and define the elements of a crisis
- Identify and define key crisis response strategies
- Identify the specific tactics employed via social media to address a crisis
- Apply crisis response strategies to specific crisis scenarios
- Create crisis communication plans via social media to address various sports-related crises

KEY TERMS

Crisis

Crisis communication plan

Crisis history

Crisis responsibility

Image repair theory

Organizational reputation

Prior reputation

Situational crisis communication theory

Social listening

Social monitoring

INTRODUCTION

A crisis is often viewed as both a destructive and a negative threat, with no redeeming value (Ulmer *et al.*, 2019). Crises, both individual and organizational, are pervasive and omnipresent. As noted by Ulmer *et al.* (2019), "organizational crises are a consistent part of our existence. We cannot prevent them and as consumers, we cannot avoid them. Worse, crises are becoming more prevalent" (p. 12). No industry sector is immune from an emergent crisis scenario, including sport. From the Chicago Black Sox World Series scandal of 1919, to the handling (or mishandling) of the COVID-19 pandemic in 2020, the sporting realm has seen its fair share of crises over the last century. While crises remain constant, the media landscape has changed dramatically in the past decade.

In the decade or so of their existence, as well described in the first 12 chapters of the book, social media sites such as Twitter, Facebook, and Instagram have become a "disruptive force in sport communication today" (Pegoraro, 2014, p. 133), shifting the balance of power among leagues, teams, athletes, and fans. Athletes have increasingly adopted social media platforms for crisis communication. Particularly, for image repair efforts because these platforms offer a direct, immediate, and interactive way to get their message across, and because they also provide athletes with control above team or league gatekeepers (Allison and Pegoraro, 2018). Athletes ranging from Lance Armstrong (Twitter — doping history) (Hambrick *et al.*, 2015); Abby Wambach (Facebook — driving under influence) (Allison and Pegoraro, 2018); and Maria Sharapova (Facebook — positive drug test) (Allison *et al.*, 2019) have used social media platforms to communicate during their individual crises with the goal of repairing their images. The rise of social media platforms present both threats and opportunities for sports organizations that encounter a crisis. Therefore, understanding crisis communication via social media is important for students, practitioners, and academics to understand better how to confront these often daunting situations.

This chapter outlines crisis communication principles, as well as how to navigate a crisis scenario in sport. An emphasis will be placed on how to employ social media platforms in order to mitigate the damage caused via a crisis. According to Coombs (2015),

> the crisis management process is varied and involves the integration of knowledge from such diverse areas as small group decision-making, media relations, environmental scanning, risk assessment, crisis communication, crisis plan development, evaluation methods, disaster sociology, and reputation management" (p. 1).

While all of the abovementioned elements will be addressed either explicitly or implicitly, this chapter will primarily focus on crisis communication, crisis communication plan development, and reputation management via social media.

INTERVIEW WITH INDUSTRY PRACTITIONER

The following section provides insights into how social media is used for crisis communication in the Sport Industry. Eline Andersen is the Senior Communications Manager for Sport Event Denmark and has over 25 years of experience in the communications function within various sports organizations.
Name: Eline Andersen
Title: Senior Communication Manager
Sport Event Denmark

(Continued)

(Continued)

Sport Event Denmark is the national sporting event organization that bids for and hosts major, international sporting events together with national federations and host cities.

Question: *Based on your experience, how has social media impacted the role of sports communication?*

Social media has changed the way we communicate within sporting events, timing has become more important than ever. Self-made communicators such as athletes, fans, media have entered the scene, claim attendance, and can set the agenda. That is why most of the major international sporting events staged in Denmark have a strong focus on how to manage social media as part of the strategic communication. Social media has added new opportunities for sports communication, which we use in all the stages from bidding for events to hosting the events. We can tailor our messages more precisely creating attention for the events.

Question: *Which social media platform(s) are preferred for generating publicity? Does it differ based upon the content being provided?*

In Denmark, the content and the target group determine the choice of social media platforms. For generating publicity about, for example, men's handball world championships, Facebook seems to be the most preferred platform, but Instagram is catching up.

Question: *Which social media platform(s) are preferred for navigating emergent crisis scenarios? Does it differ based on the type of crisis?*

For communicating crisis scenarios, the most important fact is how to reach the relevant audience. If an event has used Facebook with success, then we use the platform to redirect to the social media platforms used by the authorities in crisis situations. In Denmark, the authorities such as the police use Twitter combined with specific hashtags to communicate during crisis situations. The choice of social media platforms differs based on the type of crisis, but most importantly we use the platforms to redirect to

(Continued)

the relevant primary source of information — which could be the event website, or the social media used by the authorities.

Question: *In your organization how do you monitor engagement with your social media content? What tools and methods are frequently employed?*

In Sport Event Denmark we use different metrics to monitor the engagement with our social media content. We use the metrics and analytics provided by the platform itself and we use Meltwater and Hypefactor. For every event in Denmark, there are three major Danish partners, the national federation, the host city, and Sport Event Denmark who is responsible for hosting the event of an international federation. All the partners monitor differently, and we often use shared data.

Question: *How has your organization's social media use changed since the COVID-19 pandemic began? How do you navigate the crisis of not hosting sporting events via social media?*

We have been very cautious when communicating on social media since the COVID-19 outbreak, and we have paid special attention to the threads of our posts in order to provide timely and accurate responses. Also, we have made checklists for communicating postponements and cancellations to ensure a correct sequence for breaking the news to our audiences. We want to communicate internally before breaking the news to the media. It has not always been executed perfectly, but we have learned how to optimize and collaborate with a lot of different parties such as athletes, sponsors, volunteers, teams, officials, authorities, media while communicating during this unique time period.

SOCIAL MEDIA AND CRISIS COMMUNICATION IN SPORT: KEY CONCEPTS

WHAT IS A CRISIS?

Various definitions of a crisis exist. Coombs (2007), a leading scholar in the field, defines a crisis as "a sudden and unexpected event that threatens to disrupt an organization's operations and poses both a financial and a reputational threat" (p. 164). In the context of sport, Stoldt, Dittmore, and Branvold (2012) define a crisis as "A situation or occurrence with the potential to significantly damage a sport organization's financial stability or credibility with constituents" (p. 197). The following list provides some recent examples of crises in sport.

- Michigan State University and sexual abuse of athletes by a team doctor (i.e., Larry Nassar)
- The Olympics postponing the 2020 Olympic Games due to the COVID-19 pandemic
- Lance Armstrong engaging in doping while competing as a professional cyclist
- Maria Sharapova testing positive for a banned substance
- The University of Louisville men's basketball team funneling money to recruits through an official partner (i.e., Adidas)
- The NFL and its mishandling of recent domestic abuse incidents (i.e., Ray Rice)
- Penn State University and decades of sexual abuse of young boys by an assistant coach (i.e., Jerry Sandusky)
- FIFA Bribery Scandal during the leadership of Sepp Blatter
- Michael Vick's involvement and participation with a professional dogfighting operation
- The Houston Astros being involved in a sign stealing scandal during their run to the World Series
- The 2018 Australian Cricket National team ball-tampering scandal
- Duke University athletes being accused of sexually assaulting a stripper during a party
- An image emerging of Michael Phelps smoking marijuana from a bong (following a DUI)
- Baylor University and their mishandling of multiple sexual assault claims against football players
- Russian Doping Scandal with 51 medals stripped for doping infractions
- The NBA shutting down operations following Rudy Gobert's positive test for COVID-19

This list is by no means exhaustive. Please complete the following learning activity to build upon the examples provided.

> ## LEARNING ACTIVITY 1
>
> Based on your experiences and some quick Internet research, compile your own list of at least 10 crises (not including those just shared) that have occurred in sport within the last 10 years. Separate your list by level of competition (professional, collegiate, interscholastic, youth, etc.) and by sport (football, basketball, baseball, etc.). Review your list and try to find common trends in terms of crises across sport and level of competition. Make any observations about what you find.

ELEMENTS OF A CRISIS

Scholars have provided research that outline the multiple elements that constitute a crisis and how one should respond to a crisis. These elements include *crisis responsibility, crisis history, prior reputation, response strategies,* and *organizational reputation* (Coombs, 2007). Attribution of responsibility is vital when analyzing a crisis scenario (i.e., determining who is responsible). If an organization is perceived to be responsible for the crisis (i.e., *crisis responsibility*), the threat to that organization's reputation is heightened. In terms of *crisis history,* stakeholders are typically much more forgiving of an organization that has not been involved in crises previously. However, if an organization has a long history of involvement in crises, the ability to protect and enhance their reputation is reduced. Similar to *crisis history,* if an organization's *prior reputation* (i.e., how it has treated stakeholders in the past) is strong, navigating a crisis and rebounding from its effects will be less intensive compared to an organization that does not have a strong *prior reputation.* An *organization's reputation* is the aggregate evaluation of an organization's past behaviors among its stakeholders. Thus, if its reputation is threatened, an organization must engage in various *response strategies* in order to repair their image and the damage inflicted by a crisis.

For example, in 2017, the University of Louisville was implicated in an FBI report alleging that the university had paid US$100,000 to a high school recruit. Being named in this report made it difficult for the university to deny responsibility for its actions (*crisis responsibility*). Unfortunately, this was not the only crisis the university had been involved in. Prior to the FBI report, the university received sanctions for a scandal involving an assistant coach paying for escorts to dance and have sex with prospective recruits (*crisis history*). One could argue that both the *prior reputation* and *organizational reputation* of the university were damaged, as they had been involved in multiple scandals and crisis scenarios of varying magnitude in recent years. In the instance of the FBI scandal, the university primarily employed reducing offensiveness strategies (i.e., bolstering and transcendence), stonewalling, and rallying as their *response strategies* via social media as outlined in Table 1. Overall, there was both support and rejection of this approach among user comments (see Frederick and Pegoraro, 2018).

Table 1. Details of University of Louisville's Social Media Posts utilizing Elements of a Crisis and Image Repair Strategies used.

Text Content of the Post	Date Posted	Crisis Communication Strategy Used
A statement from Interim President Greg Postel regarding a federal investigation related to men's basketball recruiting:	9/26/17	n/a
This morning's sunrise. #WeAreUofL	9/28/17	Rallying
#WeAreUofL (+ stats and accomplishments)	9/28/17	Bolstering
University of Louisville added a temporary profile picture. (#WeAreUofL)	9/29/17	Rallying
The University of Louisville has received one of its largest grants for medical research in the school's 219-year history, a US$13.8 million award from the National Institutes of Health (NIH) to study a promising new type of adult cardiac stem cell that has the potential to treat heart failure. The announcement was made this morning. #WeAreUofL	9/29/17	Bolstering

Table 1. (*Continued*)

Text Content of the Post	Date Posted	Crisis Communication Strategy Used
We love our city! Thank you for the support Mayor Greg Fischer and team. #WeAreUofL	9/29/17	Bolstering
We are more than this. We are the many and will not collectively be defined by the transgressions of the few. It's time for us to take back our story. Help show your support:	9/29/17	Transcendence
We are going to play for the name on the front. We are in it together. — David Padgett #WeAreUofL	9/29/17	Rallying
Catch the action today! The Cards take on Murray State at 3:30 p.m. at home. #WeAreUofL	9/30/17	Stonewalling
(We have) a unified fan base ... We have a terrific set of sports programs here across the board. I'm an avid fan. — Vincent Tyra #WeAreUofL	9/26/17	Bolstering/Rallying

Source: This Table is from Frederick and Pegoraro (2018).

The above example highlights how organizations can use multiple response strategies to address a crisis. Those response strategies are defined in the next two sections of the chapter.

IMAGE REPAIR THEORY

When an individual or organization faces a crisis, they are recommended to employ the appropriate strategies to respond to the given situation. One theory that explains how individuals and organizations can navigate a crisis is referred to as image repair theory (IRT). Benoit (1997), who argued that image is essential to all organizations, developed IRT. Scholars in many other fields, such as marketing and tourism, have also supported the importance of image to an organization. Thus, when image is threatened by a crisis, the situation must be remedied. Image is threatened when the accused is held responsible for an action and the act is considered offensive (Benoit, 1997). According to Benoit, image repair consists of the following strategies (i.e., message options), which an individual or organization can use to attempt to repair the damage done by a crisis.

Denial. Within the category of denial, individuals and organizations can use *simple denial* and *shifting blame*. When *simple denial* is used, the organization or individual simply states that they did not perform the act. *Shifting blame* places responsibility for the offensive act with another party.

Evasion of Responsibility. In terms of evasion of responsibility, individuals and organizations can employ four strategies, including *provocation, defeasibility, accident,* and *good intentions*. When someone uses *provocation* (also referred to as *scapegoating*), they claim that their act was provoked by the act of another. With *defeasibility,* the accused expresses that they were lacking the requisite information to act properly (i.e., "I did not know what to do"). For *accident,* an organization will simply claim that the act was a mishap or accidental. Finally, if one employs *good intentions,* they stress that they meant well and that they did not intend to cause any harm.

Reducing Offensiveness. Reducing offensiveness consists of six different image repair strategies. These include *bolstering, minimization, differentiation, transcendence, attack accuser,* and *compensation*. With *bolstering,* an individual or organization stresses their positive attributes. *Minimization* frames the act as not serious, while *differentiation* frames the act as less offensive than other transgressions. *Transcendence* goes a step further in terms of framing an act in more favorable context, as individuals and organizations stress that their good acts far outweigh a transgression. The *attack accuser* strategy seeks to reduce the credibility of accuser. Finally, *compensation* is when an organization or individual reimburse a victim following an offensive act.

Corrective Action. The *corrective action* strategy consists of two approaches. First, the accused can attempt to restore the original state of affairs that existed prior to the crisis. Second, the accused can promise a plan to correct and solve a problem or to prevent a problem from reoccurring.

Mortification. When employing *mortification*, the accused admits responsibility and apologizes for the offensive act. This strategy is further described as confessing and begging for forgiveness.

Since Benoit's initial work in the area of image repair, multiple scholars have discovered new strategies that are independent of his original typology. These strategies include *victimization, disappoint, stonewalling, retrospective regret, conforming*, and *rallying*. When utilizing *victimization*, an individual may claim that they have been unfairly condemned by the court of public opinion without the opportunity to defend themselves (Sanderson, 2008). An organization engages in *disappointment* by expressing disappointment in the actions of the transgressors, without completely severing ties with those individuals (Len-Rios, 2010). The *stonewalling* strategy is defined as redirecting attention to insignificant details not related to the crisis (Smithson and Venette, 2013). *Retrospective regret* is when an individual expresses regret after an event has taken place and *conforming* takes place when an individual blames the culture of an institution for their misdeed (Hambrick *et al.*, 2015). Finally, *rallying* occurs when an organization implores its fan base to unite together in order to move beyond the crisis (Frederick and Pegoraro, 2018). A complete list of image repair strategies with examples are provided in Table 2.

Table 2. Image Repair Strategies & Examples.

Strategy	Example	Individual or Institution	Crisis
Denial	"We also stated unequivocally that any allegation that a sexual assault or rape occurred is totally and transparently false."	Duke University	Sexual Assault
Shifting Blame	'To say that [the] program was better than the East German doping program in the '80s? In the '70s and '80s? That's not true."	Lance Armstong	Doping

(Continued)

Table 2.   (*Continued*)

Strategy	Example	Individual or Institution	Crisis
Provocation	"When I was diagnosed and being treated, I said, 'I will do anything I have to do to survive.' And that's good. I took that attitude — that ruthless and relentless and win-at-all costs attitude — and I took it right into cycling ... and that's bad."	Lance Armstong	Doping
Defeasibility	"You know, what are you going to tell everybody who follow [sic] you, who you've inspired, what are you going to say? I did not know who to turn to, I did not know who [sic] to tell, I did not know who [sic] to trust. It was a big thing for me and I was scared. That's the truth. I was just scared and I didn't know what to do."	Manti Te'o	Catfishing
Good Intentions	"The hardest part of this whole experience is seeing my family go through it. All because of something that I did. That's the hardest part for me. The greatest joy in any child's life is to make your parents proud. The greatest pain is to know that they are experiencing pain because of you."	Manti Te'o	Catfishing
Accident	Plaxico Burress claiming that he accidently shot himself in the leg at a night club while carrying a legally owned gun as a means of protection.	Plaxico Burress	Gun Shot in Night Club
Bolstering	"Michael Phelps is a valued member of the Speedo team and a great champion."	Michael Phelps	Drug Use
Minimization	"Speedo would like to make it clear that it does not condone such behavior and we know that Michael truly regrets his actions."	Michael Phelps	Drug Use
Differentiation	"I'm going to say paying a basketball player isn't nearly as disgusting as employing and protecting a known pedophile."	University of Louisville	Paying Recruits
Transcendance	"We are more than this. We are many and will not collectively be defined by the transgressions of a few. It's time for us to take back our story. Help show your support."	University of Louisville	Paying Recruits

Table 2.   (*Continued*)

Strategy	Example	Individual or Institution	Crisis
Attack Accuser	"My official statement re: @usantidoping's latest witch hunt. [link] unconstitutional"	Lance Armstrong	Doping
Compensation	Michigan State agrees to pay US$500 million to settle the lawsuits brought forth by 332 young girls and women who were victims of sexual assault at the hands of Larry Nassar.	Michigan State University	Sexual Assault
Corrective Action	"We must also acknowledge that there have been failures at MSU, not only in our processes and operations but in our culture, and we are united in our determination to take all necessary steps to begin a new day and change the environment at the university — MSU Board of Trustees"	Michigan State University	Sexual Assault
Mortification	"I engaged in behavior which was regrettable and demonstrated bad judgment … I acted in a youthful and inappropriate way, not in a manner that people have come to expect from me. For this, I am sorry."	Michael Phelps	Drug Use
Victimization	"I think for me, it's been hard. It's been difficult. Just, not only for myself but, you know, to see your last name and just to see it plastered everywhere and that my family is experiencing the same thing. I think that is what was the most hard for me."	Manti Te'o	Catfishing
Disappoint	"This conduct was wholly inappropriate to the values of our athletics program and the University."	Duke University	Sexual Assault
Stonewalling	"Back home and Iron Maiden live is on VH1 Classic. Day just keeps getting better and better."	Lance Armstrong	Doping
Retrospective Regret	"That was just more defiance, and you know what is scary is I actually thought it was a good idea … at the time."	Lance Armstrong	Doping
Conforming	"I didn't invent the culture, but I didn't try to stop the culture."	Lance Armstrong	Doping
Rallying	"We are going to play for the name on the front. We are in it together. #WeAreUofL"	University of Louisville	Paying Recruits

SITUATIONAL CRISIS COMMUNICATION THEORY

Situational Crisis Communication Theory (SCCT) is a second theoretical approach that can be adopted to respond to a crisis. According to Coombs (2007), SCCT "provides an evidence-based framework for understanding how to maximize the reputational protection afforded by post-crisis communication" (p. 163). In SCCT, crises are referred to as unexpected events that can threaten an organization's reputation and finances. Coombs argues that crises can adversely impact stakeholders (e.g., community members, employees, customers, etc.) physically, emotionally, or financially. For example, the Penn State University scandal involving sexual abuse of young boys by a former assistant coach (Jerry Sandusky) resulted in decades of physical and emotional abuse of youth who had entrusted Sandusky to serve as a mentor. The emotional damage caused by the crisis had ripple effects throughout the local community. Additionally, the university was levied heavy sanctions including fines (US$60 million) and penalties (i.e., vacation of wins and scholarship reductions) from the NCAA as a result of the scandal and subsequent investigation.

In order to address a crisis using SCCT, one must first evaluate the type of crisis that has taken place. Coombs (2007) refers to the types of crises as crisis clusters. The first cluster is the *victim* cluster. Within the victim cluster, the organization is also a victim of the crisis (i.e., natural disaster such as the San Francisco Giants and the 1989 earthquake during a playoff game). In this instance, there is only a mild reputational threat. A recent example of the *victim* cluster would be the impact of the COVID-19 pandemic on sport. All sports organizations were thrust into a similar situation in terms of having to navigate an unprecedented event that dramatically effected all aspects of organizational operation. The second cluster is the *accidental* cluster, which is when the organizational actions leading to the crisis were unintentional. In this instance, there is a moderate reputational threat. For example, Giants's wide receiver, Plaxico Burress claimed that he accidentally shot himself in the leg at a night club with a gun that he legally owned as a means of protection (see

Glantz, 2013). Finally, there is the *preventable* cluster. In this instance, the organization knowingly put individuals at risk, took inappropriate action, or broke the law. These types of crises pose a severe reputational threat. A detailed example of a preventable crisis is the sexual abuse inflicted by former team doctor Larry Nassar while he worked for both USA Gymnastics and Michigan State University. Despite multiple warning signs and complaints against Nassar, Michigan State was slow to act on reports that the doctor was abusing young girls and young women (Kirby, 2018). That being said, three decades of sexual abuse was definitely preventable had the university acted when they were first notified of the abuse.

Once one determines the type of crisis that has taken place, the organization must choose a crisis response strategy. Coombs categorizes the majority of response strategies within three primary categories under SCCT. The three primary categories are denial, diminish, and rebuild.

PRIMARY CATEGORIES

Denial. The deny category consists of several response strategies including *attack the accuser, deny,* and pick a *scapegoat.* With *attack the accuser,* the organization confronts the party that claims the organization acted improperly. For *deny,* an organization claims that there is no crisis. With *scapegoating,* a crisis is blamed on a person or group outside of the organization.

Diminish. The diminish category consists of *excuse* and *justification.* For *excuse,* organizations minimize their responsibility by denying any intent to do harm. When employing *justification,* an organization minimizes the perceived damage caused by a crisis.

Rebuild. Within the rebuild category, an organization can utilize *compensation* and/or *apology.* For *compensation,* an organization provides money or gifts for victims. *Apology* is when an organization takes responsibility for their actions and they ask stakeholders for forgiveness.

Table 3. Secondary SCCT Strategies.

Strategy	Example
Reminder	"For your information, #PennState students are the number 1 employed grads in the nation. Fight on State!"
Ingratiation	"#PennState proved they are more than a few bad people... 10K at the vigil tonight, what a scene! #WeAre #PennStatePride #PennStateForever."
Victimage	"Sad and unfair. But also true: 409 wins wiped out by one pervert. #Paterno scandal."

SECONDARY STRATEGIES

Strategies within this category are seen as supplemental to the previously mentioned primary categories of deny, diminish, and rebuild. Secondary strategies usually involve bolstering (i.e., stressing positive characteristics). An organization can employ three strategies when engaging in bolstering. These include *reminder* (tell stakeholders about past good works), *ingratiation* (praise stakeholders and remind them of past good works), and *victimage* (stating that the organization is a victim of the crisis as well). Examples of these three strategies are provided in Table 3. Each example constitutes fan-enacted crisis communication via social media on the part of Penn State University fans during the Jerry Sandusky scandal (see Brown, Brown, and Billings, 2015).

LEARNING ACTIVITY 2

Select a sports organization of your choice that has recently been involved in a crisis. Try to select an organization that you are not that familiar with. Examine the social media content (all platforms) of that organization, particularly the content related to the crisis and answer the following questions: (i) during the crisis, did their social media content differ compared to their social media content prior to the crisis and following the crisis (if it is over)? Compare based on content, sentiment, quality, quantity, etc., (ii) what strategies (if any) did you observe that they used during the crisis via social media?, and (iii) in your opinion, was their social media use during the crisis effective at managing the crisis?

KEY SKILLS FOR PRACTICE

This section builds upon the theoretical aspects of the crisis communication outlined in the previous section and translates them into the practical skills required for crisis communication managers with a focus on social media platforms. In this section, details on how to create a crisis communication plan will be presented, including (i) how to identify a crisis, (ii) how to determine the type of crisis an organization might be facing, and (iii) understand how both of these relate to crisis management plans. Next, you will be presented with two key uses of social media to monitor your plans — social media monitoring and listening, including how each of these can be used to ensure your crisis communication strategy stays on track. Lastly, examples of successful social media communication strategies for different types of crises will be presented. Together the different parts of this section will help put the theory into practice by providing a look at the key skills needed for practice.

CRISIS COMMUNICATION PLANNING

Many organizations have a crisis communication plan in place that involves identifying the type of crisis and appropriate communication strategies for social media platforms. However, depending on the size of the organization, the plan may be less formal or non-existent. Any crisis communication plan must also be in line with the organization's overall business continuity or strategy plan, and all plans must be consistent with each other. For example, if an organization is struggling financially and is having difficulty enacting a plan to secure new sources of funding (e.g., government funds or new sponsors) when a crisis affects their organization, any communication response must be informed by the financial situation. This could result in the use of denial as a key crisis response strategy while working with stakeholders behind the scenes to keep them informed. If the organization ignored the parallel business strategy that was also being enacted within the company, the communication strategy could put the entire organization in jeopardy.

Any crisis communication plan that is developed needs to be practical and applied. This infers that the sports organization should run scenarios to test the plan, so that you can ensure that the plan will work. For example, a national sports organization (e.g., USA Cycling) might run scenarios around an athlete testing positive for a banned substance. The following provides some key practical steps to use when creating your crisis communication plan.

A Framework for Crisis Communication Plan Decision-Making

- Keep it simple
  o You do not need to make your plan complicated, make it easy to understand and follow, provide a simple step-by-step plan to use in a crisis situation.
  o For example, once you decide on a crisis response strategy (e.g., apology), a simply stated post with the apology should be crafted.
- Allocate roles and responsibilities
  o Ensure that everyone knows who in the organization is creating the content for social media channels during the crisis, who is posting it to social media, who is the spokesperson, who is answering media either on social media or on other inquiries.
  o For example, in smaller organizations, this might be the same person due to resource capacity. In larger organizations, a spokesperson is usually identified and only that person talks to the press.
- Determine how decisions are communicated and who approves them
  o There needs to be one person in the organization who is in charge to ensure no miscommunication. One voice and one message is key to crisis communication success.
  o For example, the communications manager may be the person who has to approve all statements, including that of the CEO. And, the CEO may serve as spokesperson.
- Staff need to understand their role — AND — the roles of others
  o Make it easy for your social media manager and staff to understand what their role is and what the roles of others in

communications and other areas in the organization are during any crisis. This avoids any duplication of tasks, but also ensures no missteps in your communication plan. Create a sheet with a list of individuals and their responsibilities during a crisis — the list could be based on the position held (e.g., the Director of Communications is responsible for approving all social media content during a crisis).

- Assess what is happening on Social Media
  - Your plan must be informed by the reality of what is happening. The best place to find this information out is on social media, so a key step of your plan should be to enact your social listening plan and use the information the listening plan provides to inform your crisis communication work. Do not trust the first information you find on social media, verify the source first. More detail on social listening is provided in Table 3.
- Use a Communication Decision Flowchart
  - Having a path to making a decision will help provide a safety net between a quick response or an overreaction which could result in making a mistake. It is important to get the facts right, determine the right crisis communication response, and enact the strategy across your social media platforms. An example of this decision-making flowchart is provided later on in the chapter.
- Evaluation
  - At the end of any crisis plan should be an evaluation step. You need to determine if your plan worked. To do so, you should track key benchmarks (e.g., social media sentiment, stock prices, media mentions) to know if your strategy is having the intended impact and to evaluate how your plan worked (or did not) during a crisis.
  - For example, social listening can help track sentiment change in social media conversations around a crisis, providing some indication of the success or failure of your crisis communication plan.

CRISIS IDENTIFICATION

Today's communication professional needs to be able to identify when a crisis is occurring, and what type of a crisis it is. Then, work through a plan to address the situation. When looking at identifying a crisis from a practitioner's point of view, there is a need take these theoretical findings and express them in practical terms. For instance, how do you determine what type of crisis response strategy (e.g., apology, denial) is appropriate? The first step is determining if there is indeed a crisis. Key elements of identifying if an occurrence is actually crisis include the following:

A threat to the organization: is there an immediate threat to the organization, its reputation or existence? Often social media will be the first place that a crisis will become known. Therefore, careful monitoring of organizational platforms, comments by users, and trending topics are key to identifying crises. More about social media listening will be discussed in the next section. For instance, an athlete being arrested for domestic violence would be an example of a crisis and a potential threat to the organization and its reputation. An example of a crisis that could threaten the existence of an organization would be a massive stadium collapse that has resulted in lives lost.

The element of surprise: while there is a need to have a crisis communication plan, most crises have the element of surprise to them. Crises are not planned events, but rather unplanned events that require communications practitioners to respond to, and usually initiate their crisis communication plan. The example mentioned above, of an athlete arrested for domestic abuse, would constitute a surprise that an organization would not have planned for, but rather they must respond to.

A short decision time: crisis events usual have a short window of time, usually less than a day to decide on a response strategy. This is why it is critical to have a crisis communication plan to help guide decision-making and response strategies in a short window of time. If practitioners take too long to respond, the crisis will spiral out of their control, resulting in much more damage to the organization. Continuing the example of the athlete arrested for domestic abuse, the absence of any statement and/or action from the team would result in the story staying in the news cycle longer than necessary and increase the reputational damage to the organization. Whereas a quick statement (e.g., putting the player on leave) will help to reduce the media focus on the issue and team, and perhaps switch attention to the broader issues around the crisis (e.g., domestic violence in society).

A need for change: most crises indicate that there is a need for some sort of change in the organization. The key is to first respond to and then work through the change that is needed to address the longer-term change in a parallel process. Again, based on the athlete arrest example, the first step could be releasing the statement about placing the athlete on immediate leave. This could be followed up with a message indicating that the athlete is no longer with the team (should there be more evidence brought forward) and statements from management published about a zero tolerance policy for domestic violence arrests in the organization.

SOCIAL MEDIA MONITORING AND LISTENING

Social media monitoring is defined as the "systematic process of understanding, analyzing, and reporting insights and conversations on reputation, brand position, community health, and opinion of key audience members" (Freberg, 2018 p. 96). When social media monitoring is used, it is ideally connected to the marketing objectives or business strategy outcomes (i.e., key objectives or key performance indicators (KPIs) of the organization). In turn, social media-based metrics are put in place and used to monitor social media's influence on the largest strategic objectives. For example, monitoring metrics might indicate the number of retweets or shares a sport organizations post has gotten and this would relate to the KPI of mitigating a crisis. In typical academic language, social media monitoring is more the quantitative approach to research, which would include tracking metrics and reporting increases or decreases in these numbers.

Social media listening, on the other hand, is a more qualitative approach than social media monitoring, as it is where organizations seek to learn, explore, and "uncover emerging trends, opportunities, activities, and issues" that could impact the [sports organization] either positively or negatively" (Freburg, 2018, p. 96). Social media listening gets more into the nuances of the data and content produced around a sports organisation to understand the more organic nature of the community. For example, social media listening can examine content at a more surface level (e.g., trending topics) or go more in-depth into the history of fans' interactions with the team, how engaged a fan is, how influential they are in the organizations network or community. For instance, is there one super fan for your organization that drives a lot of the content around your team and can you potentially engage this fan to move your message through their networks? Relative to social media monitoring, social media listening is more proactive in its application and requires careful monitoring when dealing with a crisis and deploying crisis communication through social media platforms. For example, initial response from social media users could be positive, and then once more information becomes available, the content could turn negative very quickly. Based on this example, social media monitoring can be used to identify when the sentiment turns negative. Feeding this information into your crisis management plan, you can then adjust your content to help turn the sentiment positive again.

Table 4 describes the difference between social media monitoring and social media listening by providing examples of how each of these could be used by sports organizations. These examples provide concrete examples of how both these approaches could be used either alone or together by a sports organization.

Table 4. Examples of How Social Media Monitoring and Social Listening can be used by Sports Organizations for Crisis Communication.

Social Media Monitoring	Social Media Listening
Monitoring key metrics (hashtags, likes, retweets) for a crisis communication post	Analyzing key trends around your sport and your team/organization
Calculating growth/loss in your community (followers) during a crisis event	Identifying influencers in your fan community

Table 4. (*Continued*)

Social Media Monitoring	Social Media Listening
Understanding your audience demographics: age/location/ activity levels/time of day to inform proper crisis communication timing and content	Examining community responses to your content on each platform. What do they like, share, view the most from your content? How does this help with crisis communication planning?
Tracking engagement, sentiment, and consumer actions (e.g., shares, clicks on profiles) across platforms — which platform is key to your crisis communication strategy? Which role should each platform play?	Understanding the sentiment (positive or negative) or tone of your fan community discussing your players, your team, league
Determine when your fans/followers are most active — when is the optimal time to post to get the best impact for your crisis communication.	Understanding your fan community, their key online behaviors (e.g., other teams/ sports they follow, brands they like, other interests). How can you activate these influencers in the time of a crisis?
Explore fans' behavioral reactions, calls to action during a crisis — what works? What does not? And feed results into crisis communication plan.	Explore new areas related to your sport or organization and integrate these as potential opportunities for future crisis communication strategy
Use evaluation and measurement data and insights to demonstrate what your social media strategy has accomplished and where adjustments are needed during a crisis and after as you debrief on the event.	Identify any hidden threats or potential crisis that could evolve based on listening to the fan community and assess potential impact on your organization

MOST SUCCESSFUL SOCIAL MEDIA CRISIS COMMUNICATION STRATEGIES

Along with the rise in use of social media platforms for crisis communications, scholars also became interested in the types of strategies used on these platforms. Reflecting on the examples

Table 5.   Examples of Crisis Communication Strategies.

Organization/ Athlete	Crisis	Platform	Strategies used
University of Louisville	FBI investigation of fraud	Facebook	Bolstering, Stonewalling, Rallying,* and Transcendence
Michigan State University	Larry Nassar Abuse Scandal	Facebook	Bolstering, Corrective Action, Mortification and Rallying*
Lance Armstrong	Performance Enhancing Drug Use	Twitter	Bolstering, Stonewalling, and Attack Accuser
Abby Wambach	Driving While Intoxicated	Facebook	Mortification & Corrective Action
Maria Sharapova	Positive Test for Banned Substance	Facebook	Denial & Shifting Blame and Reducing Credibility (Media)

provided in the previous section, Table 5 provides insights into the social media crisis communication strategies used by both athletes and sports organizations.

TRENDS AND CURRENT ISSUES

The following outline some of the current trends backed up by research in the field:

THE RISE OF SOCIAL MEDIA FOR CRISIS COMMUNICATION

A recent trend of note is sports organizations using social media platforms as their main form of communication during times of crises. For example, in the fall of 2017, when the University of Louisville (aka University 6) was implicated in the Federal Bureau of Investigation (FBI) enquiry of multiple universities and college coaches taking bribes to steer high-profile recruits to certain agents, the university used Facebook as a key part of its crisis communication strategy. During the crisis timeframe (September

26th, when the FBI investigation went public, through October 3rd, when a new athletic director was hired) the University of Louisville posted 10 times on its official Facebook page (Frederick and Pegoraro, 2018). Similarly, during the unraveling of the Larry Nassar scandal, Michigan State utilized social media, in particular Facebook, as a means to communicate with key stakeholders. During the week of the sentencing hearing of Nassar (January 16 to 27, 2018), the university created 12 Facebook posts (one on January 17, three on January 18, two on January 24, four on January 26, and two on January 27) (Frederick, Pegoraro and Smith, 2019). Therefore, in a short period of time social media platforms have become integral to any crisis communication strategy for sports organizations and athletes alike.

The second recent trend is the idea of rallying, which is a new image repair strategy identified by Frederick and Pegoraro (2018) in their investigation of the response by the University of Louisville to the FBI investigation of its men's basketball team. This strategy, which is specific to sport, was marked by university officials' calling on the larger community of fans, students, alumni, and other key stakeholders to unify and support the university and the athletic department. The purpose was to "rally" support and move beyond the immediate crisis. In this case, rallying seemed to serve as a complement to the strategies of bolstering and transcendence that were used to reduce offensiveness of the transgression. Rallying effectively adds another subtle layer to a sports organization's image repair efforts, echoing the sentiment of "We are more than this, forget the transgressions of the few, and rally behind the team." (Frederick and Pegoraro, 2018). This new strategy was also found in the Michigan State University's crisis communication strategy around the Larry Nassar abuse scandal (Frederick, Smith, and Pegoraro, 2019).

PRACTICAL PIECE

In this section, we provide practical tools to aid any sports organization in crisis communication management through social media. The first provides a flow chart to make decisions around social media posting, content, and monitoring during a crisis and the second provides a checklist to run through when a crisis emerges. These two tools are designed to be used together.

Social Media Crisis Communication Management

When a crisis or potential issue arises that can damage a sports organization, the first step as noted above is decide if this is indeed a crisis and if it is, what type of crisis the organization is facing. Once these two steps are complete, then the organization needs to engage in a decision-making process to manage the crisis. The following decision flowchart provides one example of how to work through communication decisions during a crisis, including decisions around social media posts, content, and timing. The flowchart is provided to help make decisions as you move through a crisis. As the flowchart shows, the first step is to decide if you are in a crisis and if yes — then what type of crisis is it? This will help decide on what crisis communication strategies to use and the rest of the flowchart walks you through analyzing what is happening on your social media channels, deciding whether or not to post on social media, and then advising you to continually monitor social media channels to feed back into the decision flowchart.

Social Media Crisis Communication Plan Check List

The following checklist is a practical tool for any communications manager in a sports organization to use when a crisis or issue arises. This tool is designed to be used in conjunction with the decision flowchart as well as any organizational crisis communication plan. The check list allows you to go step by step through what type of crisis you are facing, and if you are facing a full on crisis, the check list provides a list of steps to go through both for social media and offline as your crisis management plan is enacted.

Social Media Crisis Communication Plan Check List:

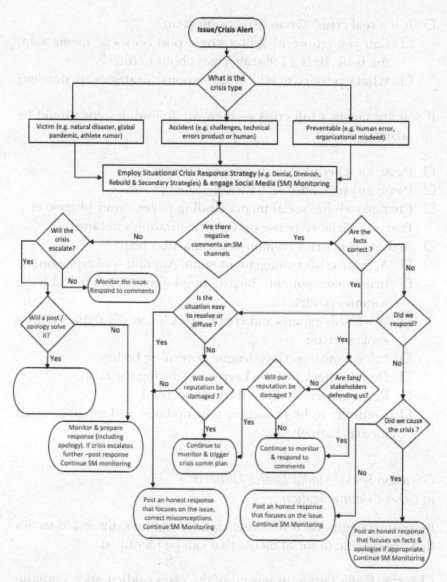

Figure 1: A Decision Flowchart for Social Media Management during a Crisis.

Source: Flowchart is adapted from Knight *et al.* (2020) and Talkwalker (2020).

☐ Is it a real crisis? Or an issue or incident?
  ☐ Can you ignore it? Will a single post on social media solve the issue, or is a full-scale crisis about to hit?
  ☐ What type of crisis is it? What response strategies are needed?

If you are facing a full crisis — then the following steps should be taken:

☐ Pause all scheduled posts on social media
☐ Pause any paid ads you have scheduled to run
☐ Change website/social media landing pages, cover photos, etc.. Post an official response on the organization's website
☐ Activate your crisis communication action plan:
  ☐ Activate crisis management team. Appoint spokesperson(s)
  ☐ Brief management, board, employees, coaches, athletes, volunteers, etc.
  ☐ Work with experts and create Q&A for media requests, prep spokesperson
  ☐ Inform owners/GMs/league governing bodies
  ☐ Double-check facts — keep a log during the crisis
  ☐ Respond personally to those concerned
  ☐ Continue to be proactive, post updates, and monitor social media channels.

Common Social Media Tactics Utilized in Crisis Communication

Beyond strategies used for crisis communications, there are tactics that are specific to social media that can be identified.

Changing Profile Picture. In several of the cases studied, sports organizations would simply choose to change their profile picture, usually putting the logo of the organization up during the crisis. Depending on the crisis, the logo maybe simply black and white in color, or adding a "frame," which might include an item such as a black armband or similar depending on the crisis.

Changing the Cover Photo: Again, this is simply a change in the cover photo on official profile pages on social media platforms or the main webpage. The photo is usually used to convey a part of the crisis communication strategy.

Statement as a Picture: This tactic involves the organization posting its official statement as pictures on social media platforms. It usually involves a simple white text on black background, or at times it has been done in the colors of the organization.

 NBA ☑
@NBA

    ⚙   👤 Follow

NBA Commissioner Adam Silver Bans Donald Sterling For Life pic.twitter.com/pDbBcs7KHn

↩ Reply   ♺ Retweet   ★ Favorite   ••• More

NBA COMMISSIONER ADAM SILVER BANS DONALD STERLING FOR LIFE

NEW YORK, April 29, 2014 – NBA Commissioner Adam Silver has banned Donald Sterling for life from any association with the Clippers or the NBA, it was announced today at a press conference in Manhattan.

Commissioner Silver has also fined Mr. Sterling $2.5 million, the maximum amount allowed under the NBA Constitution. The fine money will be donated to organizations dedicated to anti-discrimination and tolerance efforts that will be jointly selected by the NBA and the Players Association.

As part of the lifetime ban, Mr. Sterling may not attend any NBA games or practices, be present at any Clippers office or facility, or participate in any business or player personnel decisions involving the team. He will also be barred from attending NBA Board of Governors meetings and participating in any other league activity.

Commissioner Silver also announced that he will urge the Board of Governors to exercise its authority to force a sale of the team.

The discipline issued today is based on the Commissioner's conclusion that Mr. Sterling violated league rules through his expressions of offensive and hurtful views, the impact of which has been widely felt throughout the league.

A transcript of Commissioner Silver's press conference will be issued this afternoon and posted on the NBA's media website (mediacentral.nba.com).

# # #

Several of these tactics have become commonplace and are seen regularly now. During the recent crisis faced by the Washington Football team of the NFL pertaining to the changing of the team's name, we can see all of these tactics were employed by the organization:

Profile Picture Change

Source: Facebook (2000a).

Cover Photo Change

Source: Facebook (2020b).

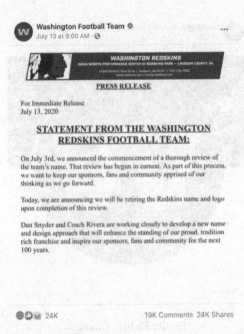

Official Statement related to the Crisis

Source: Facebook (2020c).

CASE STUDY

You currently work in the sports information department for Wabash State University. You are in charge of running the social media accounts for the athletic department. Wabash State is a Division II school located in a small (population of 15,000) college town in the Midwest. The university is located within four hours of several large cities and media markets. Wabash State has a strong athletics history. In the last 20 years, the school's football team has won three Division II championships and the basketball team has won two Division II championships. The women's soccer team is arguably the most accomplished program at the university. Since the 1970s, the team has participated in 10 Final Fours and won three Division II championships.

In the past five years, Wabash State University has been involved in multiple scandals including improper benefits (i.e., meals and

(Continued)

small amounts of cash) to athletes on the men's basketball team, negative press coverage pertaining to multiple football players intimidating a female professor for higher grades in a general education course, and a DUI for the men's soccer coach. The most recent transgression has also been the most severe. The head coach (a male) of the university's storied women's soccer team was fired for allegations of sexually abusing his athletes. A report surfaced which states that the alleged abuse took place over multiple decades. The report also alleges that some currently employed upper administration staff and athletic staff were aware of the abuse. The university is now thrust into the spotlight.

1. How would you advise the athletic department in terms of situational crisis communication theory (SCCT) and image repair (IRT) strategy utilization via social media? Provide at least three response strategies as described by Benoit (1997) and Coombs (2007).
2. Define the strategies and provide a detailed rationale why you would take this approach considering the current crisis. Which social media platforms would you utilize? What types of posts would you create to align with your strategies?

CHAPTER SUMMARY

A crisis has the ability to significantly damage an individual's or an organization's image, credibility, and standing with their constituents such as fans, sponsors, and investors. A crisis can also have a substantially negative impact on the bottom line, causing long-term financial effects in addition to a tarnished reputation among the public. Today, most crises initially unfold on social media platforms. Thus making these platforms key to both monitoring and managing any crisis a sports organization faces. A crisis represents a threat to an organization that requires the implementation of social media platforms (along with other tactics) in order to effectively repair and mitigate any damage that is incurred. One must understand that image restoration may not be achievable. Image repair should be the aim. In order to repair one's image effectively, there must be consistent monitoring of each unique crisis situation in order to wisely choose and implement the proper crisis communication strategy.

The purpose of this chapter was to provide both theoretical and practical information regarding how organizations and individuals can navigate crisis situations utilizing social media platforms. From a theoretical standpoint, this chapter defined a crisis, while outlining the elements of a crisis, as well as common crisis communication strategies as provided within image repair theory (IRT) and situational crisis communication theory (SCCT). In terms of practical applications, this chapter outlined various best practices including crisis communication planning, crisis identification, social media monitoring and social media listening, as well as common social media tactics for navigating a crisis scenario. While this chapter provided an overview of crisis communication via social media, we recommend that readers seek out additional helpful information related to this topic provided in the Key Resources section that follows.

TEST YOUR KNOWLEDGE

1. Identify the five elements of a crisis, and briefly describe each.
2. When discussing image repair, there are five primary categories with multiple strategic choices. Name the five primary categories within the image repair typology.
3. When discussing situational crisis communication theory, there are three primary categories with multiple strategic choices. Name the three primary categories within situational crisis communication theory.
4. What are some of the skills for practice as identified in this chapter?
5. What is the difference between social media monitoring and social media listening?

6. Provide, at least, three common social media tactics that organizations utilize when addressing a crisis.
7. When engaging the social media crisis communication checklist, what steps must be employed to activate the crisis communication action plan?

KEY RESOURCES

- U.S. Federal Emergency Management Agency's public service campaign — Ready: https://www.ready.gov/business/implementation/crisis.
- Talkwalker.com Crisis management templates: https://www.talkwalker.com/marketing-essentials/crisis-management-templates#.
- The Youngstown State University Crisis Communications Plan provides procedures for the coordination of communications both internally and externally in the event of a crisis situation: https://ysu.edu/crisis-communication-plan.
- 6 Effective Strategies for Communication in a Crisis: https://www.business.com/articles/effective-crisis-communication-strategies/.
- Crisis Communications in the Age of Social Media: https://www.forbes.com/sites/adriandearnell/2019/10/31/crisis-communications-in-the-age-of-social-media/#4e0f23607354.
- How to Use Social Media to Improve Crisis Communications: https://www.forbes.com/sites/forbesagencycouncil/2016/09/09/how-to-use-social-media-to-improve-crisis-communications/#2260000e2f16.
- Lessons for Crisis Communication on Social Media: A Systematic Review of What Research Tells the Practice: https://www.tandfonline.com/doi/full/10.1080/1553118X.2018.1510405.

REFERENCES

Allison, R., Pegoraro, A., Frederick, E., and Thompson, A. (2019). When Women Athletes Transgress: An Exploratory Study of Image Repair and Social Media Response *Sport and Society*, http://dx.doi.org/10.108 0/17430437.2019.1580266.

Allison, R. and Pegoraro, A. (2018). Abby Wambach: G.O.A.T. (Greatest of All Time) or Just a Goat? In Billings, A. (eds.) *Reputational Challenges in Sport*. (pp. 210–226) New York, NY: Routledge.

Benoit, W. L. (1997). Image repair discourse and crisis communication. *Public Relations Review, 23*, 177–186.

Brown, N. A., Brown, K. A., and Billings, A. C. (2015). "May no act of ours bring shame": Fan-enacted crisis communication surrounding the Penn State sex abuse scandal. *Communication and Sport*, 3, 288–311.

Coombs, W. T. (2007). Protecting organization reputations during a crisis: The development and application of situational crisis communication theory. *Corporate Reputation Review, 10*, 163–176.

Coombs, T. (2015). *Ongoing crisis communication: Planning, managing, and responding* (4th Edition). Thousand Oaks, CA: Sage.

Facebook (2020a). Washington Football Team. Retrieved from https:// www.facebook.com/washingtonnfl Accessed August 9, 2020.

Facebook (2020b). Washington Football Team. Retrieved from https:// www.facebook.com/washingtonnfl Accessed August 9, 2020.

Facebook (2020c). Washington Football Team. Retrieved from https:// www.facebook.com/washingtonnfl/photos/a.118304319573/ 10158820318159574/ Accessed August 9, 2020.

Freberg, K. (2018). Social Media for Strategic Communication: Creative Strategies and Research-Based Applications. Thousand Oaks, CA: Sage.

Frederick, E., Pegoraro, A., and Smith, L. (2019). An examination of Michigan State University's image repair via Facebook and the public response following the Larry Nassar scandal. *Communication and Sport*, https://doi.org/10.1177/2167479519852285.

Frederick, E. and Pegoraro, A. (2018). Scandal in college basketball: A case study of image repair via Facebook. *International Journal of Sport Communication, 11*(3), 414–429.

Glantz, M. (2013). Plaxico Burress takes his best shot. In J. R. Blaney, L. R. Lippert, and J. S. Smith (Eds.), *Repairing the athlete's image: Studies in sports image restoration* (pp. 187–202). Lanham, MD: Lexington.

Hambrick, M. E., Frederick, E., and Sanderson, J. (2015). From yellow to blue: Exploring Lance Armstrong's image-repair strategies across traditional and social media. *Communication and Sport, 3*(2), 196–218.

Kirby, J. (2018). The sex abuse scandal surrounding USA Gymnastics team doctor Larry Nassar explained. Vox. Retrieved from https://www.vox.

com/identities/2018/1/19/16897722/sexual-abuse-usa-gymnastics-larry-nassar-explained.

Knight, H. R., Hartman, K. L., and Bennett, A. (2020). Gun Violence, eSports, and Global Crises: A proposed model for sport crisis communication practitioners. *Journal of Global Sport Management, 5*(2), 223–241, DOI: 10.1080/24704067.2019.1576144.

Len-Rios, M. E. (2010). Image repair strategies, local news portrayals, and crisis stage: A case study of Duke University's lacrosse team crisis. *International Journal of Strategic Communication, 4,* 267–287.

Sanderson, J. (2008). "How do you prove a negative?": Roger Clemens' image repair strategies in response to the Mitchell Report. *International Journal of Sport Communication, 1,* 246–262.

Smithson, J. and Venette, S. (2013). Stonewalling as an image-defense strategy: A critical examination of BP's response to the Deepwater Horizon explosion. *Communication Studies, 64,* 395–410.

Stoldt, G. S., Dittmore, S. W., and Branvold, S. E. (2012). *Sport public relations: Managing stakeholder communication* (2nd Ed.). Champaign, IL: Human Kinetics.

Talkwalker.com (2020). Crisis Management Templates, https://www.talkwalker.com/marketing-essentials/crisis-management-templates#.

Ulmer, R. R., Sellnow, T. L., and Seeger, M. W. (2019). *Effective crisis communication* (4th Ed.). Thousand Oaks, CA: Sage.

Chapter 14

Diversity and Inclusion in Social Media and Sport

Jacob Bustad* and Oliver Rick[†]

*Towson University, United States
[†]Springfield College, United States

CHAPTER OBJECTIVES

- Develop a fundamental understanding of diversity and inclusion.
- Understand how diversity and inclusion are related to aspects of social identity.
- Critically engage with the major areas of impact regarding diversity and inclusion in sports social media.
- Understand trends and current issues that exist around diversity and inclusion in sports social media.
- Summarize the key skills needed to address diversity issues in sports social media.

KEY TERMS

Corporate social responsibility

Counterpublic space

Diversity

Ethical awareness

Hashtag politics

Inclusion

Online discrimination

Online violence

Participatory cultures

Public space

Social identity

Social media activism

INTRODUCTION

The advent of the Internet and early forms of social media in the late 1990s and early 2000s initiated a transformation in the ways that individuals and groups communicate and provided new platforms for social interaction and individual expression. Scholars writing about the potential futures of social media in this period often focused on the polarity of the positive and negative impacts of these kinds of technology, in particular regarding issues around diversity and social inclusion. These arguments proposed that the development of the Internet could potentially lead to either a 'cyberghetto,' characterized by the degradation of relationships and communication, or a 'cybertopia,' reflecting a harmony of multiple and coexisting voices and viewpoints (Ebo, 1998). Other arguments focused on how social media can be recognized as an important aspect in the development of 'participatory cultures': these include online communities (Chapter 3) such as message boards; new forms of creative expression such as digital sampling or fan fiction; shared tasks and knowledge creation such as wikis for particular subjects and topics; and the advent of different types of media such as blogs or podcasts (Jenkins, 2009).

The development of social media from this point forward has continued to demonstrate positive and negative implications for issues related to diversity and inclusion, often in relation to dimensions of **social identity** including race, ethnicity, gender, sexuality, and social class. Consider the following examples as related to the impacts of social media within the sport industry:

- Forms of discrimination expressed through social media aimed at individuals and groups (for example, racial discrimination against athletes of color, or gender discrimination against women in the sports media industry).
- Anti-discrimination campaigns and messages meant to address online discrimination produced by organizations and individuals including leagues, teams, and athletes (for example, FIFA's 'Kick It Out' campaign designed to address racism in world soccer).
- The disproportionate amount of negative social media messages aimed at female athletes in regard to their gender, sexuality, and careers in the sport industry (for example, sportswomen that endure forms of harassment through negative comments to social media content).
- The utilization of social media platforms in order to distribute and support messages related to gender equity within the global sport industry (for example, female athletes using social media toward forms of self-representation and self-empowerment).

Meanwhile, the historical relationship between sports and diversity and inclusion has demonstrated the capacity for sport to contribute to social divisions and forms of exclusion, as well as the development of togetherness and community. For example, international sports competition has brought about opportunities to link individuals and groups in regard to a shared national identity, while simultaneously creating antagonistic relationships between different national populations (Dolan and Connolly, 2018). These factors have meant that an understanding of the connections between social media, diversity, and inclusion is now a necessary aspect of the contemporary global sport industry.

In the discussion of diversity and inclusion, it will be important to first introduce the working definition of the two ideas. While diversity and inclusion have become more common terms within sports organizations, there is also persistent confusion around the definitions of these ideas, as well as the rationale for their importance for the sport industry. In response to the latter, many sports organizations have recognized that the demographics of both consumers and sport industry labor have been characterized by increased numbers of women, minorities, and varying ethnic backgrounds, and different lifestyles (Langdon *et al.*, 2002). In turn, organizations have sought to address these ongoing changes through different strategies often focused on either diversity or inclusion (Roberson, 2006). **Diversity** programs have most often been aimed at increasing the number of diverse individuals involved with the organization, through targeted recruitment initiatives and training, career development, and mentoring programs. However, many organizations have also developed a broader array of initiatives involving employee participation and community relations, and therefore have positioned inclusion as a concern both internally (in regard to hiring and human relations) and externally (in regard to the reputation of the organization and its relationship with stakeholders). For example, the NFL has recently announced a proposed policy that would incentivize developing minority coaching and management personnel, and a number of NCAA athletic directors have signed a pledge to increase the diversity of their coaching and management hires (Medcalf, 2020). **Inclusion** can therefore be understood as more wide-reaching than diversity, in that inclusion programs and initiatives seek to limit or eliminate issues not only within the organization, but also within the community and the social world in which they operate.

Within any society there exist sites that offer a **public space** of interaction for political and cultural exchange. These also include the possibility for the existence of a **counterpublic space** in which people can challenge mainstream views by developing alternative ideas. Within any moment in history, the communications technologies available to the public create the context for these dominant views and counterpublic spaces. As such, we have gone through periods where the written word, printed materials, audio mediums, and televisual platforms have been central. Generally, these have been referred to in phases of development from Web 1.0 (i.e., the original Internet Web sites) that largely carries one-way messages supplied by publishers, to social media that carries participatory and collaborative content (e.g., text, audio files, photo, video, etc.)

produced and controlled by users. This has been discussed in much more detail in Chapter 1.

LEARNING ACTIVITY 1

Through your own searching, identify at least one example of a sports organization utilizing social media to promote a particular issue or cause related to diversity and inclusion. Include a discussion of how and why social media enables the organization to communicate about the issue or cause, and how the utilization of social media contributes to the broader public relations and branding of the organization — is the organization working with other partners to address this issue or cause? Does the organization enlist particular individuals (athletes, coaches, etc.) in order to promote its stance on the issue or cause? How might social media allow the organization to communicate and interact with others in order to further this stance and address the issue or cause?

Sports media has been an integral part of the broader mediation of public and counterpublic spaces. However, there are examples of where sports media has not just existed as part of this broader evolution in media technologies but has pushed at the forefront of diversifying media more broadly. Through various advancements from mass-mediated contexts, into networked Web 1.0, and social media platforms, sport media has provided a setting for the advancement of diversity and inclusion. For example, the images of the black power protest performed by Tommy Smith and John Carlos at the 1968 Mexico City Olympics have become widespread and since their original broadcast have played a significant role in highlighting the need for increased racial justice in the US and around the world. In this case, the televisualization of sports coverage through the latter part of the 20th century and the unscripted nature of sport combined for the mass broadcast of these images.

As media technology has advanced and changed, the coverage of sports on these varying platforms has provided a setting for addressing issues of diversity. This has not been an unfettered process, or always a successful project of including diverse ideas, identities, or issues. Powerful interests have tended towards a mainstream presentation of sport, interested in presenting the most widely consumable and profitable versions of sports mediation. However, often driven from the bottom of the sports industry by athletes and fans, alternative, counter, and diverse narratives have been an important part of sports media in its many formats. For example, the work of Lewis Hamilton to raise awareness of the human rights impacts of Formula One racing has stood out as a narrative otherwise not often presented in mainstream media around the sport. Formula One (F1) has faced issues in previous media contexts regarding driver safety, tabacco sponsorship, and the sports environmental impacts. Yet, most recently and within the structures of this current social media era, Hamilton has taken the opportunities afforded by these platforms to express views that challenge the organization's silence on human rights issues, especially those around the actions of Saudi Arabia, the UAE, and Bahrain. Indeed it was just before the Bahrain Grand Prix where Hamilton "made the incendiary claim that F1 has a "consistent and massive problem" with human rights abuses in the places it visits." (Alwadaei, 2020). This statement and others from Hamilton have challenged the nature of the relationship between F1 and certain host partners and runs counter to the media output that the organization has disseminated regarding these relationships.

DIVERSITY AND INCLUSION IN SOCIAL MEDIA AND SPORT: KEY CONCEPTS

At first glance, social media platforms may seem to provide a neutral, digital space where aspects of our appearance and other elements of **social identity** — including our ethnicity, disability, gender, sexuality, race, country of origin, religion, and social class — are obscured or concealed. However, in practice, social media has demonstrated the capacity to instead magnify these dimensions of social identity. Studies have shown that race, class, and gender can structure our online experiences, including which spaces we visit (or do not visit) and which groups we engage with (or do not engage with) (Boyd, 2011). Key concepts for understanding the relationship between social media, diversity, and inclusion, therefore, focus on the specific impacts that the uses and abuses of social media have had within the global sports community. At the same time, these concepts reflect that the central issues around sport and social media have often focused on aspects of social identity, including ethnicity, disability, gender, sexuality, race, country of origin, religion, and social class.

One significant and seemingly perpetual challenge in regard to the abuses of social media within sport has been the issue of **online discrimination** against individuals and groups based on racial and ethnic aspects of their identity. We can define online discrimination as the denigration or exclusion of individuals or groups based on their social identity through the use of symbols, images, audio, video, text, and graphic representations (Tynes, 2015). Online discrimination based on race and ethnicity has been a primary issue within sport and social media, as previous studies have indicated that while the management of discrimination at sports events may have led to a decrease of in-person incidents, the prevalence of racism, intolerance, and xenophobia online and across social media platforms has continued to increase (Farrington *et al.*, 2017).

A notable example of both the perpetration and management of online racial discrimination has been evident, as noted in Chapter 12, in the case of the English Premier League, where a history of fan abuse and racism that had previously been documented at stadiums and matches is now evident via social media — after a report showing that nearly 135,000 discriminatory social media posts were made about EPL players and teams during the 2014–2015 season, the league's administrators partnered with clubs to provide guidance on social media (Kilvington and Price 2019). At the same time, non-profit and charitable organizations have also contributed to addressing online discrimination as part of a broader interest in engaging with racism in sport. One important example would be "Kick It Out", an organization that started in 1993 as "Let's Kick

Racism Out of Football" with a focus primarily on the sport in England and has since grown to a global reach including partnerships with UEFA and FIFA. In seeking to promote causes related to equality and diversity, the organization now provides many programs and services that seek to eliminate discrimination and develop the sport as more inclusive (Bennett and Jonsson, 2017).

Online discrimination also is a prevalent issue in regard to gender and sexuality, in part through the historical relationship between traditional sports media and particular ideas about the appropriate roles and responsibilities of women in the sport industry (Cooky *et al.*, 2015). Therefore, while there has been increased inclusion of women within contemporary sports media, including through social media platforms, themes related to the infantilization and sexualization of women within the sport industry more generally remain an issue (Litchfield, *et al.*, 2018). This has also demonstrated the broader problem of abuse against women within virtual spaces, wherein **online violence** — through misogyny, degradation, and threats — has been recognized as a common experience for female users (Moloney and Love, 2018). This is particularly true for women in positions of cultural popularity, including athletes, coaches, and other sportswomen who regularly report encountering hostile and threatening behaviors and comments online. In one study, for example, 12 female sports journalists described how social media has both provided new tools for communication and other aspects of their jobs, and at the same time exposed them to new forms of harassment and abuse (Everbach, 2018).

While a critical issue, the relationship between social media and online discrimination and violence should not discount the capacity of these platforms to provide opportunities for **social media activism**, including building community and consensus around more progressive issues. This has been especially evident across the global sport industry, in which individuals and groups including fans, athletes, and organizations alike have sought to use social media toward social causes and community relations. Several scholars have noted that sportswomen have utilized social media in order to more effectively control their self-representation in contrast to traditional forms of media (Toffoletti and Thorpe, 2018). This association between social media use by female athletes and forms of self-empowerment has also been documented at various levels of sports participation, indicating that social media aids sportswomen in developing and distributing representations that provide an alternative to stereotypes of women in sport (Thorpe *et al.*, 2017).

Social media activism has taken many forms across the global sport industry, and in coordination with a wide range of social issues including human rights, gender equality, and environmental conservation. One form of social media activism has emerged through **hashtag politics**, in which the hashtag (#) used originally with Twitter serves to link a message with a particular phrase — hashtag movements such as #MeToo have often demonstrated some of the capacities and limits of social media activism more broadly (Zimmerman, 2017) . The use of hashtag politics and social media activism related to sport is most commonly discussed in the context of notable athletes and events, as reflected in the following case study focusing on Serena Williams. However, social media has also been an increasingly impactful resource for individuals and groups of sportswomen from around the world. As one example, a study of 20 Muslim sportswomen from a variety of nations and sports showed that social media provided a space in which these women could challenge common assumptions and stereotypes about both their religion and their social identities (Ahmad and Thorpe, 2020).

CASE STUDY

Serena Williams is arguably the greatest women's tennis player in the history of the sport, and her dominance has resulted in multiple Grand Slam titles, sponsorships, and cultural popularity. However, the role of social media throughout her career has reflected the positive and negative aspects of these technologies, in particular in regard to issues of diversity and inclusion. As with other Black female athletes and popular figures, there is a documented pattern of online discrimination and violence aimed at Serena on the basis of her racial and gender identity, including

(Continued)

(Continued)

in regard to her physique and style of play, and her presence within the world of elite tennis (Litchfield *et al.*, 2018). These types of social media posts can therefore reflect racialized and gender-based understandings of sport and social identity that are regressive and limiting. At the same time, Serena has developed her own utilization of social media, using multiple platforms to reach her following of millions of fans and communicating messages about her career and her sponsors, as well as forms of social media activism whereby she contributes to awareness of particular issues and causes. For example, in 2020, Serena and other athletes including LeBron James worked with Nike to create the #YouCantStopUs social media campaign focused on racial equality, and Serena helped launch the #NotTheFirst campaign with Secret deodorant, bringing attention to women of color in the sport industry.

Discussion: Following this description of one athlete's involvement with social media, identify and consider your own example of at least two other athletes — how have these athletes utilized social media toward promoting forms of diversity and inclusion? How have these athletes been criticized or supported through social media in regard to their career and identity?

KEY SKILLS FOR PRACTICE

An important part of being a member of the sport industry, specifically in the role of sports management, is being able to perform in your position with an ethical set of guidelines. With the wide variety of jobs that exist in the sport industry and the complex nature of sport as an institution, being an ethical professional can be extremely challenging. These challenges range in nature, from interpersonal dimensions that have an array of legal implications, to being able to manage health and safety in often-risky environments for the many stakeholders involved in sport. Included in these ethical challenges is the ability to create an inclusive environment in which a range of diverse ideas and individuals can feel free to express themselves. The role of sports managers to ensure the institutions and spaces they manage are open to a diverse array of people, who are able to express themselves freely without fear of prejudice, be free from sexism, racism, or any other form of bigotry, is an essential part of good professional practice. Therefore, the ethical practice of a sports management professional must include the skill of **managing diversity**.

Increasingly, this ethical consideration around issues of diversity and inclusion has moved online. The very nature of social media as a read–write platform, one which also offers layers of anonymity, has made it central as a setting through which ideas on race, gender, disability, sexuality, class, etc. are voiced. This is both in a positive dimension, through which diversity has been embraced in sports social media, as well as in a negative way, where hate has been spread. For those working in sports management, the ability to engage and navigate these social media spaces around issues of diversity is a central ethical challenge. Working with the complexities and specificities of the various social media platforms is important. Being able to understand the ways in which 'real life' management decisions translate into social media spaces and communities is also fundamental. As such, being able to navigate sports social media around diversity issues not only requires a broad **ethical awareness**, but also a tangible grip on how these ideas and issues manifest themselves in the specifics of social media (Lipschultz, 2017).

In order to be able to make social media a positive and effective part of your sports business or organization, embracing diversity from the outset can be key. **Corporate social responsibility** (CSR) has long been an idea embraced in the sport industry as many organizations look to boost the positive potential of their sport, while also boosting the business performance of their organization. However, with greater awareness and action around issues of diversity and inclusion recently, many companies working in sports have done more to mobilize around this issue. Being able to build meaningful and engaged CSR programs for sports organizations is therefore a more important skill than ever before, including the ability to apply critical thinking to identify issues that need to be addressed and then working with appropriate partners to build corresponding initiatives. Therefore, while CSR programs have always been an important aspect of the sport industry, the need for producing real material outcomes from these programs is more necessary than ever.

Organizations have been working to increase their engagement with ideas of racial justice, embracing protests and calls for solidarity, including the actions of the English Premier League following its resumption in 2020 after the hiatus due to the impact of COVID-19 (the English Premier League issued a statement on the issue in June 2020 with the hashtag #NoRoomForRacism). In a similar fashion in the United States, Major League Soccer (MLS) has been working with partners to address issues of race, specifically supporting the formation of the Black Players Coalition of MLS. While these efforts are oriented toward the issue of racial justice, specifically in sport, the benefits of this work for the industry are multiple (Horting, 2019). Not only does this work create a more accessible, inclusive, and inviting space for diverse sports management talent to enter the industry, it can also extend the consumer base of a sport. Addressing issues of racism in sport, alongside issues of discrimination based on gender, sexuality, (dis)ability, etc., can aid in creating a more diverse and inclusive space for fans. Embracing CSR programs that engage with social justice issues has an array of direct impacts, but it can also signal a more inviting space for a diverse fan base. The abilities to identify appropriate causes, find partners to work with, and ensure the meaningful outcomes of CSR campaigns are critical skills. The sport industry is paying more attention to these now than ever before and the ability to blend these programs with social media as the place to take action, or as a means to provide coverage of this work, is important as well. Developing effective CSR programming and blending it into the social media work of an organization are valued skills in sport today.

Of importance for sports managers and professionals is that increasingly this form of CSR work includes or is wholly focused on social media. Many non-profits concerned with issues of diversity include some aspect of their work being focused on social media. As these platforms become significant parts of the public sphere or a place for counterpublic voices, organizations must focus attention to these settings. Potentially few non-profits focus their work wholly on diversity in sports social media, yet an organization such as Kick It Out or The Women's Sports Foundation increasingly engage with these platforms in pursuit of their missions. Recognizing the increased importance of social media for engagement with a sport, many in the sports industry are recognizing the need to address social justice issues on these platforms. For many, interacting with sports social media strongly augments their experiences of sport, or during a time like the recent response to the COVID-19, sports social media can become the central space for engaging with sport. This recognition by sports organizations has been increasing and a variety of trends in the sport industry reflect this shift.

TRENDS AND CURRENT ISSUES

DIVERSITY AND FAN-LED CHANGE

The potential of social media to allow all people to contribute on the platform equally, while not necessarily always fully realized, has opened up a greater ability for fan-led movements to form on these platforms. The ability of groups to grasp tools built into these platforms for production of content and designing for virality in messaging has established a new potential for social media in sport, where fan groups have embraced social media to augment their movements and organizing this has been oriented around a number of issues. Some of the concerns could be directly aimed at the ways their club or team is being run, they could focus on the structures of the league their team participates in, or a wide range of broader political issues. No matter what the aim of the fan group and its actions, it is important that social media has been used to boost and expand on their actions. Social media does not undermine collective grassroots action, but helps boost it, as "far from producing a generation of bedroom-bound isolates, social media in these cases appear to be bringing people together both virtually and physically in pursuit of common interests and causes." (Monagham, 2014, p. 228).

In certain cases, fan groups have embraced these social media platforms for the creation of content aimed at social justice issues, as well as subverting sports organizations' use of social media towards these issues. During the 2019 season the Portland Timbers and Portland Thorns, supporter groups mounted a protest movement against a ban on political imagery in their stadium that included the display of anti-fascist imagery and iconography (Goldberg, 2019). Using #AUnitedFront and other hashtags, these groups were able to augment in-person demonstrations that included silent protests in stadium at Timbers games with a display of white roses. Ultimately, the pressure from these fan groups resulted in a change of policy from the football clubs and the display of anti-fascist imagery from fans in stadium was no longer prohibited.

DISCRIMINATION AND GOVERNANCE

While the movements of players, fans, and coaches on issues of racial justice have been significant, their reflection in the actions of sports governance has also been key. Sports governance organizations have been increasingly aware of the need to support and protect movements that strive for justice in areas of race, gender, sexuality, national identity, etc.. While late to take action, many governing bodies or league organizations are increasingly taking steps to create policy and set precedent in these areas. The NFL has recently recognized the need to protect political action and specifically allow players their rights to express viewpoints on issues of racial injustice (Anderson, 2020). Certainly, criticism has been leveled at the league for coming to this stance late and doing so only to follow the changing climate of fan culture, ultimately protecting their financial bottom line. Yet, this action is significant and has also included a role in regulating social media. Most directly, this regulation of social media is aimed at those working in sports organizations, players, and coaches. However, it also extends to cover the actions of fans and fan groups. Governing organizations at every level are increasingly addressing the actions of fans in online spaces as well as what they do in real life. For instance, the expression of racist ideas online can have implications that are similar to those for when fans shout racist language at players in stadium. During the 2020 season, "West Midlands Police arrested a 12-year-old boy after Crystal Palace winger Wilfried Zaha received racist messages on social media ahead of the club's Premier League clash with Aston Villa" (ESPN, 2020). Working with league official's, investigations and arrests around racism online are being carried out in the same ways that in-person attacks would be dealt with. Where racist chants and comments from fans in stadiums can come with lifetime bans and criminal implications, those same remarks online are being dealt with in the same manner.

PUBLIC RELATIONS AND SOCIAL ISSUES

One issue that brings together grassroots movements and organizational change has been a recent drive to remove forms of indigenous imagery and culture that have been problematically appropriated from native cultures in North America. This has both been a proactive and reactive set of responses from sports organizations that have either been ahead of a wave of demands for change, or a slower set of shifts in policy on this issue. This means that while the appropriation of indigenous cultures within the marketing and identity of North American sports organizations has historical legacies, the use of social media to criticize or support issues related to naming and images is a more recent phenomenon. A number of examples can be identified, but the most prominent change we have seen recently in mainstream sport is the decision of the Washington DC area football team to move away from their previous name. The organization has resisted calls for change previously, employing a number of tactics to justify keeping their previous name and imagery. However, a recent resurgence in pressure from grassroots movements, utilizing social media platforms to express their demands for change, have been effective. The organization relented to this pressure to change and, while at the time of writing they are still deciding on alternative naming and branding, the team has turned to social media in part to announce these changes.

LEARNING ACTIVITY 2

Identify a social media-based CSR program from the sport industry. Review it and evaluate its success in terms of its ability to address an identified issue as well as its effects on the business success of the organization. Are these two areas of success mutually supporting? Or do they create tension in the function of the organization? Are there any other aspects you identify?

CHAPTER SUMMARY

Social media has been an increasingly common aspect of the global sport industry, and in doing so has reflected the capacity of these technologies to demonstrate both positive and negative issues related to diversity and inclusion. Social media platforms contribute to forms of online discrimination and online violence, often targeting messages of hate and intolerance toward individuals and groups based on aspects of social identity including race, ethnicity, gender, sexuality, and (dis)ability. At the same time, athletes and organizations have incorporated social media into efforts to promote their own causes and issues, resulting in a proliferation of different types of social media activism. In order to emphasize the importance of diversity and inclusion in sports social media, this chapter presented the basic concepts for understanding current trends and key examples of social media practices related to the expression and regulation of ideas concerning social identity.

While this chapter provides a foundational knowledge of these issues, further resources are available for more information on diversity and inclusion in sports social media. Please see the following "Key Resources" section. As this chapter has demonstrated, it is critical for current and future sport industry professionals to identify opportunities and pitfalls that are often inherent to social media platforms, and to develop and apply a perspective that recognizes the potential uses of social media toward forms of anti-discrimination and community engagement toward positive social change.

KEY RESOURCES

- NCAA diversity and inclusion social media campaign: http://www.ncaa.org/about/resources/inclusion/social-media-campaign.
- Academic journals: *Sociology of Sport Journal, Journal of Sport and Social Issues, Communcation & Sport,* and *International Journal of Sport Communication.*
- Periodicals: *Forbes, Sports Business Daily.*
- Sport Business Journal: https://www.sportsbusinessdaily.com/Journal/Issues/2019/07/15/Opinion/Lapchick.aspx.
- The Institute for Diversity and Ethics in Sport (TIDES): https://www.tidesport.org/.
- Tucker Center for Research on Women and Girls in Sport: https://www.cehd.umn.edu/tuckercenter/.
- Hashtag Sports: https://hashtagsports.com/.

TEST YOUR KNOWLEDGE

1. Does social media technology fundamentally alter the ways in which we communicate about issues related to diversity and inclusion? If so, what are some of these changes?
2. How much is your ethical practice as a sports manager based on navigating social media?
3. Is addressing diversity and inclusion issues on social media enough for a corporate social responsibility program? How could online action be combined with other initiatives?
4. Have fan groups really been able to make meaningful change around diversity, and how has social media helped them achieve their goals?

5. Should sports organizations' use of social media to address diversity and inclusion issues be criticized? Should these organizations be expected to be more proactive in their actions?
6. How have athletes been impacted by social media in regard to social identity? How have athletes contributed to forms of social media activism toward diversity and inclusion?

REFERENCES

Ahmad, N. and Thorpe, H. (2020). Muslim sportswomen as digital space invaders: Hashtag politics and everyday visibilities. *Communication and Sport*, 2167479519898447.

Alwadaei, S. A. (2020). Lewis Hamilton has spoken out on human rights. Formula One will have to take a stand. The Guardian, December 12, 2020. Retreived from https://www.theguardian.com/commentisfree/2020/dec/12/lewis-hamilton-human-rights-formula-one-grand-prix-abu-dhabi-regimes.

Anderson, J. (2020). Why the NFL is suddenly standing up for black lives. *Slate.* June 7 2020. Retrieved from https://slate.com/culture/2020/06/nfl-roger-goodell-black-lives-matter-players-video-kaepernick.html.

Bennett, H. and Jönsson, A. (2017). Klick it out: Tackling online discrimination in football. In D. Kilvington and J. Price (Eds.), *Sport and discrimination* (pp. 215–226). Routledge.

Boyd, D. (2011). White flight in networked publics? How race and class shaped American teen engagement with MySpace and Facebook. In L. Nakamura and P. Chow-White (Eds.), *Race after the Internet* (pp. 203–222). London, England: Routledge.

Bruns, A. (2008). *Blogs, Wikipedia, Second life, and beyond: From production to produsage* (Vol. 45). New York: Peter Lang.

Cooky, C., Messner, M.A., and Musto, M. (2015). "It's dude time!" A quarter century of excluding women's sports in televised news and highlights shows. *Communication and Sport, 3*(3), 261–287.

Dolan, P. and Connolly, J. (Eds.). (2018). Sport and national identities: Globalization and conflict. Routledge.

Ebo, B. L. (Ed.). (1998). *Cyberghetto or cybertopia? Race, class, and gender on the Internet.* Greenwood Publishing Group.

ESPN (2020). Police arrest 12-year-old over racist social media messages sent to Palace's Zaha. *ESPN,* July 12, 2020.

Everbach, T. (2018). "I realized it was about them... not me": Women sports journalists and harassment. In J. Vickery and T. Everbach (Eds.), *Mediating misogyny*. Palgrave Macmillan, Cham.

Farrington, N., Hall, L., Kilvington, D., Price, J., and Saeed, A. (2017). *Sport, Racism and Social Media*. Routledge.

Goldberg, J. (2019). Portland Thorns fans join Timbers fans in protesting ban on 'Iron Front' symbol, political displays. *The Oregonian*, August 25, 2019.

Horting, K. (2019). The Business Case For Diversity and Inclusion. *Forbes*, June 5, 2019.

Jenkins, H. (2009). *Confronting the Challenges of Participatory Culture: Media Education for the 21st Century*. MIT Press.

Kilvington, D. and Price, J. (2019). Tackling social media abuse? Critically assessing English football's response to online racism. *Communication and Sport*, 7(1), 64–79.

Langdon, D. S., McMenamin, T. M, and Krolik, T. J. (2002). U.S. labor market in 2001: Economy enters a recession. *Monthly Labor Review, 125*, 3–33.

Lipschultz, J. H. (2017). *Social Media Communication: Concepts, Practices, Data, Law and Ethics*. Taylor & Francis.

Litchfield, C., Kavanagh, E., Osborne, J., and Jones, I. (2018). Social media and the politics of gender, race and identity: The case of Serena Williams. *European Journal for Sport and Society*, 15(2), 154–170.

Medcalf, M. (2020). Multiple division I athletic directors sign collegiate coaching diversity pledge. *ESPN*, September 20, 2020.

Moloney, M. E. and Love, T. P. (2018). Assessing online misogyny: Perspectives from sociology and feminist media studies. *Sociology Compass, 12*, e12577.

Monaghan, F. (2014). Seeing Red: Social media and football fan activism. In P. Seargeant, C. Tagg (Eds.) *The Language of Social Media*. Palgrave Macmillan, London.

Roberson, Q. M. (2006). Disentangling the meanings of diversity and inclusion in organizations. *Group and Organization Management, 31*(2), 212–236.

Thorpe, H., Toffoletti, K., and Bruce, T. (2017). Sportswomen and social media: Bringing third-wave feminism, postfeminism, and neoliberal feminism into conversation. *Journal of Sport and Social Issues, 41*(5), 359–383.

Toffoletti, K. and Thorpe, H. (2018). Female athletes' self-representation on social media: A feminist analysis of neoliberal marketing strategies in "economies of visibility". *Feminism and Psychology, 28*(1), 11–31.

Tynes, B. (2015). Online racial discrimination: A growing problem for adolescents. *Psychological Science Agenda*, December 2015. American Psychological Association.

Zimmerman, T. (2017). #Intersectionality: The fourth wave feminist twitter community. *Atlantis, 38*, 54–70.

https://doi.org/10.1142/9789811237669_0015

Chapter 15

Revenue Generation and Return on Investment from Social Media in Sport

Rebecca M. Achen* and Norm O'Reilly†

*Illinois State University, United States
†University of Maine, United States

CHAPTER OBJECTIVES

After studying this chapter, you will be able to:

- Understand why measurement of return on social media investment is important
- Identify the different social media systems of measurements or metrics
- Evaluate the potential costs of social media use in an organization
- Describe the process for creating a social media measurement plan
- Create an example of a social media measurement plan

KEY TERMS

Benchmarking

Key performance indicator

Return on investment

Return on objective

Social media analytics

Social media planning process

INTRODUCTION

Generating direct revenue from social media activities and measuring the return on investment (ROI) in social media are hotly debated topics, not to mention analytically challenging ones. In the general business social media research, there is a split on whether social media needs to be measured in terms of traditional ROI (i.e., input–output model where x investment leads to y return) and whether direct revenue generation should be the goal of social media strategy. Further complicating this point is the knowledge that the measure of ROI in other sports-related marketing tactics such as sponsorship is well known to be a process and not a direct ROI model (O'Reilly and Madill, 2012). The complexity in assigning financial value to social media activities and the varying objectives for social media use across organizations are some of the factors contributing to the general lack of agreement on what social media ROI measurement means in sport and social media research.

Practically, organizations are observed struggling to truly ascribe an ROI value to a social media investment. Intuitively, they report that measurement is something that they must do, but they also report that it is hard to assess their return as it is difficult to attribute a sale to a specific social media post, a retail promotion, a brand, or some portion thereof. For instance, consider Nike's launch of the Nike Pegasus 38s in 2021, which was accompanied by a new social media campaign to enhance its image. In 2022, as part of their future planning, Nike may review their sales performance and find that they have increased sales over the Nike Pegasus 37s by 8.5% in a given year. Can that 8.5% change be attributed entirely to the social media campaign? The answer is 'no.' Changes in the market,

Nike's other marketing mix activities, improved performance of a Nike-endorsed athlete, Nike's overall brand response to social issues, and many other possible reasons could also contribute to increased sales.

However, despite the attribution challenge, there are processes that can be followed to measure the ROI of social media in a way that can inform decision-making. For instance, using Nike's example from the above paragraph, a large sample survey of new Pegasus 38 purchasers, who are asked to attribute the various possible drivers of their purchase, can allow for an estimation of the 'contribution to attribution' of the social media campaign. There would be a margin of error in such an approach but, over a large sample, it could provide strong enough data to inform an estimate of the contribution of the social media campaign to the ROI. This data can allow marketers to compare the effectiveness of social media marketing with other marketing strategies (Kumar *et al.*, 2013) and make decisions on how to spend on their marketing resources on social media in the future. Additionally, marketers can utilize this data to justify investments in social media marketing including staff, time, and content-creation tools. Further, measuring ROI from social media activities is important for justifying its use, and assessing and comparing marketing campaigns. The amount of time or money that organizations invest in social media will depend greatly on the ROI they can demonstrate (Gilfoil and Jobs, 2012).

HISTORY AND BACKGROUND

Originally, ROI was strictly a financial concept (Jobs and Gilfoil, 2014), although many business units within organizations have used the term when referring to the measurement of value brought to an organization from a given activity or line of business operations. In a very general sense, **return on investment** (ROI) means that the organization receives value for investing time, money, or other resources. A simple and direct measure of ROI subtracts the costs of an investment from the financial proceeds of that investment and divides it by the investment cost (Gilfoil and Jobs, 2012). For example, a club takes out an ad on Twitter for a promotion to sell seasons tickets for the following year. The ad used a professionally done graphic design and the club used Quick Promote, a paid Twitter service available to businesses to promote tweets. The ad is only on Twitter and a social code was shared so anyone who uses the promotion could be tracked. Following the completion of the sales cycle, reports show that 42 new season ticket packages were sold. The revenue generated (i.e., ticket sales) minus the total cost of the program (i.e., human resource time, creative, any costs due to Twitter) would be the return from that investment. However, a broader view of ROI in the social media space suggests return can be measured based on value generated from social media investments, which will depend on different objectives of an organization (Newberry and Aynsley, 2020).

Earlier chapters in this book clearly indicate that social media has grown in popularity across varied demographics over the past decade. Thus, companies across all industries have been increasingly creating social media accounts, profiles, and content across multiple platforms as a means to connect with customers. As organizations have invested more time, money, and other resources into these platforms and networks, senior managers, in turn, have stressed the need for improved data-driven evaluation of these increasing investments in social media. In a review of the research on social media and ROI, Gifloil and Jobs' (2012) early work found a range of views on ROI in social media that are important to this chapter. First, some participants suggested that measuring the ROI of social media is not possible and, thus, attempts to do so are meaningless. Second, some felt that while ROI can be measured, it should be specified in a specific way, such as measuring the investments customers make in social media, or categorizing benefits as hard or soft and detailing costs. Third, others stated that ROI can and should only be measured in financial terms. Fourth, some others suggested measuring ROI on social media should be part of a larger contextual evaluation system that seeks to measure attribution-related influences. Fifth, the last group felt measuring ROI on social media was relatively easy. This is largely due to the availability of digital analytics tools (e.g., Facebook Analytics, Twitter Analytics, Instagram Insights, YouTube Analytics) to quickly assess data and platform usage. As the varying viewpoints indicate, measuring ROI in social media is complicated and no one system or process is agreed upon by all.

SOCIAL MEDIA IMPACTS ON BUSINESS OUTCOMES

Research, across many industries, reported the positive impact of social media on business outcomes (e.g., sales, advocacy, brand equity), while not explicitly exploring return on investment. For example, using social media has a positive impact on relationships between brands and customers, intentions to repurchase, purchase behaviors, word of mouth (WOM), referral intentions, and brand equity. Researchers have provided further insights into how these impacts are realized on social media. For example, Garanti and Kissi (2019) found that brand personality represented on social media networks that is perceived to be aggressive and persistent had positive impacts on brand equity, leading to greater brand loyalty. Similarly, Walsh *et al.* (2013) found that using social media can positively impact perceptions of brand attributes for sport fans. Additionally, team identification, referral intentions (i.e., advocacy), and intentions to purchase sponsor products are positively impacted by the consumption of sports-related social media (Demeril and Erdogmus, 2016; Park and Dittmore, 2014). More specifically, higher levels of engagement, such as liking, commenting, sharing, retweeting, messaging, and other active behaviors on channels on social media can lead to:

- word of mouth (Wakefield and Bennett, 2018; Hutter *et al.*, 2013)
- greater likelihood to refer (Smith, 2013)
- greater brand awareness (Hutter *et al.*, 2013)
- higher customer loyalty (Gummerus *et al.*, 2012; Sohail *et al.*, 2020)

- increased brand equity (Godey *et al.*, 2016; Watkins, 2014)
- higher intentions to purchase (Achen, 2016, 2019; Demirel and Erogmus, 2016)
- more purchases (Goh *et al.*, 2013; Kumar *et al.*, 2016)
- more shopping visits (Rishika *et al.*, 2013)
- more website traffic (Boehmer and Lacy, 2014)
- stronger relationships (Achen, 2016, 2019; Watkins, 2014).
- higher fan identification (Watkins, 2014)

REVENUE GENERATION AND ROI FROM SOCIAL MEDIA: KEY CONCEPTS

FACILITATING REVENUE GENERATION ON SOCIAL MEDIA

While all sports organizations are not alike, most of them are looking to drive revenue generation using social media, and it is a challenging task. One important element — in practice — to consider is that many sports organization personnel may view social media as another important part of the marketing and communications mix (along with other marketing and communications tactics including, sponsorship, in-store promotions, web marketing, publicity, and advertising), where clubs, leagues, federations, events, venues, or athletes need to be present and 'out there.' However, it is challenging to attribute ROI to each specific tactic (i.e., determine what actually led to or had the most important role in the revenue generation), and most marketers view the resulting outcome as part of a vibrant and integrated promotional mix that includes all tactics and channels. This is considered a best practice in today's sports marketing world. For example, Canadian Sponsorship Landscape Study (2020), which has been evaluating sponsorship indicators in Canada over the past 13 years, reported that social media was an area of investment for brands activating sport properties in the 2012 to 2015 timeframe. However, since 2016 to 2019, it has decreased to be another channel with similar investment levels in activation to other tactics.

One way revenue could be increased is by engaging customers in ways that encourage them to share the organization's content, thereby increasing visibility and improving brand image (Goh *et al.*, 2013). Also, in seeking to reach and influence various stakeholders in the sport industry, social media is known to be one of the most relevant and growing tools available to managers today (Foster *et al.*, 2020). Specifically, advertisements on social media networks, such as Instagram and Facebook, afford organizations the opportunity to drive, and track, sales directly from social media sites. For example, Instagram shop provides a platform for sport teams and organizations to sell licensed merchandise. Sponsored content, such as Fan of the Week, contests, or fan polls, also provide additional sponsorship inventory that could be sold on social media networks. For instance, the Baltimore Ravens found a sponsor for a weekly Throwback Thursday photo, a content type that is popular and easily recognizable to fans. Selling advertisements that can be played during Snapchat, Instagram, or Facebook stories can also be a way sports teams can generate revenue directly from social media. Finally, live streams of games, practices, or events on subscribed YouTube channels provide additional potential revenue sources. Sometimes, sports organizations can combine strategies, such as the Miami Dolphins, who published a sponsored video series called "The Cutting Room Floor."

MEASURING ROI ON SOCIAL MEDIA

When measuring ROI on social media, sport managers may need to consider a non-traditional approach that focuses on non-financial outcomes that align with the goals of their social media strategy. For example, after reviewing the literature on measuring social media, Agostino and Sidorova (2016) suggested that metrics include: financial (e.g., direct sales from links on social media networks), network structure (e.g., the number of connections your followers have in their network), interactions (e.g., number of comments on content), content (e.g., relevance to the audience), and sentiment indicators (e.g., the number of positive versus negative comments on a post).

Researchers and practitioners across many industries have attempted to adapt or create metrics to measure the effectiveness of social media marketing. Kumar *et al.* (2013) proposed two metrics, customer influence effect and customer influence value. Customer influence effect is described as "the net influence wielded by a user (in a social network) in terms of his or her ability to spread positive or negative WOM through his or her direct and indirect connections" (Kumar *et al.*, 2013, p. 195). Customer influence value (CIV) is defined as the "monetary gain/loss realized by the firm that is attributable to a customer's influence effect" (Kumar *et al.*, 2013 p. 195). The calculation of the CIV involves summing the customer lifetime value (the total revenue an organization an expect from a customer over the course of their time as a customer) of all individuals who are influenced by the original poster on the social media platform. For example, the WOM connection is established between two individuals and then their posts and communication with one another are examined to see how much of the conversation centers around the product or brand. Then, sales data are used to match purchases to users, and the level of influence that they had on other customers is deemed to be their CIV. So, if customer A sent out 20 tweets about the Minnesota Lynx and purchase data indicates that a ticket holder was a Twitter follower of customer A, the purchase of that ticket holder would be value attributed to the WOM of customer A on social media. One problem with using this method to measure ROI related to WOM is that it does not consider many other sources of influence on a customer's purchase behavior including direct contact from the organization, advertisements, email communications, and the like. It also does not account for customer-level variables, such as disposable income or economic conditions, which may affect the ability of a customer to make a purchase, even if they have been influenced to do so.

Etlinger *et al.* (2012) suggested revenue impact of social media could be measured through anecdotes or examples of instances where social media influenced sales, correlation between two data-sets to examine relationships between variables, multivariate testing (i.e., comparing groups of customers who were exposed or not exposed to social media content), links and tags to attribute conversions to social media sites and content, integration with apps or software, and direct commerce on social media sites. For sports organizations, this may be as simple as using Instagram shopping to sell merchandise or track link traffic to a ticket-buying or event registration page on the main website to determine how many customers were driven to the site via social media posts. Additional research has suggested organizations measure ROI by measuring reach, sales, customer retention, customer communication, and outrage avoidance (Kaske *et al.*, 2012), or tying referral sources to net proceeds from that customer (Gould and Nazarian, 2018). Assessing customer communication or outrage avoidance is a more qualitative approach to measuring social media impact and requires the sport organization to spend time analyzing how customers are discussing them and contacting them directly on social networks and to what extent they are included in the conversations about them on social networks.

Social media ROI has also been described as a broader concept that includes many metrics and factors and may require focusing on measuring the long-term benefits of using social media and measuring customer equity built over time (Michopoulou and Moisa, 2019). The investments customers make with the brand on social media are more important and congruent with the purported long-term benefits of social media (Hoffman and Fodor, 2010). Similar to this idea, Thompson *et al.* (2014) suggested sports organizations focus on return on objective (ROO) to measure the impact of marketing on Facebook, which is a strategy that focuses on whether the marketing plan met organizational objectives (e.g., proportion of customers who believe the firm is a good corporate citizen).

Often, the functions of social media also intertwine and might include sales, customer service, business development, logistics, research and development, relationship building, public relations, and more. For example, for a college athletics department, social media may need to be assessed for separate departments, such as different teams or the marketing department, or for individual athletes or mascots. Metrics will vary depending on the use of social media. For example, measuring sales will likely require tracking link traffic to see how many individuals purchase tickets from social media links. However, relationship building may be assessed based on the number of likes on posted content or the sentiment of comments.

In thinking about how to measure social media ROI, there are clearly different views on how effective and how appropriate it is to measure. But, that aside, there is clearly an existing set of frameworks, metrics, and applications to use (as will be discussed later in the chapter). For any platform the sport organization is on, there are indicators that platforms provide (likes, retweets, views, etc.), metrics they offer for business accounts (e.g., Facebook Analytics, Twitter Analytics, Instagram Insights, YouTube Analytics) plus additional applications that can be purchased (usually at low cost) to get more detailed usage numbers (e.g., HubSpot). One way that ROI for social media campaigns could be calculated is by tracking WOM facilitated on social media and attributing it to sales (Kumar *et al.*, 2013).

PLANNING A SUCCESSFUL SOCIAL MEDIA STRATEGY

The key to building a successful social media strategy, and the subsequent measurement of that strategy, is in the social media planning process. If an organization does not know why it is using social media and what its goals are, it is impossible to determine success and how to measure that success. Clearly stated and measurable objectives are essential. For example, an athlete may want to build a following of at least 5,000 followers to help increase their sponsorship attractiveness or a National Sport Organization may want to improve its social media content by posting on all of its channels at least once a day. Once you have these articulated, you can build a social media program.

Chapter 16 focuses on the practical steps in managing social media platforms. The steps include defining goals, establishing objectives, gathering information, identifying target audience, choosing platforms, developing content, establishing content calendar, executing the plan and tracking performance, developing reports, and communicating outcomes. In this section of the chapter, some of the steps relevant to the measurement of ROI in social media will be briefly discussed. Specifically, those steps that help determine the metrics needed to measure the success of marketing efforts implemented using social media and your stated objectives.

A good social media plan should be connected to the mission, vision, and values of your organization (and brand) and tied into the strategic plan. This leads to a specification of organizational objectives and intended audiences, and making certain those objectives are measurable (e.g., Ontario Lawn Bowls Association views to increase its Facebook following from 508 in September 2020 to 5,000 by December 2022). Organizations may use social media for advertising, sales, direct marketing, public relations, promotion, news update, customer service, internal communication, or corporate communication. Organizations can focus on a combination of these purposes. Specific objectives, such as to increase brand awareness (e.g., increase followers and page likes), increase community engagement (e.g., replies, comments, shares, likes, favorites, clicks, follows, mentions), and increase website traffic, may also be created.

Defining the reasons that the organization is using social media is essential to driving measurement. Importantly, these two important aspects — objectives and audiences — are included in the same step as they often inform each other. For example, if a professional sports team has built an audience of current season ticket holders on its Facebook page, then an appropriate goal might be to improve relationships with season ticket holders by engaging them in conversations on the Facebook page. A goal to increase single-game ticket sales among new customers is not appropriate on social media if your audience is mostly current ticket buyers. The main focus should be to make sure that audiences and objectives are aligned.

Once audience and objectives have been specified, social media managers can drill down and set specific and tactical goals. In turn, these goals will drive the measurement of your social media plan. Goals should follow the SMART framework — they should be specific, measurable, attainable, realistic, and timely. These aspects are essential because they will help determine what metrics can be used to measure the success of the social media plan. Each objective may have multiple goals underneath it. For example, the objective might be to drive awareness of the sporting event, and goals might be to increase Facebook following by 10%, increase the reach of Instagram posts by 10%, and increase the shares of content on all social media platforms by 10%.

An important step in managing a social media platform is identify metrics and key performance indicators to measure each goal. As mentioned above, specific tactical goals will drive measurement choices. For instance, if the objective is to build relationships with customers, and the goal is to increase the number of comments for content on Facebook by 10% with at least 90% with positive sentiment, then the metric would be number of comments and a sentiment rating (i.e., an assessment of the positive or negative nature of the content of a given post). However, if the objective is to build awareness, and the goal is to increase page views by 10%, then page views would be the metric. Each tactical goal needs to have at least one metric to measure it, a benchmark, and a way to collect data to assess its impact on that benchmark. In considering an ROI assessment of a social media campaign, it is likely that a combination of metrics will provide you a more accurate picture of the ROI connected to a social media activity.

Once a social media manager identifies the specific metric to measure the impact of each tactical goal, they can collect the data that the metrics provide and analyze the data. In this step, organizations will need to select a frequency for collecting and analyzing the data. As you remember, Chapter 7 discussed the different data mining tools and data analysis approaches available that are relevant to this stage of social media management, collecting metrics and analyzing data. Collecting and analyzing data may differ depending on the goal and the metric. It is relatively easy to log in to an organization's Google Analytics account and view interaction or page insights data for many social media networks (e.g., Facebook's Page Insights) and this can be reviewed monthly or weekly. Using the data from analytics platforms, it is relatively easy to do longitudinal studies and assess impact of content strategies at various points in time and look at changes over the long term (i.e., for months or years). However, in the case of deeper analyses, if organizations are using improvements in relationship quality or assessments related to attribution in order to measure social media strategy, then they should consider another metric (such as an ongoing, regular survey of customers) to better understand attribution. Social media managers would have to plan carefully to be sure to get benchmarks and assessments of impact at the appropriate points in time during and post the social media effort of interest.

LEARNING ACTIVITY 1

Search online and find at least three industry blogs that discuss measuring ROI in social media in the last three years. Describe how they discuss approaching this topic on social media. Make a list of metrics and tools they discuss for measurement.

SETTING OBJECTIVES AND GOALS: KEY PERFORMANCE INDICATORS (KPIs)

Because social media platforms are different from traditional media, organizations need to explore new metrics to measure effectiveness (Schober *et al.*, 2018). A good way to approach the measurement of effectiveness is via metrics that assess goal achievement in a focused and strategic manner. One well-known method to do this is via Key Performance Indicators, or KPIs, which are indicators of your success toward reaching a goal that is important to your business and will be driven, at least in part, by the purpose and goal of your social media activity. For example, Bonsón and Ratkai (2013) suggested organizations could use likes, comments, and shares as indicators of popularity, commitment, and virality, respectively. This section will discuss the metrics for measuring social media and conclude with a chart that organizes some of the commonly used KPIs by social media goals.

An example of some of the metrics that may be useful in measuring social media are the value of the experience and value of a fan metrics. These metrics are proposed by Smith (2013) to measure the emotional impacts of content on the individual consumer's purchase and advocacy intentions. The "value of experience metric" measures the likelihood that those having positive experiences on social media pages are likely to interact on social media, purchase products, or advocate for a brand. The "value of a fan metric" measures the likelihood that people who participate in social media actions also purchase or advocate for a product.

In 2015, the Internet Advertising Bureau, the United Kingdom-based trade association that develops standards and policies for online and mobile advertising, published social media measurement guidelines. These guidelines are expansive, and some of the suggested ways to measure social media include measuring social media sites using unique visitors, cost per unique visitor, interaction rate, time spent, video installs, and relevant actions taken. Blogs can be measured using conversation size and site relevance. Widgets and social media applications can be measured using installs, active users, audience profile, unique user reach, growth, and influence. Other valuable metrics from both academic and practitioner sources that are used to measure social media include rate of follower growth, page traffic, frequency of visits, reach, number of followers, messages, time spent on page, likes, posts, reads, page visits, comments, and content shares. Specifically in sport, Abeza *et al.* (2013) suggested the level of fan involvement in a dialogue with a team on social media is a useful indicator of social media effectiveness. The authors also indicate that a specific message's flow, traffic, and frequency could be used to measure the strength of the fan's relationship with a sports organization. Thus, sports teams and leagues could also use the frequency of participation and the content of the fan's comment to value fan relationships.

While the focus of this chapter has largely been on measuring the outcomes of social media efforts, it is important to realize that determining return on investment requires that costs be calculated as well. Costs might include the costs of tools or platforms, spending on social advertisements, content creation costs including time spent, and the use of agencies and consultations (Newberry and Aynsley, 2020). While this list is not comprehensive, some common cost areas for social media are listed as follows, and a set of examples of KPIs is presented in Table 1.

1. Set-up and preparation of the infrastructure, such as technology or software costs (both time and money), costs for creating the social media plan in the form of appointing internal staff or outsourcing to another company, and for designing the home-pages or profile pages or visual look of the accounts.
2. Ongoing costs that are required to keep an active presence in social media, which might include hosting fees for platforms for managing social media sites or having advanced account options,

Table 1. Examples of Key Performance Indicators for different objectives.

Objective	Example KPIs
Increase Sales	Incoming links, direct purchases on page, lead conversion rate
Increase Brand Awareness	Number of followers, likes, page views, impressions, video views
Improve Brand Image	Positive sentiment
Increase Market Share	Comparison of followers, social share of voice
Improve Customer Relationships	Relationship quality scores, positive sentiment on content
Provide Quality Customer Service	Response times to customer complaints on social media, customer sentiment analysis, complaint resolution rate
Increase Word of Mouth	Number of shares, likes, comments, retweets, mentions, incoming links, frequency of timeline appearance
Increase Engagement	Number of shares, likes, comments, replies, retweets, mentions, hashtags used, amount of user-generated content, impressions-to-interactions ratio
Increase Reach	Number of shares, impressions, views, audience growth rate

costs of personnel to run platforms or create content, and any monitoring activity or analytics tools that the organization uses.

3. Campaign level costs that might result from designing and producing specific social media campaigns.

4. Risk factors, or implied costs related to the risk of negative social media or the loss of sales or brand value that happens when the company gets negative attention online.

There exist other frameworks for measuring social media impacts. For example, Don Bartholomew (2010) provided a framework for organizing metrics around social media that includes exposure, engagement, influence, and action and breaks down metrics for paid, earned, shared, and owned digital media. This public relations perspective provides a different way to look at how metrics meet goals within a social media strategy. For example, exposure can be measured through impressions, organic search rank, comment sentiment, and page views, among other options. The entire matrix can be found at the link in the resources section.

It is essential that practitioners not only measure what is easy or convenient to measure, but what is relevant to the organization and to its goals, ideally grounded in KPIs. Social media managers should also consider using multiple metrics to get a more holistic view of how an objective is being measured. For example, the quantity of page fans or followers may be used to measure awareness, but the manager should pair this with a measure of increase or decrease in percentage of followers. However, it is also important that managers focus on quality of metrics, instead of the quantity of metrics.

LEARNING ACTIVITY 2

Manchester United of the English Premiere League is considered one of the most effective digital marketers in professional sport. Review their social media platforms and list at least five potential KPIs that you think they might be trying to achieve with their social media content and offering.

SOCIAL MEDIA MEASUREMENT TOOLS FROM RESEARCH AND PRACTICE

Over the past decade, researchers have worked to develop measurement tools to assess organizational social media use. Miranda *et al.* (2014) created the Facebook Assessment Index (FAI) to assess a sports team's use of Facebook on three levels including popularity (the number of Facebook fans), interactivity (average number of posts made by the company, likes, comments, shares, and consumer posts answered by the company), and content. In her studies on professional sports and social media effectiveness, Achen (2016, 2019) suggested that the impacts of social media on relationship quality could be measured using the Sports Consumer–Team Relationship Quality Scale (SCTRQS), which was created by Kim *et al.* (2011). SCTRQS measures five relational constructs including trust, commitment, intimacy, self-connection, and reciprocity. If a sports organization wishes to use the SCTRQS to measure whether social media interaction is impacting customer relationships, they would first need to establish a baseline relationship quality score by sending a survey to followers on, for example, their Instagram page. Then, the organization would create a content plan designed to increase conversation and interaction on their Instagram page. After implementing this plan for a predetermined period of time, the organization could survey followers again and then connect their scores on the SCTRQS to the number of comments or likes on Instagram content by that follower during the time period. This process would allow the organization to evaluate whether their content strategy did strengthen or deepen relationships with customers.

Qualitative analysis can also be useful for organizations as it provides a better understanding of what customers think, want, and need. One such analysis that can be used to measure relationships between customers and teams is sentiment analysis, which examines the negative or positive valence of user-generated comments and content. It is important to note that although there are computer sentiment analysis programs that use linguistics to classify user comments, it often still requires someone to read, review, and evaluate what is meant by the comments, which is qualitative research.

Since engagement is an important part of impacting business outcomes, it would be useful for a framework to be available to measure engagement. However, the academic research literature does not have an agreed upon definition of engagement, although it most often includes emotional, cognitive, and behavioral involvement, and co-creation of value (Zhang *et al.*, 2017). Achen (2017) detailed that engagement on social media could be measured by exploring customer interaction, consumption, and integration. Interaction includes metrics that can be readily gathered such as likes, comments, shares, retweets, and favorites. Consumption includes additional behaviors that can by gathered on the analytics site of many social media sites, such as reading a post, visiting a link, or watching a video. Finally, integration involves the customer using information seen on social media in daily life, such as in conversations with others outside of social media or sending photos of posts to others via text messaging. The third construct would need to be measured using a survey of customers.

INDUSTRY TOOLS

The following list shares some examples of industry tools. After a quick web search for social media analytics tools, you will be inundated with different resources listing a wide range of tools, some of which are free and others involve fees. Thus, this list is shared to give you a starting point, but you are encouraged to check out the many platforms available. Many of these options include a base level free option and a more advanced paid option. Some include a free trial and you can get a feel for the tool before purchasing it.

1. Google Analytics: vast set of variables including purchase data. Free training.
2. Platform specific analytics (Facebook Analytics, Twitter Analytics, Instagram Insights, YouTube Analytics): activity tracking, historical data, reach, engagement, dashboards.

3. HubSpot: pay for service with a wide range of tools to manage content.
4. Sprout Social: social media specific monitor with detailed analytics.
5. Hootsuite: social media analytics, social listening tool.
6. Buffer: scheduling software and analytics for social media channels.

KEY SKILLS FOR PRACTICE

It is recommended that you develop the following skills to successfully measure social media efforts. First, learn the process noted in this chapter to identify objectives, set tactical goals, develop benchmarks, and put in place metrics to measure accordingly. Second, stay up to date and informed on the social media platform analytics tools (e.g., Google Analytics, Facebook Analytics) and analytical applications (e.g., NVivo and Leximancer) available and find training in analytics (e.g., Google's Skillshop, Udemy.com). Third, you need basic data analysis skills and you are encouraged to take statistics or analytics courses at your educational institution. Fourth, a working knowledge of Excel and SPSS for data analysis is needed.

TRENDS AND CURRENT ISSUES

Marketers indicate that measuring ROI is one of their top challenges (Sprout Social, 2019). One of the first issues is the lack of consistency across measurement of social media and the use of different metrics for different platforms, the fragmentation of data across multiple screens, and the fact that organizations do not own social media sites (Etlinger *et al.*, 2012). Recent academic research supports these challenges still exist, and for practitioners, it is difficult to determine the financial impacts of social media use (Michopoulou and Moisa, 2019). The aforementioned challenges are exacerbated by the sheer volume of data that exist in relation to social media and the need to create data collection and analysis methods that can handle data but are also user-friendly (Agostino and Sidorova, 2016). Because much of the practical research related to measuring social media effectiveness is proprietary, there is often a lack of transparency in methods, little description of how metrics are calculated, and an inability to measure error that limit the usability of these metrics to organizations (Lipschultz, 2020).

As mentioned above, the reliability of some metrics is in question. One issue is that some social media metrics such as likes, comments, and followers can be purchased, which makes it difficult to use them to determine the effectiveness of different content types and make comparisons to competitors. For example, organizations might choose to bolster their Instagram followers to look more credible, but these paid followers are unlikely to engage or be future customers (Cooper, 2019). Also, algorithms on social media networks determine who sees posts, when they see them, and for how long they see them, complicating measurement and comparisons of content within and across organizations (Barnhart, 2019). Additionally, some metrics, such as sentiment analysis, are text-based and subjective, which presents social media managers with challenges for presenting data to management and explaining its usefulness (Agostino and Sidorova, 2016). Further, comparing metrics across platforms (for example, Snapchat and Instagram) may be difficult because the metrics are not always comparable (Lipschultz, 2020). The measurement of social media strategy is complicated by the difficulty in determining if engagement increases purchase intentions and behavior or if already loyal customers engage on social media networks. Furthermore, impacts could be difficult to isolate, meaning their interactions with the brand outside of social media also impact their feelings toward the brand (Walsh *et al.*, 2013).

Finally, as social media changes rapidly, metrics and measurement evolve as well, further complicating connecting social media efforts to business impacts (Lipschultz, 2020). Advances in ritual and augmented reality and machine learning require social media managers to be innovative in how they measure behavior on social media networks (Lipschultz, 2020).

PRACTITIONER PERSPECTIVE

Practitioner: Katie Gillen, Manager of Social Media & Analytics with Atlanta United FC
Education: B. S., Telecommunications, University of Florida

What are your roles and responsibilities at Atlanta United FC?
At Atlanta United, I oversee all social media properties and utilize analytics from platforms to create a social strategy that reaches our fans and makes new ones. My responsibilities require me to manage and integrate content and analytics across all social media platforms we use. Specific responsibilities include: (1) Identify and deliver metrics, benchmarks, and projections for digital channels; (2) Provide competitive reporting that includes weekly, monthly, and mid-campaign analytics; (3) Lead digital marketing campaign efforts; (4) Plan, execute, and manage real-time, web-based reports and dashboards; (5) Plan, implement, manage, measure, and report organic social media marketing efforts; (6) Align content strategy, team coverage, team communications, marketing partnerships, stadium news and events, and sponsored posts; (7) Collaborate with the partnership teams to create engaging and valuable sponsorship inventory and brand integration opportunities; (8) Provide coverage for home and away matches; (9) Use reports and findings to build a social editorial calendar and innovative content; (10) Drive integrated content ideation from concept to completion; (11) Aggressively increase

(Continued)

(Continued)

overall KPI metrics; (12) Monitor best practices and trends and communicate relevant news and opportunities to internal teams; (13) Curate and share content; and (14) Manage the social team and assist with content creation, planning, and execution.

How can sports organizations utilize social media to generate revenue?

Social media can be used to generate revenue in a variety of direct and indirect ways, however, there are some issues measuring the effectiveness of revenue generation from social media when it isn't a direct link or customer journey. Some ways to use social media to generate revenue include: storytelling to create fans and ultimately get them to feel a type of emotion leading them to buy in literally and figuratively, sponsored content series where a sponsor pays to be a part of a fixed social series, and link sharing (such as shop bottom on Instagram or a shared ticketing link in a tweet).

How do you approach measuring social media efforts and determining which metrics to use?

Measuring social media efforts is done on a weekly, monthly, yearly, and project specific basis. There are also databases created specifically for things like follower growth and engagement. It is important to be able to look at data and measure historically over time. The most important metrics are reach and engagement as you cannot have one without the other. When you are reaching a large number of people and recciving a high engagement rate among those people, it means you are hitting the mark on social media. The content is resonating with your fan base and, in turn, whatever behavior or call to action you hope to achieve has a higher probability of being reached. Metrics can be determined by needs of the club and management at the time. Some executives may want to see lead generation or website traffic, and others are interested in sheer follower growth. As a social media professional, I try to guide these expectations and focus on reach

(Continued)

and engagement as key indicators of a healthy presence on social media.

What trends do you believe are important for students to be aware of in social media measurement?

Above all else, students need to be aware that social media is constantly changing, and they will need a desire and willingness to keep learning to be successful in this space. It is important to stay up to date with the latest trends, platforms, and content innovations. It's paramount to remember what the data are being used for and to present them in a way that is as an unbiased as possible. There is a trend by many to pull out individual stat lines (good and bad) to make a call about social media and its performance via analytics, which is misleading. It is our job as analysts to make sure we are reporting accurate information and ensure it is not being taken out of context or manipulated.

LEARNING ACTIVITY 3

Create a social media campaign measurement plan. Choose a sports organization and visit one of their social media pages. Create a campaign for them, define the objectives, and create a measurement plan.

CHAPTER SUMMARY

This chapter outlines the measurement of social media effectiveness for sports organizations. Measurement of social media should be driven by the organizational goals driving the use of different platforms. In many cases, this means that ROI is not measured in a traditional sense and social media managers instead must identify value outside of direct revenue impacts to determine whether their efforts on these platforms are justified. To help aid in communicating the value of social media, managers should take a strategic approach to planning a social media strategy that allows them to connect KPIs to business goals.

As social media channels evolve, sports teams are leveraging them to gain revenue and capitalizing on live streaming, sponsorship, and merchandise options that can directly generate revenue. However, social media managers should embrace a broader view of the importance of social media investments. Finally, as social media platforms mature, sports social media managers need to seek out information on trends and tools that can help evaluate and justify the resources expended on these channels.

KEY RESOURCES

- The PESO matrix for measuring social media: https://socialmediaexplorer.com/online-public-relations/the-digitization-of-research-and-measurement-in-public-relations/.
- Google Analytics training: https://skillshop.withgoogle.com/.
- Social Media Analytics tools: https://www.brandwatch.com/blog/social-media-analytics-tools/.
- Social Media Analytics tools: https://buffer.com/library/social-media-analytics-tools/.
- Other KPIs: https://blog.hootsuite.com/social-media-kpis-key-performance-indicators/.

TEST YOUR KNOWLEDGE

1. Describe the steps to creating a social media measurement plan.
2. What are KPIs and how do they tie to social media objectives?
3. Describe three industry tools for measuring social media.
4. What other tools or metrics have you seen used to measure social media effectiveness?
5. What barriers do you believe exist for sports organizations who are attempting to measure how social media impacts their profitability?

6. If you were a social media manager, what metrics would be most important or useful to you? Why?

REFERENCES

Abeza, G., O'Reilly, N., and Reid, I. (2013). Relationship marketing and social media in sport. *International Journal of Sport Communication, 6,* 120–142.

Achen, R. M. (2019). Re-examining a model for measuring Facebook interaction and relationship quality. *Sport, Business and Management: An International Journal, 9,* 255–272.

Achen, R. M. (2017). Measuring social media marketing: Moving towards a relationship-marketing approach. *Managing Sport and Leisure, 22* (1), 33–53.

Achen, R. M. (2016). The influence of Facebook engagement on relationship quality and consumer behavior in the National Basketball Association. *Journal of Relationship Marketing, 15,* 247–268.

Agostino, D. and Sidorova, Y. (2016). A performance measurement system to quantify the contribution of social media: New requirements for metrics and methods. *Measuring Business Excellence, 20,* 38–51.

Barnhart, B. (2019). Everything you need to know about social media algorithms. Sprout Social. https://sproutsocial.com/insights/social-media-algorithms/.

Bartholomew, D. (2010). *The digitization of research and measurement in public relations.* Social Media Explorer. https://socialmediaexplorer.com/online-public-relations/the-digitization-of-research-and-measurement-in-public-relations/.

Bonsón, E. and Ratkai, M. (2013). A set of metrics to assess stakeholder engagement and social legitimacy on a corporate Facebook page. *Online Information Review, 37,* 787–803. doi:10.1108/OIR-03-2012-0054.

Canadian Sponsorship Landscape Study (2020). 13th annual results. Downloaded September 13th, 2020 from www.sponsorshiplandscape.ca.

Cooper, P. (2019). Want to buy Instagram followers? Here's what happens when you do. Hootsuite. https://blog.hootsuite.com/buy-instagram-followers-experiment/.

Demirel, A. and Erdogmus, I. (2016). The impacts of fans' sincerity perceptions and social media usage on attitude toward sponsor. *Sport, Business and Management: An International Journal, 6,* 36–54.

Dholakia, U. M. and Durham, E. (2010). One café chain's facebook experiment. *Harvard Business Review, 88*(3), 26.

Dzamic, L. (2012). The hunt for the red herring: Measuring commercial effects of social media. *Journal of Direct, Data and Digital Marketing Practice, 13*, 198–206. doi:10.1057/dddmp.2011.46.

Etlinger, S., Owyang, J., and Jones, A. (2012). The social media ROI cookbook: six ingredients top brands use to measure the revenue impact of social media. *San Mateo: Altimeter Group.*

Fisher, T. (2009). ROI in social media: A look at the arguments. *Journal of Database Marketing & Customer Strategy Management, 16*(3), 189–195.

Foster, G., O'Reilly N., and Davila, A. (2020). "Sports Business Management: Decision-Making Around the Globe", 2nd Edition, Routledge (Taylor & Francis), USA.

Garanti, Z. and Kissi, P. S. (2019). The effects of social media brand personality on brand loyalty in the Latvian banking industry. *International Journal of Bank Marketing, 37*, 1480–1503.

Gilfoil, D. M., and Jobs, C. (2012). Return on investment for social media: A proposed framework for understanding, implementing, and measuring the return. *Journal of Business and Economics Research, 10*, 637–650.

Godey, B., Manthiou, A., Pederzoli, D., Rokka, J., Aiello, G., Donvito, R., and Singh, R. (2016). Social media marketing efforts of luxury brands: Influence on brand equity and consumer behavior. *Journal of Business Research, 69*, 5833–5841.

Goh, K.-Y., Heng, C.-S., and Lin, Z. (2013). Social media brand community and consumer behaviour: Quantifying the relative impact of user- and marketer-generated content. *Information Systems Research, 24*, 88–107. doi:10.1287/isre.1120.0469.

Gould, D. J. and Nazarian, S. (2018). Social media return on investment: How much is it worth to my practice? *Aesthetic Surgery Journal, 38*(5), 565–574.

Gummerus, J., Liljander, V., Weman, E., and Pihlstrom, M. (2012). Customer engagement in a Facebook brand community. *Management Research Review, 35*, 857–877. doi:10.1108/01409171211256578.

Hoffman, D. L. and Fodor, M. (2010). Can you measure the ROI of your social media marketing? *MIT Sloan Management Review, 52*(1), 41.

Holmboe, D. (2011). *How to estimate your social media return on investment.* Social Media Examiner, https://www.socialmediaexaminer.com/how-to-estimate-your-social-media-return-on-investment/.

Hudson, S., Huang, L., Roth, M. S., and Madden, T. J. (2016). The influence of social media interactions on consumer – brand relationships:

A three-country study of brand perceptions and marketing behaviours. *International Journal of Research in Marketing, 33* (1), 27–41.

Hutter, K., Hautz, J., Dennhardt, S., and Füller, J. (2013). The impact of user interactions in social media on brand awareness and purchase intention: The case of MINI on Facebook. *Journal of Product and Brand Management, 22,* 342–351. doi:10.1108/JPBM-05-2013-0299.

Internet Advertising Bureau. (2015). MRC Social Media Measurement Guidelines. https://www.iab.com/guidelines/mrc-social-media-measurement-guidelines/.

Jobs, C. G. and Gilfoil, D. M. (2014). A social media advertising adoption model for reallocation of traditional advertising budgets. *Academy of Marketing Studies Journal, 18*(1), 235.

Kaske, F., Kugler, M., and Smolnik, S. (2012). Return on investment in social media–Does the hype pay off? Towards an assessment of the profitability of social media in organizations. In *2012 45th Hawaii International Conference on System Sciences* (pp. 3898–3907). IEEE.

Kim, A. J. and Ko, E. (2012). Do social media marketing activities enhance customer equity? An empirical study of luxury fashion brand. *Journal of Business Research, 65* (10), 1480–1486.

Kim, Y. K., Trail, G., and Ko, Y. J. (2011). The influence of relationship quality on sport consumption behaviours: An empirical examination of the relationship quality framework. *Journal of Sport Management, 25,* 576–592.

Kim, Y. K., Trail, G. T., Woo, B., and Zhang, J. (2011). Sports consumer-team relationship quality: Development and psychometric evaluation of a scale. *International Journal of Sports Marketing and Sponsorship, 12,* 254–271.

Kumar, A., Bezawada, R., Rishika, R., Janakiraman, R., and Kannan, P. K. (2016). From social to sale: The effects of firm-generated content in social media on customer behaviour. *Journal of Marketing, 80,* 7–25. doi:10.1509/jm.14.0249.

Kumar, V., Bhaskaran, V., Mirchandani, R., and Shah, M. (2013). Creating a Measurable Social Media Marketing Strategy: Increasing the Value and ROI of Intangibles and Tangibles for Hokey Pokey. *Marketing Science, 3* (2), 194–212.

Lal, B., Ismagilova, E., Dwivedi, Y. K., and Kwayu, S. (2020). Return on Investment in Social Media Marketing: Literature Review and Suggestions for Future Research. In *Digital and Social Media Marketing* (pp. 3–17). Springer, Cham.

LaPointe, P. (2012). Measuring Facebook's impact on marketing: The proverbial hits the fan. *Journal of Advertising Research, 52*(3), 286–287.

Lipschultz, J. H. (2020). *Social Media Measurement and Management: Entrepreneurial Digital Analytics.* New York, NY: Routledge.

Luo, X., Zhang, J., and Duan, W. (2013). Social media and firm equity value. *Information Systems Research, 24*(1), 146–163.

Michopoulou, E. and Moisa, D. G. (2019). Hotel social media metrics: The ROI dilemma. *International Journal of Hospitality Management, 76,* 308–315.

Miranda, F. J., Chamorro, A., Rubio, S., and Rodriguez, O. (2014). Professional sports teams on social networks: A comparative study employing the Facebook Assessment Index. *International Journal of Sport Communication, 7*(1), 74–89.

Newberr, C., and Aynsley, M. (2020). How to prove and improve social medai ROI (+ Free Tools). Hootsuite. https://blog.hootsuite.com/measure-social-media-roi-business/#:~:text=ROI%20stands%20for%20%E2%80%9Creturn%20on,made%20to%20achieve%20those%20actions.

O'Reilly, N. and Madill, J. (2012). The development of a process for evaluating marketing sponsorships. *Canadian Journal of Administrative Sciences, 29*(1), 50–66.

Park, J.-A. and Dittmore, S. (2014). The relationship among social media consumption, team identification, and behavioural intentions. *Journal of Physical Education and Sport, 14,* 331–336.

Powell, G., Groves, S., and Dimos, J. (2011). *ROI of Social Media: How to improve the return on your social marketing investment.* John Wiley & Sons.

Rishika, R., Kumar, A., Janakiraman, R., and Bezawada, R. (2013). The effect of customers' social media participation on customer visit frequency and profitability: An empirical investigation. *Information Systems Research, 24,* 108–127. doi:10.1287/isre.1120.0460.

Schober, C., Rauscher, O., and Kehl, K. (2018). *Social return on investment analysis: Measuring the impact of social Investment.* London, UK: Palgrave Macmillan.

Sohail, M. S., Hasan, M., and Sohail, A. F. (2020). The impact of social media marketing on brand trust and brand loyalty: An Arab perspective. *International Journal of Online Marketing , 10*(1), 15–31.

Smith, S. (2013). Conceptualising and evaluating experiences with brands on Facebook. *International Journal of Market Research, 55,* 357–374. doi:10.2501/IJMR-2013-034

Sprout Social (2019). The Sprout Social Index Edition XVI: Above & Beyond. https://sproutsocial.com/insights/data/index/.

Thompson, A.-J., Martin, A. J., Gee, S., and Eagleman, A. N. (2014). Examining the development of a social media strategy for a national sport organisation. *Journal of Applied Sport Management, 6* (2), 42–63.

Wakefield, L. T. and Bennett, G. (2018). Sports fan experience: Electronic word-of-mouth in ephemeral social media. *Sport Management Review, 21*(2), 147–159.

Walsh, P., Clavio, G., Lovell, M. D., and Blaszka, M. (2013). Differences in event brand personality between social media users and non-users. *Sport Marketing Quarterly, 22,* 214–223.

Watkins, B. (2014). An integrated approach to sports branding: Examining the influence of social media on brand outcomes. *International Journal of Integrated Marketing Communications, 6*(2), 30–40.

Zhang, M., Guo, L., Hu, M., and Liu, W. (2017). Influence of customer engagement with company social networks on stickiness: Mediating effect of customer value creation. *International Journal of Information Management, 37,* 229–240.

Chapter 16

A Practical Guide to Social Media Management in Sport

Jessica R. Braunstein-Minkove*, Arielle Insel†, and Gashaw Abeza*

*Towson University, United States
†USA Lacrosse, United States

CHAPTER OBJECTIVES

After reading this chapter, you will be able to do the following:

- Identify the 10 practical steps in managing social media platforms
- Assess organizational goals and objectives for social media management
- Conduct an internal and external assessment to inform social media management
- Define content strategy and the role of a corresponding content calendar
- Identify strategies to track your social media performance
- Describe the role and value of reporting your outcomes

KEY TERMS

Social media management
  process

Personal use

Business account

Practical steps

Conducting assessments

Content strategy

Content calendar

Key performance indicators

Brand voice

Tracking performance

INTRODUCTION

As has been discussed in this book, over the past two decades social media has profoundly transformed the way people communicate with each other, both personally and professionally. Users join various social media platforms for different reasons, with some individual users spending hours every day on their preferred social media platform for personal use. These users consider themselves social media savvy, which creates the notion that managing social media for personal use is the same as managing a social media outlet for an organization or business. However, social media management for an organization differs from managing a personal account. Managing an organization's social media account requires professional skills and a strategic approach.

Undoubtedly, there are a number of basic similarities between the management of social media for an organization and for personal use. However, there are also significant differences. For example, on a personal account (e.g., Facebook), an individual user can change his or her social media name, unreservedly share emotions, face no need to maintain consistency in postings, and give little thought to the shares and likes received. In this scenario, personal users need not focus on the return on their social media resource investment. Also, the content of a personal account is mainly focused on broadcasting the thoughts and elements of a singular person and not necessarily about the audience. On the other hand, an organization's social media accounts are largely about reaching the audience. Unlike an account for personal use, the use of pictures, videos, hashtags, etc. for a business account is well thought out, postings are consistent, and content is purposefully aligned with an organization's overarching goals. In addition, business accounts rely heavily on data analytics and return on investment.

This chapter discusses the professional and strategic approach to managing an organization's social media platforms. In other words, faced with the opportunity to manage a social media platform of a sports team, a league, an athlete, or any other sports entity, how would a manager use it? The chapter outlines the practical steps to help these entities manage social media platforms strategically and professionally. Specifically, it discusses 10 practical steps that sports entities (e.g., sports teams) should adhere to in creating, building, and managing a social media platform.

HISTORY AND BACKGROUND

Early social media reports (e.g., Abeza, 2012; Drury, 2008) noted that organizations were reticent about the adoption of new media, including social media, around the mid-to-late 2000s. During this time period, not every organization fully agreed on the opportunities that social media could bring to their business (Martin, 2011; Waters *et al.*, 2011). While several observed social media as a new marketing opportunity, a few organizations simply considered it a form of high-tech hype (Constantinides and Fountain, 2008). Some academic works published in the late 2000s and early 2010s (e.g., Sheffer and Schultz, 2010) also questioned whether the emergence of social media brought a paradigm shift or would prove to be a passing fad. In the mid-2010s, social media began to be increasingly and widely considered an integral part of marketing communication in organizations across different sectors of the economy. The integration included the allocation of organizational resources for its strategic use and management as an essential business tactic. Today, some (cf. Menke and Schwarzenegger, 2019) argue that social media is no longer a new media but is now an established marketing communication channel.

The evolution of social media content management is briefly discussed in Chapter 1 interview with the Dallas Cowboys' Social Media Manager, Shannon Gross. The changes that have taken place over the past 10 years in social media are immense. Gross identified three significant changes in the team's management of social media. One, the team's social media platforms were previously run by an employee with the support of one staff intern. Now, most social media departments have three or four full-time people that run social media platforms. Two, the team's ownership and top management are now supportive of social media use. Support for these initiatives were more difficult to come by in the past. Three, social media departments have shifted from repurposing content to creating their own unique content, geared specifically towards social media and the various formats within its many platforms. This is a common trend in most professional sports teams' use of social media, which has clearly evolved over time. As a result of the industry's transition to one that is comfortable in, and supportive of, the social media space, it is necessary for future sports professionals to understand the various aspects of the social media management process. Therefore, the purpose of this chapter is to provide a step-by-step process, putting the concepts addressed in Chapters 1–15 into action.

PRACTITIONER'S PERSPECTIVE

Jared Hager, *Brand Manager — Lacrosse, Warrior Sports and New Balance*

Education: Bachelor of Science in Business Administration, Finance & Marketing (Bryant University); Master of Science in Sport Management (University of Massachusetts Amherst)

(Continued)

Mr. Hager is responsible for lacrosse marketing strategy for both Warrior and New Balance, out of the New Balance global headquarters in Boston, MA. Hager coordinates and executes all lacrosse marketing strategy for Warrior Sports and New Balance. He is responsible for all paid and organic social media strategy and execution, including platform focuses, content creation, and budget management.

Over the course of his career, Hager has established Warrior Lacrosse as the No. 1 brand in engagement and follower growth on Instagram in 2018, gaining 28,000 Instagram followers, outpacing the rest of the industry by 10,000. Additionally, under Hager's watch, Warrior has a 2.91% engagement rate, 0.37% better than the next closest competitor. Hager also launched the Warrior Lacrosse YouTube channel.

What is your typical day as a social media manager?

Mornings typically consist of checking performance of posts, checking comments and direct messages to see what needs to be responded to, sharing information from those comments or direct messages that need to be sent to other people within the organization. Additionally, time is spent looking at what is planned for the rest of the week to see if we need to adjust or not. Additionally, checking out posts by competitors and our athletes as well as looking for any news that we need to jump on or keep an eye on. Afternoon is focused on projects and planning. We manage our paid social media internally, so we are always checking on the performance of campaigns and whether we need to keep as is or adjust. And, there are a lot of meetings.

What is your #1 goal for managing social media for your organization?

We have different goals for both organic and paid social media. For organic, our number one goal is engagement. If they are already following us, they know who we are. So, we are not as focused on brand awareness. We want to educate people on our

(Continued)

products and entertain them with our content. For paid, our goal is brand awareness and driving traffic to our site.

How do you set your brand apart from your competitors?
It is all about content. We produce high-quality content that engages the lacrosse community. Our brand voice is edgy and confident. We put stuff out there that is more on the fringe and humor goes a long way with that.

What are three key performance indicators (KPI), or metrics, you track to determine your content performance?
#1 is engagement rate, #2 impressions/reach to create brand awareness, and #3 follower growth. We used to focus on follower growth, but it is hard to control that.

What platforms are most relevant to your organization and why?
Instagram is #1 based on the audience that is there. YouTube would be next, again just based on audience. We are trying to reach teenagers and those platforms are where our audience is. Facebook would be 3rd and Twitter, 4th, but those are weighted lower than Instagram and YouTube.

How do you use your audience insights to inform your social media content?
Our Instagram audience is 82% male with 65% of that between 13–24. So, that is who we are creating content for. And then, you use other things to determine that. What are some other brands they are following and what type of content they are putting out? We are constantly looking at those brands and trying to figure out what resonates with our audience and then using that to inform our content.

What is one of the most successful campaigns you deployed on social media?
The launch for the Burn FO with Trevor Baptiste. It was a scroll stopper. People were like, why is this lacrosse head talking. It just

(*Continued*)

---

performed really well organically. Not only did the content perform well on social media, but it also led to good sales. We've had other product campaigns that performed well on social media, but did not translate to sales. This one did both.

How do you stay on top of social media trends?
I have a few go-to sites that I like. Social Media Today is one of them. I look at Recode and Hashtag Sports a lot as well. I check these daily. I follow a couple of podcasts, too. Social Media Today has a 15-minute podcast that focuses on a single topic that is spoken about with an expert.

A PRACTICAL GUIDE TO SOCIAL MEDIA MANAGEMENT PROCESS: KEY CONCEPTS

THE SOCIAL MEDIA MANAGEMENT PROCESS

Whether you work for a small, medium, or large, local, regional, national, or international organization, social media will factor into organizational operations. Why? Social media is both accessible and easy to use and, as such, can be easily leveraged to reach a myriad of organizational objectives. Many of you may think to yourself… fantastic, I already know how to use a variety of social media platforms. I spend hours engaging with them daily! While this may be the case, managing a social media platform for personal use requires different skills and perspective than for professional use. The latter requires a different skill set and more strategic planning.

Due to the unique and constantly evolving nature of the communication channels themselves, it will never be possible to develop an evergreen, or long-lasting, social media plan. However, with a thoughtful approach, it is possible — and imperative — to have an overarching business objective for social media use. Up to this point in the book, we have reviewed the managerial, marketing, and social implications of social media in sport. Therefore, this chapter serves to address the subject from a practical perspective, presenting the 10 steps that social media managers should adhere to in order to

Figure 1: Social Media Management Process.

successfully develop, implement, and manage their social media strategies (see Figure 1).

STEP 1: DEFINE GOALS

In order to have a solid foundation from which to build, an organization must first define the reasons for utilizing social media content. Your intentions may be varied (e.g., news updates, advertising, sales, public relations, promotions, customer service, crisis communication, general communication). However, they must always link back to your overarching organizational goals. To be clear, all decisions should be grounded in the priorities established by organizational goals, which in turn are based on the mission and vision of an organization. Mission and vision define who you are and who you want to be. As such, organizational goals should drive all business decisions. Therefore, the first step will be to review your organization's strategic goals, using them to establish a set of tangible objectives, or steps to accomplish them through social media.

LEARNING ACTIVITY 1

First, select a sports organization. Then, find the organization's mission statement, vision statement, and/or any overarching strategic goals that have been established and communicated to relevant stakeholders.

NOTE: *The organization that you select for this Learning Activity should be used for the other Learning Activities throughout the chapter.*

STEP 2: ESTABLISH OBJECTIVES

More often than not, you will use social media for a number of reasons, combining tactics to meet overarching organizational goals. Therefore, the organization should set objectives that guide its social media management strategy as well as its day-to-day activity (i.e., goals = overarching/general/strategic; objectives = individual/specific/tactical). According to Sprout Social, a social marketer's top five goals for using social media are to increase: brand awareness, sales/lead generations, community engagement, brand's audience, and web traffic (Barnhart, 2020). As mentioned earlier, key performance indicators (KPI) refer to performance indicators to evaluate the success of a particular activity in which an organization or a social media team engages. The associated KPI, or metrics, that align with your goals will serve as your objectives and, in turn, indicate whether you are meeting your goals or not (see Table 1). It is pivotal to *set all* of this in advance, as this will guide the use of your time as well as your budget (social media ads, photography,

Table 1.   Social Media Goals & Corresponding Key Performance Indicators.

Social Media Goals	Examples of Key Performance Indicators
Increase brand awareness	Followers, Shares, Reach, Mentions
Sales/lead generations	Conversions, E-mail Signups
Increase community engagement	Comments, Likes, Clicks, Shares
Grow my brand's audience	Followers, Engagement Rate
Increase web traffic	Clicks, Conversions, E-mail Signups

Business Objectives → SMART Social Media Goals → KPI Metric

Figure 2:   Process of Developing Sound Social Media Objectives.

videography, graphic designer, social media managers, platforms, etc.). This process is depicted in Figure 2.

SMART goals will allow you to determine the return on investment (ROI) for both your organization and those that you partner with. This is mentioned at the planning stage, as it is necessary to determine your objectives at the beginning of a project so that you can properly evaluate them at the end. Without determining how success will be measured, how can you claim to have achieved it? For example, if your goal is to grow your brand's audience, your objective may be to increase web traffic. However, does that mean that one additional live stream of your event would equate to success? For a youth basketball program, live streaming one event may mean just that; however, for the New York City Marathon, one stream or download will not play a significant role toward their bottom line. Therefore, it is imperative that you set SMART goals (i.e., Specific, Measurable, Attainable, Relevant, Time-Bound — see Figure 3). With this, if your organization's intentions are to grow the brand, an example of a SMART social media goal would be to increase followers on Instagram by 10% within six months.

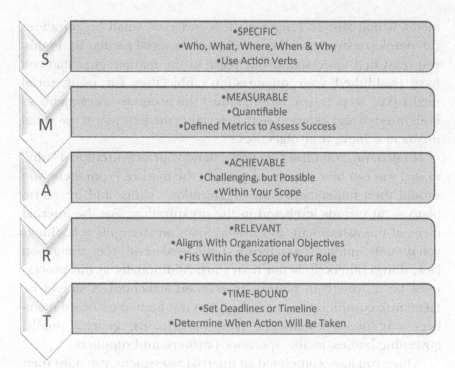

Figure 3: SMART Goals.

LEARNING ACTIVITY 2

Pick one of the goals listed in Table 1. Then (a) create a SMART goal and (b) determine the relevant KPI that will determine your goal's success.

STEP 3: RESEARCH

Individual organizations are unique. They have different personalities/characteristics, perspectives, and intentions. It is important to both understand and embrace these differences, as this will help to use social media in the best way to project those aspects of your organization's brand. One of the most exciting aspects of social media is that size no longer matters and even small organizations can develop a strong, well-known brand via social media. To do this, you must first understand your place in the market. Now that you have established your organization's objectives for using social media (i.e., Step 2), you must conduct the necessary assessments — both internal and external — to determine the best way to use social media to achieve your objectives.

In general, you must first understand your organizational "why" so that you can best assess your place in the market. From there, you should then understand your organization's short- and long-term plans — at various levels within the organization. For the internal piece of this assessment, you should focus on strengths (i.e., things you do well, unique characteristics) and weaknesses (i.e., things you lack, things others do better than you). Additionally, as this process must be thorough in nature, all relevant stakeholders should be taken into consideration, including, but not limited to: board members, employees, volunteers, fans, participants, general public, governing bodies, media, sponsors, partners, and suppliers.

Once you have completed an internal assessment, you must then look outside of your organization to address your opportunities (e.g., few competitors, emerging needs for your product/organization) and threats (e.g., actions of your competition, changes in customers' attitudes). For this, you will need to focus on both your consumers and your competition. First, you must understand who your current consumers are and both how and why they are connecting with your organization on social media. In addition to consulting internal documents and conducting research via surveys, focus groups, and other traditional methods, well-established organizations may consider social media listening tools. These tools track organic posts and online activity of social media usage, providing a greater reflection of the more casual consumer than those that would go out of their way to participate in a focus group or survey. Additionally, this organic reaction might not be skewed, as we can often see in surveys, interviews, focus groups, intercepts, etc. Specifically, individuals do not feel as though they should respond in a particular way on social media, as they might with traditional research methods. This might provide a better and more authentic picture of your general consumer.

Once you understand your consumers, you must then address your competition — both direct and indirect. To identify specific organizations in your area of business, you can opt to run a Facebook or Google search or use more specialized services (e.g., BuzzSumo, Hootsuite, SportsAtlas, Zoomph). Your competitive analysis should include an overall assessment of your competitor's social media presence in order to understand their general strengths and weaknesses, the platforms that they use most often, the type of content that they post, and how their content performs. In addition to creating a level of awareness regarding your competitor's actions, your competitive analysis will also allow you to (i) take inspiration and (ii) do it better. For example, your competitor may have a strong presence on Twitter, but they lack that influence on Instagram. This may lead your organization to put more resources into the latter, while only issuing a basic level of investment in the former. Ultimately, this leads to the most vital question — How will you set your content apart from that of your competitors? Now that you better understand your role in the market, this should be a much easier task. For example, Nike and Adidas are two of the largest sportswear brands in the world, and they are competitors. Nike has found their niche, or way to differentiate themselves, through unique storytelling. Adidas, on the other hand, has found success in their unique collaborations (e.g., English fashion designer Stella McCartney, American fashion designer Jeremy Scott). Through these initiatives, which are showcased on social media, each brand has found their place in the market.

In addition to research regarding your consumers and your competition, you should also take note of general social media trends as well as the actions of those with whom you have partnered. The actions noted above will allow for a similar type of environmental scan of general trends and sponsors/partners as well, supporting the recommendations that you make moving forward.

While a significant amount of work will go into the overall research process, your findings can be synthesized into a SWOT

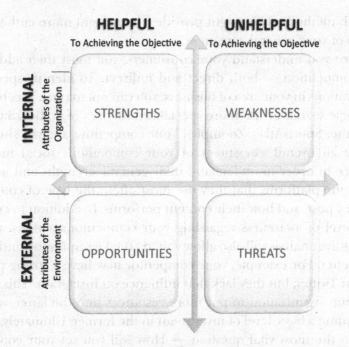

Figure 4: SWOT Analysis.

Analysis (see Figure 4) to report to others and to provide evidence to substantiate your decisions moving forward.

LEARNING ACTIVITY 3

Conduct a competitive analysis using Hootsuite's competitive analysis template (*see Resources for template link*).

Include an overarching SWOT analysis, providing an assessment from both internal and external perspectives.

STEP 4: IDENTIFY TARGET AUDIENCE

In order to be successful in any business, you must first identify who your customers are. As noted in Step 2, this will require thoughtful research, based on your organizational goals. The value in determining the right audience is that this will help you meet both your social media and overarching business goals (ticket purchases, retail purchases, article reads, etc.). Therefore, this research will inform your segmentation, targeting, and positioning activities, as it is important to determine that your intended audience is reachable, allowing you to access those who are responsive to your marketing communication efforts. For example, it might be more effective to use Facebook or Twitter to reach Gen X/Millennials, whereas Instagram or YouTube might be used more often to reach Gen Z.

While there are a variety of segmentation strategies that need to be addressed in order to break down your market (e.g., demographic, psychographic, geographic, behavioral, product usage, product benefits), the strategies used most often are outlined in Table 2.

If your organization has been using social media for some time, you can easily research audience insights through each social platform's native analytics or through a third-party platform that your organization may be using. However, if you are just beginning to use social media, there are a number of resources that you can use to better understand social media demographics and inform your social media strategy. For example, Sprout Social's resource on social media demographics can be used to inform your social media strategy. Once you understand your audience, you can better determine what type of content you will post, which platforms you will utilize, and the cadence (time/frequency) of your posts. Additionally, all of this information can ultimately be used to develop an audience persona, also called an avatar. This generalized profile (i.e., a detailed profile of your ideal customer) will allow you to

Table 2. Social Media Segmentation Strategies.

Social Media Segmentation Strategies	Examples
Demographics	Gender, Age, Location, Position/Title, Salary
Behavioral (where they consume content)	Facebook, Twitter, Instagram, YouTube, TikTok, etc.
Product Usage (when they consume content)	Time of Day, Day of Week
Product Type (how they consume content)	Short-Form Video, Long-Form Video, Photos, Articles, etc.

narrow the focus of all of your decisions moving forward (e.g., platforms, content, tone, partners, etc.). While you can develop this on your own, there are a variety of tools available to assist with this process (e.g., HubSpot's "Make My Persona" tool).

LEARNING ACTIVITY 4

Create an audience persona/avatar to use in developing your social media campaign, using HubSpot's "Make My Persona" tool (*see Resources for link*).

STEP 5: CHOOSE PLATFORMS

In order to determine which social media platforms you will be using, you will need to reflect back on your audience research. Again, the intention of this is to make sure that you are using the most appropriate tactics (and SMART goals) to reach your intended audience, meet your objectives, and reach those overarching organizational goals. With this, it is important to be aware that each platform has different types of users. A good mantra to keep in mind is "be where my audience is." As resources will determine your ability to diversify, you may not need a presence on every single social media platform. Again, this will all depend on your resources and target audience. Therefore, the following questions can help you begin to identify the best platforms for your organization:

- Why should my organization use this platform?
- Who will be reached on this platform?
- Do we have the resources to run it?
- What types of posts work best on this platform?
- How will my organization's posts be unique on this social media platform?
- Will our current strategy work well on this platform?
- Will we need to adapt our strategy for this platform?

All of these questions must be asked under the premise of meeting organizational objectives and maintaining consistent branding through your integrated marketing communication strategy.

Table 3. Sample Social Media Platforms — Strengths & Uses.

Social Media Platform	Strengths	Uses
Facebook	Largest of all the social media platforms	Best for developing general brand/company information on social media. Share articles & achieve business goals through Facebook Business (e-commerce, ads, fundraising, etc.)
Twitter	Allows the user to quickly & easily consume content by being short & to the point	Best for posting breaking news, blogs, sports play-by-plays, GIFs
Instagram	Places a larger emphasis on visual content	Best for allowing followers to engage with your brand by posting hi-res photos, videos, & behind-the-scenes stories
LinkedIn	Focuses on professional networking	Best for posting jobs, networking, & organizational news

Each social media platform has unique strengths and weaknesses and, as such, should be treated differently. Content should be specific for each channel in order to maximize its reach. Therefore, in addition to identifying your overarching strategy, you must also define your strategy for each platform. For example, if you are targeting a young American audience, you may want to put more focus on platforms like Instagram, TikTok, and Snapchat instead of LinkedIn. Table 3 identifies the strengths and uses a sample of four social media platforms (i.e., Facebook, Twitter, Instagram, LinkedIn).

LEARNING ACTIVITY 5

Determine the appropriate platform(s) that will be used for specific audiences, referencing your previous research to substantiate this recommendation (see Learning Activity 4).

STEP 6: CREATE AND CURATE CONTENT

At this point within your social media strategy, all of the work that you have completed should provide you with a solid foundation to understand and create the type of content that you plan to share. Here, you will also decide what content will be created (i.e., developed by/for your organization directly) or curated (i.e., content from external sources that is shared with your audience). While this step will be fun, as this is where the majority of your creativity can be used, your content development should be guided by your organization's goals, brand identity, audience insights/competitive analysis, and the following questions: What goals or challenges does my audience have? How will I/we help solve them? For example, data indicates that only 4% of sports coverage is dedicated to women's sports. Just Women's Sports (a San Francisco based multi-platform digital media company) saw an opportunity to solve an audience's challenge by covering exclusively women's sports. Through their social media channels, they feature women's highlights, podcasts, interviews, game coverage, and more.

Leveraging your organization's branding guidelines, you need to create a consistent look and feel across your social media platforms to make your content more easily recognizable. As with any other aspect of your integrated marketing communication plan, you must use the correct logo/s, colors, and similar graphics. The NFL's Baltimore Ravens established a look among their social media content that fits their team brand, which is tough, gritty, and hardworking. Besides, as you scroll through their social feeds, you will notice each photo, video, or graphic has consistent branding, from font to colors and the way the photos are filtered. Additionally, you will need to optimize your social platforms by properly setting up each profile. For this, thoroughly fill out all profile fields and always use high-quality images with the correct size recommendations for each platform.

With a multitude of content ideas, be realistic about what you are able to produce. You may want to create visually stunning graphics, but you do not have access to a graphic designer. Or, you may work at an organization whose graphic designer and videographer have limited bandwidth. Therefore, it is important to have a mix of realistically creatable content that is still innovative and engaging. No matter what your resources look like, it is your job to ensure that your content is both engaging and high-quality. Think back to the audience insights you found. Your content should resonate well with your target audience(s). While you may need to satisfy your organization's business goals with promotional/sales content, be sure to mix in entertaining and informative content for your audience to engage with. Peloton, a provider of live and on-demand streaming fitness classes, uses technology, content, and instructors to empower their community through fitness. On social media, they offer a perfect mix of content by frequently highlighting the accomplishments of their users (user-generated content), while also mixing in their own educational and promotional content. Some examples of content that you can add to your offerings include articles and blog posts, behind-the-scenes looks, company news, contests and giveaways, customer photos, GIFs, influencer content, infographics, league/conference/NGB content, memes, polls and surveys, previews and teasers, product photos, sponsor and partner content, takeovers, tips and tricks, user-generated content, and video (live or pre-recorded).

While it is important to create innovative content, you cannot forget that a major defining characteristic of social media is that it is, in form and function, social. Interact with your followers by engaging in conversations. Answer their questions. Comment back on their posts. One powerful aspect of social media is that you can imbed opportunities for feedback in an organic way, asking your followers for feedback and more ideas for content. For example, you can use Twitter or Instagram Polls, asking followers their opinions on the latest item your organization has for sale.

As important as it is to create high-quality visual content for your social media platforms, it is also important to consider copy writing. Put differently, it is not just what you say, but how (and where) you say it. With this, it is imperative that you remember that each social media platform is unique and should be treated as such. For example, the content you write for Twitter should not necessarily be the same content you share on Facebook. If you would like, for instance, to share a live play-by-play update of a game's results, Twitter is likely to be your best option even though you can also do that on Facebook. On the other hand, if you want to start a conversation regarding your community service activities, opt for Facebook. Finally, while your organization's needs should guide your content management, you must always maintain an awareness of your target audience as you develop your content to distribute on each platform.

Though not exhaustive, some general recommendations include: be consistent, use trending stories, optimize your social profiles, use automated-scheduling for social media posts, consider paid content, join community groups, do not leave messages unanswered, do not let platforms stay quiet for too long, do not overwhelm followers with too much content, and do not forget the social aspect of social media. Additionally, it is always important to consider your brand's voice when communicating via social media. Brand voice is the distinct personality a brand takes on in all of its communications. It will give your social presence more personality, help keep your content consistent, and stand out from your competitors. Finally, do not forget that social media is fast-paced. Therefore, it is vital to keep up with trends, participate, and be authentic.

LEARNING ACTIVITY 6

Define your content strategy for each platform selected in Learning Activity 5.

STEP 7: ESTABLISH A CONTENT CALENDAR

No matter your social media goals, planning and structure will help to eliminate some of the day-to-day stress that can arise. Rather than struggling to find shareable content on a daily basis, a content calendar will allow you to strategize for pre-planned messaging, freeing up resources for the development of last-minute initiatives.

Depending upon the type of organization you work for, a yearlong calendar may be appropriate, while smaller organizations/projects might rely on monthly calendars. In general, it is suggested that at least a month's worth of content is scheduled for the release of material.

In general, it will be important for you to have a plan in place for when you will share content in order to yield the most favorable results. For example, if you are in charge of social media for a professional sports team, your audience will likely be on one of your social media platforms right before, during, and after a game. You must consider the best time for posting based on your audiences' behavior. If necessary, to confirm go back to the data for your target audience when planning your calendar. In addition to a more general schedule, you must also determine the cadence of content. This refers to how often you should post each day and each week. With the fast-paced nature of Twitter, it is generally appropriate to post through the platform most often. To pull from our previous example, a professional team may use Twitter to post play-by-play updates, but only post a game recap on Facebook.

Once you have determined the timing and frequency of your content, the next step is to create a content calendar. You can use the likes of a Microsoft Excel worksheet to set up a content calendar. Another platform is Monday.com, which allows for easy collaborations with your social media team. Once a calendar is set, use a scheduling tool to plan/schedule posts in advance rather than having to constantly update during the day. Some platforms have these tools embedded, including Facebook and Twitter. For example, Facebook's business pages include a native scheduling tool and Twitter allows for the use of Tweetdeck. Unfortunately, not all platforms have associated tools. However, scheduling is still possible through third-party providers like Hootsuite. Once you have developed your calendar, make sure that you update it as often as necessary (i.e., weekly, monthly) to make sure that it continues to meet your needs. Helpful categories include: (a) content type, (b) content format (e.g., text plus photo, graphic design, video, GIF), (c) associated content format (e.g., mentions @, hashtags), (d) calls to action (e.g., like/follow us, learn more, share now, comment now, visit website), (e) platform type (e.g., Facebook, Twitter, Instagram, Snapchat, LinkedIn, TikTok), and (f) description (e.g., specific actions and tasks, responsible person).

By developing a content calendar in advance, it will provide you with a bit more flexibility to interact with followers, keep up on the latest trends, or to post content that is more timely and cannot be prepared in advance.

LEARNING ACTIVITY 7

Plan a one-week content calendar for at least two of the social platforms for your organization. Make sure that you address both timing and cadence. As a reminder, the selected platforms and calendar must be appropriate for your previously identified audience.

STEP 8: EXECUTE, PLAN, AND TRACK PERFORMANCE

Now that your strategy has been planned, it is time to execute. Whether you are the lead for one project or have multiple projects to balance, the previous steps should help ensure that you are prepared in a thorough and organized manner. This will give you the ideal platform to successfully achieve all of the goals outlined in your calendar.

During the execution phase, it is vital to simultaneously track your results. This will allow you to understand how your content is performing and how it measures up against your goals and objectives. Most often, you will have an annual review. However, there are a variety of other time-bound evaluation cycles. Time-bound evaluations are often associated with specific projects. They are also helpful and should be built into your calendar as well. One way to track your progress is through the use of a tool like a Gantt Chart, an illustrated project schedule, to determine the progress of a project. However, if you prefer, you may choose to use any number of programs that assess social media metrics (e.g., Sprout Social,

HubSpot, Buzz Sumo, Google Analytics) to track the value of the initiative in meeting goals. Whatever type of tracking program you deem best for your organization, it is imperative that your specific evaluation cycle(s) are determined during the development of your SMART goals so that you know both how and when to assess for successes or failures.

For the evaluation itself, you will use the KPI metrics listed in Step 2. A number of platforms will provide you with the resources to complete this assessment. For example, Twitter, Facebook, and Instagram offer their own native analytics that dive into the majority of metrics you will search for. However, there are also third-party platforms to help with this effort (Hootsuite, Sprout Social, etc.). When analyzing your results, always go back to what you noted as your primary objectives and the associated KPI that you determined you would use to gauge success. With this, your primary goal will be to take note of what performed well and what may not have performed well. Ultimately, the data will provide a rationale for you to adjust your content strategy, when necessary.

Social media is constantly evolving so, as noted at the beginning of the chapter, it is important to remember that it will never be possible to develop a fixed social media plan. Given this unique nature, it is acceptable to be reactive and adjust your approach quickly. However, you should also take the time to be proactive and adjust your long-term plans as needed (see Step 10). In general, do not be afraid to make changes to your social media strategy so that it better reflects new trends, insights, technology, and goals. While we will discuss overarching adjustments in the final step, you should continually monitor and make minor modifications to ensure that you are working towards your goals.

LEARNING ACTIVITY 8

Determine what you will evaluate for your report (Step 9) and draft an evaluation schedule that aligns with the content calendar that you prepared for Learning Activity 7.

STEP 9: DEVELOP A REPORT AND COMMUNICATE OUTCOMES

As with any other aspect of operations, it will be necessary for you to report on your progress and performance. Luckily, you have already begun this process through the previous steps (i.e., identification of relevant objectives, development of SMART goals, creation of an audience persona, specified target audience, and the key performance indicators that were tracked).

Whether you work with a team of social media managers, a big marketing department, or the VPs of your company, it is important to communicate your efforts and results to all relevant internal and external stakeholders. Discuss with your team how often they would like to see reporting so that you can plan ahead and know what to expect. Weekly? Monthly? Quarterly? Yearly? In addition to review cycles, it is important to be aware of who you will be reporting to and what their preferred presentation style may be. For example, your direct boss might want a presentation of all findings — both written and oral — while the VP of Marketing might be more interested in an executive summary of the report that highlights your accomplishments against the goals and objectives established in the planning process. As this might be your opportunity to make requests for additional staff (e.g., video editors, photographers, graphic designers) and equipment (e.g., software, analytic tools), it is your responsibility to both demonstrate your commitment to organizational objectives and justify organizational investment to continue to innovate through these reports.

Additionally, if you fail to accomplish any particular goals, you need to be prepared to justify that with concrete evidence. This is also a good time to evaluate how your content performed. If it did not perform as expected, discuss why it did not meet expectations, and adjust your content strategy. For example, if you receive on average of 50k impressions for video content on Instagram, but a recent post only garnered 20k impressions, discuss with your team why that content may not have resonated with your audience. In general, this would be the time to propose remedial strategies to continue to aid in the development of strengths and minimization of weaknesses.

LEARNING ACTIVITY 9

Prepare the outline of a report that you would develop to assess the social media plan developed in these steps. Do not forget to state your audience and revisit your SMART goals.

STEP 10: ADJUST

As the social media space evolves so quickly, it is important to keep that fluidity in your role as well. Therefore, the final phase of this process is to adjust your actions. While small adjustments can (and should) be made regularly, the intention of this final step is to make any major adjustments necessary to continue to meet your social media goals. This may be reflective of a single post that simply did not resonate with your audience, or a larger campaign, like launching registration for an event that may not have received the intended purchase level that you had projected. Whatever the case, this adjustment period should take place at the conclusion of your social media calendar and evaluation period in order for you to move on to the next period of success.

Some may see results, and therefore adjustments, as somewhat of a good/bad binary. They may say, "we did well" or "we failed miserably." In practice, there are examples of incredibly successful outcomes as well as significant losses. However, results tend to land along more of a spectrum from amazing to horrendous. With that note, one needs to keep in mind that adjustments can be made to improve performance moving forward. For example, your outcome might be outstanding. Your messaging was on point, you reached your targeted audience, and your KPI reflected a positive ROI for both your organization and the partners involved in your project. That is remarkable. However, that does not mean that you should rest on your laurels. It is your responsibility to take this momentum, adjust or update, and continue to innovate. Perhaps, the next step with this messaging might be aligning with a new content creator or influencer that shares your values and mission or conducting a competitor analysis to see how you compare. There is always room for growth, so use this step to reflect on ways for you to continue to innovate. Rather than a positive response, you might also find that your results lead you back to the beginning, a feedback loop that warrants a complete refresh in understanding and action.

Social media might not be the highest priority for every organization. However, it is the means by which most people receive their messaging today and that is not to be taken lightly. Therefore, whatever the result of your assessment may be, this is the time to adjust and make sure that your next wave of initiatives continues to represent your organization in a way that helps it reach its overarching business goals.

LEARNING ACTIVITY 10

Develop a scenario (good or bad) that would require an adjustment in your social media strategy. Determine what step you would need to return to in the social media management process to make this adaptation and provide a brief overview of what your recommendations would look like from that point through Step 10.

CASE STUDY: US LACROSSE

US Lacrosse (USL), a 501c3 non-profit and the national governing body (NGB) of men's and women's lacrosse in the United States, has provided national leadership, structure, and resources to fuel the sport's growth and enrich the experience of participants since 1998. During the first two decades of US Lacrosse's existence, lacrosse has been one of the fastest-growing team sports in the country at all levels. Since 2001, total participation has increased 227% (US Lacrosse, 2018).

With the rise in popularity of lacrosse, more and more lacrosse businesses and organizations have emerged in the United States. While none of these businesses are in direct competition with US Lacrosse, some have similar business objectives, including training

(Continued)

for coaches, providing equipment and financial grants, and other forms of local community support.

Herein lies the problem. US Lacrosse offers many programs and services to fuel the sport's growth; however, many in the lacrosse community are not as aware of what US Lacrosse does as compared to local organizations. US Lacrosse provides millions of dollars a year in support of the sport through grants, hundreds of clinics for youth players'/coachs'/officials' development, safety studies to ensure a safe sport for players, and other initiatives. While all of this is true, the lacrosse community is simply not aware of all of these actions. US Lacrosse believes that this is partly due to the fact that it has been more focused on growing the sport than on promoting its own brand. Therefore, the time has come to educate its audience, using social media to do so.

Discussion: With a primary audience of parents, coaches, & officials, aged 35–55, US Lacrosse is developing a brand awareness campaign for social media that will aim to better promote who and what USL does as an organization. As a decision-maker for the NGB, how should you use social media to differentiate USL from others and better promote who you are as an organization? Specifically:

1. Which social media platforms should you use?
2. What type of content should you integrate into your campaign [focusing on the interests of your primary audience(s)]?
3. Which metrics will determine the success of your campaign?
4. What should your unique brand tone and voice be?
5. What type of call to action will help strengthen your campaign?

CHAPTER SUMMARY

While the social media management process is vitally important, over time it will be more like second nature and you will not necessarily progress through each step of the process in such a formulaic manner. However, each phase will continue to play into your practices moving forward. While this is the case, it is vital to understand that, in addition to your plan relying on your organization's overarching objectives, you should always start and end with your organization's mission, vision, and goals. Additionally, you should always remember that social media is a continually evolving medium. Therefore, its fluidity should be reflected in your adaptability.

All organizations have different objectives and resources for their social media practices. Therefore, it is your job to make an impact with the resources you have on hand (or can gain access to). Professional sport teams and leagues may have full-time social media staff devoted to creating video content, graphic design works, and more; however, many others are working with limited resources to pull together the most impactful messaging with a minimal budget. While this is the case, greater resources do not always equate to greater success in social media content management. Creativity in developing content that appeals to your audiences is essential, and your creative content can go viral if it has the potential to capture the interest of a wider audience outside of your following. Therefore, to ensure you end up on the winning side of the social media game, planning is imperative. In sum, while your role may change over time, our hope is that this process provides a foundation with which you can develop a solid base to communicate your organization's message via social media.

RESOURCES

- Hootsuite: Conducting a competitive analysis (template): https://blog.hootsuite.com/competitive-analysis-on-social-media/.
- HubSpot: Persona generator: https://www.hubspot.com/make-my-persona.
- Opendorse: Social media in sports marketing: https://opendorse.com/blog/social-media-in-sports-marketing/.
- Video Guru: What is the right length for a video? https://www.vdo.guru/so-what-is-the-right-length-for-a-marketing-video/.

- Sprout Social Media
  — Setting/achieving social media goals: https://sproutsocial. com/insights/social-media-goals/
  — Social media demographics to inform your brand: https:// sproutsocial.com/insights/new-social-media-demographics/.
  — How to use social media to keep sports fans engaged: https://sproutsocial.com/insights/social-media-in-sports/.

TEST YOUR KNOWLEDGE

1. Why is it important to understand your organization's mission when developing your social media strategy?
2. Define the characteristics of a SMART goal?
3. What type of research is necessary to develop your plan and why?
4. What role does your target audience play in selecting platforms?
5. Identify three unique types of social media content and explain how they can be implemented, and scheduled, to meet your stated objectives.
6. What key performance indicators would you recommend using to evaluate your progress?
7. Who might you need to report your progress to and why?

REFERENCES

Abeza, G. (2012). An exploratory study of the opportunities and challenges of social media in meeting relationship marketing goals in sport organizations. (Unpublished Masters thesis). University of New Brunswick, Canada.

Barnhart, B. (2020). How to build your social media marketing strategy for 2020. Sprout Social. https://sproutsocial.com/insights/social-media-marketing-strategy/.

Constantinides, E. and Fountain, S. (2008). Web 2.0: Conceptual foundations and marketing issues. *Journal of Direct Data and Digital Marketing Practice, 9*(3), 231–244.

Drury, G. (2008). Opinion piece: Social media: Should marketers engage and how can it be done effectively? *Journal of Direct Data and Digital Marketing Practice, 9*(3), 274–277.

462   *Social Media in Sport*

Martin, A. (2011). Social media success requires more than just showing up. *SportBusiness Journal.* http://www.sportsbusinessdaily.com/Journal/Issues/2011/04/18/Opinion/Martin-column.aspx.

Menke, M. and Schwarzenegger, C. (2019). On the relativity of old and new media: A lifeworld perspective. *Convergence, 25*(4), 657–672.

Sheffer, M. L. and Schultz, B. (2010). Paradigm shift or passing fad? Twitter and sports journalism. *International Journal of Sport Communication, 3*(4), 472–484.

US Lacrosse (2018). *Participation report.* https://www.uslacrosse.org/sites/default/files/public/documents/about-us-lacrosse/2018-participation-report.pdf.

Waters, R., Burke, K., Jackson, Z., and Buning, J. (2011). Using stewardship to cultivate fandom online: Comparing how National Football League teams use their websites and Facebook to engage their fans. *International Journal of Sport Communication, 4*(2), 163–177.

Afterword

Paul M. Pedersen, PhD, Professor, Indiana University;

Editor, *International Journal of Sport Communication (IJSC)*

As you have come to the end of this groundbreaking and engaging book, I am most certain that you are — just as I am — very well aware of how important social media is to sport communication and, more broadly, sport management. You are also now fully cognizant that this importance is growing, expanding, and amplifying each year, accelerated by COVID-19 and the ever-digitizing world around us. Thus, because you have read this insightful and timely book, you are now well informed on this topic and ready to further enhance your use and understanding of social media in your professional life.

How important is social media scholarship within the field of sport studies?

In the "early" days of social media, there were many scholars who held that the activity and engagement surrounding this new area would soon fade away and that researching such a perceived novelty had limited value. Now, just a dozen or so years into the research surrounding this "fad", there might be a few scholars who still feel this way, but if that is the case, they simply would be wrong. After having read this book, I am convinced that you would agree.

Social media has impacted the sport industry in so many ways, ranging from the financial, promotional, informational, and cultural to careers, policies, sales, and opportunities for interactivity. The impact will only increase in the coming years as established social media platforms evolve and new ones are embraced by sport industry stakeholders. This impact has been studied by many sport scholars — including the four leading editors of this book and many of the chapter authors — and it is imperative and prudent that the myriad aspects of social media in the sport industry continue to be examined. The resulting scholarship — including this publication — should be building on the body of knowledge in the area and assisting sport industry practitioners in their efforts to be more effective and efficient in the management, marketing, and promotion of their sport entities. Due to the proliferation of social media platforms which the editors and authors delve into in this book, as well as the ever-changing nature of the social media offerings (which you also read about in the preceding chapters), and the overall use of social media by sport industry stakeholders (athletes, coaches, fans, teams, leagues, managers, events, governing bodies, etc.), there is a need for continued — and even increased — social media scholarship within the field of sport studies. As you have learned in this book, social media is applied to major and minor sport entities alike, and has become a key driver of the decisions in sport organizations of any size. In order to support my point, let me take a few paragraphs to give you examples of social media in both a major and a minor sport organization.

How versed should a professional working in a major sports club be in social media?

While employees of some areas (e.g., finance, accounting) of professional sports might not be required to have any involvement with social media, without question those working in any job related to marketing or communications in professional sports must be well versed in social media. This is obvious for those working in social media departments or running the social media accounts for professional sports clubs, but it is also true for those who are not posting or sending out social media messages. At a minimum, they need to be following social media platforms in order to stay informed (a sport communication professional should not be the last to know and not at least following social media accounts is a guarantee of not being up-to-date and fully engaged). Ideally, they need to use social media as a source of what fans are thinking and feeling about the club, its players, the coaches, the sponsors, the brand, and so much more. Considering the scope, magnitude, and extent of social media use in the sports world today, employees who embrace and use social media are needed throughout professional sports, and indeed in all of sports, from national sport organizations to youth sports. While the usages might be different (e.g., maybe simply informational at the lower levels), social media is highly effective for promotional outcomes, interactivity, and a host of other benefits.

I would add that any sport industry professional who does not participate in social media is doing themselves (and their organization) a disservice because of all the benefits they are missing out on. The chapters in this book, written by a set of authors who are among the best in our field, are all the evidence I need to support this point.

How versed should a professional working in a minor sports be in social media?

Minor sports are sport entities (including teams, leagues, governing bodies, athletes, coaches, and beyond) that would have received minimal to no focus in a pre-digital landscape. However, this is not to imply (as indicated in Chapter 5) that these sports are "minor" in and of themselves. Some examples may include national federations who represent low profile Olympic sports, such as equestrian, table tennis, and triathlon. Reaching their audiences through the traditional media outlets such as national television is still a long shot for most minor sports organizations. Social media — with the opportunities it presented for source publicity (i.e., where the sport entity could inform and promote on its own through social media platforms rather than rely on the traditional mass media — changed this challenge dramatically for minor sports.

For example, professionals working at DII (and even DIII) level athletic departments, might not get the publicity provided by the media, but they are able to use social media to get their messages out to their stakeholders. Thus, such sport industry professionals most definitely need to be well versed in social media. In addition to the limited coverage provided by the mass media, professionals working for "minor" sport entities need to be skilled and experienced in using social media mainly because, among other reasons, they will be working with social media platforms due to their low resource cost. It would be rare for a professional at DII or DIII level of intercollegiate athletics to not be engaged — and most likely heavily engaged — with social media platforms through the postings of the athletic department, teams, and many other stakeholders (e.g., student-athlete, athletic director, sponsors, etc.). Specifically, they use social media to reach audiences with common interest and address their demands directly, by extension, helping serve as a hub for a target audience of a specific sport.

MY RECOMMENDATIONS

To build on the content of the book, I would like to provide some advice for those of you readers who are seeking a career in sport.

First, there are many opportunities "out there" for you to pursue a social media career within the sport industry. While there is plenty of competition for positions in this area, there are many ways that you can set yourself apart from your peers and be competitive for such opportunities. Obviously, and this goes without saying, you need to have an interest in communication overall and in social media in particular. If there is limited interest in communicating and engaging with others, then a social media career might not be the best way to go. However, let us assume that if you read this book, you have this box checked.

Second, beyond the interest in social media (as well as an interest in sport, but that too goes without saying for those who have finished this book), you must be able to write well and that comes from past experiences (writing, re-writing, studying language, taking communication courses, etc.) as well as reading. Even if the posts are photos or graphics with few words and even if the space is limited for a quick tweet, being well-versed in writing will help you to not make mistakes that will work to undermine your abilities and focus (e.g., taking the time to proofread).

Third, you need to (as early as possible) volunteer to assist the social media activities wherever and whenever you can. If you are a student, volunteer for social media activities surrounding your university athletic department, one of the teams attached to your athletic department, a club team, or intramural offerings. Next, I would advise to work towards maybe even running a social media account for one of those entities. This will aid in developing your writing skills, allow you to participate in social media content creation and scheduling, build your networking with social media professionals, and support you in developing skills in creative areas (e.g., graphic design, photography, multimedia editing). As I have learned, these are all areas that you can and should work on while in school (and preferably with the athletic department or some sport entity). A more formal route would be interning in the social media department, which I also highly recommend.

The good news here is that each of the chapters in this book has a Key Skills for Practice section that you can go back and refer to, to make sure that you have developed the necessary skills to run a professionally managed social media account for an organization. As you recall from the last chapter, running a personal social media account is different from managing an organization's account.

FINAL THOUGHTS ON THE BOOK

As I have tried to point out above (and I am sure you realized as you were going through the chapters), this book is a novel, substantial, and significant addition to the field of sport studies. What is covered in this book (touching all aspects of the sport industry) and the individuals involved (prolific editors and authors) demand that this book be on the shelf of sport scholars and practitioners. I am pleased you have read it. In terms of the content, the book starts with a well-constructed introductory chapter. It then truly covers social media in the sport industry as the chapters cover everything from marketing, decision-making, data management, and the legal issues to crisis communication, and diversity and inclusion. Those involved academically (scholars, researchers, professors, students, etc.) and in the field (i.e., sport industry practitioners) will benefit from this expansive and exhaustive social media publication. While reading the last chapter, you went through a practical guide to social media management that includes 10 practical steps that one should adhere to in managing a social media platform. I would further emphasize that the second chapter is an excellent resource for those of you who want to further explore and refer back to research about the impact of social media on the sport industry.

It is not surprising that the content of the book is outstanding. That is because this publication is led by four prolific sport scholars. The book's editors — Gashaw Abeza, Norm O'Reilly, Jimmy Sanderson, and Evan Frederick — have studied and published an astounding amount of social media and sport industry research. They are leading social media scholars and they have assembled an outstanding cast of diverse, international scholars who range from prolific veteran researchers to emerging investigators, to join them as authors. Assembling such a team is challenging, but the editors have pulled it off and the final product is an exhaustive and engaging look at social media in the sport industry.

Paul M. Pedersen, PhD, is Professor of Sport Management within the Department of Kinesiology in the School of Public Health at Indiana University at Bloomington (IU). He has worked as a sports writer, sport management consultant, and sport business columnist. Pedersen's primary areas of scholarly interest and research are the symbiotic relationship between sport and communication, and the activities and practices of various sports organization personnel. A research fellow of the North American Society for Sport Management (NASSM), Pedersen has published 10 books (including titles such as

Sport and the Pandemic, Strategic Sport Communication, Handbook of Sport Communication, and *Research Methods and Design in Sport Management*) and over 110 articles in peer-reviewed outlets such as the *Journal of Sport Management, European Sport Management Quarterly, Sport Marketing Quarterly, International Journal of Sports Marketing and Sponsorship, Sociology of Sport Journal, International Review for the Sociology of Sport,* and *Journal of Sports Economics.* He has also been a part of more than 125 refereed presentations at professional conferences and more than 50 invited presentations, including invited addresses in China, Denmark, Hungary, Norway, and South Korea. He has been interviewed and quoted in publications as diverse as *The New York Times* and *China Daily.* Founder and editor-in-chief of the *International Journal of Sport Communication,* he serves on the editorial board of seven other journals. A 2020 distinguished alumni award (Florida State University, College of Education) recipient and 2011 Golden Eagle Hall of Fame (East High School in Pueblo, Colorado) inductee, Pedersen lives in Bloomington, Indiana, with his wife, Jennifer, and their two youngest children, Brock and Carlie. Their oldest children and their spouses (Hallie, Liam, Zack, and Megan) live in Bloomington and Chicago.

About the Contributors

Andrew C. Billings (Ph.D.) is the Ronald Reagan Chair of Broadcasting and Executive Director of the Alabama Program in Sports Communication at the University of Alabama. He received his Ph.D. from Indiana University. He has published 20 books and over 200 academic journal articles and book chapters, the large majority of which pertain to issues of sports media content and societal influence.

Ann Pegoraro (Ph.D.) is the Lang Chair in Sport Management and currently holds an appointment as a Full Professor in the School of Hospitality, Food, and Tourism, in the Gordon S. Lang School of Business and Economics at the University of Guelph. Dr. Pegoraro is also the co-Director of E-Alliance, the Research Hub for Gender Equity in Canadian Sport. Dr. Pegoraro's research focuses mainly on sports consumers, marketing, and communication, including how different forms of media are used to establish connections with consumers of sport at all levels from amateur to professional. Her research has been published in different academic journals. Dr. Pegoraro's recent work in digital media and innovation is focused on analytics, gender, and diversity.

Ari Kim (Ph.D.) is an Assistant Professor in the Department of Kinesiology at Towson University (TU). Before joining TU, Dr. Kim had taught at the University of North Florida and worked as a marketing research consultant at Kantar TNS. Her research interests focus on consumer behavior in sport, specifically examining the role of new technology (e.g., sports data analytics) in sport marketing, and sports fans' media consumption behaviors. Her research has been published in outlets such as *International Journal of Sport Communication* and *International Journal of Sport Management and Marketing*.

Arielle Insel is the Senior Manager of Marketing and Brand Strategy at USA Lacrosse, the national governing body of the sport, where Arielle manages organizational marketing initiatives and oversees social media marketing. Her hard work and dedication coupled with her high energy has been instrumental in helping USA Lacrosse engage the entire lacrosse community to build heightened awareness of its mission. Arielle resides in Baltimore, Maryland, with her husband Joel and their French bulldog, Bailey.

Beth A. Cianfrone (Ph.D.) is a Professor of Sport Administration at Georgia State University. She is the Coordinator of the Sport Administration M.S. program and Associate Director of the Center for Sport and Urban Policy. Her research focus is on the areas of sport marketing communications and consumer behavior. She is a North American Society for Sport Management Research Fellow and the 2019 Sport Marketing Association Stotlar Award recipient.

Christos Anagnostopoulos (Ph.D.) is the Deputy Head of Business and Management School at University of Central Lancashire (Cyprus) and an Associate Professor in Sport Management at Molde University College (Norway). Christos is an editorial board member in nine academic journals serving sports management and marketing and has published over 40 peer-reviewed articles in outlets such as the *Journal of Sport Management, European Sport Management Quarterly, Nonprofit Voluntary Sector Quarterly, Journal of Brand Management,* and *Voluntas.* He is notably interested in sports governance, corporate social responsibility in and through sport, as well as in the way sports organizations use social media.

David Cassilo (Ph.D.) is a former sports journalist turned academic. After earning his B.A. at Villanova University (2010), David completed a Master's degree in journalism at Northwestern University (2011). He received his Ph.D. from Kent State University. He then worked as a digital media and magazine reporter. David is now an Assistant Professor at Kennesaw State University. His research interests largely focus on media portrayals of health issues in sport, specifically examining concussions and mental health. David's other research areas include race and sport as well as social media usage. His work has been published in several academic journals and has been presented at academic conferences.

David Wagner (Ph.D.) is a Professor of International Business and Digital Business at Munich Business School and Academic Director of the Master Program in Sports Business and Communication. He is an Associate Director at MUUUH! Next and heads the Research Committee of the German Association for Community Management (BCVM). He has authored numerous journal articles, conference papers, and book chapters; he is also an active reviewer for leading international conferences and journals. Details about current projects, publications, and speaking engagements are available on his website: https://kpsquared.org/.

Elisabetta Zengaro received her Ph.D. in Communication and Information Sciences from The University of Alabama, researching mental health communication and stigma in college sports. Her research and teaching interests include sport and health communication. She earned her Bachelor's degree in Journalism and Master's degree in Sport and Human Performance from Delta State University, where she worked in sports media as a graduate assistant for Delta State Athletics.

Jacob Bustad (Ph.D.) is an Assistant Professor in the Department of Kinesiology at Towson University. His primary research and teaching interests are in the fields of sport management, physical cultural studies, the sociology of sport and urban studies. Specifically, he is interested in sport and physical activity within urban environments, sport and globalization, and sport and social inclusion.

Jessica Braunstein-Minkove (Ph.D.) is an Associate Professor in the Department of Kinesiology at Towson University, where she teaches courses in sport marketing and professional development. Her primary research focus is in the areas of sport marketing communications and consumer behavior, examining activities that organizations engage in to impact consumers' perceptions of the brand (e.g., brand personality, athlete endorsers/influencers, market demand,

and social media). She also studies curricular and co-curricular practices that impact preparedness (e.g., internships, high-impact practices). Her research has been published in a number of sports-related academic journals, and she has presented at various national and international conferences.

Kelsey Slater (Ph.D.) is an Assistant Professor at North Dakota State University. She recently completed her Ph.D. at Mississippi State University, where her dissertation focused on how sport for development and peace organizations based in Africa use social media to achieve their organizational and development goals

Kevin Hull (Ph.D.) is the Sports Media Lead and an Associate Professor in the School of Journalism and Mass Communications at the University of South Carolina. He received his Ph.D. from University of Florida. Before entering academia, Kevin was a television sports broadcaster who covered the Super Bowl, Stanley Cup, and various other major sporting events.

Lauren Burch (Ph.D.) is a Senior Lecturer in Sport Business and the Programme Director for the Sports Analytics and Technology M.Sc. at Loughborough University London, where she teaches courses in sport analytics and statistics. Burch earned her Ph.D. from the School of Public Health at Indiana University Bloomington in 2012. Her research interests include digital media, brand authenticity, and personal branding. Her research has been published in such journals as *Sport Management Review, International Journal of Sport Management and Marketing,* and the *Journal of Sport Management.*

Matt Blaszka (Ph.D.) is an Associate Professor at Indiana State University (ISU) within the Department of Kinesiology, Recreation, and Sport. He primarily teaches sport marketing, sponsorship, and sales. His research has focused on social media, marketing, and wearable fitness trackers. He received his Ph.D. in Sport Management from Indiana University. Outside of ISU, he is the Director of Community Soccer with the Cutters Soccer Club in Bloomington, IN.

Matthew H. Zimmerman (Ph.D.) is an Assistant Professor at Mississippi State University. His scholarly interests pertain to the effects of New Media and Social Media on interactions between sports organizations and sports consumers. This includes platforms such as Facebook, Twitter, YouTube, Instagram, online message boards, media website comment sections, and sports-themed video games. Dr. Zimmerman's goal is to build on, apply, and develop existing theory on such interactions in regard to the relationship between sports organizations and their target audiences.

Melinda R. Weathers (Ph.D.) is an Associate Professor in the Department of Communication Studies at Sam Houston State University in Huntsville, Texas. Her scholarly interests include intercultural communication, gender and women's health issues, and new communication technologies. She received her Ph.D. from George Mason University. Dr. Weathers' research has encompassed a range of topics addressing issues related to messages within relational, institutional, societal, and health contexts. Her research regarding social media and sport communication has been published in journals such as

Communication and Sport, Sport Management Review, Communication Quarterly, and *Journal of Sports Media.*

Oliver Rick (Ph.D.) is an Assistant Professor in the Department of Sport Management and Recreation at Springfield College. His research agenda has three main strands: critical analyses of sports media and communication, globalization processes in sport, and urban physical activity cultures.

Petros Parganas holds an MBA and DBA from the Edinburgh Business School, Heriot-Watt University, UK, and is currently the Global Head of Football in the Digital Marketing Analytics Department of adidas. Prior to this position, he has been working in academia and was teaching sport marketing courses at various universities and colleges. His research interests lie in sports brand management, sponsorship, and social media and his research appeared in various international journals.

Rebecca M. Achen (Ph.D.) is an Assistant professor of Sport Management in the School of Kinesiology and Recreation at Illinois State University. She graduated with her Ph.D. in sport management from the University of Kansas. Prior to that, Rebecca received her Master's degree from Winona State University and her Bachelor's degree from Southwest Minnesota State University. She has many years of work experience in higher education administration and sports marketing and sales. Her research focuses on the effectiveness of social media as a relationship marketing tool in professional sports. She also engages in the Scholarship of Teaching and Learning.

Edward (Ted) M. Kian (Ph.D.) is Professor and the Welch-Bridgewater Chair of Sports Media at Oklahoma State University. A former professional sports journalist for newspapers, websites, media relations, and radio, Dr. Kian's research focuses primarily on sport communication, specifically the framing of gender, sex, and LGBT in media content, social media, and Web 2.0, and attitudes and experiences of sports journalists. He has authored or co-authored three books, and more than 100 journal articles, conference papers, and invited book chapters. Dr. Kian's research, journalism, and expertise has been cited by outlets such as 60 Minutes and *The New York Times*.

Yiran Su (Ph.D.) is an Assistant Professor of Sport Management and Policy at the University of Georgia. Her research interests lie in the areas of business analytics and brand management with a focus on sport and new media contexts. Her research program is interdisciplinary in nature and pushes the traditional boundaries of her field to emphasize the importance of critical scholarship.

Yoseph Mamo (Ph.D.) is an Assistant Professor of Sport Management in the Department of Human Performance and Sport Sciences at Tennessee State University. Dr. Mamo's research interest is to examine the outcomes and impacts of sports organizations' corporate social responsibility (CSR) activities in the digital age. Specifically, his recent research has focused on a range of modern analytical techniques such as text mining and natural learning processing to understand ordinary citizens' voices and better understand public perceptions of sports organizations' CSR efforts. He received his Ph.D. from Louisiana State University. His work has appeared in the *Journal of Sport Management*, *Journal of Sport Behavior*, and *Journal of Global Sport Management*.

Index

CPSIA information can be obtained
at www.ICGtesting.com
Printed in the USA
BVHW070116270721
612698BV00002B/2

9 789811 237652